The Beatles, Drugs, Mysticism & India

Maharishi Mahesh Yogi - Transcendental Meditation

~ Jai Guru Deva OM ॐ

Paul Mason

Premanand

PREMANAND
premanandpaul@yahoo.co.uk
www.paulmason.info

First published by Premanand 2017
© Paul Mason 2017, 2018, 2020
ISBN: 978-0-9562228-9-3

Cover and contents design by Premanand

Acknowledgements

To John, Paul, George, Ringo, Maharishi & Donovan, and all the others who were there, especially... Mike Dolan, Millie Drummond, Carole Hamby, Richard Blakely, Terry Gustafson, Paul Saltzman, Per Gunnar Fjeld, Jerry Stovin, Yavar Abbas, Alan Waite, Joe Lysowski, Jerry Jarvis, Rosalyn Bonas, Karin Hegendörfer, Pattie Boyd, Ajit Singh of Pratap Music, the tailor of Lakshman Jhoola, Andreas Müller, Gypsy Dave Mills, Brahmachari Satyanand, Geoffrey Baker, Shambhu Das, Paul Scrivener & Raj Varma.

Invaluable support, suggestions and assistance from family... Kathy Mason, Ben Mason, Richard Mason & Gabriel Mason.

Fantastic support from friends ... Theo Fehr & Francisca Janus, Tony 'Suradeva' Evenson, Sue Jenkinson, Tony Martin, Stuart Norfolk, Phil Cowan, 'Stash' Prince Stanislaus Klossowski de Rola, Tormod Kinnes, Brahmachari Raghvendra's niece; Gesu Aftab, Odd Bull Indramurti, Frauke Meier-Siems, Holger Mielke, Kyle Anderson, Bjarne Ulrich Hansen, Phil Goldberg, Robert Jayan Petzing, Lisa Lindberg, Diane Rousseau, Tom Anderson & Gina Catena. And Dan Friedman, Robert Sanders and Lothar Heggmair of the Guru Dev Legacy Trust.

And many, many thanks to all the well-meaning people who have given their feedback, who have therefore helped to shape or re-shape the project.

Illustration art

Original artworks - *'George & John on TV'*, and *'Leaving'* - by Kathy Mason.

Photo credits

Grateful thanks go out to Carole Hamby for donating the transparencies she took in India to this project and for Douglas Gowan's Bangor photos too, and to Theo Fehr for offering use of Gertrud Soares de Souza's Collection. Thanks to Frauke Meier-Siems for sending the photos of Georg Meier-Siems. Also to Richard Blakely for access to his collection, and to Vincent Daczynski for generously passing over rights to all the transparencies taken by Charlie Lutes in India, and to Paul Scrivener for sharing his photos. Well done Tony Evenson for sharing his collection, and to Holger Mielke.

And for 'permissions', warm thanks go to Paul Keene at www.avico.co.uk, Per Gunnar Fjeld, and Paul Saltzman at www.thebeatlesinindia.com/

Chapters

THE BEATLES

John Lennon
Paul McCartney
George Harrison
Ringo Starr

Chapter One
Help!

It's Thursday, 25th February 1965, and The Beatles - John, Paul, George and Ringo - are enjoying the sun, sand and sea of the Bahamas whilst there for the filming of their second movie.

John - 'The first time that we were aware of anything Indian was when we were making Help!.'
'… we were in the Bahamas filming a section and a little yogi runs over to us. …. this little Indian guy comes legging over and gives us a book each, signed to us, on yoga. We didn't look at it, we just stuck it along with all the other things people would give us.'[1]

George - 'We were on our bikes on the road, waiting to do a shoot, when up walked a swami in orange robes: Swami Vishnu Devananda, the foremost hatha yoga exponent. It was on my birthday.'[1]
'I didn't look at the book in detail for some time, but at a later date I found it and I opened the cover, and it had a big OM written on it.'[2]

Ringo - 'A hell of a lot of pot was being smoked while we were making the film. It was great.'[1]

Paul - 'We showed up a bit stoned, smiled a lot and hoped we'd get through it. We giggled a lot.'[1]

As with The Beatles' first movie, *'Hard Day's Night'*, this second film is also a comedy. The new film is again directed by Richard Lester with a script written by Marc Behmm. The storyline this time is that John, Paul, George and Ringo get involved with an Indian sect who hunt down The Beatles in order to retrieve a ring related to their sacrificial rites in service of their goddess, 'Kaili'. Eleanor Bron plays Ahme, the cult's High Priestess. The leader of the cult is a man named Clang, played by actor Leo McKern, who is at times really quite convincing as a sermonising holy man.

Swami Clang (speaking to a clergyman) - 'Oh, goodness me, yes! Sex is creeping in; it's being thrown at you. You see it everywhere, in the bazaars, in the marketplaces, in the temple even. And you wonder they turn up their noses at a mystical impulse?'[3]

The sect is obviously a parody of the centuries-old and much-feared cult of *Thuggee,* organised teams of thugs, professional robbers and assassins, who claimed to be devotees of the goddess Kali, sometimes depicted as eight-armed.

According to an on-screen caption - The Beatles are *'seeking enlightenment'* about one of Ringo's rings, and the world famous group visits the Rajahama, an 'Oriental' restaurant, where the house band serenades customers with versions of Beatle tunes. Curiously, John Lennon is served a bowl of soup in which he finds a pair of thin-rimmed round spectacles; a result of what appears to be deadly mayhem in the kitchen.

George - 'We were waiting to shoot the scene in the restaurant when the guy gets thrown in the soup and there were a few Indian musicians playing in the background. I remember picking up the sitar and trying to hold it and thinking, "This is a funny sound."'[4]

John - '…and on the set in one place they had sitars and things - they were the Indian band playing in the background, and George was looking at them.'[1]

With regard to The Beatles and their use of pot; it was back in August 1964 when Bob Dylan introduced The Beatles and their manager, Brian Epstein, to marijuana. But this was not the first time they had gotten high with drugs, the group had long been resorting to pep pills in order to keep up and awake, in fact John Lennon claims his use of artificial stimulants goes back to when he was 17 years old.

John - 'I was a pill addict until Help!, just before Help! where we were turned onto pot and we dropped drink. Simple as that. I've always needed a drug to *survive*. The others too, but I always had *more*, I always took *more* pills and *more* of everything, cause I'm *more* crazy.'[5]

And recreational drugs are surprisingly easy to obtain legally, just a matter of knowing how.

Paul McCartney is living at the family home of his actress girlfriend, Jane Asher, and one day when Paul is suffering from a bad cold, Jane's father, a medical consultant, explains to Paul how he might self medicate.

Dr Richard Asher - '"You take off the top and place it on your little finger, like so." He demonstrated. "Then you take a sniff with each nostril as per normal; then, after you've finished with it, you can unscrew the bottom and eat the Benzedrine."'

Paul - 'We learned about that stuff up in Liverpool but hearing it coming from him was quite strange.'[6]

❀ ❀ ❀

In the spring of 1965, John and George, along with wives, Cynthia Lennon and Pattie Boyd, discover a new high, a relatively unknown drug called lysergic acid diethylamide, know by its initials, LSD.

Cynthia - 'It was when a friend of George's slipped us an LSD "micky-finn" that I finally realized I was on my own. It was a horrifying experience that I will never forget, an "Alice in Wonderland" experience. I felt as though the bottom was beginning to fall out of my world. I never felt closer to insanity than I did then…'[7]

John - 'A dentist in London, put it.. laid it on George, me, and our wives, without telling us at a dinner party at his house. He was a friend of George's, and our dentist at the time. And he just put it in our coffee or something. And we went… he was saying; "I advise you not to..", he didn't know what it was, it's all the thing, sort of, that sort of … middle-class London swingers, or whatever, hadn't all heard about it and they didn't know it was different from pot or pills. And they gave us it and he was saying, "I advise you not to leave", and we thought he was trying to keep us for an orgy in his house and we didn't want to know, you know.'[8]

Pattie - 'We drank the coffee but by then we were really keen to get away.
John said: "We must go now. Our friends are going to be on soon. It's their first night."
Riley [the dentist] told him: "You can't leave."
"What are you talking about?" asked John.
"You've just had LSD. It was in the coffee."
John was absolutely furious. "How dare you f****** do this to us," he said.
George and I said: "Do what?" We didn't know what LSD was.
John said: "It's a drug." As it began to take effect we felt even more strongly that we didn't want to be there.
We were desperate to escape. Riley said he would drive us but we ignored him and piled into my Mini, which seemed to be shrinking. All the way to the club the car felt smaller and smaller, and by the time we arrived we were completely out of it.'[9]

John - 'This guy [John Riley] came with us, he was nervous, he didn't know what was going on. We were going crackers. It was insane going around London on it.'
'When we entered the club, we thought it was on fire. And then we thought it was a premiere, but it was just an ordinary light outside. We thought, "Shit, what's going on here?" And we were cackling in the street, and then people were shouting, "Let's break a window." We were just *insane*. We were just out of our heads. We finally got in the lift and we all thought there was a fire in the lift. It was just a little red light, and we were all *screaming* - it was hysterical. We all arrived on the floor, 'cause this was a discotheque that was up a building. The lift stops and the door opens and we're all going "Aaahhh" [*loud scream*], and we just see that it's the club, and then we walk in, sit down, and the table's elongating.'[1]

Pattie - 'As the doors opened, we crawled out and bumped into Mick Jagger, Marianne Faithfull and Ringo. John told them we'd been spiked. The effect of the drug was getting stronger and stronger, and we were all in hysterics.'[9]

George - 'We'd just sat down and ordered our drinks when suddenly I feel the most incredible feeling come over me. It was something like a very concentrated version of the best feeling I'd ever had in my whole life. It was fantastic. I felt in love, not with anything or anybody in particular, but with everything. Everything was perfect, in a perfect light, and I had an overwhelming desire to go round the club telling everybody how much I loved them - people I'd never seen before.'[1]

The crazy revellers somehow manage to get back to George's house.

Cynthia - 'John and I weren't capable of getting back to Kenwood from there, so the four of us sat up for the rest of the night as the walls moved, the plants talked, other people looked like ghouls and time stood still. It was horrific: I hated the lack of control and not knowing what was going on or what would happen next.'[10]

John - 'And then George's house seemed to be, you know, just like a big submarine. I was driving it, they all went to bed. I was carrying on, on me own, it seemed to float above his wall, which was eighteen foot, and I was like driving 'em.'[8]

❀ ❀ ❀

The incident has been a shock to all concerned, but rather than file a report with the local police, John and George decide to keep quiet about the incident, in fact they are curious to find out more about LSD and have another 'trip'!

❀ ❀ ❀

At zero hour, just before the release of the new Beatles film, a decision is made to drop the working title of the movie - *'Eight Arms To Hold You'* which refers to the multi-armed image of Kaili revered by the cult.

John Lennon tells cousin Stan Parkes of the news.

John - 'God, they've changed the title of the film: it's going to be called "Help!" now. So I've had to write a new song with the title called "Help!"'[11]

'But now these days are gone. I'm not so self-assured
Now I find I've changed my mind and opened up the doors'
- Excerpt of lyrics to *'Help!'* by John Lennon & Paul McCartney

George - 'John and I had decided that Paul and Ringo had to have acid [LSD], because we couldn't relate to them any more. Not just on the one level - we couldn't relate to them on any level, because acid had changed us so much. It was such a mammoth experience that it was unexplainable: it was something that had to be experienced, because you could spend the rest of your life trying to explain what it made you feel and think. It was all too important to John and me. So the plan was that when we got to Hollywood, on our day off we were going to get them to take acid. We got some in New York; it was on sugar cubes wrapped in tinfoil and we'd been carrying these around all through the tour until we got to LA. Paul wouldn't have LSD; he didn't want it. So Ringo and Neil took it, while Mal stayed straight in order to take care of everything.'[1]

Paul - 'I really was frightened of that kind of stuff because it's what you are taught when you're young. "Hey, watch out for them devil drugs." So when acid came round we'd heard that "you're never the same. It alters your life and you never think the same again", and I think John was rather excited by that prospect. I was rather frightened by that prospect. I thought, Just what I need! Some funny little thing where I can never get back home again. I was seen to stall a little bit within the group. There was a lot of peer pressure. Talk about peer pressure. The Beatles.'[1]

The Beatles have been touring North America, and on Tuesday, 24th August 1965, they are relaxing at the house rented from Zsa Zsa Gabor, at 2850 Benedict Canyon, Beverly Hills, in Los Angeles, California.

George - 'I had a concept of what had happened the first time I took LSD, but the concept is nowhere near as

big as the reality, when it actually happens. So as it kicked in again, I thought, "Jesus, I remember!" I was trying to play the guitar, and then I got in the swimming pool and it was a great feeling; the water felt good.'
'Dave Crosby and Jim McGuinn of The Byrds had also come up to the house, and I don't know how, but Peter Fonda was there. He kept saying, "I know what it's like to be dead, because I shot myself." He'd accidentally shot himself at some time and he was showing us his bullet wound. He was very uncool.'[1]

Peter Fonda (actor) - 'I remember sitting out on the deck of the house with George, who was telling me that he thought he was dying. I told him that there was nothing to be afraid of and all that he needed to do was relax. I said that I knew what it was like to be dead because, when I was 10 years old, I'd accidentally shot myself in the stomach and my heart stopped beating three times while I was on the operating table because I had lost so much blood.'
'John was passing at the time and heard me saying, "I know what it's like to be dead." He looked at me and said, "You're making me feel like I've never been born. Who put all that shit in your head?"'[12]

> *'She said, "I know what it's like to be dead."'*
> *'I said, "Who put all those things in your head?"'*
> - Excerpt of *'She Said, She Said'* by John Lennon & Paul McCartney

John - 'We still didn't know anything about doing it in a nice place and cool it and all that, we just took it. And all of a sudden we saw the reporter and we're thinking, "How do we act normal?" Because we imagined we were acting extraordinary, which we weren't. We thought, "Surely somebody can see." We were terrified waiting for him to go, and he wondered why he couldn't come over, and Neil [Aspinall], who had never had it either, had taken it, and he still had to play road manager. We said, "Go and get rid of Don Short," and he didn't know what to do, he just sort of sat with it. And Peter Fonda came, that was another thing, and he kept on saying, "I know what it's like to be dead." We said, "What?" And he kept saying it, and we were saying, "For chrissake, shut up, we don't care. We don't want to know." But he kept going on about it.'
'Paul felt very out of it 'cause we were all a bit cruel. It's like, "We're taking it and you're not." We couldn't eat our food. I just couldn't manage it. Picking it up with the hands, and there's all these people serving us in the house, and we're just knocking it on the floor - oh! - like that.'[5]

George - 'That is another thing: when two people take it at the same time; words become redundant. One can see what the other is thinking. You look at each other and know.'[1]

Though Paul McCartney is wary of LSD, Ringo, on the other hand, is more open to trying it.
Ringo - 'I'd take anything. John and George didn't give LSD to me. A couple of guys came to visit us in LA, and it was them that said, "Man, you've got to try this." They had it in a bottle with an eye-dropper, and they dropped it on sugar cubes and gave it to us. That was my first trip. It was with John and George and Neil and Mal. Neil had to deal with Don Short while I was swimming in jelly in the pool. It was a fabulous day. The night wasn't so great, because it felt like it was never going to wear off. Twelve hours later and it was: "Give us a break now, Lord."'[1]

❀ ❀ ❀

Cynthia - 'When John was tripping I felt as if I was living with a stranger. He would be distant, so spaced-out that he couldn't talk to me coherently. I hated that, and I hated the fact that LSD was pulling him away from me. I wouldn't take it with him so he found others who would. Within weeks of his first trip, John was taking LSD daily and I became more and more worried. I couldn't reach him when he was tripping, but when the effects wore off he would be normal until he took it again.'[10]

❀ ❀ ❀

Shortly after the premiere of The Beatles' *'Help!'* film, an LP (Long Playing record) of new Beatles' music is released with some added bonus tracks; Indian instrumental versions of three Beatles tunes scored by Ken Thorne - *'A Hard Day's Night'*, *'Can't Buy Me Love'* and *'I Should Have Known Better'* - performed on *tabla*, *surbahar*, *tamboura*, and *sitar* played by Diwan Motihar who also features on two other *'Help!'* instrumentals, the *'James Bond Intro'* and *'The Chase'*.[13]

❀ ❀ ❀

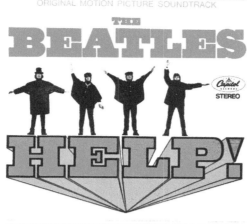

David Crosby and Jim McQuinn of The Byrds, fellow LSD trippers from L.A., draw George's attention to the records of Ravi Shankar, an Indian classical musician who plays the *sitar*.

George - 'So I went and bought a sitar from a little shop at the top of Oxford Street called Indiacraft - it stocked little carvings, and incense. It was a real crummy-quality one, actually, but I bought it and mucked about with it a bit.'[1]

⊛ ⊛ ⊛

In October 1965, whilst in the EMI recording studios at 3 Abbey Road, St. John's Wood, North-West London, The Beatles tackle a song with the working title of *'This Bird Has Flown',* and George wishes to add an interesting accompaniment to complement the rather obscure lyrics.

George - 'Anyway, we were at the point where we'd recorded the Norwegian Wood backing track (twelve-string and six-string acoustic, bass and drums) and it needed something. We would usually start looking through the cupboard to see if we could come up with something, a new sound, and I picked the sitar up - it was just lying around; I hadn't really figured out what to do with it.'[1]

When George breaks one of the instrument's strings, it is suggested he phone the Asian Music Circle to see if someone there might help. It falls to Ringo to make the call, which is answered by Ayana Angadi.

Shankara Angadi, Ayana's son - 'He [Ayana] was heard shouting into the telephone: "Yes, but Ringo who?" As luck would have it, we did have some sitar strings in the house, and the whole family went down to the studio at Abbey Road and watched them record, from behind the glass. My mother drew several sketches of them recording "Norwegian Wood", which are still in the family.'[14]

John - 'George had just got the sitar and I said, "Could you play this piece?"'
'I asked him could he play the piece that I had written, you know, "Dee diddley dee dee, diddley dee dee, diddley dee dee," that bit. But, he was not sure whether he could play it yet because he hadn't done much on the sitar, but he was willing to have a go. As is his wont, he learned that bit and dubbed it on after that.'[5]

> *'She told me she worked in the morning and started to laugh,*
> *I told her I didn't and crawled off to sleep in the bath.'*
>
> - Excerpt of *'Norwegian Wood (This Bird Has Flown)'* by John Lennon & Paul McCartney

John - '*Norwegian Wood* is my song completely. It was about an affair I was having. I was very careful and paranoid because I didn't want my wife, Cyn, to know that there really was something going on outside of the household. I'd always had some kind of affairs going, so I was trying to be sophisticated in writing about an affair, but in such a smoke-screen way that you couldn't tell.'[15]

Together John and Paul write a song called *'Word'*.

'Say the word and you'll be free
Say the word and be like me'

- Excerpt of *'Word'* by John Lennon & Paul McCartney

Paul - 'We smoked a bit of pot, then we wrote out a multicolored lyric sheet, the first time we'd ever done that. We normally didn't smoke when we were working. It got in the way of songwriting because it would just cloud your mind up - "Oh, shit, what are we doing?" It's better to be straight. But we did this multicolor thing.'[6]

Some months after John and George had taken their first LSD trip, Paul McCartney decides to try some himself. He is 'turned on' by his friend, the Honorable Tara Browne, the 20-year old son of an Irish peer (a member of the House of Lords). When Paul 'drops' the acid it is at Tara's mews house in Belgravia, and he does so in the company of various mutual acquaintances including Pretty Things drummer Viv Prince.

Nicki Browne (Tara's wife) **-** 'Because it was Paul's first time, he [Tara] felt it was important for him to stay lucid just in case Paul had a bad trip. And what Paul did was he spent his whole trip looking at this art book of mine called *Private View*. He wasn't interested in any of the females there. He wasn't interested in listening to music either. He just stared at this art book.'[16]

Paul - 'We stayed up all night. It was quite spacey. Everything becomes more sensitive.'[6]

In December 1965, Paul takes some time off from working with The Beatles in order to visit relatives up in Liverpool, and friend Tara, who arrives in his AC Cobra sports car, joins him there. Tara is a motor racing enthusiast but is happy enough to go joy riding with Paul on a pair of rented mopeds (low powered motorcycles).

Paul - 'We were riding along on the mopeds. I was showing Tara the scenery. He was behind me, and it was an incredible full moon; it really was huge. I said something about the moon and he said "yeah", and I suddenly had a freeze-frame image of myself at that angle to the ground when it's too late to pull back up again: I was still looking at the moon and then I looked at the ground, and it seemed to take a few minutes to think, "Ah, too bad - I'm going to smack that pavement with my face!" Bang!
There I was, chipped tooth and all, it came through my lip and split it.'
'In fact that was why I started to grow a moustache.'[1]

❀ ❀ ❀

The next markedly experimental recording made by The Beatles is another John Lennon composition, *'Rain'*, which, though there appears to be no *sitar* on it, has some real surprises such as the unusual use of a drone accompaniment and the startling inclusion of backward vocals on the last verse.

'Can you hear me, can you hear me?
sdaeh rieht edih dna nur yeht semoc niar eht fi.'

- Excerpt of *'Rain'* by John Lennon and Paul McCartney

John - 'Somehow I got it on backwards and I sat there, transfixed, with the earphones on, with a big hash joint.'[15]

' We'd done the main thing at EMI and the habit was then to take the songs home and see what you thought, a little extra gimmick or what the guitar piece could be. So I got home about five in the morning, stoned out of me head, I staggered up to me tape recorder and I put it on, but it came out backwards, and I was in a trance in the earphones, what is it -- what is it? It's too much, you know, and I really wanted the whole song backwards almost, and that was it. So we tagged it on the end. I just happened to have the tape the wrong way round, it just came out backwards, it just blew me mind. The voice sounds like an old Indian.'[17]

❀ ❀ ❀

In early 1966, Evening Standard reporter Maureen Cleave secures the chance for a coveted interview with John Lennon. Whilst they talk, John plays Maureen a record of Indian music, but he doubts that she has been playing much attention to it, even after twenty minutes.

John - 'You're not listening, are you? It's amazing this -- so cool. Don't the Indians appear cool to you? Are you listening? This music is thousands of years old; it makes me laugh, the British going over there and telling them what to do. Quite amazing.'

He holds other strong opinions too.

John - 'Christianity will go. It will vanish and shrink. I needn't argue about that; I'm right and I will be proved right. We're more popular than Jesus now; I don't know which will go first -- rock 'n' roll or Christianity. Jesus was all right but his disciples were thick and ordinary. It's them twisting it that ruins it for me.'

'I've read millions of books, that's why I seem to know things.'

Though he uses his mind a lot, John Lennon confesses he is not physically active.

John - 'Physically lazy. I don't mind writing or reading or watching or speaking, but sex is the only physical thing I can be bothered with any more.'

He lives with his wife, Cynthia, and 3 year-old son, Julian, in an affluent area of Weybridge, Surrey, known as 'Millionaire's Row'.

John - 'Weybridge, won't do at all. I'm just stopping at it, like a bus stop. Bankers and stockbrokers live there; they can add figures and Weybridge is what they live in and they think it's the end, they really do. I think of it every day -- me in my Hansel and Gretel house. I'll take my time; I'll get my real house when I know what I want.'

'You see, there's something else I'm going to do, something I must do -- only I don't know what it is. That's why I go round painting and taping and drawing and writing and that, because it may be one of them. All I know is, this isn't it for me.'

John opens up about a lot of topics, and in the course of this meeting with Maureen Cleave he expresses disappointment with her.

John - 'You never asked after Fred Lennon. He was here a few weeks ago. It was only the second time in my life I'd seen him -- I showed him the door. I wasn't having him in the house.'[18]

So, what about the women in John's life, how does he get on with wife, Cynthia, who he married several years ago when it was discovered she was pregnant?

John - 'I would get fed up now and then and I would start thinking the "Where is she" bit. I'd be hoping that the "one" would come. Then I'd get over it again.'[19]

As a child John was extremely fond of his mother, Julia, though it was not she but his Aunt Mimi who raised him. Tragically, when John was only 17 years old, he witnessed his mother struck and killed by a car driven by an off-duty policeman. Paul McCartney also lost his mother, Mary, when he was young, at the slightly younger age of 16 years old. And apparently Ringo's upbringing had its problems too, as he saw little of his father whilst growing up. But George has been more fortunate in that he has had the benefit of being raised by both his parents whom he still remains close with. Interestingly, whilst George's mother, Louise, was pregnant with him she would sometimes listen to *'Radio India'*, a Sunday morning radio show.

Louise Harrison - 'I always used to fiddle with our wireless to get Indian music. I'd tuned into Indian stuff once by accident and I thought it was lovely, so after that I was always trying to get it on the wireless. I'm not saying this has affected George. This was all before he was born…'[20]

❀ ❀ ❀

It was just a matter of time before another pop group would decide to record a song featuring the *sitar*, and it happens on Tuesday, 8th March 1966, after musician Harihar Rao happened to bring his *sitar* into RCA Studios in Los Angeles. Seizing the opportunity The Rolling Stones' founder, Brian Jones, suggests that the group add the instrument to the group's recording of *'Paint It Black'*, and Brian settles down to play a very rocked up *sitar* line to the song. Mind you this is not the first time The Rolling Stones have experimented with exotic sounds, for several months ago they used an Indian instrument on *'Mothers Little Helper'* - Brian played *tamboura* throughout, creating an unfamiliar drone sound.

The desire to experiment has really taken a strong hold on The Beatles, and George sets about finding out more about Indian music, leading him to get further involved with the Asian Music Circle in London.

Pattie - 'George didn't want to meet new people or go to new places. He was happy to visit my old friends and our families, but he was wary of newcomers—unless they were musicians. One evening some months before we had been invited to dinner by a Mr. Angardi, who ran the Asian Music Circle in London, and his English wife, who painted a large portrait of the two of us, for which we sat on several occasions. Mr. Angardi wanted George to meet a sitar player called Ravi Shankar. Ravi was well known in classical-music circles and a hero in his own country, India. They talked music all evening and George was awestruck.

Soon afterwards Ravi came to Kinfauns to give George a sitar lesson. At one point the phone rang and George put down the sitar, stood up, and went to answer it, stepping over the sitar as he did so. Ravi whacked him sharply on the leg and said, "You must have more respect for the instrument."

The technique involved in playing the sitar is quite different from anything George had known before: he had to sit on the floor for hours, cross-legged, with the bowl of the gourd resting on the ball of his left foot. In no time at all his legs were in agony.'[21]

Ravi Shankar - 'The special attraction to sitar suddenly came about when the Beatles and the Rolling Stones and some other pop groups used it in recordings of their songs.

'Then in June 1966, at a friend's house in London, I met George Harrison and Paul McCartney of the Beatles. I found them to be very charming and polite young men, not at all what I had expected.

'George explained to me he had no real training with the sitar, but had done some experiments with it on his own, using his knowledge of the guitar as a background, and he expressed, very sincerely, his desire to learn from me to play the sitar.'

'He asked me to his beautiful house in Esher, outside London, and a few days before I had to leave England, I gave George his first lesson in Indian music. I found him to be quite sensitive and quick. I visited him once more before leaving for India, when he had requested me to play for a few mutual friends and, of course, the other three Beatles.'[22]

❀ ❀ ❀

In July 1966, Donovan, a singer/songwriter musician friend of The Beatles, releases a new single, dedicated to John and Paul, called *'Sunshine Superman'*, the reverse side of which is *'The Trip'*. Both songs seem to contain allusions to personal drug use.

> *'I said, "Girl, you drank a lot of drink-me but you ain't in a wonderland"'*
> *'The whole wide human race has a-taken far too much methedrine.'*
> - Excerpts of *'The Trip'* by Donovan Leitch

❀ ❀ ❀

Prior to the release of their new LP, The Beatles play concerts in Japan, and the Philippines (where they find themselves in a situation in which they begin to fear for their lives). On their way back to London they stop off in India and check into the Oberoi Hotel in Delhi.

George - 'Before the tour was planned, I had an arrangement made that on the return journey from the

Philippines to London I would stop off in India, because I wanted to go and check it out and buy a good sitar.'
'Somewhere between leaving London and going through Germany and Japan to the Philippines, one by one the others had all said, 'I think I'll come, too.'
'Well, it will be "OK. At least in India they don't know The Beatles. We'll slip in to this nice ancient country, and have a bit of peace and quiet."
'So we got off. It was night-time, and we were standing there waiting for our baggage, and then the biggest disappointment I had was a realisation of the extent of the fame of The Beatles - because there were so many dark faces in the night behind a wire mesh fence, all shouting, "Beatles! Beatles!" and following us.
We got in the car and drove off, and they were all on little scooters, with the Sikhs in turbans all going, "Hi, Beatles, Beatles!" I thought, 'Oh, no! Foxes have holes and birds have nests, but Beatles have nowhere to lay their heads.'
'The next day I bought a sitar. I had a guy bring them over - again we couldn't really get out easily. I bought a sitar off a man called Rikhi Ram.'[1]

The Beatles who arrived in Delhi on their way from Manila seen at Palam on Tuesday.

When the new Beatles LP, 'Revolver', is released on Friday 5th August 1966, the group's fascination with studio experimentation is very evident - it's as though the group has gone through a mysterious transformation and become a different entity. They sound vastly more interesting, with so many unusual ideas bubbling away, that one might suggest they have become an altogether different group, as though they have stepped out of their black and white phase and suddenly gone into colour as *The Studio Beatles*!
One of their new tracks, originally given the working title *'Granny Smith'* (the name of an apple), is a decidedly Indian sounding composition, containing some deeply philosophical lyrics written by George Harrison.

'A lifetime is so short
A new one can't be bought'

- Excerpt of *'Love You To'* by George Harrison

A musician from the Asian Music Circle, Indian *tabla* player Anil Bhagwat, is paid £35 for the session, for assisting George on *'Love You To'*.
Anil Bhagwat - 'George told me what he wanted and I tuned the tabla with him. He suggested I play something in the Ravi Shankar style, 16-beats, though he agreed that I should improvise. Indian music is all improvisation.'[23]

From their appearance and behaviour these days, people are beginning to suspect that The Beatles are dabbling in drugs, and several of the tracks on *'Revolver'* seem to refer to artificial stimulants - *'Doctor Robert'*, *'She*

Said, She Said', 'I'm Only Sleeping' and *'Tomorrow Never Knows'* - the latter utilising an array of loop tapes and swirling vocals.

The lyrics of *'Tomorrow Never Knows'* seem to be directly influenced by *'The Psychedelic Experience',* a book co-authored by Timothy Leary, Ralph Metzner and Richard Alpert, a guide to dealing with ego-loss after the taking of LSD. Interestingly, the book is based on an ancient treatise called *'Tibetan Book of The Dead'* which offers advice to the dying. Leary's book gives such guidance as, *'Trust your divinity, trust your brain, trust your companions. Whenever in doubt, turn off your mind, relax, float downstream.'*

John - 'Leary was the one going round saying, take it, take it, take it. And we followed his instructions in his "how to take a trip" book. I did it just like he said in the book, and then I wrote "Tomorrow Never Knows", which was almost the first acid song.'[1]

> ***'Lay down all thoughts, surrender to the void, that you may see the meaning of within.'***
> - Excerpt from *'Tomorrow Never Knows'* by John Lennon and Paul McCartney

Paul - 'Well, see we wrote the song. See it was a very funny song from the start because John came up with the lyrics to it and he'd just been reading *"Tibetan Book of the Dead"* and he was dead impressed by it, you know, very impressed, and he decided that he'd, erm, write a song, and we only had one verse. I think we stretched it to sort of two verses, and we couldn't think of any more words cos we'd sort of said it all, what we wanted to say, in about two verses. So we had to try and work out how to sort of do it, and how to make it different. So I decided to do some of those, those loops that I'd been doing on my own tape recorder, and they're just tape loops, and I'd been making 'em. So I just took along a bag full of six tape loops to the session and we just tried them and mixed them in and brought them in, in those places. So it was sort of vaguely my idea that bit of it.'[24]

John - '… The Book of the Dead. I'd never seen it in my life. I just saw Leary's psychedelic handout - it was very nice in them days.'

'The expression "tomorrow never knows" was another of Ringo's. [A "hard day's night" being another earlier example] I gave it a throwaway title because I was a bit self-conscious about the lyrics.'[1]

George - 'Indian music doesn't modulate, it just stays. You pick what key you're in, and it stays in that key. I think 'Tomorrow Never Knows' was the first one that stayed there: the whole song was on one chord. But there is a chord that is superimposed on top that does change: if it was in C, it changes down to B flat. That was like an overdub, but the basic sound all hangs on one drone.'[1]

❀ ❀ ❀

John Lennon's comments to Maureen Cleave made to her many months before, about Christianity, have since become public knowledge, and though in Britain they are met with indifference, elsewhere, in the States, many people react with shock and anger. In the Bible Belt of America, protestors congregate in public protest with slogans such as *'JESUS LOVES YOU, DO THE BEATLES?', 'JESUS DIED FOR YOU, JOHN LENNON', 'GOD SAVE the BEATLES',* and many indulge in public displays of Beatle record burning.

Clearly, the situation is serious, and it puts The Beatles under a lot of pressure, so the pressure is on John to offer up an explanation for his comments.

On Thursday, 11th August 1966, The Beatles give a Press conference.

John - 'I just happened to be talking to a friend and I used the word Beatles. I just said that they are having more influence on kids and things than anyone else, including Jesus, but I said it in a way that is the wrong way.'

'I'm not saying that we're better or greater, or comparing us with Jesus Christ as a person or God as a thing or whatever it is. I just said and it is wrong . . . and now it's all this . . . I'm not anti-God, anti-Christ. I am not anti-religion . . . I believe in God, but not as an old man in the sky. I believe what people call 'God' is something in all of us.

'I apologize if it will make you happy. I still don't know quite what I've done. I tried to tell you what I will do, but if you want me to apologize, if that will make you happy, them I'm sorry.'[25]

The Beatles' shock announcement

Just a few days later, on Monday, 29th August 1966, The Beatles appear at Candlestick Park, San Francisco, California, the last date in their 3rd tour of U.S.A., then afterwards make a surprise announcement saying that they will stop touring!

Tony Barrow (Beatles' Press Officer) - 'Coming out of San Francisco that night, getting aboard the charter flight to fly back to LA, one of the first things that George Harrison said when he leant back in the plane and took a drink was, "Well, that's it. I'm finished. I'm not a Beatle any more!"'[12]

❀ ❀ ❀

Gentlemen of Leisure

Now The Beatles have put an end to all the screaming and mayhem of 'Beatlemania', all four of them will no doubt have more time on their hands and will therefore be free to develop and pursue their own individual interests. John quickly decides to take up a role in a new Dick Lester film, *'How I Won The War'*, a black comedy anti-war movie that's due to be shot in the autumn of 1966. And George too finds himself absolutely free to accept an offer, in his case a long vacation in India with Indian musician Ravi Shankar, the maestro *sitar* player whom he met in London back in June.

A few words about Ravi Shankar

Born in Benares, India, in 1920, the son of an eminent barrister and scholar, Ravi Shankar was initially given the Bengali name Rabindro Shankor Chowdhury, but he later took to shortening his name to 'Ravi', a Sanskrit word meaning 'the sun'. At the age of just 10-years-old Ravi joined his brother, Uday, the world famous choreographer, in Paris, France. Ravi studied at a French Catholic school there, also learning dance and various instruments whilst he lived with his brother. Several years later Ravi returned to India in order to study the *sitar* under his musical *guru*, Ustad Allauddin Khan, in order to master the instrument to a high proficiency.

But despite Ravi's obvious talent, his life has had its hurdles, and at one time he became so depressed he even began writing suicide notes - one for his family and one for the police. But before taking his own life he decided to play one last concert, for the Prince of Jodhpur.

Prior to the performance he sat dejectedly, musing on how people would view his death.

Ravi Shankar - 'Then, while I was sitting and practicing, someone knocked at the gate and came in to speak to me. Very humbly, he explained that he was not speaking for himself; he was travelling with his *guru*, and his *guruji* had to go to the bathroom! The man recognized me, since I was sitting with my sitar, and he became even more apologetic for disturbing me. I dried my tears and began to ask a few questions. I learned that this man's *guru* was a *mahatma* ("great soul") known as Tat Baba. I immediately got up and became very attentive, for I had heard this name before and had been told that this man was a very great yogi and a saintly person. The fellow went on, explaining that just as they were passing by our house, the *guru* had asked him to stop the car so that he could go into the nearest house.

And quite simply, that is how I met the person who changed the course of my life - not only on this one day, but many times thereafter.'[22]

❀ ❀ ❀

George - 'What happened to me was that Ravi Shankar wrote to me before I went out to Bombay, and in the letter said, "Try to disguise yourself - couldn't you grow a moustache?" Not that it's going to disguise me, but I've never had a moustache before, so I'll grow it.'[1]

On Wednesday, 14th September 1966, George and his wife, model Pattie Boyd, embark on a six-week trip to India, and after arriving at Bombay airport they are met by Ravi who takes them to the hotel where they book in as "Mr. and Mrs. Sam Wells".

Ravi Shankar - 'They registered for a suite at the Taj Mahal Hotel under a false name, but as it turned out, one young Christian page boy happened to recognize them and truly, within twenty-four hours, almost all Bombay came to know that George Harrison was there.'

'Things reached such a state that we had to call a Press conference to explain that George had not come as a Beatle but as my disciple, and he asked to be left in peace to work on his music with me.'[22]

The day after the Press conference, a BBC radio correspondent obtained an interview with George, during which he explained his religious views.

George - 'I believe much more in the religions of India than in anything I ever learned from Christianity. The difference over here is that their religion is every second and every minute of their lives - and it is them, how they act, how they conduct themselves, and how they think.'[26]

He is quoted in the *Times of India* too.

George - 'I am here not as a Beatle. I have come here just as plain George Harrison to learn the sitar and something of Indian classical music.'[27]

Fortunately for George, his appeal for fans to leave him alone has the desired effect, and he is able to go out on Saturday night to watch a performance by Ravi Shankar, at Santa Cruz in Bombay, without being mobbed.

George - 'I stayed in a Victorian hotel, the Taj Mahal, and was starting to learn the sitar. Ravi would give me lessons, and he'd also have one of his students sit with me. My hips were killing me from sitting on the floor, and so Ravi brought a yoga teacher to start showing me the physical yoga exercises.'[1]

Shambhu Das (George's personal *sitar* tutor) - 'But they kept changing his room but there were still people who were bothering him, and then finally, we decided to leave the city, go to a very isolated place.'[28]

Pattie - 'Ravi was respected all over India: his students would bow down at his feet.'
'Ravi told us that sometimes he would go into a meditative state and not know consciously what he was playing.
We visited many jewels of India with him - the Taj Mahal, Jodhpur, Jaipur, Agra, Delhi, temples with ancient carvings of gods and goddesses in love, fighting and sometimes disguised as demons. We met some holy men who were more than a hundred years old, and sadhus who live in abject poverty. We visited the sacred ghats of Benares, where people are cremated and have their ashes scattered in the Ganges.'
'We went to a festival of Kumbh Mela, the most sacred of all Hindu pilgrimages which attracts millions of people from all over India.'[21]

George - 'I went to the city of Benares, where there was a religious festival going on, called the Ramlila [Ram *'leela'* meaning, the 'play' of Rama]. It was out on a site of 300 to 500 acres, and there were thousands of holy men there for a month-long festival. During this festival the Maharajah feeds everybody and there are camps of different people, including the sadhus - renunciates. In England, in Europe or the West, these holy men would be called vagrants and be arrested, but in a place like India they roam around. They don't have a job, they don't have a Social Security number, they don't even have a name other than collectively - they're called sannyasis, and some of them look like Christ. They're really spiritual; and there are also a lot of loonies who look like Allen Ginsberg. That's where he got his whole trip from - with the frizzy hair, and smoking little pipes called chillums, and smoking hashish. The British tried for years to stop Indians smoking hashish, but they'd been smoking it for too long for it to be stopped.
I saw all kinds of groups of people, a lot of them chanting, and it was a mixture of unbelievable things, with the Maharajah coming through the crowd on the back of an elephant, with the dust rising. It gave me a great buzz.'[1]

Pattie - 'Among many others, we met Ravi's spiritual guru, Tat Baba, who explained the law of *karma* to us both - the law of action and reaction, or cause and effect.'[21]

George - 'When I was in India, I met Ravi's spiritual guru. He was great; he's a hundred and forty-five, but he only looks about forty, and he only looked like that because he was bald - he'd shaved all his hair off. He was talking about karma and samskara. Karma is your actions and your reactions, past, present and future, like "Whatever a man sow, that shall he also reap," what Jesus said. And samskara is like the sum of all that karma at the end of one incarnation, and that determines where you're at for your next incarnation.'[29]

Shambhu Das - 'So, Ravi Shankar says, "Let's go to Kashmir." Kashmir is a haven, bottom of the Himalaya, part of the Himalayas. And there's this nice lake, surrounded by the hills, and there is nice houseboats, fancy houseboats. So, he rented a very luxurious houseboat, where you get a living room, dining room and bedroom, in the boat itself. Very nicely decorated, very western system. So, we lived there almost seven weeks.'[28]

George - 'When we were on the houseboat in Kashmir, owned by a little guy with a white beard called Mr Butt, it was really cold in the night because it was on a lake right up in the Himalayas. Mr Butt would wake us up early in the morning and give us tea and biscuits and I'd sit in bed with my scarf and pullover on, listening to Ravi, who would be in the next room doing his sitar practice - that was such a privileged position to be in.'[30]

To Mr. Butt - with thanks for a very peaceful stay at Clermont, special thanks to Rahman - who served us exceptionally well! My wife and I were whelmed by it all.
Good wishes for the future
George Harrison

Gulam M Bhatt - '... there would be music heard from that houseboat from the crack of dawn, right through the day. We organised *shikara* [flat bottomed boat] rides for both of them.'[31]

Ravi Shankar - 'I had already introduced George to Yogananda's book *Autobiography of a Yogi*. He was totally enchanted by it, and he also had brought some other books on Indian philosophy, including Vivekananda's *Raja Yoga*, which my brother Rajendra had given him.'[30]

Swami Vivekananda is famous most particularly for his speech at the Parliament of the World's Religions in Chicago U.S.A., on Monday, 11th September 1893.

Swami Vivekananda - 'Sisters and Brothers of America, It fills my heart with joy unspeakable to rise in response to the warm and cordial welcome which you have given us. I thank you in the name of the most ancient order of monks in the world; I thank you in the name of the mother of religions, and I thank you in the name of millions and millions of Hindu people of all classes and sects.

My thanks, also, to some of the speakers on this platform who, referring to the delegates from the Orient, have told you that these men from far-off nations may well claim the honour of bearing to different lands the idea of toleration. I am proud to belong to a religion which has taught the world both tolerance and universal acceptance. We believe not only in universal toleration, but we accept all religions as true. I am proud to belong to a nation which has sheltered the persecuted and the refugees of all religions and all nations of the earth. I am proud to tell you that we have gathered in our bosom the purest remnant of the Israelites, who came to Southern India and took refuge with us in the very year in which their holy temple was shattered to pieces by Roman tyranny. I am proud to belong to the religion which has sheltered and is still fostering the remnant of the grand Zoroastrian nation. I will quote to you, brethren, a few lines from a hymn which I remember to have repeated from my earliest boyhood, which is every day repeated by millions of human beings: "As the different streams having their sources in different paths which men take through different tendencies, various though they appear, crooked or straight, all lead to Thee."

The present convention, which is one of the most august assemblies ever held, is in itself a vindication, a declaration to the world of the wonderful doctrine preached in the *Gita*: "Whosoever comes to Me, through whatsoever form, I reach him; all men are struggling through paths which in the end lead to me." Sectarianism, bigotry, and its horrible descendant, fanaticism, have long possessed this beautiful earth. They have filled the earth with violence, drenched it often and often with human blood, destroyed civilization and sent whole nations to despair. Had it not been for these horrible demons, human society would be far more advanced than it is now. But their time is come; and I fervently hope that the bell that tolled this morning in honor of this convention may be the death-knell of all fanaticism, of all persecutions with the sword or with the pen, and of all uncharitable feelings between persons wending their way to the same goal.'

George - 'Ravi had a really sweet brother called Raju, who gave me a lot of books by wise men, and one of the books, which was by Swami Vivekananda, said: "If there's a God you must see him and if there's a soul we must perceive it - otherwise it's better not to believe. It's better to be an outspoken atheist than a hypocrite."'[1]

Chapter Two
Strawberry Fields, White Lightning & Orange Sunshine

Paul - 'After recording sessions, at two or three in the morning, we'd be careering through the villages on the way to Weybridge, shouting "weyhey" and driving much too fast. George would perhaps be in his Ferrari - he was quite a fast driver - and John and I would be following in his big Rolls Royce or the Princess. John had a mike in the Rolls with a loudspeaker outside and he'd be shouting to George in the front: "It is foolish to resist, it is foolish to resist! Pull over!" It was insane. All the lights would go on in the houses as we went past - it must have freaked everybody out.

When John went to make "How I Won the War" in Spain, he took the same car, which he virtually lived in. It had blacked-out windows and you could never see who was in it, so it was perfect. John didn't come out of it - he just used to talk to the people outside through the microphone: "Get away from the car! Get away!"' [1]

Work continues on the production the *'How I Won the War'*, in which John Lennon plays Private Gripweed. John uses much of his time on location writing and re-writing his new composition, *'Strawberry Fields Forever'* a tune that features the sound of the *swarmandal*, an Indian zither or autoharp.

> **'There's no one on my wavelength, I mean, it's either too high or too low,
> That is you can't, you know, tune in, but it's all right, I mean it's not too bad'**
> - Excerpt of early lyrics for *'Strawberry Fields Forever'* by John Lennon & Paul McCartney

During the filming of *'How I Won the War'* John has been wearing 'National Health' spectacles in order to compensate for his longstanding shortsightedness, and in so doing inadvertently finds a very individual style for himself. Then, stoned on a special bar of chocolate, John creates a parody of the Shroud of Turin, with an image of himself wearing glasses, and entitles the result 'Shroud of Tourin'! Coincidentally, John's 'granny glasses' are very similar to the spectacles discovered in his soup during the restaurant sketch of the *'Help!'* movie. [288]

Cynthia - 'I was glad he was being creative, but his drug-taking hadn't stopped and too often he was lost to me. Still, I clung to the times when he was his old self, hoping that the real, loving John would return. One morning at breakfast he pointed out an article in the newspaper to me. It was about a Japanese artist, Yoko Ono, who had made a film that consisted of close-up shots of people's bottoms. "Cyn, you've got to look at this. It must be a joke. Christ, what next? She can't be serious!" We laughed and shook our heads. "Mad," John said. "She must be off her rocker." I had to agree. We had no understanding at all of avant-garde art or conceptualism at that point and the newspaper went into the bin.' [10]

Of course, the individual Beatles' artistic interests are not restricted to music and films alone, but to art generally. Indeed, John Lennon's personal appreciation of visual art can be traced right back, at least to his teen years when he attended Liverpool College of Art where he got to mix with the bohemian set. All the Beatles are interested in experimenting with their music, but this does not prevent John suggesting that '*avant-garde* is French for bullshit'.

On Monday, 7th November 1966, John Lennon attends a London art gallery, and is given a preview of Yoko Ono's exhibition, *'Yoko at Indica'*. Indica is owned and run by Marianne Faithfull's husband, artist John Dunbar.

John - 'There was an apple on sale there for two hundred quid; I thought it was fantastic - I got the humor in her work immediately. I didn't have to have much knowledge about avant-garde or underground art, the humor got me straightaway.'
'.. neither of us knew who the hell we were, she didn't know who I was, she'd only heard of Ringo, I think, it means apple in Japanese.

'John Dunbar insisted she say hello to the millionaire. And she came up and handed me a card which said "breathe" on it, one of her instructions, so I just went [*pant*]. This was our meeting.'[5]

Yoko - 'I didn't know who he was. And when I found out I just didn't care, I mean, in the art world a Beatle is - well, you know. Also he was in a suit and he looked so ordinary.'[19]

Apparently though, Yoko had already met with Beatle Paul some month's earlier when she solicited him on behalf of *avant-garde* artist John Cage, for some handwritten Beatle lyrics.
John - ' I don't remember her at the gallery at all. I was stoned. Then she called me up. She wanted scores of my songs for some book.'[19]

Barry Miles, owner of Indica Books - 'She knew exactly who they were. She'd already approached Paul for some John Cage manuscripts she wanted. He wouldn't give her anything, but suggested she go to John. But she told John she'd never heard of the Beatles and he believed her.'[33]

John Cage, born 1912, is a respected composer and *avant-garde* artist who has studied Indian thought and Zen Buddhism.

❀ ✤ ❀

John - 'Nothing much happened at that first meeting. I assumed she was just a 36-year-old Japanese lady artist whose interest in a young multi-millionaire was that he might finance some of her future exhibitions.'[34]
'The next time we met was at a Claes Oldenburg opening, with a lot of objects like cheese-burgers made out of rubber and garbage like that. When we met again, we sort of made eye contact.'[12]

Yoko - 'We started to bump into each other in places. Liverpool Art School asked me to come to lecture and do a performance. I told that to John, when I met him. He thought that was great. "So you're going to Liverpool?" He moved his eyebrows up and down a couple of times - like Groucho Marx - and looked at me warmly.'[25]

And Yoko obtains the hand-written colourised lyrics of *'The Word'* by John and Paul, with its stoned doodles in yellow, purple, pink and red.

Cynthia - 'We didn't discuss Yoko Ono again until one night when we were lying in bed, reading, I asked John what his book was. It was called *Grapefruit* and looked very short. "Oh, something that weird artist woman sent me," he said.
"I didn't know you'd met her."
John looked up. "Yeah, I went to her exhibition, John Dunbar asked me. It was nutty."'[10]

Yoko - 'Finally, there was a call from him that he'd like me to come to Kenwood. And a car was sent for me, and I went and I was thinking, "What is this about?" He said he'd read Grapefruit, and he wanted to know whether he can get this Light House on the sales list in Grapefruit.'
'Appearing under "Architectural Works" in the book's spoof merchandising list, Light House is described as "a house constructed of light from prisms, which exists in accordance with the changes of the day".
'And he wanted to build that in his garden. It's very sweet… but it's conceptual.'[35]

❀ ✤ ❀

The *Daily Mirror* of Friday, 11th November 1966, includes an interview with George Harrison.
George - 'We've been resting and thinking. It gave us a chance to re-assess things. After all, we've had four years doing what everybody else wanted us to do. Now we're doing what we want to do. But whatever we do, it has got to be real and progressive. Everything we've done so far has been rubbish as I see it today. Other people may like what we've been doing, but we're not kidding ourselves. It doesn't mean a thing to what we want to do now. People live too easily in a plastic world. They think they are doing something, but when they peg out, they've done nothing.'[12]

Tara Browne has recently become co-owner of *Dandie Fashions*, a men's boutique about open in the King's Road, in Chelsea, and he is also about to inherit a fortune, £1,000,000 to be precise. Yet, despite his wealth and position, Tara has worries; and like his close friend Brian Jones, he has intimated that he doesn't expect to live very long. So when Brian and Tara set about creating personalised *mandalas,* spiritual visualisations of their lives, they are likely attempting to take stock and make sense of their life experiences thus far.

Kathy Etchingham (a girlfriend of Jimi Hendrix) - 'On the night of the 17th December 1966 Jimi and I went to a party. Brian Jones had come round and insisted we should go to a party to see his friend Tara Browne before he went off to Ireland for Christmas. We arrived late and met Tara Browne and his girlfriend, the model Suki Potier who had both been spending that day with Brian, and they chatted with us around the dining room table. We exchanged phone numbers and said we would keep in touch and then they left.'[36]

Having borrowed a sports car for the weekend, Tara takes Suki out for a midnight drive. Suddenly he swerves as *'a large low car had come quickly across the road', 'appearing from nowhere',* and the young couple crash into a stationary vehicle, leaving Tara with severe head injuries. The Press publish a photograph which appears to show Tara's Lotus Elan, its tyre treads caked in ice, broken bonnet and bumper smashed into the rear of an old black Riley RM saloon car, wreckage strewn about the frosted tarmac.
Gilbert Potier - 'He saved my daughter's life, I am convinced of that. It appears he swung the car in an attempt to save Suki from the full force of the crash. It was a very gallant act. It's tragic it should have cost him his life.'[37]
Brian Jones, who on hearing of Tara's death weeps - 'I am numbed. It's ghastly. He was so full of life.'[16]
Whether or not Tara was 'on' anything or not can only be a matter for conjecture since blood tests for drugs are fairly basic.
Stash (a mutual friend of Brian and Tara) - 'Since Tara protected Suki when they crashed, it does not seem to me that whether or not he was high is relevant.'[38]

⊛ ⊛ ⊛

On the evening of Wednesday, 28th December 1966, BBC television screens the premiere of Jonathan Miller's star-studded dramatisation of Lewis Carroll's *'Alice in Wonderland',* commissioned for the popular *Wednesday Play*. Soon the audience is drawn into Alice's struggle to deal with the bewildering mind-bending, conscious-altering consequences of ingesting the mysterious *'drink me'*, and share her dreamlike experiences as she loses all sense of time and space, drifting about in a state of fear, wonder and confusion. The original soundtrack by Ravi Shankar features imaginative use of Indian and western instrumentalisation which has the effect of deepening the sense of surreal dreaminess that abounds in this heady, slightly disturbing drama.

⊛ ⊛ ⊛

John - 'I was reading the paper one day and I noticed two stories. One was the Guinness heir who killed himself in a car. That was the main headline story. He died in London in a car crash. On the next page was a story about 4000 potholes in Blackburn, that needed to be filled.'[15]

'Well, I just had to laugh
I saw the photograph'
- Excerpt of *'A Day in the Life'* by John Lennon & Paul McCartney

Paul - 'He'd been reading the *Daily Mail* and brought the newspaper with him to my house. We went upstairs to the music room and started to work on it. He had the first verse, he had the war, and a little bit of the second verse.'
'The verse about the politician blowing his mind out in a car we wrote together. It has been attributed to Tara Browne, the Guinness heir, which I don't believe is the case, certainly as we were writing it, I was not attributing it to Tara in my head. In John's head it might have been. In my head I was imagining a politician bombed out on drugs who'd stopped at some traffic lights and he didn't notice that the lights had changed. The "blew his mind" was purely a drug reference, nothing to do with the car crash. In actual fact I think I spent more time with Tara than John did.'[6]

John - 'Paul's contribution was the beautiful little lick in the song "I'd love to turn you on,"…'[15]

Take 2 of *'Day in the Life'* ends with a long drawn out *'OMMMMMMM'* lasting about 5 seconds.

Chapter Three
Expand Your Conscious Mind

Paul McCartney is asked to contribute a composition to be played at the 'Million Volt Light and Sound Rave', an event organised by several of Tara's friends, design associates Binder, Edwards and Vaughan, who have recently given Paul's piano a facelift by painting a strikingly colourful design all over it. The sounds at the 'Rave' or 'happening' will activate some 15 light projectors, which will automatically screen coloured shapes. Paul hopes to get The Beatles involved in making this soundtrack.

Paul - 'So we were set up in the studio and we'd just go in every day and record. So I said to the guys, "It's a bit indulgent but would you mind giving me 10 minutes? I've been asked to do this thing". I said, "All I want you to do is just wander round all of the stuff; bang it, shout, play it, and it doesn't need to make any sense. Hit a drum, then wander on to the piano, hit a few notes and just wander round." So that's what we did, and then we put a bit of echo on it, and so it's very free.'[39]

The finished product, advertised as 'Music composed for the occasion by Paul McCartney', is an *avant-garde* recording of about 14 minutes long, described as *'the combination of a one-take track plus numerous overdubs, so that by its end it included distorted, hypnotic drum and organ sounds, a distorted lead guitar, the sound of a church organ, various effects (water gargling was one) and perhaps most intimidating of all, John and Paul screaming dementedly and bawling aloud random phrases like "Are you alright?" and "Barcelona!".'[23]

This form of music is not new, in fact composer Frank Zappa's TV debut, on the *Steve Allen Show* in 1963, showed him organising an impromptu performance of cacophonic random sounds. And John and Paul's apparently meaningless shouting finds precedent in playright Eugène Ionesco's *'théâtre de l'absurde'* 1950's dramas that explore shifts in consciousness. At the end of Ionesco's *'The Bald Prima Donna'*, for instance, the cast shout and scream absurd and random lines, such as *'Silly gobblegobblers, silly gobblegobblers.'*, *'Marietta, spot the pot!'*, *'Krishnamurti, Krishnamurti, Krishnamurti!'*, and *'The pope elopes! The pope's got no horoscope. The horoscope's bespoke.'*

David Vaughan (a friend of Paul's) - 'I asked Paul to do it and I thought he would make more of it than he did; I thought this was a vehicle for him, if anything was. My trouble is, I expect everybody to drop everything. I forget other people have got things on.'[6]

'That organ is exactly how I used to see him. I used to picture him as a maniac from the seventeenth century: one of those brilliant composers who'd suddenly been reincarnated into this century, let loose with modern technology. A lot of people thought Paul McCartney was shallow. I didn't see him as that at all, I saw him as very very deep. He had this open fire with a big settee in front of it, there would be no lights on, and he'd be playing music at top volume. I used to sit there watching him for hours. I think that's the real him; this real deep, dark ... I thought, Who knows what he could do if they'd leave him alone for a bit? Because he could absorb a lot without encountering any mental block, he could express that Machiavellian, European horror.'[6]

❀ ❀ ❀

In February 1967, whilst her husband George is off playing with The Beatles, recording *'A Day In The Life'*, his 21-year old wife, Pattie, finds she has rather too much time on her hands spent alone at 'Kinfauns', the couple's luxury bungalow in Esher, Surrey. Relief comes in a visit from her best friend, fellow fashion model, brunette Marie-Lise Volpeliere-Pierrot.

Sitting in the kitchen, thumbing through recent newspapers, Pattie gets to looking at the small ads and spots one in particular, sandwiched amongst offers of accommodation, sales of Turkish cigarettes, Victorian chairs, and Persian, Indian and Chinese carpets. The ad Pattie spots is surrounded by a cluster of appeals from well-meaning charities in search of generous donors. The advertisement she lights upon is for a technique of meditation, and has been placed by an organisation located in Grosvenor Place, London, just a stone's throw from Buckingham Palace, the official residence of the Queen of England.

> **TRANSCENDENTAL MEDITATION** of
> Maharishi Mahesh Yogi; for further information regarding this technique write to Spiritual Regeneration Movement Foundation, 20 Grosvenor Place, London, S.W.1. BELgravia 8994.

Pattie - 'I thought I'd really like to look into, or study, something that is more meaningful in my life, something sort of on the spiritual path. And I saw a tiny advertisement in the *Sunday Times*, in England, advertising talks about meditation, about Transcendental Meditation.'[40]

The advertisement for meditation arouses both the young women's interest:-

Pattie - 'I had a yearning to take up chanting, meditation or something spiritual - I suppose after the experience of India - and she felt much the same. Something was missing from our lives, we decided.'[21]

So Pattie and Marie-Lise together decide to attend an introductory lecture in Central London, at Caxton Hall, a grand red brick building in Westminster (in which, two years earlier, Beatle Ringo Starr's marriage to Maureen Cox had been solemnised).

Pattie - '… and I went along with a girlfriend, and we really enjoyed it.'[40]

After the lecture, the two friends enroll on a course to learn how to meditate, and are advised that on the day of their 'initiation' (when they will be taught to meditate) they each should bring an offering of cut flowers, some fresh fruits, a clean white handkerchief and a donation of one week's earnings. Jet Fairly, a middle-aged no-nonsense woman, who in her time might well have been a poster girl for the Land Army, meets and greets them and politely asks them to remove their footwear. Jet then watches as the glamorous young women set about taking off their very fashionable 'Jesus Boots' of plaited suede, struggling to unfasten the thongs that tie them. After successfully divesting themselves of their high boots they attend a short ceremony, and are then given instructions as to how to practice Transcendental Meditation. After sitting to meditate long enough to get a taste for the process, they are given further instructions, and it is suggested to Pattie and Marie-Lise that they practice this meditation twice daily for about twenty minutes each time.

Pattie - 'I loved meditating and I found the effects remarkable; I really did feel more alert and energetic. It did what it said on the bottle - it was life-changing. I couldn't wait to tell George.
As soon as he came home I bombarded him with what I had been doing and he was really interested.'[21]

When John Lennon hears about Transcendental Meditation, he is initially sceptical.

John - 'She said, "They gave me this word but I can't tell you, it's a secret". And I said; "What kind of scene is this if you keep secrets from your friends?"'[41]

❀ ❀ ❀

The Beatles continue recording their new LP, which is to be built up around a concept Paul has come up with, where they envisage themselves as an entirely different group, a band even.

Paul - 'It was the start of the hippy times, and there was a jingly-jangly hippy aura all around in America. I started thinking about what would be a really mad name to call a band. At the time there were lots of groups with name like "Laughing Joe and His Medicine Band" or "Col Tucker's Medicinal Brew and Compound", all that old Western going-round-on-wagons stuff, with long rambling names. And so… I threw those words together: "Sgt Pepper's Lonely Hearts Club Band".

I took an idea back to the guys in London: "As we're trying to get away from ourselves - to get away from touring and into a more surreal thing - how about if we become an alter-ego band, something like, say, "*Sgt Pepper's Lonely Hearts*"? I've got a little bit of a song cooking with that title."'

George - 'I felt we were just in the studio to make the next record, and Paul was going on about this idea of some fictitious band. That side of it didn't really interest me, other than the title song and the album cover.'[1]

> **'You gave me the word, I finally heard**
> **I'm doing the best that I can.'**
>
> - Excerpt of *'Getting Better'* by John Lennon & Paul McCartney

On Tuesday, 21st March 1967, The Beatles are in the studio working on a track called *'Getting Better'*, but John is not his usual self and when he takes a turn for the worse The Beatles' producer, George Martin, gets concerned.

George Martin - 'We were overdubbing voices on one of the Pepper tracks, and John, down in the studio, was obviously feeling unwell. I called over the intercom, "What's the matter, John? Aren't you feeling very well?" "No," said John.

I went down and looked at him, and he said, "I don't know. I'm feeling very strange."

He certainly looked very ill, so I told him, "You need some fresh air. Let's leave the others working, and I'll take you outside."

The problem was where to go; there were the usual five hundred or so kids waiting for us at the front, keeping vigil like guard-dogs, and if we had dared to appear at the entrance there would have been uproar and they would probably have broken the gates down. So I took him up to the roof, above Number Two studio. I remember it was a lovely night, with very bright stars. Then I suddenly realised that the only protection around the edge of the roof was a parapet about six inches high, with a sheer drop of some ninety feet to the ground below, and I had to tell him, "Don't go too near the edge, there's no rail there, John." We walked around the roof for a while. Then he agreed to come back downstairs, and we packed up for the night.'[42]

George Martin has no inkling at all as to what is up with John.

John - 'I thought I was taking some uppers, and I was not in a state of handling it. I can't remember what album it was but I took it and then [whispers] I just noticed all of a sudden I got so scared on the mike. I said, "What was it?" I thought I felt ill. I thought I was going cracked. Then I said, "I must get some air." They all took me upstairs on the roof, and George Martin was looking at me funny. And then it dawned on me. I must have taken acid. And I said, "Well, I can't go on, I have to go." So I just said, "You'll have to do it and I'll just stay and watch." I just [became] very nervous and just watching all of a sudden. "Is it alright?" and they were saying, "Yeah." They were all being very kind. They said, "Yes, it's alright." And I said, "Are you sure it's alright?" They carried on making the record.'[8]

Paul - 'I thought, Maybe this is the moment where I should take a trip with him. It's been coming for a long time. It's often the best way, without thinking about it too much, just slip into it. John's on it already, so I'll sort of catch up. It was my first trip with John, or with any of the guys. We stayed up all night, sat around and hallucinated a lot.

Me and John, we'd known each other for a long time. Along with George and Ringo, we were best mates. And we looked into each other's eyes, the eye contact thing we used to do, which is fairly mind-boggling. You dissolve into each other. But that's what we did, round about that time, that's what we did a lot. And it was amazing. You're looking into each other's eyes and you would want to look away, but you wouldn't, and you could see yourself in the other person. It twas a very freaky experience and I was totally blown away.

There's something disturbing about it. You ask yourself, "How do you come back from it? How do you then lead a normal life after that?" And the answer is, you don't. After that you've got to get trepanned or you've got

to meditate for the rest of your life. You've got to make a decision which way you're going to go.
I would walk out into the garden - "Oh no, I've got to go back in." It was very tiring, walking made me very tired, wasted me, always wasted me. But "I've got to do it, for my well-being." In the meantime John had been sitting around very enigmatically and I had a big vision of him as a king, the absolute Emperor of Eternity. It was a good trip. It was great but I wanted to go to bed after a while.
I'd just had enough after about four or five hours. John was quite amazed that it had struck me in that way. John said, "Go to bed? You won't sleep!" "I know that, I've still got to go to bed." I thought, now that's enough fun and partying, now ... It's like with drink. That's enough. That was a lot of fun, now I gotta go and sleep this off. But of course you don't just sleep off an acid trip so I went to bed and hallucinated a lot in bed. I remember Mal coming up and checking that I was all right. "Yeah, I think so." I mean, I could feel every inch of the house, and John seemed like some sort of emperor in control of it all. It was quite strange. Of course he was just sitting there, very inscrutably."[6]

❈ ❈ ❈

A group of designers, known collectively known as The Fool, are chosen to create a wonderfully colourful and imaginative cover for *'Sergeant Pepper'* and when it is finished The Beatles love it. But the artwork has been made to the wrong dimensions, so, after discussion followed by indecision, their cover artwork is discarded in favour of a fresh commission. Only their design for the record's paper sleeve is retained.

Original cover design by The Fool for the *'Sergeant Pepper's Lonely Hearts Club Band'* LP

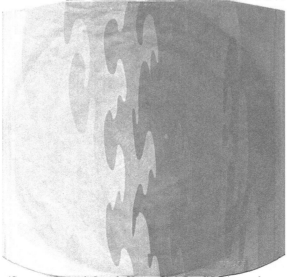

'Sergeant Pepper's Lonely Hearts Club Band' LP inner sleeve

Under the direction of gallery owner Robert Fraser, a new sleeve for *'Sergeant Pepper'* is designed, this time by artists Peter Blake and Jann Haworth. The front cover is a brilliant piece of Pop Art, rather reminiscent of a school photograph, but instead of classmates it uses the likenesses of many of those who have left an impression on individual members of The Beatles, and on the designers of the cover. Pictured are such notables as Oscar Wilde, Lewis Carroll, Mae West, and, modern celebrities such as actresses Marlene Dietrich and Marilyn Monroe, and world champion boxer Sonny Liston, who stand out most prominently.

'Sergeant Pepper's Lonely Hearts Club Band' **LP cover**

But not all of The Beatles' individual suggestions are adopted.
Peter Blake - 'John had put Hitler and Jesus on his list.'
'That was John's sense of humour. There had been the "Christ" controversy by then, so I think it was John just being naughty again.'[43]

Notwithstanding, a life sized photographic image of Hitler is created and placed at the centre of the front row, though after a re-think it is discarded and replaced with 'Tarzan' Johnny Weissmuller. At the insistence of Sir Joseph Lock, the head of EMI Records, Mahatma Gandhi is also removed, as Sir Joseph doubts that the record cover would otherwise be printed in India. Nevertheless, several other Indian thinkers remain on the cover - all George's choices - characters featured in Paramahansa Yogananda's *'Autobiography of a Yogi'*.

Mahatma Gandhi at the *'Sergeant Pepper'* **photo session**

Paul - 'Those Indian people have amazing stories. There's one called Yogananda Para Manza, who died in 1953 and left his body in an incredibly perfect state. Medical reports in Los Angeles three or four months after he died were saying this is incredible; this man hasn't decomposed yet. He was sitting there glowing because he did this sort of transcendental bit, transcended his body by planes of consciousness. He was taught by another person on the cover and *he* was taught by *another*, and it all goes back to one called Babujee [Babaji] who's just a little drawing looking upwards.

You can't photograph him - he's an agent. He puts a curse on the film. He's the all-time governor, he's been at it a long time and he's still around doing the transcending bit.

George says the great thing about people like Babujee and Christ and all the governors who have transcended is that they've got out of the reincarnation cycle; they've reached the bit where they are just there; they don't have to zoom back.

The Yogi goes through millions of things to realise the simplest of all truths, because while you are going through this part, there's always the opposite truth. You say, "Ah well, that's all there is to it then. It's all great, and God's looking after you." Then someone says, "What about a hunchback then, is that great?" And you say, "OK then, it's all lousy." And this is just as true if you want to see it. But the truth is that it's neither good nor lousy; just down the middle; a state of being that doesn't have black or white, good or bad.

I think George's awareness has helped us because he got into this through Indian music - or as he calls it, "All India Radio". There's such a sense of vision in Indian music that it's just like meditation.'[44]

'When you've seen beyond yourself then you may find
Peace of mind is waiting there.'

- Excerpt of *'Within You Without You'* by George Harrison

On *'Sergeant Pepper'* the group can be heard deploying a wonderfully wide array of instruments and sound effects, but the real surprise, the track of particular note is an Indian sounding number entitled *'Within You, Without You'* by George Harrison. George's composition is a deeply reflective number on which George sings and plays an acoustic guitar. He is accompanied by an array of Indian musicians from the Asian Music Circle in London playing stringed instruments such as *sitar*, *dilruba*, *tamboura* and *swarmandal* to the constant beat of *tabla* drums. On the session, George instructed producer George Martin as to how he wanted the string orchestration for violins and cellos to be arranged.

John - 'George has done a great Indian one. We came along one night and he had about 400 Indian fellas playing there … it was a great swinging evening, as they say.'[1]

George Martin - 'There are some Indian musicians who worked on "Sgt. Pepper" who still haven't been paid simply because George doesn't know their names.'[45]

It is easy to overlook the fact that the *Sergeant Pepper* LP contains only this one song by George Harrison.

George - 'For me it was a bit tiring, or it was a bit boring, because ermm, I mean, I had a few moments in there that I enjoyed, but generally I didn't really like that album much. My heart was still in India, you know, I mean that was the big thing for me, when that happened in '66. It was, after that, everything else seemed like hard work, you know, it was a job. It was like doing something I didn't really want to do. I was losing interest in being Fab at that point.'[46]

'Before then everything I'd known had been in the West, and so the trips to India had really opened me up. I was into the whole thing; the music, the culture, the smells. There were good and bad smells, lots of colours, many different things - and that's what I'd become used to. I'd been let out of the confines of the group, and it was difficult for me to come back into the sessions. In a way it felt like going backwards.'[1]

❀ ❀ ❀

George Harrison's friend and *sitar* tutor, Ravi Shankar, is these days so much in demand in America, that he has decided to move and live there, in California, where he appears at the Monterey Pop Festival alongside Jimi Hendrix, Otis Redding, The Who, Canned Heat, Country Joe & The Fish, and many other notable groups.

❀ ❀ ❀

John Lennon is nowadays being seen wearing a curious 'talisman', a long leather necklace with daisy shapes, indigo blue glass rings, swirl cones and metal eyelets.

John - 'I've had a lot of time to think, only now am I beginning to realize many of the things I should have known years ago. I'm getting to understand my own feelings. Don't forget that under this frilly shirt is a hundred-year-old man who's seen and done so much, but at the same time knowing so little.'[47]

George - 'People are very, very aware of what's going on around them nowadays. They think for themselves and I don't think we can ever be accused of under-estimating the intelligence of our fans.'[47]

❀ ❀ ❀

'Sergeant Pepper's Lonely Heart Club Band', The Beatles' long awaited new LP, immediately becomes the talk of the town. At The Troubadour café in Earl's Court, London, the double cover is displayed above the counter and the record plays continuously.

The new Beatles record provides listeners a fascinating fantastic aural trip through intertwined multi-tracked recordings, and many believe they detect hidden meaning in the lyrics. Rumour has it that these days, not only are The Beatles taking drugs but they are also inciting others to take them and that within the lyrics to songs on *'Sergeant Pepper'* are coded messages to their fans about drug use, and the BBC (British Broadcasting Company) promptly bans airplay of *'A Day in the Life'*, on account of the words *'I'd love to turn you on'*. It is not just the BBC responds; Scotland Yard is getting increasingly interested in the personal habits of The Beatles and other popstars.

Mick Jagger - 'The music that's being done now - not only "Pepper" - has been influenced by drugs, LSD, pot. That's damned obvious. A lot of freaky people are playing a lot of freaky music without LSD, but the drug has had an influence on music. Take "A Day In The Life": nothing in there is specifically about drugs, yet it's all about drugs.'[48]

Paul - 'A song like *"Got to Get You Into My Life,"* that's directly about pot, although everyone missed it at the time. …*"Day Tripper,"* that's one about acid (LSD). *"Lucy in the Sky,"* that's pretty obvious. There's others that make subtle hints about drugs, but, you know, it's easy to overestimate the influence of drugs on the Beatles' music.'
'Just about everyone was doing drugs in one form or another and we were no different, but the writing was too important for us to mess it up by getting off our heads all the time.'[49]

Stones' lead singer Mr Jagger, 24, has been accused of illegally possessing four tablets containing amphetamine sulphate and methylamphetamine hydrochloride. Guitarist Mr Richards, also 24, is charged with allowing his house to be used for the purpose of smoking cannabis.

- *BBC News* Wednesday, 10th May 1967.[50]

Brian Jones and friend 'Stash', Prince Stanislaus Klossowski de Rola, are arrested too, for possession of cannabis and cocaine. After the bust, Stash is invited to stay at Paul McCartney's London home.

Paul - 'I did cocaine for about a year around the time of Sgt. Pepper.'
'Coke and maybe some grass to balance it out. I was never completely crazy with cocaine.'
'I'd been introduced to it and at first it seemed OK, like anything that's new and stimulating.'
'When you start working your way through it, you start thinking: "Mmm, this is not so cool an idea," especially when you start getting those terrible comedowns.'[49]

❀ ❀ ❀

The Beatles are working on a new song, *'All Too Much'*, written by George, a celebration of his experiences of LSD.

*'It's all too much for me to take
The love that's shining all around here'*

Extract from *'It's All Too Much'* by George Harrison

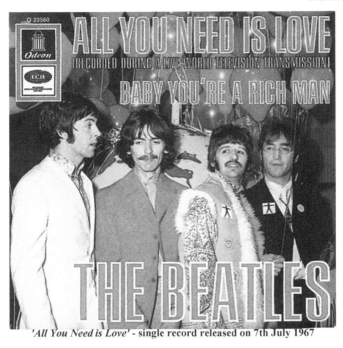

'All You Need is Love' - single record released on 7th July 1967

The Beatles' new single is another recent composition, *'All You Need is Love'*.

On Friday, 16th June 1967, barely a week after the release of the *'Sergeant Pepper's Lonely Heart's Club Band'* LP, 25 year-old Beatle Paul McCartney admits to having taken LSD.
Paul - 'After I took it, it opened my eyes. We only use one tenth of our brain. Just think what we all could accomplish if we could only tap that hidden part! It would mean a whole new world. If the politicians would take LSD, there wouldn't be any more war, or poverty or famine.'[51]

Several days later, an ITN reporter tackles Paul about his statement on LSD.
Reporter - 'Do you think that you have now encouraged your fans to take drugs?'
Paul - 'I don't think it'll make any difference. I don't think my fans are going to take drugs just because I did, you know.'[3]

Paul - 'I remember a couple of men from ITN showed up, and then the newscaster arrived: "Is it true you've had drugs?" They were at my door - I couldn't tell them to go away - so I thought, "Well, I'm either going to try to bluff this, or I'm going to tell him the truth." I made a lightning decision: "Sod it. I'll give them the truth."
I spoke to the reporter beforehand, and said, "You know what's going to happen here: I'm going to get the blame for telling everyone I take drugs. But you're the people who are going to distribute the news." I said, "I'll tell you. But if you've got any worries about the news having an effect on kids, then don't show it. I'll tell you the truth, but if you disseminate the whole thing to the public then it won't be my responsibility. I'm not sure I want to preach this but, seeing as you're asking - yeah, I've taken LSD." I'd had it about four times at that stage, and I told him so. I felt it was reasonable, but it became a big news item.'[1]

John - 'It was a long time before Paul took it. And then there was the big announcement. I think George was pretty heavy on it. We were probably both the most cracked. I think Paul's a bit more stable than George and I. I don't know about straight. Stable. I think LSD profoundly shocked him.'[5]
'I never felt any responsibility being a so-called idol. It's wrong of people to expect it.'
'There's an illusion that just because somebody buys your record that they're going to do what you tell them. It doesn't work that way.'[1]

The Sunday Times of 24th July 1967, carries an advertisement with a petition to 'Legalise Pot', signed and paid for by The Beatles.

'The law against marijuana is immoral in principle and unworkable in practice.'

The Sunday Times, 24th July 1967.

The Beatles seem determined to draw attention to their personal drug use, as do the many people who lend their names to the petition, amongst them The Beatles' manager, Brian Epstein.
Brian Epstein - 'I really believe that pot, marijuana or hash, whatever you like to call it, is less harmful, without question, than say, alcohol.'[12]

The petition is also signed by other eminent people; film director Jonathan Miller, broadcaster David Dimbleby, artist David Hockney, politician Brian Walden MP, and many others, including jazz performer George Melly. The main impetus behind the petition is the arrest of John 'Hoppy' Hopkins, the popular editor of International Times (IT), the foremost British 'underground' newspaper. But the petition also comes as a response and acknowledgement of other arrests amongst the 'hip' community, including pop stars such as Donovan, charged with possession of 'Indian hemp', and members of The Rolling Stones, who have been prosecuted for drug related offences. There is no denying it, in pop music circles drugs are becoming very pervasive, and that these days everyone seems to want to get 'high'.

So, when it comes to 'artificial stimulants', what are the options? Well, pot is a plant that grows wild in many countries, whereas most other available drugs are produced in laboratories and then pressed into tablets etc.

Pot
Cannabis is the compounded pollen of the marijuana plant, which in some countries grows in the wild, hence the terms 'grass' and 'weed'. The most popular 'turn on' seems to be the smoking of 'joints', hand-rolled cigarettes containing cannabis resin (often referred to as 'hashish'). When smoked, pot seems to confer an increased sense of personal well-being, and moves individuals more easily to laughter.

Uppers & Downers
In order to get a 'buzz', some resort to amphetamine drugs such as Dexydrine, Benzadrine, Drynamil and Methedrine, drugs more commonly referred to as 'uppers' or 'speed'. Speed is a stimulant, a consciousness-altering drug, which can give users the impression of having greater energy, increased self-confidence, greater creativity and well-being. However, in order to sustain and prolong these effects it is necessary to escalate the dosage, and before long the user is beset by the negative side effects; physical, mental and social problems. For those who wish to counteract the 'come down' from speed, or else to get really 'stoned' or 'blocked', then 'downers' are used, barbiturate pills such as Mandrax and Mogadon, which relax and seem to help lessen inhibitions but which also lower awareness, with resultant slurring of the speech and drowsiness.

Acid
LSD or 'acid' differs from other social drugs in that it is seldom taken in order to get 'high', but usually by those desirous of having a mental adventure or 'trip'. Alike to amphetamine, LSD alters the consciousness, but its effects differ significantly, in that though there can also be a highly increased sense of well-being - sometimes exaltation - there is also a tremendous heightening of the senses, and sometimes a changed inner perspective of inter-dependence and co-existence. A common perception amongst LSD users is of having a very profound experience. But, on the down side, there is the very real danger that those who take LSD might be visited by experiences of high anxiety, paranoia, hallucinations and confusion; hence LSD is commonly referred to as the 'heaven and hell' drug. Doses of LSD are often given enticing 'brand' names, as for example, 'White Lightning', 'Orange Sunshine'. 'Blue Cheer' and 'Strawberry Fields'.

Gear
Heroin, 'H', 'Horse' or 'Junk', is not the drug of choice for many, other than those who are heedless of the dangers of drug dependency, of becoming a drug addict (a junkie), and the likelihood of an early death.
Cocaine, 'coke' - is also highly addictive.

John - 'We didn't really shove our LP full of pot and drugs, but I mean there was an effect. You were more consciously trying to keep it out. You wouldn't say; "I had some acid, baby, so groovy," but there was a sort of feeling that something happened between *Revolver* and *Sgt. Pepper*.'[41]

By now The Beatles are not only taking drugs they are also dabbling with *mantras* - words of power. In fact, by all accounts, they have been spending much of the time of their recent holiday to Greece together, tripping out on LSD and chanting 'Hare Krishna' whilst sailing about in a luxury yacht. Inspiration for the chanting came after George came across an LP record entitled *'Krishna Consciousness'* by Swami A.C. Bhaktivedanta.

Hare Krishna, Hare Krishna
Krishna Krishna, Hare Hare
Hare Rama, Hare Rama
Rama Rama, Hare Hare
Hare Krishna Mantra

The chanting of *'Hare Krishna, Hare Rama'* is endorsed by the influential New York beat poet Allen Ginsberg, who has moved to San Francisco and says of the chanting; *'It brings a state of ecstasy.'*

Both 'Krishna' and 'Rama' are held to be the names of historical persons who are also believed to have been *'avataars'*, divine living manifestations of God. *'Hare Krishna'* means 'Lord Krishna', with *'Hare'* being pronounced 'Haa-ray'. There are several Scriptures dedicated to Rama and Krishna; one is the story of 'Lord' Rama as told in the epic poem *Ramayana*, another is the story of 'Lord' Krishna as told in the *Maharbharata*, which also contains the *Bhagavad-Gita*. *'Gita'* means 'Song', and is an account of a conversation between Lord Krishna and his friend Arjuna, a warrior. *Shrimad Bhagatam* is another religious text related to Lord Krishna, with further stories of his life and teaching.

Amongst those experimenting with drugs is a tendency to want to 'live in the now' and they have a desire to obtain 'expanded consciousness', a term also used by those who practice meditation. Some are experimenting with their own versions of meditation, concocting methods with the help of drugs, incense, candles and music, whilst others seek out books on *yoga*, mysticism and meditation teachings, in the subtle hope of finding a way to enjoy a permanent 'high'.

In early August 1967, George flies to Los Angeles to visit Ravi Shankar at the L.A. branch of his Kinnara School of Music ('Kinnara' being the name of a mythological celestial musician, half-man, half-horse). A few days later, George and Pattie move on to San Francisco to visit one of Pattie's younger sisters, Jenny, who has recently split up with her boyfriend, Mick Fleetwood, drummer with John Mayall's Bluesbreakers. Jenny is now helping to run a shop in San Francisco and when George and Pattie arrive she joins them and their friends for a stroll around the Haight Ashbury district, wandering out amongst the 'Hippy' community. Unsurprisingly, George is instantly recognised whereupon he obligingly agrees to his giving an impromptu performance on guitar, and he is repeatedly offered drugs by passers by.

Earlier that day, before going about on the walkabout, George had taken some 'acid' but without really considering the likely consequences. The experience of meeting local Hippies, whilst he is tripping, unsettles George deeply, making him question deeply the Hippie counterculture lifestyle based as it is on the widespread use of recreational drugs such as marijuana, amphetamine and LSD. It's not that he's against taking drugs, it's just that he is repelled by the 'druggie' lifestyle he encounters in San Francisco, where Timothy Leary's exhortation to *'Turn On, Tune In, Drop Out'* seems to have become adopted religiously, inspiring an outbreak of round-the-clock drug-taking amongst young people.

George - 'There were so many nice people that I saw. It was obvious, you can see people who just vibrate a little happiness. And then there's the other sick part of it where you see people so out of their minds with drugs and who really believe the drug's the thing that's doing it. That's the sad bit and that overpowered the good bit for me.'[41]

Questions over the validity of drug-taking continue to weigh on George's mind, and on his return to Britain he confides his reservations about taking LSD to fellow Beatle, John Lennon.

George - 'Throughout that period I was quite close to John (although people always saw the Lennon-McCartney aspect). We were the ones that had had "The Dental Experience" together.'[1]

John - 'I said "Well, it's not doing me any harm, I'll carry on." But I just suddenly thought, I've seen all that scene. There's no point and if it does do anything to your chemistry or brains? Then someone wrote to me and said that whether you like it or not, whether you have no ill-effects, something happens up there. So I decided if I ever did meet someone who could tell me the answer, I'd have nothing left to do with it.'[41]

John's music is becoming ever more imaginative and way out. In late August author Hunter Davies visits him.

Hunter Davies - 'I remember being at John's house in Weybridge, and we were swimming round the pool and, several streets away, you could hear a police siren going, "da-da, da-da, da-da, da-da," and John started humming this, and playing with those two notes.'[52]

The simple rhythm of the siren is somehow similar to that of a chant.

'Element'ry penguin singing "Hare Krishna"
Man, you should have seen them kicking Edgar Allan Poe.'

- Excerpt from *'I am the Walrus'* by John Lennon and Paul McCartney

Hunter Davies - 'The rhythm had stayed in his head and he was playing with putting words to it. "Mis-ter, Ci-ty, p'lice-man, sit-tin, pre-tty".'
'He'd written down another few words that day, just daft words, to put to another bit of rhythm. "Sitting on a cornflake, waiting for the man to come."'[52]

Whilst writing *'I am the Walrus'*, John has in mind the walrus of Lewis Carroll's poem, *'The Walrus and the Carpenter'*, from *'Through the Looking-Glass and What Alice Found There'*.

John - 'I went back and looked at it and realized that the walrus was the bad guy in the story and the carpenter was the good guy. I thought, Oh, shit, I picked the wrong guy. I should have said, "I am the carpenter."'[15]

Chapter Four
Not Just a Matter of Sitting Down Quietly

In 1967, during his eighth world tour, Maharishi Mahesh Yogi, the founder of the Spiritual Regeneration Movement and the International Meditation Society, announces his intention to return to India permanently.

Pattie - 'Then, joy of joys, I discovered that Maharishi was coming to London in August to give a lecture at the Hilton Hotel.'[21]
'This seems to have been a sudden decision. It wasn't in any of our literature that he was in London or even coming to our Bangor conference. When I heard it, I said to George, look, we've got to go.'[53]
'I was desperate to go, and George said he would come too. Paul had already heard of him and was interested.'[21]

Further encouragement to meet the Maharishi comes from a recently recruited Beatles assistant, Alexis Mardas.
Cynthia - 'A young Greek entered into our lives during this period, John Dunbar, Marianne Faithfull's husband, introduced him to John. Dunbar praised this young man's attributes to the skies. Alexis Mardas was an electronics engineer - "Magic Alex". Magic because of his so-called wonderful, way-out inventions. His hair was as blond and as angelic as his style.'[12]
'"Magic Alex" was really out to impress and it was his need to impress that led him to introduce us all to another kind of magic, meditation. The Maharishi Mahesh Yogi was in London giving lectures on his own particular brand of Transcendental Meditation. Alex had heard of him before and suggested that The Beatles go along to the lecture.'[12]

Another associate of The Beatles, upcoming local sculptor David Wynne, also mentions Maharishi.
George - 'I had seen David Wynne again, and had been talking to him about yogis. He said he had made a sketch of one who was quite remarkable, because he had a lifeline on his hands that didn't end. He showed me a photograph of this fella's hand and said, "He's going to be in London next week doing a lecture." So I thought: "Well, that's good. I'd like to see him."'[1]

So George sets about ordering tickets, making a block booking for his immediate family and associates, at a cost of 7/6d (seven shillings and sixpence) per person, a sum that could buy one 30 cigarettes, or 5 pints of draught beer. For a little less money one might choose to purchase a copy of the latest 45rpm single release by The Beatles, entitled *'All You Need Is Love'*, a song performed on the *'Our World'* programme, the first live international satellite television production, broadcast to as many as 700 million people.

> *'Nothing you can do but you can learn how to be you in time*
> *It's easy.'*
> - Excerpt from *'All You Need Is Love'* by John Lennon & Paul McCartney

❀ ❀ ❀

On Thursday, 24th August 1967 - it is a bright hot summer's day - a flight carrying Maharishi Mahesh Yogi touches down at London Airport. Maharishi is scheduled to appear that evening on the BBC Television current affairs programme *'24 Hours'* where he will answer a series of questions from resident host, Michael Barratt.

Maharishi sits cross-legged in the studio, in his hand a single rose.
Barratt - 'Maharishi, Good evening. Why are you now giving up your lectures around the world?'
Maharishi - 'I think I have established my system of Transcendental Meditation, and have trained quite a number of people in every country. And now I should take care of India, because this Transcendental Meditation is as much needed in India as in other parts of the world.'
Barratt - 'But do you think that in these other parts you have achieved as much as you hoped?'
Maharishi - 'Hmmm, not quite that much, but the basic ground has been prepared for all the people to be peaceful and happy and more energetic in their life.'

Barratt - 'You once said, if I can quote you, I think it's a direct quote; "Even if only one tenth of the adult population meditated for short periods each day, it would not take more than a few months to remove the entire accumulation of tension in the world."'

Maharishi - 'I am absolutely convinced about it!'

Barratt - 'These are your words, yes.'

Maharishi - 'People should be told, every home and every man should be aware that it is very easy for everyone to take his mind deep within the thinking process and thereby expand the capacity of the conscious mind, and improve his efficiency in thinking and in action.'

Barratt - 'Can you explain how I might do this? How do I, in practical terms, begin?'

Maharishi - 'I have established this International Meditation Society, and SRM Foundation of Great Britain, here, and we have many, many centres to teach this. It takes about half an hour to let a man experience the subtler phases of a thought, and the moment he feels subtler aspect of a thought, his mind expands.'

Barratt - 'He can't do this at home, listening to you now, or I couldn't do it here in the studio.. ?'

Maharishi - 'No, it has to be learned with a few.. within a few instructions.'

Barratt - 'It's not just a matter of sitting down quietly and ....'

Maharishi - 'No, no, far from that, because sitting quietly will make the mind dull. One has to know how to reduce the thought below thinking level and experience the finest state of the thought. This experience is very simple and very natural, but it has to be learned.'[3]

❀ ❀ ❀

Later, Maharishi arrives at the Main Ballroom of The Hilton, a newly-built hotel on Park Lane, in Mayfair, Central London, where about a thousand seats have been laid out for the evening lecture. Elsewhere, in the hotel annexe, Maharishi engages with the press, answering their questions and posing for photographs. But Maharishi doesn't always quite understand the questions, and on one occasion he mistakes a reference to the 'flower people' as *something to do with Interflora'*, a company that sells and distributes flower arrangements. However, on the topic of drugs he is very clear.

Maharishi - 'I am not in favour. It is wrong that expansion of consciousness has been associated with this thing. Expansion of consciousness results in improved efficiency at all levels, whereas the results of these drugs do not verify that.'[54]

The audience starts to arrive, and soon all the seats are filled, leaving latecomers only to resort to sitting on the floor in front of the stage.

Maharishi sits himself on a low sofa crossed-legged upon a deerskin and prepares to address the sell-out capacity crowd via the microphone set immediately in front of him.

George - 'All of a sudden there was this man from India. Not in a flash of lightning or anything, but there in the Hilton Hotel.'[55]

Amongst those eagerly listening to Maharishi is Beatle Paul McCartney and his girlfriend, actress Jane Asher, Mike McGear (Paul McCartney's brother), Beatle John Lennon and his wife, Cynthia Lennon, Pattie Boyd, Beatle George Harrison and his sister-in-law Jenny Boyd. There is also an empty seat at the end of row, presumably intended for Ringo who is right now with his wife Maureen, in nearby Queen Charlotte's Maternity Hospital where she has recently given birth to their second child, Jason. Someone else has seated themselves there listening attentively to Maharishi, who explains his theories, explaining, for instance, that for a forest to be green each tree needs to be watered, and that each man must find inner peace for there to be peace in society.

Albert Goldman (an author) - 'Talking in a high-pitched voice, interspersed with odd little giggles, he launched into an endorsement of transcendental meditation. "This practice," he warbled in a high reedy voice, "will alone bring one to the complete fulfillment of one's life." Demanding but "one half hour a day," transcendental meditation's effect could be detected immediately. "Rejuvenation is there!" enthused the monk. "Within two or three days, the face of a man changes." The maharishi's claim must have made every Beatle zoom in on the old man's face. God knows, he wasn't a beauty. His complexion was dusky, his nose broad, his hair long, greasy, and unkempt, his beard a cotton boll stuck on his chin. Yet the man was right! He *had* a glow on his face.'[56]

Maharishi - 'Transcendental Meditation is to provide that which every young man wants, and the need of every young man is joyfulness in life, happiness, harmony, love. Umm? Universality, international, due to these fast jets, non-stop jet flight for here and there, a situation we have created for our younger generation to feel that the whole world is there, they fly there, and they fly there, and they go here and they go this - the joy of life.'
'Even though this meditation is an individual approach, but for anything to be significant on a mass scale, the approach has to be individual. If we want to make the whole.. the whole garden green, it's necessary to water every root. Without watering every root, dreaming and scheming and making all sorts of schemes to make the garden green: waste of time.'
'Expansion of consciousness. When we think of this, then what we find these.. particularly those who are acquainted with the philosophy of Transcendental Meditation, or with the principles of it, as the mind experiences the finer state of thought during meditation, the breath becomes slower, slower, slower, slower. As the mind enters finer activity of finer thoughts the breath becomes finer and finer, metabolism decreases, metabolic rate becomes less and less and less. The entire system gets rest. Complete rest. The rest that the system does not get even in deep sleep. Because the breath is slowing in deep sleep and the whole metabolism is functioning. Hmm. In meditation, because the mind goes to a finer level of activity, the body follows the pattern of the mind, and gets to that most tranquil state, in a very natural way. And because the way of centralising, giving complete rest to the body is so very natural, and not sudden, but slow, gradual, yet quick but natural. The whole system becomes rejuvenated.
Within two or three days the face of a man changes. Changes means; all the sadness and worries and deep-rooted stresses, appears to be happier, some more joyfulness, more life appears on the face. This is because all the physiological influence of Transcendental Meditation to bring complete rest to the ever-functioning machinery of the body.'[3]
Amongst the many topics which Maharishi raises is a brief mention on the topic of drugs.

Maharishi - '… if the change in the nervous system could be brought about through some physical means, it should be possible, theoretically, to experience that bliss consciousness, which is transcendental consciousness, called *"samadhi"* in the language of *yoga*. Hmm? Or self-realisation. It could be possible, it should be possible through the use of the drugs to bring that tranquilising effect. And tranquilising effect of that, of that nature, where the whole system becomes absolutely normal, not functioning yet ready to function, in its all alertness, steady alertness of nervous system will give us the experience of transcendental consciousness.
So, Transcendental Meditation does not infuse any means of tranquilising or.. the nervous system does not induce any physical means to control this n.. nervous system and reset it to reflect bliss consciousness. The practice is only mental, mind goes deeper and deeper and deeper, but the body follows that pattern and with that complete rest of the body and mind, reju.. in a natural way, rejuvenation results. And with that, the experience of inner being brings joyfulness, happy, jolly mood, in a sensible manner.
The drugs which I have heard, they produce some happy mood, some sorrowful mood, but, when the influence of the drug is gone, the body remains the same, the man remains the same, it doesn't change the character. Huh? That shows, the use of these drugs,- which are known in today, it does not produce a harmonious homogenous influence in the nervous system to bring about that bliss consciousness. Because one good experience of bliss consciousness changes the whole field of life. Because it not only makes the mood happier but makes one more energetic, more intelligent, more creative, much more sensible, alert, but these drugs seem to have a.. the influence on, one-sided aspect of life, hmm? Its, they effect the psychology of man, some understanding, some happy mood, some powerful mood, something, but it remains in the field of thinking or feeling. It does not create an overall influence on all spheres of life. But the principle is acceptable, and the desire for the youngsters, and even the desire for the many elderly people with all this big publicity about what is happening, what is happening. Even the elderly people might begin to try; "Let me see, let me try, even though I don't speak to my friends, but let me see for myself what happens." (laughs) But Transcendental Meditation is something.. something sensible, more sensible, which does not influence.. which does not influence any aspect of nervous system unduly, hmm? It produces very natural effect on the **whole** of the personality, **whole** of the nervous system, the **whole** of the metabolism falls and falls and the whole, the whole system becomes tranquilised, refreshed, rejuvenated, regenerated. Hmm? This is the principle of Transcendental Meditation.'
'It's a joy to express, that this complete philosophy, and the technique of it, the practical aspect of it, has now very profoundly been established in society, and that is what has encouraged me to take leave from the west, hmm? And devote a year of my activity in India, and then go into silence.'[3]

Pattie - 'Maharishi was every bit as impressive as I thought he would be, and we were spellbound.'[21]

George, to journalist Peregrine Worsthorne - 'That's the first time anybody has talked about these things in a way I understand.'[57]

So, George, John and Paul are now eager for a personal meeting with Maharishi.

Maharishi - 'Now in that lecture I found quite a lot of questions about drugs, here and there and there .. And I, I replied as I reply.

Then when the lecture was over, and the whole thing stopped, some man came from behind the stage and said "The Beatles were listening you, and they want to hear you, they want to meet you".

I said. "Tomorrow morning I'm going to Wales, and it's already eleven in the night, there won't be any time."

But he said, "It's very important they should talk to you".

I said, "When they can talk to me?"

Then he said, "Can't they come on the stage?"

And I said "Alright, then draw the curtain". The curtain was drawn; I sat again on the stage. They came - I had been hearing some, some word "Beatle", from California, and I thought they may be boys, may be ten years, twelve years. (laughter)

But here came, they came, the boys, moustaches and all that.

And then the man who came before, he introduced, "These are The Beatles", one, two, three, like that. Then I sat and talked to them for about fifteen minutes, and I said "You have created a magic attraction in your name, so you should do something for the youngsters."

They said, "We want to do, tell us to do, and we'll do."

When I said, "First you experience this meditation and then try to become teachers."

They said, "We'll do everything, we want to experience. Tell us now."

I said, "Now is twelve o/clock you must be feeling sleepy. I'll be in Wales for three days, and .." But I said "You don't have to come there, there are about twenty teachers in London, here is healthy centre."

They said "No"; they want to learn from me.

I said, "Then come there."

There were some pressmen, listening to our talk from behind the curtains, and the news went around the Press that The Beatles will be going [with] Maharishi, to Wales, to start meditation.'[58]

Paul - 'We'd seen Maharishi up North when we were kids. He was on the telly every few years on 'Granada's People and Places' programme, the local current-affairs show. We'd all say, "Hey, did you see that crazy guy last night?" So we knew all about him: he was the giggly little guy going round the globe seven times to heal the world.'[1]

John - 'We thought, "What a nice man," and we were looking for that. I mean, everyone's looking for it, but we were all looking for it that day. We met him and saw a good thing and went along with it. Nice trip, thank you very much.

The youth of today are really looking for some answers - for proper answers the established church can't give them, their parents can't give them, material things can't give them.'[1]

But it is odd that despite their having known of Maharishi Mahesh Yogi and Transcendental Meditation for many years, it has taken the announcement of his retirement to get The Beatles to go along to see him. And now that they are fired up with curiosity about how to meditate, they spurn the offer to obtain guidance from a trained teacher of the Spiritual Regeneration Movement, and insist on receiving Maharishi's personal tuition, even though it means travelling with him to Wales.

George - 'I was actually after a mantra. I had got to the point where I thought I would like to meditate; I'd read about it and I knew I needed a mantra - a password to get through into the other world. And, as we always seemed to do everything together, John and Paul came with me.'[1]

Maharishi - 'Join me tomorrow at one of my schools of meditation in Bangor, North Wales. We will make room for you somewhere on the train.'
John - 'There's always the luggage rack.'[12]

Chapter Five
Mystic Special

Ringo - 'At that time Maureen was in hospital having Jason, and I was visiting. I came home and put on the answerphone, and there was a message from John: "Oh, man, we've seen this guy, and we're all going to Wales. You've got to come." The next message was from George, saying, "Wow, man - we've seen him. Maharishi's great! We're all going to Wales on Saturday, and you've got to come.""[1]
'I rang Maureen in hospital. She said I had to go. I couldn't miss this.'[53]

John - 'Cyn and I were thinking of going to Libya, until this came up. Libya or Bangor? Well, there was no choice, was there?'[1]

❀ ❀ ❀

Shirley du Boulay is the Producer of a popular radio programme called *'Woman's Hour'*, broadcast on the BBC Home Service, and since Shirley practices Transcendental Meditation it is natural for her to want to share her interest with listeners.

Shirley du Boulay - 'One of the people with whom I worked regularly was the controversial journalist Malcolm Muggeridge, witty, outrageous, for many years a devout and determined atheist but at the time on the brink of becoming a Christian.
'I asked him if he would like to interview the Maharishi and he was attracted by the idea. But unfortunately the BBC was not.
'I returned to Malcolm with the news and to my delight he said, "Well, let's do it anyway".
'So we arranged a day, I managed to borrow a BBC tape recorder and we met to record the interview in a house near the Albert Hall in London.'[59]

On Friday, 25th August 1967, Shirley hosts a frank and lively exchange between Malcolm Muggeridge and Maharishi Mahesh Yogi, who makes a brief mention of his meeting the night before.

Maharishi - 'Yesterday I was very happy to see The Beatles. They were so deeply interested in this deep thought of inner life. I was just surprised, to find their interest in this Transcendental Meditation. After the lecture they talked to me for about an hour.'

Muggeridge - 'I don't want to dash your feelings, but one of them said that, before talking to you, some days ago, that it is of course through the drug, LSD, that he had been able to understand the nature of God and everything.'[3]

Shirley du Boulay - 'We recorded for about an hour, then, as we left, I promised to try again to interest the BBC in the tape.'
' I was planning to go to Bangor for a weekend's seminar with the Maharishi, so I put the tapes in my case and set off for Euston.'[59]

The decision, by The Beatles, to accompany Maharishi to Wales, has been made in the heat of the moment, and will result in their missing their next recording session, at De Lane Lea Studios, arranged for seven o'clock this evening. The arrangement is now for The Beatles to meet Maharishi at Euston Station - the main London railway terminus for trains coming and going to the Midlands and the North West of England - and for them all to travel to Wales on the 'Three Five', the five past three stopping train for Holyhead.
Well ahead of time, the short slight figure of a smiling Indian gentleman in sandals walks slowly and purposely to the correct platform - Platform 13 - and he moves with an almost regal gait - this is of course 'His Holiness' Maharishi Mahesh Yogi. He carries no baggage but instead clutches a large bunch of colourful fresh flowers to his chest - chrysanthemums, carnations and roses. Beside him is a very much taller man, his assistant, a fellow Indian, Brahmachari Devendra. Like his master he has long dark hair and a full dark beard, and in his hands he holds a small suitcase and a lightly rolled deerskin.
Though the Bangor train is already standing at the station, Maharishi makes no attempt to board it, and instead stops to talk to a reporter.

Reporter - 'The Beatles seem to be among your supporters now, how do you feel about that?'

Maharishi - 'I think they're a great promise for the younger generation, because if The Beatles take up this Transcendental Meditation, they are the ideal of energy and intelligence in the younger generation, and that will really bring up the youth on a very good level of understanding and intelligence. I'm very happy about it that they heard my lecture last evening and they talked to me for about an hour after the lecture. They seem to be very intelligent and alert.'[46]

But when asked as the current whereabouts of The Beatles he appears to become confused, and is at a loss to explain their non-appearance at the station.

Then Paul McCartney strolls onto the platform, in the company of Rolling Stones' singer Mick Jagger and girlfriend Marianne Faithfull, escorted by a London 'Bobby' (a local uniformed policeman). Ironically, not long ago this fashionable couple were involved in a drugs bust in which 19 policemen descended on the Sussex house of Rolling Stone Keith Richards. Since then salacious tales of her as 'Miss X' have spread, suggesting she was naked when the police arrived but that she then wrapped a fur rug round herself, which she let slip from time to time. Today, Marianne walks several paces behind Paul and Mick, her eyes fixed on the policeman at whom she smiles. Not only is she dressed but is turned out very fashionably in dark trousers and belt with large buckle, blouse, a printed pattern jacket. For his part Mick is dressed in dandy fashion, with crushed velvet trousers, psychedelic print shirt and light coloured tailored casual jacket. He grins whilst being photographed, and he has good reason to smile, for by the efforts of others, the severe 6 months prison sentence passed down on him has been quashed, and he is now FREE!

Paul McCartney too is looking 'with it', and is wearing an embroidered high collared Indian style shirt, dark trousers, and is looking quite relaxed. Two assistants flank him - Neil Aspinall, who has known Paul since they were kids, and Peter Brown, who has been manager Brian Epstein's personal assistant for many years.

Finding their seats on the train, Paul sits down opposite Mick and Marianne, and enjoys a chat and a cigarette with them while they all wait for the rest of the gang to turn up. But the other three Beatles are still on the road, being driven up from Surrey in John's astonishingly bright yellow psychedelic 'Roller' (1965 Rolls-Royce Phantom V) the bodywork of which has been painted by gypsies to a design by Marijke Koger of The Fool, with dahlias and delphiniums, depicting the flowers of autumn. Even the hubcaps have received attention, have been embellished with rotating speed lines. Far out, really far out, Man! The interior of the vehicle has been customised too, equipped with a writing desk, radiotelephone, television, refrigerator and record player, and the back seat of the 19-foot long limousine has been modified to be able to convert into a double bed.

Fortunately for the celebrity passengers the train has been delayed for six minutes, due to a need to change the engine, else it would already have departed. Under the watchful gaze of a series of policemen positioned along the way, John Lennon, Ringo Starr & George Harrison come running across the concourse and onto Platform 13, hurrying past the gazing bystanders and a uniformed sailor there. Peter Brown follows after them, suitcase in hand, with Pattie Boyd, Jenny Boyd & Cynthia Lennon trailing closely behind.

Cynthia - 'It was a bright, sunny morning when we set off. I was ready early, but Pattie, George, and Ringo were coming in our car, and were late. By the time Anthony [chauffeur Les Anthony] drew up at the station entrance we were cutting it fine and had five minutes to catch the train. John leapt out of the car with the others and ran for the platform - leaving me to follow with our bags. It was the result of years in which he'd taken it for granted that others would see to all the details. I followed him as fast as I could. The station was mayhem, with fans, reporters, police and passengers all milling around.'[10]

Photographers grab a series of shots of the stars as they hurriedly walk towards the train - flashbulbs bursting forth, bright white light popping and bouncing on the scene. A British Railways employee opens the door of the nearest carriage and Ringo gets in, then John, and then George, with one hand clutching his *sitar* close to him and the other he carrying a small dark suitcase. A policeman stands watching, waiting, and now moves forward to close the door, but before doing so greets Pattie and Jenny and gives them a helping hand to climb aboard. Then, only five seconds after The Beatles have clambered on, the train starts moving off. Quickly, Peter Brown darts up, climbs the steps and deposits a large suitcase aboard, quickly backing down and off again. But in so doing he blocks Cynthia who is standing behind him.

Beatle wife misses the train

Mr. John Lennon's wife, Cynthia, was stranded in tears at Euston station yesterday as her husband left by train with the three other Beatles for Bangor. She was held up in a mass of screaming girls who were waving goodbye to the group.

The Beatles, with Mr. Mick Jagger and Miss Marianne Faithfull, were travelling with an Indian mystic, Maharishi Yogi, exponent of Transcendental Meditation. The party, which included Miss Jane Asher, were on their way to hear a series of lectures by the Maharishi.

The group arrived late at Euston after a traffic holdup.

Mrs. Lennon was held up by the fighting girls. Her worried husband, dressed, like the rest of the group, in a multi-coloured Indian shirt, shouted from a carriage window: "Run, Cindy, run."

The white-robed Himalayan mystic known to the Beatles as "His Holiness", said: "The Beatles are very intelligent boys—I'm sure meditation will help them. And their interest in my work will help it to spread to the youth of all countries. That will do good for the whole world."

Cynthia - 'John, realising that something was missing from his baggage, poked his head out of the window, and other heads sprouted their way out to see what was happening. John's face was a picture. He just couldn't believe what was happening: *'Tell him to let you on; tell him you're with us!'*[7]

Beatles' assistant Neil Aspinall arrives on the scene and grabs hold of the door, trying to assist Cynthia to get onto the moving train. John is heard yelling through the window; *'Jump, jump'*, but the Bobby starts to push on the carriage door and as he does so the British Railways employee and another gentleman join in, and together they push, making sure the door gets slammed well and truly shut.

Cynthia - 'It was all so stupid. It was in our car that we drove at break-neck speed to the station. It was I who was ready hours before anyone else, yet I was the one who was barred from scrambling onto the train as it began to move out of the station.'[7]

To ensure that no one makes a last minute effort to get on, the dutiful policeman hurries to keep pace with the train whilst another policeman walks slowly but purposefully towards him. The train is gains speed and is starting to move quite fast now. Cynthia attention is focused on her husband John.. *'... his face a disappearing blur as the train rattled into the distance.'*[7]

Peter Brown and Neil Aspinall try to console the tearful Cynthia, and a solution is soon arrived at with Neil offering to give Cynthia a lift to Bangor. Peter Brown decides to go to see his boss, Brian Epstein, at his Chapel Street address, just around the corner from the SRM centre in Belgravia. Peter and Brian then drive to Brian's country house in Sussex where, with another colleague, they intend to spend the weekend. Brian has been having health problems of late, and has recently been undergoing rehabilitation for his addiction to pep pills, in particular 'uppers' (amphetamines), and related problems with 'downers' (barbiturates), which he uses to deal with his insomnia.

Clearly, all the Beatles' staff had already made plans for the Bank Holiday weekend, so, The Beatles' decision to travel by themselves by public transport to Wales has left them without support, they are now rather concerned about getting mobbed, and none of them dare to venture out of the compartment they being too scared even to go to the lavatory!

John - 'It's like going somewhere without your trousers on.'[53]

Anyway, The Beatles settle themselves down - not amongst the luggage as John had suggested, but on the comfy upholstered seats of a well appointed First Class compartment. They are accompanied on this journey by their biographer, writer Hunter Davies, (prompted by a late night phone call from Mike, Paul McCartney's brother). In his early thirties and a little older than The Fabs, Hunter is smartly dressed in suit, pin-striped shirt and tie; a journalist by trade he make notes of the journey.

Hunter Davies - 'The Fans rushed to the train when we stopped and shoved autograph books through the windows and doors; quite a killing for the fans, getting such a batch of heroes, all in the same spot at the same time. Most of them dutifully signed, except John, who soon said he was fed up.'[53]

Elsewhere in the *'Flower Power Express'* train, Maharishi Mahesh Yogi is sitting talking with meditator and artist Geoffrey Baker. Maharishi wants to give each Beatle a copy of his book, 'The Science of Being and Art of Living', and he puzzles for a moment before asking Geoffrey a question.

Maharishi - 'How many are the Beatles?'[60]

The Beatles themselves are still wary of venturing out of the relative safety of their compartment, but Hunter Davies decides to pop out, stretch his legs and discover Maharishi's whereabouts in another compartment, a First Class 'No Smoking' compartment.

Hunter Davies - 'Maharishi was sitting cross-legged on a white sheet laid out on the seat by his followers. He bounced up and down when he laughed, which was most of the time. He admitted he'd never heard any Beatle music in his life. He had been told they were very famous, and so was Mick Jagger, but he got very confused about him being a Rolling Stone. He didn't know what that meant.
The Beatles eventually went into his compartment. He laughed a great deal as he chatted with them. He illustrated his talk by taking a flower in his hand and saying it was really all sap. The petals on their own were an illusion, just like the physical life.'[53]

Ringo - 'The Maharishi had no idea who we were and thought we were other travellers, devotees, whatever. As soon as he found out, he thought it would be good if we did a world tour - and we weren't touring then! - to pass on his message.'[61]

Copyright: Avico Ltd.

They all chat a while, then it is time for Mick Jagger and the ladies to meet with Maharishi, so The Beatles take off and go off to have some tea in the Buffet Car. In an attempt to give The Beatles some privacy, the attendant ropes off an area for them, which works quite well. Whilst the train halts at Chester General station, George pours a cup of tea from the stainless steel teapot. A couple of fans push through.
Two teenage boys - 'What are you going to Bangor for? Are you playing there?'
Ringo - 'That's right. On the Pier Head at 8.30 Second House. See you.'[53]
Of course he is joking, but there *is* a pier at the seaside town of Bangor, Garth Pier, a very long pier indeed.

At 7.50pm, just over four and a half hours after leaving London, the *'Mystic Special'* slowly pulls into the seaside town of Bangor. But at the sight of so many people waiting on the station platform, there is immediately talk amongst The Beatles of travelling on to the next station instead, in order to avoid the crowd - so clearly they have *some* experience in such matters! It is touch and go as what to do for the best, but Maharishi, who is not yet aware how fabulously famous The Beatles are, assures them that if they keep with him then everything will be all right.
Paul - 'Yeah, we got up there. There was a big crowd at the train station, and there was a crowd to meet us. We all sort of wandered through in our psychedelic gear.'[46]
It takes quite a long time for John, Paul, George, Ringo, Mick Jagger, Maharishi, and his assistant, to pass through the crowds on Bangor Station's Platform 3, and to deal with the Press reporters and the film crew, but thankfully no one is mobbed, in fact it is all relatively civilised.
Hunter Davies -'On the platform, rather lost and bemused amongst all the screaming kids, was a handful of Maharishi's followers, waiting to welcome him to the conference. They were bowled aside by the crowds, screaming at the Beatles.'[53]

The Beatles move in for a quiet weekend

...but Bangor has other ideas

Left, a tea-time huddle between Beatles Paul, Ringo and John as they travel north on the London Holyhead express to attend the Bangor conference on meditation. And above, fourth member of the group George Harrison pours a cup of tea, during the trains halt at Chester General station.

by D.P. reporters
Iowerth Roberts & Tony Tucker

Bangor teenagers screamed a welcome last night to the Beatles who had moved into the town for a quiet weekend of meditation.

Even before the train emerged from the tunnel into Bangor station, the screams started.

They reached a crescendo the old familiar, "We want as a thousand throats shouted Ringo."

On the platform—all armed with flowers—were followers of Maharishi Mahesh Yogi, Himalayan mystic, founder of the International Meditation Society, who is giving a series of lectures at Bangor. The Beatles will be there to hear him.

As photographers tried to take pictures of the Maharishi, surrounded by the Beatles and Mick Jagger and Marianne Faithfull, autograph books were handed to the Beatles.

Outside the station more

MARIANNE FAITHFULL

than 1,000 people, young and old, waited, and the screaming and shouting became continuous as the party appeared.

No special arrangements

A dozen policemen vainly tried to keep order as the party drove in taxis to the Normal College where the conference is being held.

Outside the college, hundreds more teenagers, screaming and shouting, waited.

But even as they arrived there was no certainty as to where the visitors would spend the night.

No special arrangements had been made by the college for the Beatles. "As far as we are concerned, the Beatles are attending this conference as private citizens. The conference was booked with us in the normal way," said Mr Gwyn

Thomas, the college registrar.

At the college the welcome was totally different. The 300 followers of Maharishi were silently standing around, waiting for the founder of their movement and his guests.

Then there was an hour-long meditation session in the John Phillips Hall.

In the centre of the flower-bedecked platform on a white seat was the Maharishi, quietly giving instructions from time to time.

The Beatles sat to his right—probably the first time they had ever been on a platform without having to perform. With a background of flowers they presented a colourful picture. Paul was wearing a flesh-coloured shirt and green trousers. John Lennon was in a bright multi-coloured striped shirt and pink trousers. Ringo Starr in a green floral shirt with dark trousers and George also in a many-coloured patterned shirt with light blue trousers.

In the front row sat Mick Jagger, Marianne Faithfull and Patti Boyd.

The Beatles and other followers at the conference will spend most of the day in meditation, but the Maharishi will talk individually at some time or other with each of the 260 to 300 followers.

Court in the first class

For nearly four hours on the train between Euston and Bangor the Maharishi held court in the first class compartment.

His disciples: Beatles Paul, George, John and Ringo. The four sat, flower shirted and intent in a non-smoker. In the midst squatted the Maharishi, cross-legged on a white

bear skin rug and holding a flower.

Their conversation ranged from music to Communism—the Maharishi did most of the talking—interspersed with his high-pitched giggle.

The Maharishi and his followers on the train—the Beatles were but a few of the total number —were making a pilgrimage to Bangor.

There, the spiritual regeneration movement through transcendental meditation, were holding a seminar. And the Maharishi, affectionately known as His Holiness, is their leader.

What brought the Beatles? They were not at all sure.

Said John "It is difficult to analyse. I'm not quite sure where it is leading but he is worth listening to."

George Harrison was equally uncertain of the direction in which transcendental meditation might lead him. But he was more urgent about it.

"It is now that matters.

And we are listening now. To-morrow will follow on its own accord."

The Beatles only just made it on to the 3.05 from Euston.

Minutes earlier, His Holiness had arrived, and was greeted on the platform by some of his more anonymous followers with bunches of flowers. In fact they all chose to remain anonymous.

One who said she would rather not give her name, told me it was normal to give flowers to holy men in India.

Another—"No, I'd prefer not to tell you my name"—found that meditation had given her a new confidence in herself.

A tremendous influence

"Problems don't seem nearly so enormous," she said. "I used to be shy. Now I don't care a hang."

Also on the train was Beatle wife Patti Boyd, and pop singers Marianne Faithfull and Mick Jagger.

But they stayed in their first class compartment, with the blinds drawn against the prying eyes of

excited holidaymakers.

"I've really nothing to say," commented Mick Jagger. Marianne Faithfull pouted prettily and repeated the formula.

Meanwhile, back in the non-smoker, the conversation went on.

"The Beatles," His Holiness said, "have a tremendous influence. They must use it wisely. They are ideal to the younger generation. Through this meditation, if they take it up, they could bring up the youth of to-day to a higher understanding of life."

Not at all put out by the proceedings was the ticket collector, Mr Edward Kohler, of Princes Park, Liverpool. Fighting his way along the crowded corridor he said: "It's the first time I've had the Beatles on my train. I've seen them before, of course, in Liverpool, you know."

Mr Kohler wore a pink carnation in his button-hole.

"In sympathy?" I asked.

"No, it was given to me by one of the followers. Got to be with it, you know."

The wife who was left behind; and Flower power makes its way to North Wales.—Page Four.

The Maharishi Makesh Yogi sits with Mick Jagger during the journey to Bangor.

- Daily Post 26th August 1967

At the earliest opportunity, The Beatles are whisked off by hire car, and in minutes they are being welcomed at the University of Bangor by assorted leading lights of the SRM, including Jet Fairly.

George - 'When we first went to Bangor, we met all these meditators, and it's so obvious, just by seeing the people, that they give off this peace and happiness.'[12]

Cynthia Lennon arrives by car and is met with hugs and kisses, but also has to bear the jibes such as; *'If you want to know the time ask a policeman, but don't miss the train while you're doing it.*'[7]

❀ ❀ ❀

There are about 300 people attending the 10-day meditation course at Bangor, but standing about in the grounds are many, many more, members of the Press corps, dozens of fans, and several uniformed policemen. The leader of the British movement, Eileen Forrestal, has even enlisted the assistance of a 17 team of security guards and 3 Alsatian dogs.

Hunter Davies - 'Maharishi himself seemed to be enjoying all the commotion and excitement. He was very kind and considerate to all the Press and TV men. He very smartly agreed with them to have a Press conference, after he'd spoken privately to the conference members.'[53]

Reporter - 'The people here think of you as a saint, what is it that you preach?'
Maharishi - 'I preach a simple system of Transcendental Meditation which gives the people the insight into life and they begin to enjoy all peace and happiness. And because this has been the message of all the saints in the past, they call me "saint".'
Reporter - 'You seem also to have caught the imagination of the pop stars in this country.'
Maharishi - 'What is this "**pop** stars"?' (laughter)
Reporter - 'People who sing, people who sing with guitars. Have you anything to say about that?'
Maharishi - 'I find they.. You mean The Beatles! (laughter) I found them very intelligent and young men of very great potential in life. And they.. during my stay here, they'll look into some meditation, and if they find it does bring more energy and more intelligence and relief from stress and strains, then they will be leaders for the next coming generation to spread this message of peace and harmony. There's a great potential in them.'[3]

The evening lecture is abuzz with anticipation; everyone is looking about to see if they can see The Beatles. When Paul, John, Ringo and George walk in, they make their way to seats up on the stage where they sit looking just a little self-conscious. The womenfolk and Mick Jagger have it a little easier, occupying as they do the seats in the front row.

Susan Lawrence - 'We knew Maharishi was coming to the course, but were surprised and delighted to hear that The Beatles were coming with him.
That evening Maharishi and The Beatles entered the calm and silent hall, they looked surprised, as it appeared unusual for them not to be screamed at by fans or pursued by Press and photographers.'
'… Maharishi gave a very inspirational talk, both I and many others were in tears, thinking that with The Beatles practising TM it would lead to a major expansion of interest and with that we hoped a major positive effect on the world…'[38]

The Beatles and the rest of the audience all gaze with rapt attention at Maharishi who sits beside a blackboard, the stage is decked with vases of seasonal blooms. The news media is allowed a limited access to the lecture so film cameras are brought in and directed at Maharishi, at the celebrities and at the rest of the audience. Then, after this evening's lecture comes a hastily convened Press conference, during which Maharishi is met with a barrage of hostile questions from reporters from national and local papers.
Unphased, Maharishi takes the questions in his stride and confidently restates the fundamentals of his teaching.
Maharishi - 'One sits down comfortably, in a chair or wherever one wants, and, he uses a thought that he has been given, especially for himself, and he starts experiencing the subtler state of thought.'
Reporter - 'Are you experiencing the subtler state of thought at this moment?'
Maharishi - 'No. I am out in the gross field.' (laughter)
Reporter - 'What do you have to do to attain this state of thought?'
Maharishi - 'Just a few instructions from a trained teacher and one begins to experience it.'
Reporter - 'How long does it take?'

Maharishi - 'About half an hour.'

Reporter - 'And how do you know when it's happened?'

Maharishi - 'Ah, one begins to feel relaxed, from, right from the beginning one begins to feel some improved level of well-being.'[3]

But notwithstanding Maharishi's attempts to explain his teachings clearly, this is the first contact many of the reporters have with the idea of 'meditation' so they can be forgiven for being a bit confused, especially when The Beatles are now claiming they have given up drugs!

Hunter Davies - 'They thought the Beatles must be involved in some publicity stunt. They couldn't believe they were serious about Maharishi, whoever he was. They were belligerent in their questions, almost as if they expected the Beatles to admit they were just doing it all for a laugh. The Beatles were cheered loudly by the congregation when they made it clear, at the expense of the Press's ignorance, that they were very serious indeed.

John found a reporter's notes afterwards in one of the college's telephone booths. It had the heading "Paul, George, Ringo, John Lennon and Jagger" plus details of what each had been wearing. "You've taken over from me," said John to Mick Jagger, pointing out how the reporter had named each of them.. "I just used to be called Lennon when I was wicked. Now I'm John Lennon. I haven't yet reached the next stage of being John. You're still Jagger."'[53]

The VIP's and their womenfolk are tired and hungry, but they decide to pass on the canteen food in favour of joining Hunter Davies in search of a late night restaurant. They find the Senior Chinese Restaurant, located in the centre of town, where mercifully The Beatles are not recognised.

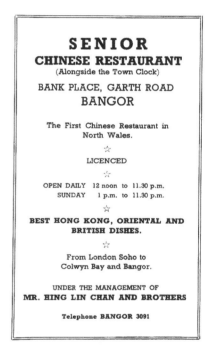

Hunter Davies - 'It was late at night, in a very small provincial town, and we could find only a Chinese restaurant open. When the bill finally came, I realized I had not enough money, nor had anyone else. The Beatles never carried money, just like the Royal Family, and this time they were without their normal aides and assistants who carried the purse for them.

The Chinese waiter was becoming very upset, thinking we were all going to walk out without paying, when George suddenly put his bare foot on the table. He had taken off his sandals and was examining the sole of the shoes. There was a slit at the front and from it he withdrew £20, more than enough to settle the bill. He had put the money there for such emergencies, months if not years previously, and forgotten about it until that evening.'[53]

The revellers, amongst them four of the most famous people on the planet, now return to Normal College to spend the night in dormitory accommodation.

Cynthia - 'The lodgings provided at Bangor were less than luxurious, but very adequate for us all. It was marvellous feeling like a student again. We entered into the whole experience with a great spirit of adventure.' 'That night was spent unpacking and anticipating, with a great deal of excitement, our initiation into meditation with the Master himself. Mick Jagger and Marianne Faithfull were also in on the new mental turn-on. We were all very happy and impatient to get on with it.'[7]

Paul - 'It was a bit funny going to those camps because it was like going back to school. Just the nature of it meant staying in a classroom and we'd been used to our nice comfortable homes or hotels so to be staying in an old school on a camp bed was a little bit disconcerting.'[6]

Chapter Six
Initiation

Saturday, 26th August 1967.

Cynthia - 'The following morning we were introduced to our fellow meditators and teachers. The atmosphere was tranquil and full of well-being - an all-embracing feeling of friendship and unity.'[7]

John - 'Mick came up there and he got a sniff and he was on the phone saying: "Send Keith, send Brian, send them all down." You just get a sniff and you're hooked.'[41]

But Mick Jagger and Marianne Faithfull are returning to London by the 10.25am train, as Marianne needs to get back to see her very young child, Nicholas, and Mick is expected at Olympic Sound Studios for a recording session with The Rolling Stones for their forthcoming LP.

❀ ❀ ❀

The primary reason why The Beatles are attending this course at Bangor is for them to have the opportunity to learn how to meditate. But before they learn, it is first necessary for them to attend a couple of talks; an introductory talk, and after that, a preparatory talk, to enable them to become familiar with what meditation is, and what it is not.

Transcendental Meditation is a system of meditation, which is generally practiced twice daily, once in the morning and again in the evening. In order to learn how to meditate, a trained teacher of meditation is needed and such a teacher is known as an 'initiator'. On the day of 'initiation' the 'initiate' brings along several prescribed 'offerings', flowers, fruit, a fresh clean white cotton handkerchief and a donation. There is a short interview with the teacher, during which the teacher gets to know a little more about you. Once this exchange is completed the initiation proper can then proceed.

Immediately prior to being taught to meditate there is a short ceremony known as a '*puja*', during which the initiator murmurs a traditional Sanskrit composition and performs a ritual set of offerings in front of a portrait of Guru Dev, a revered Indian sage. Following this ceremony the initiate is instructed to understand how effortlessly thought occurs, and is then given a *mantra* (a sound that is meaningless to the initiate) and guided on how to use this *mantra* to good effect in meditation.

'In this meditation, we do not concentrate; we do not try to think the mantra clearly. Mental repetition is not a clear pronunciation. It is just a faint idea. We don't try to make a rhythm of the mantra. We don't try to control

thoughts. We do not wish that thoughts should not come. If a thought comes, we do not try to push it out. We don't feel sorry about it. When a thought comes, the mind is completely absorbed in the thought.'

'When we become aware that we are not thinking the mantra, then we quietly come back to the mantra. Very easily we think the mantra and if at any moment we feel that we are forgetting it, we should not try to persist in repeating it. Only very easily we start and take it as it comes and do not hold the mantra if it tends to slip away.'

'Noise is no barrier to meditation. Even in a noisy market, it is possible to be thinking thoughts and whenever we can think, we can meditate. So one can think the mantra comfortably even though aware of outside noises. We just innocently favour the mantra and do not try to resist noise in any way.'

'It is easy and simple. It is just the normal, natural process of thinking the mantra and taking it as it comes. Now, this is how we will meditate, easily, morning and evening.'

According to Maharishi, this meditation does not involve autosuggestion and is a natural process which can be verified scientifically. The process naturally yields benefits, so it is unnecessary to make any sudden changes to one's philosophy, religion or lifestyle.

After initiation, having enjoyed a sustained experience of meditation, the new initiate is advised to get on with his or her life as normal. Before leaving the teacher, the white cloth handkerchief is given back to the initiate along with a flower bloom and a piece of fruit. It is suggested that the initiate return for several more teaching sessions during which sustained experience and deeper understanding about meditation is gained.

❀ ❀ ❀

Ringo - 'When I first met him, it was in a room, cos it was in a university, so we were like in dorms, you know, in a dormitory, we were all with him, and err, it was, it's one of those mind altering moments of your life, because the man was **so** full of joy, you know, and happiness and, it just blew me away. That he, you know, on my best day I never felt like he looked. Err, it was so far out, he was so.. I said "so I want some of that!" you know what I mean. Oh, it's the best thing that could ever happen.'[62]

Paul - 'The actual ceremony in Bangor when we got given the mantra was nice. You had to wait outside his room as he did people one by one, and then you got to go into the inner sanctum, just a room they'd put a lot of flowers in and a few drapes around, and lit a few joss sticks. You had to take some cut flowers to Maharishi as some sort of offering. It was all flowers with Maharishi, but flowers were the symbol of the period anyway so it was very easy. So you got your flowers, you took your shoes off and went into a darkened room where Maharishi was. It was quite exciting. It reminded me of Gypsy Rose Lee's tent in Blackpool - "Come inside!" - Santa's grotto or something. Maharishi explained what he was going to do, he said, "I'll just do a few little bits and pieces …" however he put it, of this and that, little incantations for himself, then he said, "I will just lean towards you and I'll just whisper, very quietly, your mantra." He gives you your mantra and he's only going to say it once and you repeat it once, just to check you've got it, and he says, "Yes, that's it." And he said, "The idea is that you don't mention that to anyone ever again, because if you speak it, it will besmirch it to some degree; if you never speak it, then it's always something very special."'[6]

Ringo - 'I was really impressed with the Maharishi; I was impressed because he was laughing all the time. and so, you know, we listened to his lectures and we started meditating, we were given our *mantras*.'[46]

After the initiation, The Beatles and their entourage emerge from the main building of the university, and the Press pounce hungrily upon them. But all four Beatles appear untroubled and calm, each carrying a flower in his hand and what appears to be a rolled up handkerchief, all seemingly happy to chat with journalists and to sign autographs for fans.

The Beatles and the women then withdraw to their own quarters, where at 2 o/clock they are served some Indian curry.

After lunch, at 3 o/clock Paul and Ringo oblige the Press by offering up a progress report, with George and John making an appearance holding their copies of *'Science of Being and Art of Living'*, a book of the Maharishi's teachings, compiled in 1963.

❀ ❀ ❀

The Press seem to be publishing fairly favourable reports.

Daily Sketch reporter - 'Whatever he is, Maharishi is a delightful personality. He has a sharp brain, argues brilliantly, sometimes with simple, direct stories, sometimes with farout concepts. He bubbles over into laughter frequently. He tells the Beatles that the rich man is there to relieve the burdens of society. It is only difficult for a rich man to enter the kingdom of heaven if he just sits there and contemplates his wealth. "Christ said the kingdom of heaven is within you and that is all I am saying".'[63]

The *Daily Mail* carries coverage of last night's lecture.

DAILY MAIL,

How His Holiness descended from the hills of Kashmir and came to Bangor last night, picking up sundry Beatles and Rolling Stones on the way

IN BANGOR LAST NIGHT WITH THE MAN THEY CALL MASTER...THE BEATLES

Picture by DENIS THORPE.

THE MYSTERY shrouding the background of His Holiness Maharishi Mahesh Yogi, who preached his doctrine of meditation and the simple life to the Beatles this week, deepened yesterday.

by MICHAEL LITCHFIELD

Each of his names means the same thing in India — "The Greatest" or "Great Saint."

Maharishi, 56, white-robed and bearded, founded the International Meditation Society nine years ago—in Britain.

He started in humble surroundings when he first decided to teach the Western world of the simple life—a small flat in Knightsbridge.

Five years later he was at the Piccadilly Hotel, where he gave a lecture to 900 people, each paying 2s. 6d.

This week he was staying at the Hilton Hotel, in Park Lane, where 1,500 people, including the Beatles, paid 7s. 6d. each to hear his theories.

This was advertised—by a publicity and public relations firm representing him in Britain—as his farewell public appearance before retiring to a "life of silence" in Kashmir.

Lectures

After making his "farewell public appearance," last night, he was travelling by train to Bangor, Caenarvonshire—with the Beatles and Rolling Stone Mick Jagger—for five days of lecturing.

He claims that he now has a following throughout the world of some 100,000 people, each of whom contributes a week's salary to the cause. Sometimes the people are poor — sometimes they are Beatles.

Asked about his 47 years before he realised his true calling, he said: "I was in the hills with my master. Then I came down from the hills to the people."

His master, according to his smart publicity brochure, was Swami Brahmananda Saraswati Maharaj, Shankaracharya of Jyotirmath.

Again all those words, except the last, mean the same in India—a disciple, Jyotirmath, say his publicity agents, is a place. The place does not appear in the *World Gazeteer*, and it is not known to officials at India House.

Maharishi says there is nothing religious about his philosophy of simple meditation. Why does he call himself His Holiness? He said: "Holiness is just a quality of life."

The money from people's salaries, he said, helps him to travel around the world lecturing and to set up centres wherever he visits.

He claimed, and still does, that his form of meditation will release world tension and avert war.

He said much the same on long-playing records released at 32s. 6d. a time.

Strange

Each new follower is given a word to think about, and this, he claims, releases "inner tensions." The word for everyone is different, and must be kept a secret.

After having an audience with Maharishi, three young English girls went to the Yoga Centre, in Hampstead Gardens, London, N.W.3, and revealed they had each been given the same word, an Indian word—Rama, which means "without any illusion."

Mr. Nandi, principal of the centre, said last night: "It seems strange that they should be given a word to think about of which they don't know the meaning or understand one word of the language. How on earth could they derive any benefit from that?

"It seems wrong that there should be so much propaganda and commercialism attached to something that is meant to be spreading the simple life.

"In no other form of meditation society have I ever heard of followers being expected to give a week's salary. The income must be enormous.

"India is a poor country and needs help. I wouldn't have thought the Hilton was exactly the place to preach any doctrine to any of the poor anywhere."

An official of the British Meditation Society said: "Vast sums of money are needed to promote our work."

Why is Maharishi returning to the Himalayas when his work is unfinished?— "Because the master calls," he said.

48

In order to protect The Beatles from unwelcome intrusions from the Press and from fans, course members are called upon to assist in various way; with Shirley du Boulay being given some quite specific tasks.

Shirley du Boulay - 'We were assigned various jobs to protect them; I remember I was asked to be sure that Marianne Faithfull did not go topless to see the Maharishi. I was also deputed to act as a waitress for our visitors - they would have been mobbed if they had tried to reach the canteen where the rest of us were eating.'[59]

A car draws up outside the front of the college. Once it is parked the occupants of the vehicle emerge, a crew of three Asiatic looking visitors who walk the distance into the college, laden with eight ready-prepared meals neatly stacked on trays. It isn't difficult to guess who the meals are intended for!

Henry Grossman, the famous American photographer also visits, and gains access to The Beatles, of whom he takes many shots as they socialise with other students. Amongst those in the kitchen is a young Italian called Paolo Ammassari, a meditator who has driven all the way from Scandinavia to be here.

Paolo Ammassari - 'I came from Denmark, driving a German car, with other two friends: Ulla and Fabio Posada, with the purpose to join Maharishi in Bangor for a course in meditation. I started TM [Transcendental Meditation] in 1964 and in these times I followed Him in all His steps in Europe.'[64]

Paolo spends time with The Beatles and their entourage.

Paolo Ammassari - 'During the meeting in the small dining room of the college, with John, we spoke about two points: Nazca land drawings [Nazca is in Peru] and about the possibility of some degree of spirituality not linked to religions.'[64]

This evening, Paul, George, Ringo and John attend another lecture in John Phillips Hall, and once again, as the guests of honour, they sit in a row up on the stage, each with his hardback copy of one of Maharishi's books resting on his lap. Meanwhile, the ladies, Jenny, Jane, Cynthia, Marianne and Pattie, sit in their places in the front row. Maureen Starkey has only just been discharged from hospital, so is not present at Bangor.

Paolo Ammassari - 'During the lecture, the hall was crowded, and a few people had some questions to forward in a very sympathetic, respectful and, I can say, in an unexpected sweet way. Maharishi spoke about the way in which Transcendental Meditation drives the familiarity of the meditator to states of "Transcendental Consciousness" and, with the regular practice of it, to an establishment of deep "Cosmic Consciousness". The audience was absolutely fascinated by the Maharishi's speech.'

'The Beatles didn't speak, they were just listening with pleasure and attention. The audience was focused on Maharishi's speech, but the presence of the Four was giving an exceptional atmosphere of charm and joy.'[64]

Chapter Seven
Negative Feelings Would Impede Brian's Journey

Sunday, 27th August 1967.

The Beatles' sojourn with Maharishi Mahesh Yogi, which started with their meeting him at The London Hilton and has stretched to travelling with him by train to Wales and staying in Bangor, now enters into its fourth day. The Beatles have all been initiated into Transcendental Meditation and now intend to stay here with Maharishi and his students for several more days.

Paul - 'Then trying to learn to meditate. It's not that easy, you don't just pick it up like that, it's an effort and you've got to be involved, so it was like going back to school.'[6]

'It was like a summer camp, and you spend your first few days just trying to stop your mind dealing with your social calendar, you know, whatever's coming up. But it was good. I eventually got the hang of it, we all got the hang of it.'[46]

⊛ ⊛ ⊛

Today, The Beatles and their party are to spend some further time with Maharishi, and this morning brings a big surprise, that George Harrison intends to give an informal recital for Maharishi. George brings along his *sitar*, sits down cross-legged on the carpet and begins to tune up, then proceeds to demonstrate his proficiency at playing this Indian classical instrument. For the uninitiated, even holding this instrument correctly can pose a serious challenge, let alone the tuning of it, for, unlike the 6-string guitar that George is accustomed to playing, the *sitar* can have as many as 23 strings. But George is becoming more familiar with the *sitar*, having practised on it regularly for many months now.

Copyright: Avico Ltd.

Several other meditators are here to enjoy this impromptu performance; spectators include Paolo Ammassari, and Colin Harrison, an amateur photographer.

After the *sitar* recital, there is a photo session with Henry Grossman, who is here in Bangor to capture some shots of The Beatles with Maharishi. The Beatles and the ladies wear a bewildering diversity of colourful fabrics and designs, with some of the patterns quite simply stunning. The room has been decorated with an astonishing profusion of flowers; gladioli, roses, carnations, chrysanthemums, and dazzling dahlias, all artfully

Copyright: Avico Ltd.

arranged in generous bouquets. Pure whites and vibrant colours - sharp, citrus lemon, golden yellows tangerine oranges and reds - all hot colours, no blues. Maharishi, who is seated in front of a colour portrait of his master, Guru Dev. holds a single blossom - an oyster pink dahlia. The stars sit at ease, each with a hardback copy of one of Maharishi's books placed in front of him, a commentary on the first six chapters of the *Bhagavad Gita ('The Lord's Song'),* an Indian Scripture, Henry also wishes to photograph The Beatles alongside their womenfolk, but before the session Cynthia decides to change out of her polka dot trousers. Then Henry proceeds to take some beautiful photos of the colourful group. When the photo session is finished the group return to their hostel for a late lunch.

After their meal they all go out again into the bright sunshine to spend some time in the college grounds where, alas, the flowerbeds have been virtually denuded of blooms due to fans stealing them to give to their idols! Whilst The Beatles, womenfolk and newfound friends are enjoying the fresh air, they hear the distant sound of a telephone ringing. The ringing continues; and Jane, realising it is coming from the porter's lodge back in their dormitory building, decides to go inside to investigate. The caller is Brian Epstein's assistant, Peter Brown, who has apparently been given this phone number by Pattie Boyd, in case of emergencies, and as Peter wishes to speak to Paul McCartney urgently, Jane immediately calls Paul to the phone.
It soon becomes obvious to everyone that Paul has received some very bad news.

Pattie - 'We were stunned when Paul, ashen-faced, repeated what he had been told. It had to be a mistake. Paul and George were in complete shock. I don't think it could have been worse if they had heard that their own fathers had dropped dead. The unthinkable had happened. Brian had found them, believed in them, moulded them, turned them into millionaires and made them famous the world over. He had looked after them, pandered to their every whim, protected them, guided them, advised them. He was their friend, their enabler, their hero. He was irreplaceable.'[21]

Ringo - 'In Bangor we heard that Brian had died. That was a real downer because of the confusion and the disbelief: "You're kidding me!" Your belief system gets suspended because you so badly don't want to hear it. You don't know what to do with it. If you look at our faces in the film shot at the time, it was all a bit like: "What is it? What does it mean? Our friend has gone." It was more "our friend" than anything else. Brian was a friend of ours, and we were all left behind. After we arrived there with hope and flowers - now this.'[1]

Apparently, Brian's Spanish butler, Antonio, tried without success to raise Brian on the intercom at his Belgravia home, and having met with no success called up Peter Brown who quickly went round to the house. The door to Brian's bedroom was broken open, only to reveal the awful truth, of Brian lying lifeless on his bed. As yet there are no clues as to how this young, charming and successful entrepreneur has met this fate. Brian is only 32-years old; how could anyone have foretold his death?

Marianne Faithful - 'We wanted to know about other disciplines of living. What the Maharishi told us was something to do with individuality, something whereby you could live without other people. The strangest thing about that was... that, at the moment they were being given a philosophy in which they could live their lives as individuals, at that very second, Brian died, the one who'd wanted them to be as a group.'[3]

Pattie - 'We had been on our way to Maharishi who was going to talk to us privately - and suddenly that seemed the right thing to do so we kept the appointment. We needed someone wise and spiritual to tell us what to think. We were lost. I even thought, idiotically, Maharishi is so amazing, maybe he can bring Brian back to life. He couldn't, of course, but he was calm. He talked about reincarnation, but he said, too, that negative feelings would impede Brian's journey. His spirit was with us, and to release it, we must be joyful for him, laugh and be happy. It was hard to feel any joy that day, but it was an enormous help to have someone to turn to, who knew with such certainty how we should cope. I can't help thinking it was no coincidence that we were with Maharishi when Brian died. Someone up there was looking after us.'[21]

As it happens, after having taken Cynthia up to Bangor, Neil Aspinall decided to remain in the area and enjoy a short vacation, so he was not far from The Beatles when the news of Brian Epstein's death became known.

Neil Aspinall - 'I had heard on the car radio that Brian had died.
'I went to where the guys were with Maharishi. I said to John that Brian had died, and he said, "I know - isn't it exciting?" and I thought, "What?" But they were all in a state of shock.'[1]

Paolo Ammassari - '.. they were deeply concerned at the news. They went to Maharishi and the farewell was quiet and sad.'[64]

Paul and Jane are the first to leave for London, taking off in a chauffeur driven Daimler limousine and leaving John, George and Ringo go to deal with questions from the waiting reporters. Eventually they venture out front and asked about their feelings and about their immediate plans.

Reporter - 'Have you a tribute that you would like to pay to Mr. Epstein?'

John - 'Well you know.. We don't know what to say. We loved him and he was one of us.'

George - 'You can't pay tribute in words.'

Reporter - 'What are your plans now?'

George - 'To return to London, and do whatever we can.'

Reporter - 'I understand that Mr Epstein was to be initiated here tomorrow.'

John - 'Yes.'

Reporter - 'When was he coming up? Was he coming up this afternoon?'

George - 'Tomorrow, just Monday. That's all we knew.'

Reporter - 'Had you told him very much about the Spiritual Regeneration Movement?'

George - 'Well, as much as we'd learned about spiritualism and various things of that nature, then we tried to pass on to him. And he was equally as interested as we are, as everybody should be. He wanted to know about life as much as we do.'

Reporter - 'Did the Maharishi give you any words of comfort?'

John - 'His meditation gives you confidence enough to withstand something like this, even the short amount we've had.'

George - 'There's no real such thing as death anyway. I mean, it's death on a physical level, but life goes on everywhere and you just keep going. Really! But.. so the thing is, it's not so disappointing .. it is and it isn't .. you know? And the thing about the comfort, is to know he's .. okay!'

Reporter - 'Had you spoken to him since your, since you became interested this weekend?'

John & Ringo - 'No.'

George - 'I spoke to him Wednesday evening, the evening before we first saw Maharishi's lecture. And he was in great spirits'.

Reporter - 'And when did he tell you that he'd like to be initiated?'

George - 'Well, when we arrived here on.. - was it on..? - .. Friday, we got a telephone call later that day to say that Brian would follow us up and be here Monday.'

Reporter - 'Do you intend returning to Bangor before the end of this conference?'

George - 'We probably won't have time now, because Maharishi will only be here till about Thursday and we'll have so much to do in London that we'll have to meet him again some other time.'

Reporter - 'I understand that this afternoon Maharishi conferred with you all. Could I ask you what he, what advice he offered you?'

John - 'He told us that, uh, not to get overwhelmed by grief, and to.. whatever thoughts we have of Brian to keep them happy, because any thoughts we have, have of him will travel to him wherever he is.'

Reporter - 'Had he ever met Mr. Epstein?'

John - 'No, but he was looking forward to meeting him.'[3]

Poster by Hapshash & Coloured Coat (Michael English & Nigel Weymouth)

One of Brian's most recent ventures has been to lease a wonderful 1930's theatre in London's Shaftesbury Avenue and turn it into a music venue, arranging music nights for top acts such as Rock 'n' Roll star Chuck Berry, and singer/songwriter Donovan. Today's show at the Saville Theatre features several acts, the psychedelic blues group The Jimi Hendrix Experience, Tomorrow (featuring Keith West), and The Crazy World of Arthur Brown. The theatre management decides to cancel the second house as 'a mark of respect' for Brian.

❀ ❀ ❀

Jenny Boyd - 'George and Pattie, and the rest of The Beatles. We all went to Wales together to meet Maharishi, and on our way back George asked me whether I wanted to go to India.'
'So I said "I'd love to go to India, it'd always been a dream of mine to go to India".'[65]

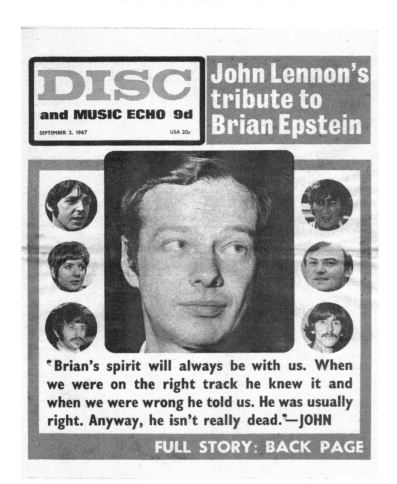

Chapter Eight
The Beatles' Academy Of Meditation

The following day, Monday, 28th August 1967, Ringo and John are in sombre mood sitting in John's garden when they receive a visit from a reporter from a music paper. After talking about the loss of Brian Epstein they open up about their newfound interest in Transcendental Meditation.

Ringo - 'I go a lot on transcendental meditation - I wish we'd heard about it before we ever went on those tours. They were such a drag and a strain that we just needed something like this.

We got little sleep, and some form of mental relaxation is what we missed. Now we know this form of meditation could have helped a lot.

This meditation can be used by everyone. It isn't just because we have the freedom that we can do it - people in 9 to 5 jobs can use it, because it can be done any time, and it can help people unwind and do their jobs properly. This is a very upsetting time for us, but we've got it under control, I hope. People say; "Why aren't you wearing a black tie?" It isn't disrespectful just because we don't wear black ties. It's what's in your mind that counts. You can be wearing a flowered shirt or a black tie, but neither governs what you're thinking.'[66]

John - 'His spirit is still around, and always will be. It's a physical memory we have of him, and as men we will build on that memory. It's a loss of genius, but other genius's bodies have died, as well, and the world still gains from their spirits.

It is up to us, now, to sort out the way we, and Brian, wanted things to go. He might be dead physically, but that's a negative way of thinking. He helped to give us the strength to do what we did, and the same urge is still alive.

He was due to come up to Bangor and join us in these transcendental meditations with the Maharishi, it's a drag he didn't make it....'

'We're all going to India soon for a couple of months to study transcendental meditation properly.

'We want to learn the meditation thing properly, so we can propagate it and sell the whole idea to everyone. This is how we plan to use our power now - they've always called us leaders of youth, and we believe that this is a good way to give a lead.

'We want to try to set up an academy in London and use all the power we have got to get it moving.

The whole world will know what we mean, and all the people who are worried about youth and drugs and that scene - all these people with the short back and sides - they can come along and dig it, too.

'It's no gospel, Bible-thumping, singalong thing, and it needn't be religion if people don't want to connect it with religion. It's all in the mind. It strengthens understanding and makes people relaxed.'[66]

The Beatles' decision to take tutelage under Maharishi Mahesh Yogi might come as a shock to many, for it seems so unlikely that The Beatles need any tips on philosophy, they are known for being free thinkers and being able to think for themselves. The very idea of their sitting around meditating is puzzling to many, for it sounds that 'meditating' is just another word for 'doing nothing'! However, as The Beatles have already discovered, quietening the mind and finding inner relaxation takes a bit of understanding and practice, so it's really convenient that they have had the opportunity to take time off and gain a clear idea about how to meditate.

Paul - 'It was like a summer camp, it was like a school that they'd taken over, and you sit around and he tells you how to do it, and er, you go up to your room and try and do it, and of course you can't. The first half hour you've got a *mantra* to meditate on, and you're thinking on, going "bloody hell, that train journey was a bit much wasn't it? Oh sorry, *mantra*, duh di-duh di-duh di-da - bloody hell, wonder what our next record's going to be? Well you know I try.." Oh, stop, stop, stop, and you spend all your first few days just trying to stop your mind dealing with your social calendar, you know, whatever's coming up. "He's a funny bloke that Mahar... oh, no." But it was good.'[46]

❀ ❀ ❀

Mick Jagger returns to Bangor in order to learn meditation and to spend time with Maharishi, and he joins in the class photos being taken by local photographer Douglas Gowan.

A new teen magazine, *INTRO*, is soon to be published which will include in its first issue an interview with Beatles George and John, who are happy to talk about their interest in meditation.

George - 'Pattie started it all really.

'She joined the Maharishi place a long time ago. We'd been looking for this thing and suddenly it's there.'

John - 'Bangor was incredible, you know. Maharishi reckons the message will get through if we can put it across. What he says about life and the universe is the same message that Jesus, Buddha and Krishna and all the big boys were putting over.'

George - 'But with meditation you don't have to bother with religion or anything. When you come out after meditating in the morning, you forget it completely and let it work for you.'

John - 'Yeh, and there's none of this sitting in the lotus position or standing on your head. You just do it as long as you like. (In a heavy accent) Tventy minutes a day is prescribed for ze verkers. Tventy minutes in the morning and tventy minutes after verk. Makes you happy intelligent and more energy.'

George - 'It helps you find fulfilment in life, helps you live life to the full. Young people are searching for a bit of peace inside themselves.'

John - 'The main thing is not to think about the future or the past, the main thing is just to get on with *now*. We want to help people do that with these academies. We'll make a donation and we'll ask for money from anyone we know with money, anyone that's interested, anyone in the so-called establishment who's worried about kids going wild and drugs and all that. Another groovy thing: everybody gives one week's wages when they join. I think it's the fairest thing I've ever heard of. And that's all you ever pay, just the once.'

'With Brian dying it was sort of a big thing for us. And if we hadn't had this meditation it would have been much harder to access and carry on and know how we were going.

'Now we're managers, now we have to make all the decisions. We've always had full responsibility for what we did, but we still had a father figure, or whatever it was, and if we didn't feel like it - well, you know, Brian would do it.'

George - 'We've all come along the same path. We've been together a long time. We learned right from the beginning that we're going to be together.'

John - 'Even if you go into the meditation bit just curious or cynical, once you go into it, you see. We weren't so much sceptical because we'd been through that phase in the middle of all the Beatlemania like, so we came out of being sceptics a bit. But you've got to have a questioning attitude to all that goes on. The only thing you can do is judge on your own experience and that's what this is about. You know, I'm less sceptical than I ever was.'

George - 'We don't know how this will come out in the music. Don't expect to hear transcendental meditation all the time.'[41]

INTRO is also to include a contribution by Maharishi.

Maharishi - 'The interest of young minds in the use of drugs, even though misguided, indicates their genuine search for some form of spiritual experience.

'With the interest of The Beatles and The Rolling Stones in Transcendental Meditation, it has become evident that the search for higher spiritual experience among the young will not take long to reach fulfilment. But it is for the older generation to provide facilities for the teaching of Transcendental Meditation.

'It is an indication of the progress that The Beatles are thinking of having their own academy for teaching, in London to start with, and I congratulate the Archbishop of Canterbury who has expressed his satisfaction with The Beatles' interest in Transcendental Meditation.

'The youth of today need the support of their elders and I hope they will extend their grace.'[41]

❀ ❀ ❀

Actually though, The Beatles are not the only pop stars interested in Maharishi and the technique of meditation. Mike Pinder is a member of another successful pop group, The Moody Blues, and Mike is also a friend of John Lennon, and interested in meditation. It was Mike who introduced John to the Mellotron, a fantastic experimental keyboard, the keys of which trigger a bank of tape loops of just about any instrument imaginable. John has already used the Mellotron to great effect on The Beatles' really way-out single *'Strawberry Fields Forever'* and is still exploring its potential.

An article is published, with a photo of John in his home studio, which suggests that John has changed since learning to meditate, and become very relaxed, *'the easiest Beatle to talk to'.*[67]

john's music room

them to life are; a Farfisa organ, a small piano, and a Mellotron. Also scattered around the room are various guitars—many with weird and wonderful psychedelic patterns flowing all over their bodies.

John Lennon's one-man band.

FAVOURITE

I have often wondered how one particular instrument manages to become the favourite of Beatle Lennon. But although I have asked him the question many times I have never yet got a straight answer. John's reply is usually: "Mal just got it for me." or something similar.

He's also got lots of old musical bits and pieces stacked up in various places; a saxophone minus a mouth piece; a violin with only one string hanging loosely along its body.

John moved around the instruments giving us a quick solo on the organ, a tinkle on the piano, some strums on the guitars and some crazy antics on the non-working sax and violin.

JOHN Lennon has changed. The raw, restless, sharp son of Merseyside has been replaced by a new, very successful pop star and international celebrity.

He has learnt to meditate.

But, whether this is entirely due to the influences of that celebrated, and much-publicised, Himalayan mystic, Maharishi Mahesh Yogi, no one knows. But whatever the cause, the result is plain to see.

RELAXED

John is very relaxed, the easiest Beatle to talk to, and far more understanding.

He meditates in his garden, perched on a buttress, which juts out from the broad terrace behind his Weybridge home, staring at his favourite tree, a big silver birch, which stands serenely some 30 ft away in his wooded garden.

He also meditates on music. And this meditation has probably earned him more than

John seems very happy with a new sound he has discovered on his Mellotron.

all the thoughts of dozens of top business men put together.

I believe that John has always found it more difficult to get down to his song writing task than Paul. Ideas seem to pop into Paul's head with surprising regularity, while John's flow of musical genius is harder to catch.

Like all the other Beatles

he has a special room in his house, set aside for the hard work of composing the hit songs, which are going to vibrate through millions of loudspeakers all over the world very shortly after their birth in a smallish room at the top of John's mansion.

John's room has taken longer to put together than

inside and when you pull these knobs and press the keys they start playing". The next 10 minutes were pure Lennon as John worked out a dozen variations of every theme that came into his head, grinning at us whenever the noises became particularly fantastic.

John is one Beatle who has gone through many phases since his group first brought out a disc called "Love Me Do".

What's his current mood? Well, outwardly Hippy! But, take a look at that badge he has got stuck on his shoulder in one of the pictures, I think it reveals a lot. It reads "I still love the Beatles".

MELLOTRON

But the instrument which obviously fascinated him—because of its usefulness to him in his song writing—is the Mellotron. He pushed in a few knobs, pulled out some bars, depressed a key at the base end and a throbbing rhythm filled the room. He quickly changed to a waltz tempo. "It's all done by tapes," he explained, "there are dozens of reels of tapes

George's or Paul's, it is also much more comprehensive and well set up.

The first thing you notice on entering, is the battery of five tape recorders ranged along a shelf on one side of the room.

The other occupants, standing around waiting for their master's magic touch to bring

John with his hand-painted Gibson jumbo.

Like The Beatles, The Moody Blues are also interested in experiencing enhanced levels of consciousness, and their new guitarist and singer Justin Hayward, who replaced Denny Laine (singer on *'Go Now'*), has been looking into the merits of Transcendental Meditation.

Justin Hayward - 'In the early part of '67 we'd started to read those books on Transcendental Meditation. The Beatles were the leaders of that particular club in London that we all went to. We didn't get the Maharishi, though, we got the Indian waiter from down the road. But we really were looking at that mind-expanding stuff, and the TM turned it into a religion. It was a proper way of life - better than just hanging around and being stoned all the time.'[68]

'We went to the TM Center at the same time that The Beatles did. Four of us went: me, Mike [Pinder], Graeme [Edge], and Ray [Thomas]. We went through the whole process.'[69]

Perhaps Justin's use of the word *'religion'* needs to be put in context, for it is stated again and again that one does not need to be religious to practice Transcendental Meditation, nor is the practice a religion. But Justin is by no means alone in seeing the search for mind expansion as a religious act, though others see it differently, as just a regular exercise, comparable to cleaning one's teeth.

Actually, there are many on the pop scene that are getting involved in Transcendental Meditation, though not all are making it known to their fans. Back in the spring of 1965, The Doors pop group was formed after keyboardist Ray Manzarek, guitarist Robby Krieger and drummer John Densmore met at an introductory meeting for Transcendental Meditation in Los Angeles. As with The Beatles, The Doors discovered meditation via psychedelic drugs, naming their group after Aldous Huxley's classic, *'Doors of Perception'*, which is itself a reference to a William Blake poem.

> **'If the doors of perception were cleansed every thing would appear to man as it is, Infinite.**
> **For man has closed himself up, till he sees all things thro' narrow chinks of his cavern.'**
> - Excerpt from *'The Marriage of Heaven and Hell'* by William Blake (1757-1827)

Maharishi's directions on to how to meditate - *'Take it easy'* and *'Take it as it comes'* - find their way into one of The Doors' 1966 song, *'Take It As It Comes'*.

Joe Hagan (journalist) - '"There wouldn't be any Doors without Maharishi," says Densmore, who recalls the guru as "this androgynous little weird fairy dude" who emanated "a palpable love vibe".'[70]

Certainly, Maharishi speaks a lot about love, in fact he has written a poem called *'Love'*, which was recorded and released as one whole side of a gramophone record issued back in 1963. Here is a short excerpt.

Maharishi - 'Love as love is universal. Personal love is concentrated universal love. Ah. My heart flows when I say; "personal love is concentrated universal love". The ocean of universal love flows in the stream of individual love. What a blessing in life. The heart in whom the universal consciousness has dawned, is able to have the force of the unbounded ocean of universal love, even in the stream of personal love. Those who are restricted in their ability to love, those whose love flows only in restricted channels of isolated objects or individuals, those who can only like this or that. Those who have no awareness of universal consciousness in their hearts are like small ponds where the love can flow only as ripples and not as waves of the sea. Such is the love of most of us. We love today, and rise to fight tomorrow.

'Let us not bring shame to love. Let us rise to love forever more and more. When an ocean flows in love, it flows in peace within. When a shallow pond moves to rise high in waves of the ocean, it only stirs the mud at the bottom, and the whole serenity of the pond is spoiled. When a heart, shallow as a pond, seeks to rise high in waves of love, it creates a muddle and brings out the mud that was so far gracefully hidden underneath. To enjoy the ocean of love, we have to improve the magnitude of our hearts and gain the depth of an ocean, unfathomable and full.

'Let us give this status of an ocean to our heart before we let loose of our love to be tossed about by the blowing winds. And having gained the status of the deep, let us open the heart for the ocean of love to flow, and let it flow in fullness. The mighty waves of love will rise in grace and hail the glory of the multiple creation with the bliss of the unity and peace within.

'And how do we improve the depth of our heart? By probing deep into the purity of our being. By exploring the finer regions of the impulse of love that murmurs in the silent chamber of our heart. By diving deep into the stillness of the unbounded, unfathomable ocean of love present within our hearts. By a simple technique of self-exploration, or by what is commonly known as "the transcendental deep meditation". It is easy for every one of us to fathom the unfathomable magnitude of the ocean of love present within, and forever enjoy the fullness of heart, in the fullness of life.'[3]

Scots born Donovan Leitch is a poet, songwriter and guitarist, famous for the hit singles *'Catch the Wind'* and *'Colours'*, he is also a pal of The Beatles and has even contributed a line to *'Yellow Submarine'* - *'Sky of blue and sea of green'* - and appeared on the world-wide transmission of *'All You Need is Love'*. Inspired by beat writers such as Jack Kerouac and Allen Ginsberg, and the mystical essays of Alan Watts, Donovan has been exploring Zen meditation and Eastern thinking.

Donovan - 'George called me and said, "He's here."'[71]

'I saw my friends The Beatles on the television going down to see him. I made a note to look into it.'[72]

⊛ ⊛ ⊛

Maharishi is scheduled to fly to Europe before the end of the 10-day Bangor course.

Camilla Drummond (a meditator) - 'Yes, I was there too! Didn't have anything to do with Beatles, they were just there.. The pivotal moment for me was giving Maharishi a flower as He was leaving, He stopped to take it & said "just enjoy" & time stood still for me, my mind went blank & my life as it was was over! Everyone was disappearing fast & I remember frantically looking for someone to ask when I could see Him again. Finally someone told me I'd have to go to India to see him.. ..'[38]

But before leaving Great Britain for India, Maharishi has plans to meet up with The Beatles in London.

On Thursday, 31st August 1967, The Beatles and their entourage including Ringo's wife, Maureen, and Paul McCartney's brother, Mike McGear, lead singer of a pop trio of comedic musical poets called The Scaffold, converge on the luxurious London home of one of Maharishi's devotees, Jemima Pitman, at Albert Place, Kensington. Paul and Jane lounge on a sofa, and John sits on the carpet beside Maharishi, whilst the others sit on chairs around the vast sitting room. Another of Maharishi's devoted followers, Hermione Cassell, is there too, sitting near to the bay window on a chair beside Ringo. Everyone is paying attention to Maharishi.

Reporter - 'He looks beneficently about the room; first at the mop-headed Beatles, who have made his name almost as famous as their own: John Lennon with his ten-cent spectacles, Ringo in his white suit and multicolored shirt, George Harrison with his beads, Paul McCartney with his lime-green jacket. His gaze takes in Mick Jagger of The Rolling Stones, Jane Asher, McCartney's girl friend; then moves around the room which is a sea on intent, upturned faces.

And we, in turn, return the gaze. And wait for Maharishi Mahesh Yogi to speak.'[73]

Seated crossed-legged on a large armchair, Maharishi composes himself before addressing the group and the members of the Press who have been given permission to attend.

On this occasion, Maharishi chooses to explain some points about the use of the *mantra*, the sound that is given to each new meditator at his or her initiation. He does not illustrate the points by using a genuine *mantra* and instead he takes as his example the sound 'Boom', a sound without any real meaning other than by association.

Reporter - ""First," says Maharishi, "you have got to forget what 'Boom' means. Simply say; 'Boom-boom-boom-boom-boom' into nothingness." He does it, eyes tightly shut, fingers gently wafting, "You see?"

'What sort of words does he give to his followers to contemplate?'

'"A simple word or a syllable. One to which their vibrations respond."

'Will he volunteer such a word?'

'"No. You are here as an inquirer, not a follower. The word would be meaningless to you, as the phrase 'transcendental meditation' is meaningless to most outsiders. How do you describe the taste of jam to one who has not tried it?"'

You find yourself watching The Beatles. Everyone is watching The Beatles. They watch Maharishi.

"Has anyone had a remarkable experience since the last meeting?" Maharishi asks.

George Harrison puts a hand up. He does it in a rather shy way. Everyone applauds.

"Has anyone newly seen the light?" asks Maharishi.

A hand goes up. It belongs to Mrs John Lennon. More applause.

Paul McCartney speaks up. He talks for quite a time. He explains how each of The Beatles tried drugs in their quest for mind expansion. It didn't help. Since coming to the meetings, they have realized the futility of drugs.'[73]

So, what specific benefits might one derive from this meditation?

John - 'Put very simply - detachment. An emptying of the mind of those endlessly self-regarding thoughts that sabotage your energies and destroy your peace of mind.'[73]

Mick Jagger comments on Maharishi's teaching about the attainment of global peace, which states that attaining individual peace of mind is the very basis of securing World Peace.

Mick Jagger - 'What Maharishi teaches is this. When a man's mind is not peaceful, whatever he does or thinks creates vibrations in the atmosphere. The sum of these tense vibrations finally explodes into calamities like war. There is only one way to neutralize the atmospheric tensions, he believes, and that is to reduce them at source - in individuals.'[73]

And George Harrison, perhaps the most enthralled by Indian thinking amongst this audience, is convinced that meditation has already brought significant improvement for him.

George - 'Well, for a start it's expanded my consciousness so that I'm at last able to change my attitudes.'[73]

He goes on to explain some elements of his personal philosophy, ideas which are certainly not contained in any literature of the Spiritual Regeneration Movement.

George - 'I believe that all our actions are motivated by fear. Fear is the first thing that we experience when we emerge from our mothers.

'We live by compulsions, and the neurosis of compulsion is based on fear. All sin is fear-motivated, and all forms of aggression, materialism, and lust are means of trying to calm the fear within us.'

'He [Maharishi] believes that meditation is a means of removing fear, so that we can become content just by being.

'I believe that through meditation you develop a far deeper power of communication with other people, and this has huge sociological and political implications.

'It is also the one thing that could help to bridge the gap between the generations that is now so wide. Wide because the young are using concepts that older people do not understand, and because older people resent the young having a freedom they never had.

'I know that by saying this I am sticking my neck out. And I am not in a position to say that I *know* meditation to be true. But I don't think we can afford the luxury of sneering at something which *could* provide the answer.'[73]

❀ ❀ ❀

George - 'When Brian died, I had so many spiritualists calling me up, saying, "Brian Epstein wants to talk to you." In fact, I think I talked to him more after he died than I did when he was alive.'

Paul - 'George and John got a call from a medium who said that Brian was trying to contact us and that he had something to say to us. We didn't want to pass up any channels, so John and George went along to the séance. But, they didn't believe it at all. There was nothing in it.'[12]

⊛ ⊛ ⊛

Friday, 1st September 1967.

John, George and Ringo are due to meet at Paul's house in Cavendish Ave, St. John's Wood, London, for a discussion about The Beatles future.

Tony Barrow (Beatles' Press Officer) - 'While he and I waited for the rest of the Beatles to arrive, in St John's Wood, Paul confessed to me that his biggest fear was whether or not the group could possibly get back to work again or if they'd drift off to India, and without the leadership of Brian Epstein and without any immediate jobs that needed doing, that the Beatles would no longer work together after that.'[74]

At their meeting, The Fab Four discuss the way forward, with Paul suggesting that they put their plans to visit India on hold for the time being, and embark on their own film project, home-movie style with hand-held cameras. The movie project is an idea Paul has been fostering for some time. Actually, since The Beatles stopped touring, it has largely been Paul who has been steering the group, it was his idea for The Beatles to record as *Sergeant Pepper's Lonely Hearts Club Band*. But in the early days of The Beatles it was always John who was viewed as leader, he enjoyed being the boss of his 'gang' of friends and had enjoyed it since he was a child.

John - 'The sort of gang I led went in for things like shoplifting and pulling girls' knickers down.'[75]

'I was aggressive because I wanted to be popular. I wanted to be the leader. I wanted everybody to do what I told them to do, to laugh at my jokes and let me be the boss.'[53]

These days though John seems content to let Paul initiate new ideas, in spite of the fact he then finds himself under pressure to write new songs hastily in order to have material for any new project.

The current proposal involves hiring a coach, filling it with friends and touring around the countryside, and filming whatever takes their fancy. The basic idea seems to have been triggered by the real life tale of Ken Kesey, author of *'One Flew Over The Cuckoo's Nest'*, and his friends, the Merry Band of Pranksters, who, in 1964 motored around the United States on a bus painted out with psychedelic patterns. Kesey's crazy trip was a drug-fuelled escapade as most of the Pranksters were high on LSD. Driver of the bus was Neil Cassady (the inspiration for Dean Moriarty, the star of Jack Kerouac's 1957 novel *'On The Road'*). By comparison, the Beatles new project will be decidedly tame, being centred as it is on the idea of a traditional British tradition of a 'mystery tour', where passengers have no clear idea where they are going; the sort of trip that can just turn into a booze up and a pub-crawl.

⊛ ⊛ ⊛

Today John Lennon responds to a letter he has received from his father, Alf 'Freddie' Lennon - who in truth he hardly knows - and in the reply he tells him; *'I'll get in contact before a month has passed - after that I'm going to India a couple of months…'*

⊛ ⊛ ⊛

Maharishi is set to return to India but before doing so he intends to visit some SRM centres in Europe.

John Coleman (author) - 'When he finally left London for Holland and more lecture engagements, his farewell at Heathrow airport was as captivating a performance as any he had yet given.

'According to one paper the teacher of Transcendental Meditation had omitted to meditate beforehand on the advisability of buying an airline ticket in advance. He bought one and got his luggage weighed just five minutes before his flight was due to leave. Then he couldn't find his passport, "a situation," said the Daily Mirror, "which he resolved after a short meditative session."'

'An anxious BEA girl implored him to hurry, then, thinking he was trotting along behind her, turned to find him distributing flowers among the crowds who had come to see him off. He gave his last, breathless, news conference to the London journalists as he ran across the tarmac to the waiting plane, which eventually left twenty minutes late.'[76]

THE BEATLES, DRUGS, MYSTICISM & INDIA

On Friday, 1st September 1967, Maharishi leaves Heathrow for Holland. In Amsterdam Maharishi is to speak at the 'Concertgebouw' (the 'Concert Hall'), and to meet him there are Mick Jagger and Brian Jones of The Rolling Stones.

The following day, when Maharishi flies on to Bremen, in West Germany, his faithful assistant Brahmachari Devendra accompanies him, and Brian Jones travels along too. Dressed as they are in flower power fashion, Brian stands out from the rest of the other passengers, as do his travelling companions, one of whose friends is Michael Cooper, who had photographed the montage of faces for The Beatles' *Sergeant Pepper* record cover at his Chelsea studio.

❀ ❀ ❀

These days the Press is giving a lot of column inches to The Beatles' involvement with Maharishi Mahesh Yogi, but they seem incapable of conveying a clear impression of just what Transcendental Meditation is about. Perhaps this is because the Press finds it difficult to distinguish between The Beatles' practice of a self-help technique (which has been around for years), and the perception they have become pupils of an Indian mystic who is teaching them how to think.

Pop journalist Keith Altham brings up the subject of The Beatles with Jimi Hendrix, who Paul McCartney enthusiastically calls 'Fingers Hendrix'.

Keith Altham - 'We talked of the Maharishi Mahesh Yogi, whom the Beatles have lately adopted (or vice versa).'

Jimi Hendrix - 'I don't really believe that this transcendental meditation is much more than day-dreaming. If you really believe in yourself you can think it out on your own; you don't need someone else!'[77]

Judging by the lyrics to one of his recent songs, Jimi would be the last to condemn day-dreaming.

> *'Some people say;*
> *"day-dreaming's for all the lazy minded fools, with nothing else to do"*
> *so let them laugh, laugh at me.'*
>
> - Excerpt of *'May This Be Love'* by Jimi Hendrix, recorded April 1967.

❀ ❀ ❀

George Harrison writes a letter to his mum, Mrs. Louise Harrison (née French). [78]

Dear Mum,
Thanks for your letter last week, and if it's any comfort to you, don't worry about me and don't think anything negative about Maharishi. Because he's not phoney, it's only the bullshit that's written about him that's phoney. He's not taking any of our money, all he's doing is teaching us how to contact God. And as God isn't divided into different sects as our religious leaders here make out by their prejudices, then it doesn't affect my dedication to Sacred Heart in any way, it only strengthens it. But we will help to spread this teaching so anybody can attain this, and new generations will grow up to have this right from the start. Instead of going through the ignorance that seems to dominate everything and anyone at the moment, causing them to feel it's mysticism or something strange or black magic. Don't think that I've gone off my rocker because I haven't. But I now love you and everybody else much more than ever. So it's not that bad is it? -

---

Generally speaking it is not easy for Beatle fans to be able to get access to any of the group, but it happens that one enterprising fan manages to get a letter through to John Lennon (after obtaining his address from her boss who supplies flowers to Brian Epstein's office). She writes to John about her spiritual search, and he responds by hand-written letter, postmarked 6th September 1967.

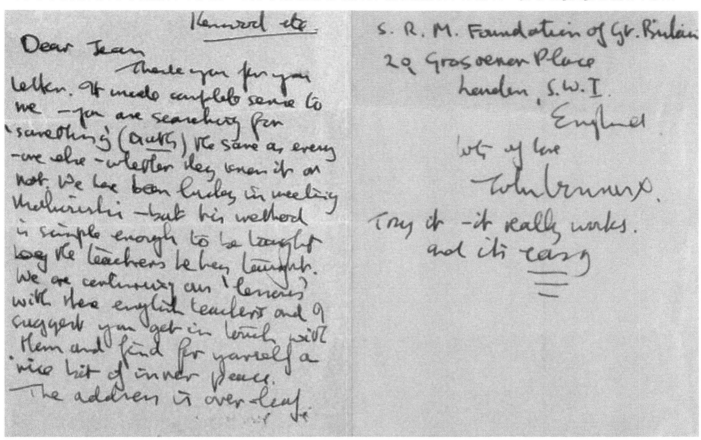

<u>Kenwood etc.</u>
Dear Jean,
Thank you for your letter. It made complete sense to me - you are searching for 'something' (Truth) the same as everyone else - whether they know it or not. We have been lucky in meeting Maharishi - but his method is simple enough to be taught by the teachers he has taught. We are continuing our 'lessons' with these english teachers and I suggest you get in touch with them and find yourself a nice bit of inner peace. The address is overleaf.

S.R.M. Foundation of Gt. Britain
20, Grosvenor Place
London, S.W.I.
England.
Lots of love
John Lennon x.
Try it - it really works.
and its <u>easy</u>

During the first week of September The Beatles visit the studios several times, recording a handful of new titles. Unusually for them, they begin working on an instrumental track, provisionally titled *'Aerial Tour Instrumental'* which is to be jointly credited to the four of them, and on it John uses the amazing multiple tape loop Mellotron keyboard to conjure up the sounds of trumpets and flutes.

❀ ❀ ❀

The Beatles are invited to a séance.
Pattie - 'Shortly after Brian's death, a couple wrote to George and John saying that Brian was trying to make contact with us. The wife was a medium and could conduct a séance. But, they said, it was vitally important that we told no one about it because some Venusians would join us, and if anyone got wind of their visit, the military would kill them.'

'We waited and waited. There was no sign of the Venusians. Were we sure we hadn't told anyone? Yes. Then the husband sat in front of a big old-fashioned radio, like something out of a 1940's movie, put on earphones and fiddled with some knobs, saying things like "V6, V6, come in, V6 ..." The Venusians, he announced, had said they weren't coming after all, but they would contact us at another time. He and his wife were so disappointed, but we dared not look at each other for fear of cracking up.

We were ushered into a big dark room where we sat round a circular table. Suddenly the wife was talking in a weird voice as though she had been taken over by a spirit.'[21]

Cynthia - 'The bellowing voice identified itself as a Red Indian spirit. He spoke loud and clear about many things and future happenings but didn't mention anyone by name until he asked, "Is there a Cynthia one here?" My heart pounded fit to burst, I found it almost impossible to swallow.

"Is there a Cynthia one here, you must listen to her. The Cynthia one will lead the way."'[7]

Pattie - 'She talked about people on the other side, people who were coming forward, who wanted to speak to us. She had Brian with her, she said. He was saying he was all right, we were not to worry about him - and he wanted us to know that he had not committed suicide. I so wanted to believe her, and so did George, I think, but she got a few things wrong for me: she was pretty accurate in the things she told Cynthia, but John pooh-poohed the whole thing. When it was over, and the spirits had left her, she looked drained.

Her husband told us that because the Venusians hadn't come, they wouldn't charge us, and we said goodbye. Outside we howled with laughter.'[21]

John, to Cynthia - 'And who wants to listen to you anyway; he must be mad!'[7]

⊛ ⊛ ⊛

Brian Epstein died from "incautious overdose" of drug, says Coroner

Brian Epstein the 32-year-old manager of the Beatles, was killed by the accumulative effect of bromide in a drug he had been taking for some time, it was stated yesterday at an inquest in London.

In recording a verdict of "Accidental death" the Coroner, Mr Gavin Thurston, said death was due to poisoning by Carbrital, due to an incautious self-overdose.

Mr Epstein, a man of considerable business affairs who lived a life of pressure, had been taking sleeping tablets for a long time, and had "perpetual trouble with insomnia," he said.

Mr Epstein, chairman of N.E.M.S. Enterprises, was found dead in bed on August 27 at his home in Chapel Street, Belgravia, London.

Dr Robert Donald Teare, pathologist, said of the bromide traces he found:—"It indicates that Mr Epstein must have been taking bromide in some form, presumably by Carbrital, for a long time. This level can be achieved only by the continued use of Carbrital."

He had found a trace of an anti-depressant drug and barbiturate and bromide. The barbiturate level in the blood was "a low fatal level."

Bromide had an accumulative effect, Dr Teare said. About evidence that Mr Epstein had been drowsy, he stated:—"It would certainly fit in with a high bromide level."

Answering the Coroner, Dr Teare said it might make a man "careless, injudicious."

Asked how long Mr Epstein had taken Carbrital regularly, Dr Teare replied:—"I would roughly have said weeks rather than days."

The level of bromide contained in Carbrital indicated repetition rather than a single dose.

Police Inspector George Howlett said Mr Epstein was lying dead on a single bed, dressed in pyiamas, and with correspondence spread out over an unoccupied single bed beside him.

Mr Epstein's butler said the locked door of the bedroom was broken open after he could get no reply from him.

At last the reason for Brian Epstein's death is to be made public, and on Saturday, 9th September 1967, *The Times* newspaper reports the Coroner's verdict of accidental death, attributed to the cumulative effects of a long-standing over-dependence on the use of barbiturates. Though it is good that he did not commit suicide, for anyone close to Brian this news can give them but cold comfort.

Brian never married, indeed he didn't appear to have been overly attracted to the opposite sex, leading many to suppose The Beatles' song, *'You've Got to Hide Your Love Away'* is a song about him.

> ***'Everywhere people stare, each and every day, I can see them laugh at me,***
> ***and I hear them say; "Hey, you've got to hide your love away".'***
>
> *- Excerpt of 'You've Got to Hide Your Love Away' by John Lennon and Paul McCartney*

The Beatles have lost a dear friend and valued colleague, but they are determined to forge ahead and do what they do best, which is to make music.

Late in September, from 25th-27th September 1967, The Beatles are set to record a track entitled *'Fool On the Hill'*. During the sessions, two Japanese journalists, Rumiko Hoshika, a reporter, and Koh Hasebe, a photographer, visit the studio and get to hear The Beatles work in progress. John also gets a visit, from the avant-garde Japanese artist Yoko Ono whom he has been keeping in contact with since their meeting at Indica Gallery in November 1966.

John - 'I used to bring her out to the house when my wife was here. We were just friends. I respected her work and I knew she was having trouble with her husband. I tried to teach her how to meditate.'

Yoko - 'I was getting very famous at that time. My career was going well but my husband and I were fighting about who would answer the phone. He always wanted to answer the phone so that he could be into everything. 'I always thought of him as my assistant, you see, but he wanted it to be both of us. All I wanted was someone who would be interested in my work. I needed a producer.'[19]

Yoko - 'There were times when he [John] would call me. My guess was that he was in the studio where they [The Beatles] had to wait for the engineer to prepare the tapes or whatever.'
'I was always wondering why he called me. There was many people who used to call and just chat. He wasn't chatty - "Hi". Then silence. I wasn't chatty either. There was a lot of silences in the phonecall.'[80]

Lizzie Bravo (an ardent Beatles fan) **-** 'I vividly remember the first time I saw her: John had been on the phone for a while asking this person if he/she would like to come to the recording session. He even asked the doorman for the address (yes, John didn't remember the address to the studios!) - 3 Abbey Road - and said he would see this person in half an hour. A cab arrived and out came this short oriental lady all dressed in black (trousers and top - a sweater, I believe), with long hair.'[81]

There's an ambiguity about who the song title refers to, who is the 'Fool on the Hill'? It could be seen to be about its writer, Paul McCartney, who when given Tarot readings by Marijke Koger (of The Fool collective), is said to often pull the 'The Fool' card. According to fellow Fool member Simon Posthuma, the Fool card, more properly known as Arcana Zero, *"represents Truth, spiritual meaning, and the circle which expresses the universal circumference in which gravitate all things."*

But the lyrics of *'The Fool on the Hill'* seem also to relate to Maharishi who noted, on one occasion, that to someone watching, the sun appears to be going down of an evening, even though it's widely accepted that the earth is actually turning around. The other lyrics of the song also seem also to relate to Maharishi, telling of the derision he sometimes faces and the way he deals with it.

> ***'He never listens to them,***
> ***he knows that they're the fools.'***
>
> *- Excerpt from 'The Fool on the Hill' by John Lennon and Paul McCartney*

Paul - ' *'Fool on the Hill'* was mine and I think I was writing about someone like the Maharishi. His detractors called him a fool. Because of his giggle he wasn't taken too seriously. It was this idea of a fool on the hill, a guru in a cave, I was attracted to. I remember once hearing about a hermit who missed the

Second World War because he'd been in a cave in Italy, and that always appealed to me.'[6]

Paul - 'You know, "Fool on the Hill", to me, is like anyone who's not listened to. Originally it was kinda like a guru figure, from the days of Maharishi, and things like that. But, I mean you can, to me you can uh substitute anyone - Jesus would do - you know, as a person who in his time was called a fool, but who was actually rather smart.'[82]

Maharishi puts pen to paper and in green ink drafts out a telegram:-

---

**Telegram to**   _**Indira Gandhi Prime Minister of India, New Delhi India**_

Mother India your spiritual heritage now is the front page news of the world's press due to Beatles being blessed by it they are coming with me for three months to be in the academy of meditation Shankaracharya Nagar Rishikesh and would you consider personally blessing them at your residence on arrival in Delhi A documentary film for world wide release will be made by BBC or other company. Govt. of India may appeal to the youth of the world by according them an official reception at the airport on the basis of their being MBE Members of the British Empire

During coming weeks I will be touring Europe will be happy to receive your reply care Spiritual Regeneration Movt Foundation of Great Britain 20 Grosvenor Estate

**Maharishi Mahesh Yogi**

Chapter Nine
On The Road Again

The Beatles have by now hired a coach, in which they intend to take themselves and their guests out on the road for a magical mystery tour. On Tuesday, 12th September 1967, filming starts and the coach pulls out of London, heading out for the open countryside and off to leafy Devon, to the coastal resort of Teignmouth where they stay overnight at the Royal Hotel. The next day they visit the naval port of Plymouth before continuing their road trip, crossing over the Tamar River into Cornwall and driving to Newquay on the North Coast, where George Harrison is interviewed for the BBC radio show, *'Scene & Heard'*.

George - 'The contract we signed with United Artists is for three films, two of which we've done. The third one, the thing is, we can do it any time we want. We haven't so far done the film because we didn't want to make a film just to make some money. We wanted to do a film that might mean something to either us or to the people who go to watch it. So the thing is, over the last year or two since "Help", we've had thousands of ideas but they've all been "Help" and "Hard Day's Night" revisited. It's no good. We've got to have something good, how we visualize the film. It's got to be at least the difference between the song "Help" and "Sgt Pepper," as the movie has got to be that progressed too. So we haven't made it until we feel it's right... and I think we should start it 'round about next February. And if we do, we'll probably end up by not having a big production team film it all.'

Miranda Ward (reporter) - 'Rather like you're doing this one.'

George - 'Yeah. This part that we've been doing is mainly just to tie the whole show together, because it's called a Magical Mystery Tour, then this is just a typical coach tour, but anything can happen. You see, that's the difference because it's magic, then we can do anything. So these parts, these sequences, we just had a few ideas. It's mainly just to show the people getting on the coach and a few little things that happen during the course of the coach trip.'

Miranda Ward - 'How does it feel to be out on the road again as "The Beatles"?'

George - 'Uhh, yes. I dunno. I've never really known what it's been like as The Beatles. (laughs) Because, you see, The Beatles is still something abstract as far as I'm concerned. You know, it's something that other people see us as The Beatles, and I TRY to see us as The Beatles but I can't.'

Miranda Ward - 'At the beginning, didn't you feel like a Beatle?'

George - 'Uhh, I suppose I did, yeah. In fact I do sometimes, you see, when it's in the midst of all this and people are saying "Beatles this" and "Beatles that," then I've got to accept the thing that they think I'm a Beatle. I'm willing to go along with it, you know, if they want me to be a Beatle then I'll be one.'

Miranda Ward - 'When did you first start becoming interested in Indian culture and religion?'

George - 'Probably about two years ago, and uhh... I don't really know exactly when, but when I first noticed that I was interested with the music first of all, I think, and along with that I'd heard stories of people in caves. Yogis, as they're known. People levitating and de-materializing. (laughs) And doing all sorts of wonderous things. And then, through the music... with meeting Ravi (Shankar), it was great because he's a *brahmin* which is a high sect. And uhh, just all the groovy people are *brahmins*, like the scientists, religious people and musicians, and all those. And then in the end, I'd like to become this myself. I'd just like to have this quality that these people have, which is a spiritual thing. And I think with us having all the material wealth that we need... you know, the average person feels that if they had a car and a telly and a house, and that's where it's at. But if you get a car and a telly and a house and even, you know, a lot of money, your life's still empty because it's still all on this gross level. And what we need isn't material, it's spiritual. We need, sort of, some other form of peace and happiness. And so, that's why the Indian people all seem very peaceful and as though they have found something, because they haven't had the material wealth. They've had to look at themselves for some answer, and they've found it inside themselves.'[83]

The Beatles remain in Newquay for several days, shooting further footage of movie film for their forthcoming film, to be called the *'Magical Mystery Tour'*.

❀ ❀ ❀

THE BEATLES, DRUGS, MYSTICISM & INDIA

On Sunday, 17th September 1967, the BBC Home Service broadcasts a half-hour radio programme entitled *'The Spirit and the Flesh'*, an edited cut of Shirley du Boulay's recording, in which Malcolm Muggeridge quizzes Maharishi on various aspects of the philosophy behind the technique of Transcendental Meditation.

Maharishi - 'I want to make progress more fulfilling and more useful to life by the impact of inner silence and increased energy at the same time. We want peace, but not at the cost of progress, and life, but peace that will be the basis of greater activity and yet life in greater fulfilment and more joyfulness. This is what the Spiritual Regeneration Movement has brought, this philosophy, and this is not a new philosophy, I count it to be just the interpretation of the original text of the philosophy of life contained in the books of every religion.'[3]

Naturally, during the interview, Maharishi can't resist mentioning his meeting at the Hilton the night before.

Maharishi - 'And ... yesterday I was very happy to see the Beatles, they were so deeply interested in this deep thought of inner life. I was just surprised to find their interest in this Transcendental Meditation.'

But the mention of The Beatles only sets Muggeridge off, and gets him onto the topic of drugs, and he openly challenges Maharishi to clarify his position concerning recreational drugs amongst young people.

Muggeridge - 'But do you imagine that sucking a drug is going to.. is going to produce the result? No, no, no, no, no.'

Maharishi - 'No. But then we must supply them with some tangible, simple, natural means to glorify all aspects of their personality and life. If the religious people and religious practices and churches and all that goes with it, if they are not able to satisfy the need of the youngsters for that experience of higher consciousness then they must fall into this and into this, into this. But what is important there for us is the desire in the youngsters for some experience of higher nature or experience of some bliss consciousness. If Christ has said that, "Kingdom of Heaven is within you", a young man of today wants to verify where is that Kingdom of Heaven within me.'[3]

⊛ ⊛ ⊛

A couple of days later, Maharishi appears before a studio audience on an hour-long TV chat show with Les Crane in Los Angeles, California, and presents his views.

Maharishi - 'Misery and suffering does not belong to life. Only, not able to live full value of life, people fall into suffering and misery.'

'Weakness is the basis of all sorrow and suffering.'

'Transcendental Meditation is a simple natural way to make a man to develop his full mental potential.'[3]

Maharishi describes himself as a *'very simple natural man'*.

Les Crane - 'You have been a monk all of your life?'

Maharishi - 'Yes.'

Les Crane - 'You're a life-long celibate, is that right?'

Maharishi - 'Yes, I'm a life celibate, as a monk.'

Les Crane - 'Celibacy is part of Transcendental Meditation? Maharishi?'

Maharishi - 'It's not a part of Transcendental Meditation, it's err, it's my life.'

Les Crane - 'But I mean for those who wish to practice, do they also have to practice celibacy?'

Maharishi - 'Hundreds of thousands of householders, husband and wife meditate together.'

Les Crane - 'You don't have to give up though, do you?'

Maharishi - 'Nothing we have to give up, only we add on, add on, add on.... to life.'

Les Crane tells Maharishi of an article in the current issue of *Time* magazine article, on The Beatles, in which Maharishi is described as a *'cherubic seer with shoulder-length locks'*.

Les Crane - 'I have never met any other *guru*, but you are the cutest *guru* I've met. You are so full of joy and life, it's just beautiful. Anyway, apparently..'

Maharishi - 'It goes with the message of Transcendental Meditation.'

Les Crane - 'You mean everyone gets this happy that practices Transcendental Meditation?'

Maharishi - 'They do.'

Les Crane - 'Well The Beatles say you changed their life dramatically. How did you get together with The Beatles?'

Maharishi - 'I was speaking in Hilton in London, and towards end of the lecture I knew that Beatles were hearing the lecture and they want to talk to me. Next day I was to go to Wales to conduct the course there, and I called them on the dais and talked to them, and they said they had tried so many things, along with all these drugs and all that, for some higher spiritual experience. And in my talk they heard that this higher spiritual experience can be gained very easily and comfortably without any restrictions of habits and all that, through Transcendental Meditation.'[3]

Amongst the audience is suave actor Ephrem Zimbalist Jnr, who is well known for starring in the television series 'FBI'. He has been practicing Transcendental Meditation for quite some time.

Ephrem Zimbalist Jnr - 'It has a tremendously refreshing and revitalising effect; as Maharishi said, it's complete rest, and more, it builds the.. it seems to build all the positive values. One comes out of meditation, not only rested but also strengthened in those values.'[3]

One of Maharishi's closest aides also appears in the programme. He is Jerry Jarvis, a former landscape gardener, now head of an organisation called the Students International Meditation Society (SIMS), a complementary organisation to the Spiritual Regeneration Movement (SRM) run by Charlie Lutes, a businessman who met with Maharishi shortly after he first visited the shores of the U.S.A. in 1959 and is said to have been the first in Los Angeles to have been taught meditation by Maharishi. Over the years Maharishi has set up a total of three organizations to promote and teach Transcendental Meditation - Spiritual Regeneration Movement (SRM), International Meditation Society (IMS) and Students International Society (SIMS).

America, and Los Angeles in particular, is really the centre of Maharishi's operation, for it was the U.S.A. that he travelled to from India in the late 1950's, and it was in Los Angeles that he stayed with the Olsons, a wealthy family living in a Hollywood suburb.

❀ ❀ ❀

Whilst Maharishi is back in Los Angeles, one of his followers hears that Donovan is appearing locally at the Hollywood Bowl, and so he invites him to hear Maharishi.

Donovan - 'I arrived and took a place in the back of the auditorium, not wanting to be recognised. On stage was a podium behind which hung a large black and white photograph of a powerful Yogi, the Maharishi's own teacher, Guru Deva. The Maharishi sat cross-legged on the platform, a microphone before him and a few flowers in his hand, with which he caressed his face now and again. He spoke eloquently about the Science of Being, presenting the possibilities of his transcendental meditation in a most entertaining way. His infectious laughter punctuated the discourse, and this helped endear him to the assembled multitude. For my part I could not but like this guy.

'Just before the Maharishi finished his "show" (and it was very much a performance) the fan in the suit came to fetch me and asked if I would like to go backstage and meet him.

'Standing in the wings, I watched as the Maharishi wound up, inviting the audience to join him in his movement and discover the hidden potential within us all. I saw him rise from his podium and leave the stage to a round of applause.

'Moving sedately, he walked slowly to the wings, dressed in a flowing cotton robe, his long dark hair and beard flecked with silver strands. As he clicked nearer on his wooden sandals, I heard him ask his aide, "And who is this?" in his sing-song way. I heard the aide reply, "Like the Beatles."

'Well, I was flattered to be compared to me mates.

'The Yogi came to meet me. Moments of embarrassment followed as I stood in the presence of a Guru. Sensing my plight, the Maharishi invited me to visit him where he was staying in Beverly Hills. "Come and see me soon."'[84]

Donovan decides to take up the invitation, however, when he pulls up in his chauffeur driven car and enters the large residential house, he finds others waiting, but it is not long before he is shown in to see Maharishi.

Donovan - 'I was ushered into the dimly lit room. The Maharishi sat cross-legged on a deerskin on the carpeted floor. His aide departed and the Yogi motioned for me to sit likewise. He adjusted his cashmere shawl and settled himself, his limpid eyes bidding me to relax. I did so and entered his vibe.

'A calming influence came over me as the Maharishi gazed down at the floor and spoke of the attitude I should adopt to receive my Initiation. He breathed long and slow and I became aware of the stillness of the room. The windows were shaded and the world outside seemed to slip away. He said, softly, "Close your eyes and breathe as I do." I followed his instruction and drew air into my lungs through my nose, expelling my breath slowly. With no effort at all I entered his world, and then he said, "Say the word inside." I repeated the word after him. "No," he said. "Say the word inside." I felt myself fall deep down within and kept falling, down and down, into a place I had never gone before. I gave myself up to his instruction, remembering that total obedience to a Guru is essential.

'After a time, which I had no way of measuring, the Maharishi spoke again and said, "Slowly open your eyes," I opened my eyes and returned to the world. But it wasn't the same world. I felt displaced as I came to and realised that I had been Initiated.

Somehow an aide knew it was over, entered the room and said, "The Grateful Dead are next." Maharishi laughed and said, "They should not call themselves the Grateful Dead, they should call themselves the Grateful Living."'[84]

⊛ ⊛ ⊛

On Wednesday, 20th September 1967, the *Daily Express* publishes an informative article, which gives readers a rough idea of what The Beatles are likely to be getting involved in when they go to India. According to the piece they are to be trained as teachers of meditation, on a course that has three distinct phases:-

'Phase One is the get-ready phase; featuring talks and lectures by Maharishi.

'Phase Two, you meditate for longer periods ("increasing the clarity of the experience so that explanation can be precise"), and Maharishi explains the nature of the experiences you have had. In this phase everything becomes very quiet and gentle.

'Phase Three, as in the last stage of a Turkish bath, you are brought gradually back into active life; meditation is reduced, you are sent for drives into the country, or shopping, or bathing in the Ganges…'[85]

But right now The Beatles trip to India is on hold as they are busy with their current project, the filming of their road trip around England. They travel to an airfield in West Malling, Kent, and dressed in their hippie clothing they perform *'I Am the Walrus'*. Once indoors, John, Paul, George and Ringo join dozens of dancers to create an amazingly glitzy presentation of another new song, *'Your Mother Should Know'*.

Chapter Ten
Go Fix Your Own House

Early in the morning of Friday, 29th September 1967, popular broadcaster David Frost is at London's Heathrow Airport, ready to interview Maharishi on a stopover on his way from Los Angeles to Scandinavia. Noticing that flowers surround Maharishi, David is curious about their significance.

Frost - 'Everywhere there's flowers, why do you use a flower as a sort of symbol of what you're saying?'

Maharishi - 'Not actually a symbol but I think flowers are for decoration that people put around. And, flower also presents my message. The message is - enjoy all the glories of outer life and also enjoy the honey of life present in the inner being. Bliss consciousness should not be lost when one is enjoying the outer material glories of life.'

Frost - 'And how does a flower sum that up?'

Maharishi - 'The outer beauty attracts the honey bee (laughs) and it knows the technique of going deep, enjoys the honey and goes out.'[3]

Frost goes on to question Maharishi closely about his teachings and about the method of meditation he teaches.

Frost - 'Could you tell, what is the difference, basic difference between Transcendental meditation, as you talk about it, and..'

Maharishi - 'All the other methods prevalent in the market.'

Frost - 'Well yes, or even just sitting around and thinking.'

Maharishi - 'You see. The basic difference is that other methods try to concentrate, control the mind. All.. almost all the methods prevalent are to control the mind, want the mind to go deep within, thrust the mind. But this control is unnatural. Transcendental Meditation uses a natural faculty of the mind to go deep, and that natural faculty is to go to a field of greater happiness.'

'Experiencing the subtler state of a thought takes the mind to the source of thought. Here thoughts start as an air bubble from the bottom of the sea and coming up it becomes big enough to be appreciated on the surface.'[3]

Frost is also curious to know if the teaching Maharishi is spreading has some sort of moral code.

Frost - 'Do you, to the people that come to you, say that certain things are right and certain things are wrong?'

Maharishi - 'No, nothing, nothing. Only we tell them just start experiencing the subtler state of thought, and experiencing the source of thought which is a tremendous reservoir of energy and intelligence. When I say that the source of thought is a reservoir of energy and intelligence, what I mean is .. See, a thought has energy due to which it flows and it has intelligence due to which it takes a direction. So the source of thought must be a tremendous reservoir of energy and intelligence. Conscious mind going to that field, becomes filled with greater energy and intelligence and this is what makes a man more efficient in life.'[3]

David Frost's line of questioning seems to assume that Maharishi is teaching a philosophy, whereas his mission is to spread a system of meditation, a method that requires no adherence to any particular philosophy or religion. This is why Maharishi initially encouraged The Beatles to learn this meditation at the London SRM centre from one of the many trained teachers, because it was not necessary for them to learn any philosophy from Maharishi. But David sees all practitioners of Transcendental Meditation as 'followers' of Maharishi Mahesh Yogi, as if all those who meditate necessarily need to take advanced courses with Maharishi himself, which they do not.

Before winding the interview up, Frost finds time to ask a very direct question concerning the *mantras* used in Transcendental Meditation.

Frost - 'Is that the same sound that you give to each person?'

Maharishi - 'No. Each person gets different, but we don't have as many sounds as we have men in the world, so they are grouped together.'

Frost - 'How many sounds are there?'

Maharishi - 'Oh there are lots of sounds.'

Frost - 'I mean, hundreds, or thousands, or ...?'

Maharishi - 'You could say thousands.'[3]

✸ ✸ ✸

David Goggin is a Californian Beatles fan who has sailed to England in order to pursue his "Junior Year Abroad." His intent is to locate John Lennon's home and when he finds it he introduces himself to the housekeeper, Dot, only to be informed that John is sleeping. Indeed, John has been working well into the night with The Beatles, putting the finishing touches to *'Aerial Tour Instrumental'*

Later in the day David returns, and this time Dot allows him in suggesting he wait in the garage until John comes down. When the master arrives, attired in *'a green linen suit with tiny mirrors embroidered in an Indian fashion'*, David proudly shows him the embroidered portrait of John on the back of his jacket, with two sequins for eyes.

David Goggin - 'I was shown to a sofa and looked out on the scenery as John sat at a kitchen table eating eggs and fried tomatoes. He was eating alone, so I grabbed my bag and notebooks and joined him. I told him about the brain wave experiment I had managed at UCI, and spoke about meditation, rock and roll light shows, and my idea for a Zen western.'

John - 'We've got to head into London to do the David Frost program. Would you like a lift?'[86]

Along with Peter Brown, John and David climb into the gypsy painted yellow Rolls Royce and are driven to George Harrison's house. As the journey continues George takes the time to explain to David about the various states of consciousness, and writes down details of them in David's journal; and recommends he reads *Autobiography of a Yogi*. When the car arrives at the Studio One in Wembley, John and George are ushered through the waiting crowds and through to the studio where David Frost awaits them.

❀ ❀ ❀

Announcer David Frost addresses the studio audience.

Frost - 'Welcome back! From the Maharishi to his followers; during a short break in a lengthy Beatles film and recording session earlier this evening, we managed to abduct John Lennon and George Harrison.'[3]

George and John are dressed in bright colours though viewers are unlikely to realize this, as they will view the programme on monochrome television sets providing only black and white images. George and John sit adjacent to David Frost, and listen to him attentively, taking turns to respond to his questions.

George takes the opportunity to explain how the system of meditation works, almost delivering a full introductory talk on Transcendental Meditation. John, who sounds remarkably down to earth in his attitude, and tries really hard not to oversell the practice of meditation, really ably supports George's efforts.

John - 'Well, the worst days I have on meditation are better than the worst days that I had before without it.
'You don't feel you have more knowledge or anything. Well, maybe you do, I can't feel that exactly. You just feel more energetic, you know, just simply for doing work or anything.
You just come out it, it's just "Whooah. Let's get going!" you know.'

George - 'The real thing is, it takes a lot of practice to arrive at the point, if you can remain there permanently.'
'We're not saying that this meditation is the only answer, it's obviously not. *Yoga* incorporates lots of different techniques, but the whole point is that each soul is potentially divine..'

John makes a trumpet sound, which provokes laughter - '.. .. ..'

George - '.. *Yoga* is a technique of manifesting that, to arrive at point that is divine.'

Frost - 'How would you..? I mean.. What differences would you say there were between Jesus, say, and the Maharishi, for instance?'

John - 'Well, I don't know, you know. I don't.. Maharishi doesn't do miracles, you know, for a kick-off. (laughter) I don't know how divine or how, you know, super-human or whatever it is he is, at all. But I mean Jesus was.. . .'

George - 'Jesus was a divine incarnation. Like some of the people like Christ and Buddha and Krishna, and various others, are divine the moment they're born. That is, they've achieved the highest thing, and they choose to come back to try and save a few more people. Whereas others manage to be born just ordinary, and attain their divinity in that incarnation.'

John - 'So Maharishi was probably one of them, you know, who was born quite ordinary, but he's working at it.' (laughter and applause from audience)

Frost - 'And, how do you think, in fact, this, the Maharishi, this meditation can for instance help the world's problems?'

John - 'Well, if everybody was doing it, it would just be. . .'

George - 'It's the same, same thing that Jesus said about "go and fix your own house", and it's solved, everything's fixed up then. If you sort yourself out, everybody needs to go home and find out for themselves, and fix up all their personal problems. Then no other problems exist, because they only cause the problems that exist in the world. It's all each person, individual, it's just up to him to do it.'

Frost - 'The word, for instance, the word 'God', I mean, has, does it mean something different to you now than it did before Maharishi?'

George - 'It means all sorts of things to me. I mean, the first concept of a man in the sky, well I kicked that one a few years ago, but I got back to that now, 'cos it's the man in the sky as well, if you like. It's just everything, the whole thing, it's just everything, every aspect of creation is part of God.'[3]

George and John's decision to appear on primetime television proclaiming the benefits of Transcendental Meditation, is providing viewers a good opportunity to find out more about The Beatles' newfound enthusiasm for the practice. But what effect is meditation going to have on The Beatles' music?

Frost - 'Are you finding, now we've grabbed you in the middle of a day of a recording sessions and so on, are you finding a difference in yourselves as you work, in what you work at, and how you work?'

John - 'All the differences in Pepper and all that were in retrospect, you know. It wasn't, sitting there thinking, oh, we had LSD, so we'll make a little tinkle on this, you know, it all. .'

Frost - 'Oh no, no, no; as you look in retrospect to what you did yesterday?'

John - 'We can't see. We can't see what we've done now.'[3]

George and John are excellent ambassadors of Transcendental Meditation, but the frequent mention of Christian and Hindu theology shows George to be very involved in Indian beliefs generally, something John seems to be concerned about, thinking that this will confuse viewers who might not know much about meditation. But George just can't seem to contain his enthusiasm for talking about Hindu teachings.

George - 'Well, I believe in reincarnation. I mean, it's just something that I feel exists, that what you sow you reap, so when you die, I mean life and death are still only relative to thought, there's no such thing really, you just keep going. I believe in rebirth, and then you come back and go through more experience and you die and you come back again and you keep coming back until you've got it straight. (laughs) That's how I see it.'

Frost - 'And then what?'

George - 'Well, the ultimate thing is to manifest that divinity so that you can become one with the Creator. I mean, it sounds pretty far out, talking about things like that, but that's just what I believe.'

John - 'Yeah, I believe the same, but it's just when we're talking about meditation and that, it's frightening really for people who haven't done it, or still, who fancy the meditation but they hear all that coming back and all that up there. So, you know, I'd sooner put it over and forget about that. Just that, put it over.'

George - 'Because that's not really important.'

John - 'That happens anyway, you know.'

George - 'The whole point of his meditation is for now, you know, because it's now, all the time, it's present, and past's got nothing to do with it.'

John - 'Not to live to get into heaven by being a good boy, or to go to hell, just to live better as you're living, do whatever you're doing better. And live now, you know, not looking forward to the great day, or whatever it's meant to be.'

Frost - 'And there we must leave it. John and George, thank you very much indeed.'

George & John - 'Thank you.'[3]

John's smile turns slowly to a stare as he gazes out intently at the audience. And then he gestures with his hands outstretched.. in the manner of a wizard casting a magic spell, and then he starts incanting some incomprehensible utterance.

And slowly George smiles, and the audience starts to respond, at first hesitantly and awkwardly, offering up a rousing round of applause.

After the show John and George head off for the recording studio, and David tags along.

David Goggin - 'We entered the large Studio Two, which had a staircase leading up to the control room that looked down on the large recording area. Up in the control room I was introduced to George Martin.'[86]

Various new songs are listened to; *'Your Mother Should Know'*, *'Cry Baby Cry'*, *'Mean Mr. Mustard'*, bits of *'Fool On The Hill'*, and the basic recording of *'I Am The Walrus'*.

David Goggin - 'Ringo was reading a *Beano* comic book and fiddling with a radio tuner.'[86]

John is interested in the voices coming from the radio and feels inspired to record them and mesh them with the basic recording of *'I Am The Walrus'*.

David Goggin - 'It was a serious play being broadcast live and this caused a lot of interest and merriment. The console had big shifters that looked like gear shift knobs, and it was John who seemed to be running the show.'[86]

The broadcast is a Shakespearean tragedy, *King Lear*, starring Sir John Gielgud.

Before he leaves David asks the group if they could all sign his journal.

John - 'What would you like me to say?'

David Goggin - 'Just something witty and intelligent.'

> *'Here is something witty*
> *and intelligent,*
> *Having a wonderful time*
> *from*
> *John*
>
> *That goes for me Paul McCartney*
>
> *Good Luck for Edinburgh University*
> *George Harrison*
>
> *Love and Best Wishes*
> *from Ringo ☆ Starr'* [86]

The recording session is not over yet; John stays to overdub an organ part for *'Your Mother Should Know'* and does not leave until 5 o/clock in the morning.

Chapter Eleven
It's All Relative

Amazingly, only a few days after appearing on *David Frost Programme*, on Wednesday, 4th October 1967, George and John are back on television, again putting forth their case for Transcendental Meditation.

Frost - 'And now we return to the subject we dealt with on Friday when we talked to the Maharishi, and then we talked with John Lennon and George Harrison and we welcome them back very much indeed again tonight.' 'First of all though, one subject that lots of people have referred to, and we talked about a little in fact after the programme, talking about meditation and the Maharishi in general, after the programme on Friday, is the whole area is . . . what would you say, would you say that your lives have altered since the Maharishi, that they've got more meaning or purpose, or more fun or something?'

George - 'I think our lives have been altering all the time, that's what life is, it's one continuous alteration, and you keep altering until you've made yourself perfect, or as near perfect as you're capable. But, we have altered a little more, probably, since meeting Maharishi, because we've got something more to work on now. I mean, before we've known . . I've been under the impression that meditation and *yoga*, things like that, have held the answer, personally, and yet I haven't actually had any formal teaching, whereas when Maharishi came around, there he was, ready to teach us.'

John - 'Yeah, well I mean we said that last week. It's just that the good days are very good and the bad days are okay, you know. It's just through tapping me source of energy.'

Frost - 'And I mean, has it altered your attitude to something like money, was money ever satisfying and it isn't now, or what?'

John - 'No, it's not all . . what I meant about the money last week was, before we sort of "made it", as they say, money was partly the goal but it still wasn't a, sort of, "let's get some money." But, we sort of got, suddenly had money, and then it wasn't all that good, you know.'

George - 'By having the money we found that money wasn't the answer. Because we had lots of material things that people sort of spend their whole life to try and get. We managed to get them at quite an early age. And it was good really, because we learned that that wasn't it. We still lacked something, and that something is the thing that religion is trying to give to people.'

Frost - 'And now that you've got meditation, would you..? Now you have that plus.. Would you be as happy now if all the money were taken away?'

George - 'Yeah, I'd probably be happier actually, because it's the . . if you have some income, then you have some income tax and if you have a big house, you have all the other things, headaches that go with it. So, naturally, for every material thing you gain, there's always a little loss, whether it's mental or in some other way. You get a headache for everything you own, so if you don't own anything, you've got a clear mind.'

John - 'You'll get them all saying, "give it away," now.'

George - 'Yeah.' (audience laughs)

'You see, his [Maharishi's] meaning for this meditation is to . . so that people don't alter their day-to-day routine, but through the meditation their routine will naturally become influenced by the meditation experience, so they can keep all their material wealth and things like that that they have. It's just that this gives them some spiritual wealth to go with it, and with that you're able to put the material wealth more into the true perspective. Instead of.. I mean you can use all the material things, like we've got them and it's nice to have them, but we don't really believe in them, whereas some people, who haven't the material things, they tend to believe in them.'

Frost - 'But if you were to choose at this moment between having meditation and all that goes with it, and having all your possessions, you would choose to give up the possessions?'

George - 'Yes.'

Lennon nods in agreement.

Frost - 'Can you..? You were explaining, sort of after the program was over on Friday, that, I mean, I was, what the eventually aim of it is and the eventual aim of life is and the eventual point with meditation that you hope to reach?'

George - 'Well, with this expansion of consciousness, that these three states that we live in at the moment, like sleeping and waking and dreaming. They're all known as relative states, because it's all relative. Transcendental Meditation takes you to that transcendental level of pure consciousness. But by going there often enough, you bring that level of consciousness out onto this level. Or you bring this level onto that level. But, the relative, plus that level, becomes Cosmic Consciousness. And that means that you're able to hold the full bliss consciousness in the relative field, so you can go about your actions all the time with bliss consciousness.'

Frost - 'Yes . . . and can you go as though. . ?'

George - 'And there's a higher one, yes, they go higher and attain what's known as "God Consciousness" and then higher still to one known as "supreme knowledge" where the people who know about supreme knowledge know about all the subtle laws that control the universe.

Consequently, they're able to do all those things that are called miracles. In actual fact, a miracle is just having knowledge of supreme law.'

Frost - 'And so these people are able to do miracles, are they, when they reach this point, also able to live longer and do this?'

George - 'Yes, well there's lots of cases; there's a book I've been reading about a *yogi* known as Sri Puri Baba. He lived to be 136, and when he was 112, he got cancer of the mouth, and started smoking cigarettes and got rid of it.' (audience laughs)

George - 'And there's another one, there's one who's in the Himalayas at this very moment and he's been there since . . I mean, it sounds pretty far out, you know, to the average person who doesn't know anything about this, but this fellow's been there since before Jesus Christ, and he's still here now in the same physical body.'

John - 'Same suit.'

Frost - 'So, from before Jesus Christ. He's still there?'

George - 'They get control over life and death. They have complete control over everything, having attained that higher state of consciousness.'

Frost - 'And this is eventually the aim of anyone who takes that meditation?

George - Yeah.'

Frost - 'But a long, long time ahead.'

George - 'Well, I think Maharishi's. . .'

John - I mean, they don't mean this life, you gonna get that miracle scene. That happens later, a few more lives, maybe, you might get.'

Frost - 'When you've returned a number of times.'

John - 'Yeah.'

Frost - 'Yeah.'

George - 'But his plan is so that people from the age of say 15 practice it. By the time they're our age they've already attained Cosmic Consciousness, that is, the state of bliss.'

Frost - 'Stage three, as it were. Yeah.'

George - 'And then, they're at an age where they can go and act, and manage to change the world a little bit for the better. Rather than sort of waiting 'til you're almost dying, then thinking, you know, "What is it? We've got to find out where we're going, what's all this thing about death?" And then they start panicking, and then it's a bit late. The whole point is to try and find it out at this age and then you've got your whole life to go and act upon it.'

Frost - 'And then, you set about doing something about the world around you.'

George - 'Well, obviously, that if you believe in certain things, and other people aren't, as it were, harmonizing with these laws. It's all the thing about the Ten Commandments, all that, it's that sort of thing that certain people have laid down laws, or they've said that these laws exist and we live within these laws anyway, whether we like it or not. We're controlled by these divine laws. So, if you harmonize with the laws, then everything's much nicer, and nature tends to support you.'[3]

Two converts and a sceptic

Frost - 'Right. At that point can we throw it open to our audience here.

Frost directs his attention to John Mortimer QC, a well-known dramatist, writer, and senior barrister.

Frost - 'John, have you got some comment to make at this point?'

John Mortimer - 'Yes. First of all, I don't accept universal divine laws, that's a difficulty, but I think you've really got to judge these beliefs by their pragmatic effect, and the amount of good they're going to do in the world. And what worries me, very much about this attitude, is that it seems to be tremendously self-involved, and finally, tremendously selfish.

And, the idea of sitting very quietly perfecting yourself, while everybody else goes to hell around you appears to be not really. . '

John - 'But it's 20 minutes in the morning, so's you can go out and do something about all the. .'

George - 'You're not listening to what we said, I mean. .'

John Mortimer - 'But you see, this kind of doctrine of universal love, in a way seems to me to end up by not really caring about anybody very much.'

George - 'Well, that's your point of view.'

John Mortimer - 'What I think one needs is a little, well-aimed loathing at things like President Johnson and Ronald Reagan and so on, and not sitting in San Francisco watching the flowers grow, and letting Governor Reagan be elected perhaps for the presidency of the United States.'

John - 'Well, that's not the same thing, you know, I mean, that's . . . watching the flowers grow in Haight-Ashbury is not what we're talking about.'[3]

Various other members of the audience wish to have their say, and amongst them is Juan Mascaró, a 70-year old Sanskrit scholar who has translated various Eastern texts into English.

Juan Mascaró - 'May I say a word?'

Frost - 'Yes, of course.'

Juan Mascaró - 'A few moments of silence every day, of deep silence, can only be good, do good to us all, in this world of noise, first. Second, from the.. in these moments of silence, once we are conscious of something deep in us, which is our own being in eternity, independent of our becoming in time, then we have had the greatest and deepest experience of our life. Third, if in that moment we can feel that our object is to receive the love of the universe that brought us here and to give something of this love to all, at all times in all places, if we can, and if not we struggle to do it. It can only be good.'

Frost - 'John?'

John Mortimer - 'Well, again, it's very, very self-involved. You want to get peace, you want to enjoy peace, you want to enjoy placidity. You think the universe is something which has independent love for you, I don't happen to agree. I think the universe is a soulless, biological thing, and it's up to us to improve it. And we're not going to improve it if we're going to stay quite still, enjoying peace and perfection.'

John - 'But nobody's saying stay still all day, are they?'

Audience member - 'Some of us here are Quakers and we've been practicing what some people would call a form of meditation, which has driven the Society of Friends into action.

Now, after last week's wonderful program, we're very impressed and people have been saying to us, there's a couple of lads there who are natural Quakers. Now, do they think they're Quakers?'

George - 'Well, it's all the same. This is the point we've got to try and get over to people, that religion.. there's only one God and they're all a branch of the same thing. And the sooner people get over this sectarianism, the better, you know. I mean, I'm a Quaker, I'm a Christian, and I'm a Buddhist, and I'm a Hindu. And it's all the same.'

Audience member - 'Well, that's what Quakers have been saying for the last 300 years. . the spark of the divine is in all of us.'

Another audience member - 'Is this something you must do on your own, or does it lead you into community action?'

George - 'Well, you must do it on your own to attain your own bliss state, naturally.

It's something that Jesus said, something about "go and fix your own house first," and that's what you've got to do. Everybody goes and fixes themselves up, and when they're all straight, then they're all able to act together, because we're all one, anyway, whether you like it or not.'[3]

The *David Frost Programme* is scheduled to cover some other topics, but in the event it is decided to extend this debate on meditation for the remainder of the show.

David Frost, to John and George - 'Do you think it's fair, what's been said so far by John Mortimer and so on, suggesting that meditation is selfish?'

John - 'I don't see how it's selfish, if we've no need to be here. You know, I mean we don't sort of dig doing TV for the fun of it. We're here just because we want, you know, we believe in meditation. So that's not very selfish.'

George - 'And we can sort of maybe help a few other people to understand that it's, you know, that it's easy.'

John Mortimer - 'But we've got no need to be here either, really.' (audience laughs)

John - 'We're not claiming you're selfish though.'

John Mortimer - 'And I would like to understand, I think that perhaps we should try and get it a little clearer, what we're talking about. If we're talking about a mystical religious belief, which I think that George Harrison is because he talked about the divine laws.. .'

George - 'It's not mystical.. .'

John Mortimer - 'Well, let me just finish this. Then that's one thing, which I would dispute, but I would like to ask John Allison [another member of the audience, seemingly an initiate of Transcendental Meditation], whether really this has got anything to do with a belief in God at all. Because if all we're talking about is a technique of self-examination that you can perform over shaving in the morning and then go out and help mankind more as a result of having done it, then nobody in their senses would dispute that it was a very excellent thing to do. Are we talking about that, or are we talking about a universe which has some hidden laws and a hidden creator, who manifests himself only to people like Mr. Harrison and the Maharishi when they get into a state of trance, that's what I want to know.'

George - 'Well, let's face it, these laws that you say, hidden laws, they are hidden, but they're only hidden by our own ignorance. And the word mysticism is . . just been arrived at through people's ignorance. There's nothing mystical about it, only that you're ignorant of what that entails.'

John Mortimer - 'Everybody with any religious belief has always thought that everybody else was ignorant about its mystical value. But are we really talking about mysticism, or are we talking about a technique of improving yourself, which is totally scientific and rational?'[3]

He clearly has a point. Is Transcendental Meditation a simple self-help technique, learned in a matter of minutes, which will naturally assist the practitioner to greater inner happiness and success in life? Or, is Transcendental Meditation really a gateway to learning more about Indian beliefs, and if so, would the meditation yield its results even to one who knew nothing about Maharishi's beliefs? Put more simply, if one were to learn Transcendental Meditation and yet ignore or even disagree with all or any of the views of Maharishi Mahesh Yogi, might one still derive great benefit from the practice?

Though the lively debate continues for some time, these fundamental questions are not answered. But what is apparent is that that George is uncomfortable with John Mortimer's repeated use of words such as 'mystic', 'mystical' and 'mysticism'. But many people use these words in a positive way, so could it be that Maharishi has instilled in him a dislike of these words, on the basis that they can be said with a negative bias?

George - 'Mystic, mystic, all the time! You know, there's nothing mystic about mystic, you know, it's just a word that people have invented because they don't understand it.'

Frost - 'But alright then, John, what is then the difference would you say between John Lennon before meditation and John Lennon after a few weeks of meditation?'

John - 'Well, before I wouldn't have been here. I've got more energy and more happiness. I don't know about intelligence. I'm just happier, you know, I'm just a better person, and I wasn't bad before.'

George - 'I'll second that.' (audience laughs)

John - 'Thank you George, thank you.'

Frost - 'And that there, with personal testimony, is where we must leave it.'[3]

Μυστικός *mystikos* = One who has been initiated.

Mysticism is popularly known as; union with God or the Absolute. In the 13th century the term *unio mystica* came to be used to refer to the 'spiritual marriage,' the ecstasy, or rapture, that was experienced when prayer was used 'to contemplate both God's omnipresence in the world and God in his essence.' In the 19th century, under the influence of Romanticism, this 'union' was interpreted as a 'religious experience,' which provides certainty about God or a transcendental reality.[194]

Chapter Twelve
The Kingdom of Heaven Within You

The *Daily Mirror* of Friday, 6th October 1967, carries an interview with Maharishi, conducted in a hotel suite in Falsterbo, Sweden, wherein he is asked 'the *$64 question'* of why are The Beatles turning to meditation.

Maharishi - 'There are certain things that cannot be gained from the outer sphere of living. They know they lack something in their lives, but they cannot pin-point it.

'They have millions, cars, fine houses - then what, then what?' he mused. 'They have told me they have been seeking for something more - maybe a greater peace and serenity. They have told me that there is no one in the Western world to whom they can turn.'

Reporter - 'But supposing you did not exist - what would happen to the Beatles then?'

More infectious laughter from His Holiness.

Maharishi - 'They would remain seeking Beatles!' he sang.

Reporter - 'And supposing after meditation they decide to give up pop music in favour of higher spiritual things?'

Maharishi - 'I cannot think why they should,' he laughed. 'Transcendental meditation does not reject the material world - it merely helps to acquire greater happiness within it. Anyway, they will always be able to sing the song of life!'

Reporter -'Are you a rich man?'

Maharishi - 'I have nothing.'

❁ ❀ ❁

Several days later, on 9th October 1967, *The Daily Sketch* offers its readers a clearer insight into this question by publishing an interview piece called *'What I Believe - by Beatle John'*.

Anne Nightingale - 'Are you deliberately using the power of the Beatles to spread the word about transcendental meditation?'

John - 'Yes, because we've never felt like this about anything else. We want the younger generation, especially, to know about it. It's for everyone. For "householders" as the Maharishi calls them. Just for ordinary people. You don't have to be some sort of freak to meditate. We've got to convince people we are not mystic... get through our million images to show people that what we can do, anyone can do.'

Anne Nightingale - 'Are you convinced that meditation will last your life, that it won't be just a phase?'

John - 'I've got some reservations, of course, but I'm convinced it works in the way they say it works. There's a lot more to learn yet. But I'm willing to find out. You don't have to have a great faith or anything. The whole thing is so simple - as though it's too marvellous to be true. You think: "Why haven't I heard about it before?" But in fact, it's been around for a long, long time.'

Anne Nightingale - 'The Beatles must have been the target for every cult imaginable. What made this so different for you?'

John - 'It was always the same package before - Billy Graham stuff. Of course everyone's trying to reach the same thing ultimately. But the Maharishi's way is natural, not unnatural. You can make it with meditation if you're a Christian, a Mohammedan or a Jew. You just add meditation to whatever religion you've got. It runs alongside Christianity amazingly. Re-read it now, you know, what it's about. The kingdom of heaven within you. It IS within you.'

Anne Nightingale - 'People have been a bit doubtful about the moral issues with transcendental meditation...'

John - 'Obviously you put your own code of ethics into it. No one really wants to go around killing and having orgies.'

Anne Nightingale - 'People like Malcolm Muggeridge have questioned the validity of the Maharishi's meditation...'

John - 'And where is Malcolm Muggeridge at? The Maharishi is a completely happy man. Malcolm Muggeridge isn't.'

Anne Nightingale - 'Would you have found meditation so acceptable if you hadn't taken LSD?'

John - 'It's all been misconstrued. We dropped LSD weeks before we met the Maharishi. We were looking for something more natural. But all that has been said about us building gold palaces in India is rubbish. Everyone thinks we are going to freak out into the hills forever! All meditation means to us is that we have more output in our work. More energy for things like recording and filming. It would have worked just the same if we hadn't taken LSD.'

Anne Nightingale - 'What do you feel about the religious aspect of the flower movement?'

John - 'I can understand religion now. I might have come to that conclusion anyway at 25 or 26. But now I understand it - realizing that The Church Of England and all those things, they're government. We all rejected that. I'm not against organized religion if it's organized by religious people and not just by politicians disguised. But they've got themselves into the position of any big company - they lose touch. I've realized religion is personal. It's "Do as you would be done by" really.'

Anne Nightingale - 'Does it involve a superior force, a God?'

John - 'It's an energy. I don't and never did imagine God as one thing. But now I can see God as a power source - or as an energy. But you can't see any kind of energy... only track it on radar or things like that. You can be aware of your own energy and all the energy that's around you. All the energy is God. Your own energy and their energy, whether doing god-like things or ungodly things. It's all like one big jelly. We're all in the big jelly.'

❀ ❀ ❀

On Wednesday, 11th October 1967, a London art gallery hosts an exhibition advertised as *'Yoko Ono ½ Life'*, which is set to continue over a month, until 14th November. The exhibition seems to be Yoko's solo project, but visitors are being shown only half the story.

John - 'I gave her the money to back it and the show was - this was in a place called the Lisson Gallery, another one of those underground places. For this whole show, everything was in half: There was half a bed, half a room, half of everything, all beautifully cut in half and painted in white. 'It was presented as "Yoko Plus Me" - that was our first public appearance. I didn't even go to see the show. I was too uptight.'[5]

And Yoko is seen again at the recording studio with The Beatles.

Lizzie Bravo (Beatles' fan) **-** 'Yoko … I have her down as being there definitely on October 6th and October 19th.'[87]

❀ ❀ ❀

It appears that ABC Television in America is under the impression that Maharishi can get The Beatles to appear on a television show with him, someone needs to step in and clear up the misunderstanding.

Peter Brown (Beatles' aide) **-** 'I called the Maharishi in Malmö, in Sweden, where he was lecturing, and explained the problem to him, but his answers were obscure and indefinite. I decided to fly to Malmö to insist that he should not represent the Beatles as being part of his projects. There the Maharishi greeted me warmly but only giggled and nodded and chattered on like a mouse on speed as I laid down the law.'[88]

On Saturday, 14th October 1967, accompanied by Peter Brown, George and Paul fly out to see Maharishi at the Falsterbohus Hotel, in Falsterbo, to discuss The Beatles' plans to visit India. The visitors are wearing winter coats, the summer of flower power and love beads and bells is but a memory now - but after his arrival at the hotel Paul changes into fresh clothes and is seen sporting a floral shirt, and the colourful waistcoat he had worn at Bangor. When interviewed by Åke Wihlney for Sveriges Television, both Paul and George seem to be in exceptionally good spirits.

Dagens Nyheter 15th October 1967

Falsterbo invaderas Världspress står i kö

Från DN:s utsände medarbetare

FALSTERBO, lördag. Beatles-pojkarna George Harrison och Paul McCartney stod plötsligt framför hotelldirektören Karl-Gustaf Ericsson på Falsterbohus.

— God dag, sade Harrison.

— Vi behöver var sin svit, sade McCartney.

Detta hände milt sagt plötsligt och på lördagseftermiddagen.

Nu är det fullt pådrag i denna annars vindpinade och övergivna sommaridyll.

Men plötsligt börjar det att krylla av vishetstörstande nybörjare i parkas och autografblock. Hotelldirektören, som denna weekend utstrålar lugn och godhet, får en pärs. Det rycka hela tiden i stora entrédörren. Det gluttat genom fönster. Det smyga och kika och fnittras. Beatles i Falsterbo! Stora larmet har gått.

Beatles vishetslärare har kurser på Falsterbohus. Han heter…

Åke Wihlney - 'We're glad to have you here.'
Paul - 'Thank you.'
George - 'Thank you.'
Åke Whilney - 'We do appreciate your music. And the…'
George holds a chrysanthemum up to the face of the interviewer for him to sniff.
Åke Whilney - 'That's good.'
Paul - 'The smell of the flowers.'
And their genial host, Maharishi, seems contented too.
Maharishi - 'I am very happy, very relaxed, there is nothing which would bother me at any time.'[89]

❀ ❀ ❀

But when George and Paul visit to a local restaurant they are refused service on account of not being properly dressed, as they were not wearing ties!

Peter Brown - 'We met the Maharishi and tried to explain to him that he must not use their names to exploit his business affairs, and that they definitely would *not* appear on his TV special, but the Maharishi just nodded and giggled again. "He's not a modern man," George said forgivingly on the plane home. "He just doesn't understand these things."'[88]

Chapter Thirteen
Arrive Without Travelling

In a letter sent by George Harrison from Kinfauns, Claremont Drive, Esher, Surrey, dated 21st October 1967, George responds to a note he has received from a fellow meditator named Colin whom he met on the Bangor course. George refers to Maharishi as *'Mahashi'*, which is the way those close to the teacher call him; based on the Sanskrit spelling of the word, which in the Devanagari alphabet is rendered as महर्षि, transliterated as 'Maharshi'.

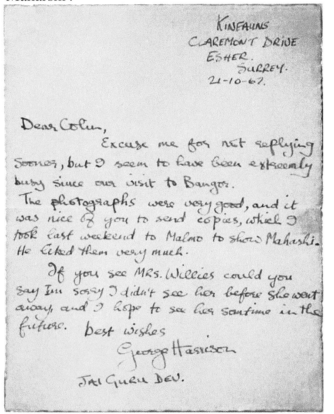

KINFAUNS
CLAREMONT DRIVE
ESHER.
SURREY.
21-10-67.

Dear Colin,
        Excuse me for not replying sooner, but I seem to have been extreemely busy since our visit to Bangor.

        The photographs were very good, and it was nice of you to send copies, which I took last weekend to Malmo to show Mahashi. He liked them very much.

        If you see MRS. Willies could you say I'm sorry I didn't see her before she went away, and I hope to see her sometime in the future.
                best wishes
                George Harrison
                JAI GURU DEV.

The Beatles are not alone in spreading the word about meditation, Bob 'The Bear' Hite, the front man of Canned Heat, a psychedelic American blues band, advises fans to *'"Sit back and meditate" as the Maharishi says'*, and The Grateful Dead appear to be endorsing Maharishi too. According to an article in *The Village Voice*, a New York weekly, in the issue of 9th November 1967, entitled *'What's New in America? Maharishi and Meditation'* Maharishi and meditation are becoming very big news in America nowadays.

'When John Lennon said last winter that the Beatles were more popular than Christ, it brought only a chorus of outrage. But it may have been prophetic. Recently Bob Weir, guitarist for the Grateful Dead, seemed to echo Lennon's comment in a different way. "It's the best answer," he said. "It's to us today what Jesus was saying 2000 years ago."

'Weir was speaking of the message of Maharishi Mahesh Yogi, 56, a tiny, Indian mystic whose disciples include not only Weir and the Beatles but a star-studded cast ranging from Donovan and the Rolling Stones to Mia Farrow and Shirley MacLaine. The Doors, now the top rock group in the Billboard charts, first met at a transcendental meditation meeting in Los Angeles two years ago. With 2000 students waiting anxiously in Berkeley for their introductory lectures and initiation, it looks now that Maharishi may become more popular than the Beatles.'

- *The Village Voice* [90]

The Beatles are still working on their *'Magical Mystery Tour'* film, and the idea is, that when it's finished, they will be free to make that trip to India to see Maharishi. But in the meantime they find time to hang out with friends and acquaintances.

American born film director, Joe Massot, first met The Beatles back in 1965, during the making of their first movie, *'Hard Day's Night'*, and in 1966 he directed a successful short film featuring The Beatles and Jenny Boyd, called *'Reflections On Love'*, about 'swinging London'. His current project is also centred on the swinging younger generation, but this time it is a full length movie, *'Wonderwall'*, starring Jack McGowran, as a middle-aged professor, and a leading lady who is an up and coming English 'dolly bird', an actress called Jane Birkin, who famously appeared in Michelangelo Antonioni's *'Blow Up'* showing more of her body than was seen to be decent at the time in mainstream cinema. Massot has also employed the Dutch collective, The Fool, to appear and to paint colourful sets. The actual filming is by now almost complete, but appropriate music is needed.

Joe Massot - 'I had various choices, the Bee Gees were interested in doing something and came to Twickenham Studios to see me. It seemed the movie had created a vibe as Graham Nash also wanted to join in. George told me that he had been working on "Magical Mystery Tour" helping out, but that was Paul's project...that he would like to do something solo. So I told him he would have a free hand to do anything he liked musically. That was what interested him in the picture.'[91]

George - 'Joe asked if I would do the music and I said "I don't know how to do music for film" and he said, "Anything you do I will have in the film" and those were the terms on which I agreed to do the work.'[92]

Mal Evans - 'His first job was to go and see an unfinished, but roughly-edited, version of the film so that he would be familiar with the story and the changing atmosphere of every scene. Each time the film was run through for him George noted down everything he was watching. He worked out that about an hour's music would be needed. He timed each sequence carefully until he had a list of "situations" where he thought music should be heard in the background. There is one part of the film where a girl is seen crying. So George jotted down "Sad scene for 3 minutes. Girl cries for first 2 minutes 35 seconds."'
'All this was done at Twickenham before George set up his first recording sessions. At home he made tape-recorded outlines of bits of themes, the first scraps of tunes which were growing in his mind for the various parts of "Wonderwall".'[93]

❀ ❀ ❀

On Thursday, 16th November 1967, Juan Mascaró, the Sanskrit teacher whom George met whilst appearing on the *David Frost Programme* back in October, sends him a copy of his inspirational book, *'Lamps of Fire: Spirit of Religions'* and writes a note saying that he has recently heard The Beatles' record *'Within You Without You'* and has enjoyed it. He closes his letter with a postscript saying;
'P.S. Might it not be interesting to put into your music a few words of TAO, for example No. 48, page 66 of LAMPS?'

48. THE INNER LIGHT
'Without going out of my door
I can know all things on earth
Without looking out of my window
I can know the ways of heaven
For the farther one travels
The less one knows
The sage therefore
Arrives without travelling
Sees all without looking,
Does all without doing.'

The Tao TE Ching XLVII - Rendered by J. Mascaró

❀ ❀ ❀

On Wednesday, 22nd November 1967, George Harrison starts working at EMI's studios in Abbey Road, London, on this his first solo recording project. Since there is very little dialogue in the *'Wonderwall' film*, the music sometimes has to serve as a commentary to a scene or sequence. Initially, George works with a *tabla* player and two flautists, taping pieces such as *'Swordfencing'*, *'India'*, *'Backwards Tabla'* and *'Backwards Tones'*.

George - 'I had a wind-up stopwatch and I viewed the film to "spot-in" the music with the watch. I wrote the timings down in my book then I'd make up a piece, record it and when we'd synch it up at Twickenham, it always worked. It was always right.'[94]

❀ ❀ ❀

The Beatles' friend, Donovan, is only too familiar with the role of being a solo artist, and has amassed so much new material that his record company has decided to release a double-LP, *'Gift From a Flower to a Garden'*, packaged in a box. It has been decided to illustrate the cover with photographs of Donovan and friends (including Jenny Boyd) selected from a location shoot at Bodiam Castle. On the back cover of the box-set is a colour photograph of Donovan seated with Maharishi, hands touching. The picture is captioned; 'His Holiness Maharishi Mahesh Yogi and the Author'.

The inside of the box bears a poetic message from Donovan to his fans that includes a passage condemning the use of drugs, which comes as quite a surprise. He says:-

> *'I call upon every youth to stop the use of all Drugs and banish them into the dark and dismal places.*
> *For they are crippling our blessed growth.*
> *Must you lay down your Fate*
> *to the Lord High Alchemy*
> *In the hands of the Chalk and the Drug*
> *Magic circles he will spin*
> *and dirges he will sing*
> *through the transparency of a*
> *Queen Ant's Wing*
> *Yes, I call upon every youth to stop the use of all Drugs and heed the Quest to seek the Sun.'*

But how many of his fans will understand Donovan's declaration has been provoked by his association with Maharishi and his conviction that Transcendental Meditation will prove a viable alternative to taking drugs?

❀ ❀ ❀

Christmastime is here again!

For several years now, it has been a tradition that John, Paul, George and Ringo record a seasonal offering for members of The Beatles' Fan Club. This year, on Tuesday, 28th November 1967, The Beatles go into EMI Studio 3 to create their 5th Christmas record. The finished recording starts with John shouting *'Interplanetary Remix Take 444'*, followed by a curious montage of crazy self-indulgent comic sketches inter-spliced with a specially written Beatles Christmas song;

'Christmastime is here again, ain't been round since you know when.'

The seasonal recording ends with John reciting a poem to the tune of Auld Land Syne; *'And Christmas time is all, and your bonnie clay us through. Happy breastling to you people all our best from me to you. When the beasty brangom button to the heather and little inn. And be strattened oot in matether to yer arms once back again. Och away, ye bonnie.*[13]

⊛ ⊛ ⊛

George is very keen to include more Indian music on the *'Wonderwall'* project; and in particular he wants to deploy the sound of the *shehnai*, an Indian wind instrument similar to the oboe. Ideally, he needs to travel to India and work with session musicians there, but the budget for creating the music is only £600. This is a problem, and George writes to Shambhu Das, his *sitar* teacher, who is in constant contact with, to explain and asks to be sent some of his favoured incense sticks, *Special Durbar Agarbatti*.

A double-EP of 11 tunes from the *Magical Mystery Tour* movie is released prior to the screening of the film.

KINFAUNS.
CLAREMONT DRIVE.
ESHER.
SURREY
ENGLAND

30/11/67.

Dear Shambhu,

Thank you for your very quick reply.

At the moment I am having difficulty with the people from the film company and I can't go ahead now until that buisiness is cleared up. I still think I will come to Bombay, but now maybe not until after 1st January. I will write to you again when I know the exact time I can come, and I will le give you enough time to arrange these things, and also tell you how many musicians of each kind I will require. Can you tell me what the equipment is like in the independent studio? Is it 1, 2, or 4 tracks.

Lots of congratulations for you & Gowri for your baby, that really was a big surprise. I hope you are all very well.

I will keep you in touch, as to what [and when] I will do about this music
Lots of love from
George.
Sorry about my delay, but I really can't do anything until I am sure that they pay for all these things.

THE BEATLES, DRUGS, MYSTICISM & INDIA

The *Melody Maker* music paper of Saturday, 2nd December 1967, carries an interview with Ringo in which he makes it clear that going to India is not just about getting further training in meditation.

Jack Hutton - 'Is the Maharishi Mahesh Yogi a big thing in your life?'

Ringo - 'Yes. I got to a point where I wondered what I was and what it all was. This looks like answering those questions like nothing else can. I think they'll be the right answers.'

Jack Hutton - 'Are you prepared to spend a considerable time in India to do so?'

Ringo - 'Yes. It's the only way. It would be nice if you could sit around and the answers were brought to you but you've got to find them. Seek and ye shall find, as George keeps saying!'

Jack Hutton - 'Some people are sceptical about the Maharishi asking a week's wages.'

Ringo - 'Yes, my uncle said that - "He's after yer money, lads." But a week's wages is only a lot when they talk about people like us because they think we make a million a day. But for an ordinary man it's twenty quid, fifteen quid. And that's a fair bargain - one week of your working life you give the Maharishi gives you something for the rest of your life.'

Jack Hutton - 'What do you think you get out of it?'

Ringo - 'A lot of peace and answers. It's not going to come in a week you know.'[95]

❀ ❀ ❀

In an interview in early December, George Harrison really opens up about his interest in Indian music.

Reporter - 'The things you've said in interviews, I guess the accepting that Indian music is only part of it.'

George - 'Yeah, but for me the Indian music was a stepping stone for the spiritual things, because the music really is very much spiritual. It depends how spiritual the performer is, who's playing it, and also the type of raga that's being played. The music is, it's really, there's no words because it's guided so subtle, and I've found that like most things, the more that you know about it, the more you see there is to it.'

Reporter - 'When you first heard it, how much did you know about it?'

George - 'I didn't know anything about it at all.'

Reporter - 'When was that?'

George - 'About two or three years ago now.'

Reporter - 'And how did it happen that you heard it?'

George - 'I heard a few people over a period of about eighteen months mention to me Ravi Shankar, I just kept hearing his name. And a friend of mine in America said, "You ought to listen to this." So I went home and bought the record of it, I couldn't believe it. Because really, it's hard to explain, I just felt as though I knew it, somehow. I'd never heard it before as far as I know, never heard it before in this life.'

Reporter - 'Is it totally foreign to your own musical experience, was it a brand new thing that you had to learn?'

George - 'Not really, it's like any music, you start with do re mi fa so la ti do and all the exercises, whatever it is, you learn the finger exercises. Same as sitar, sa re ga ma pa dha ni sa, which is the same.'

Reporter - 'And how many scales are there?'

George - 'I think there's a lot.'

Reporter - 'And how many do you think you know? I mean, I'm just curious.'

George - 'Oh, I don't know, you see. I think there's about 72 basic ones, but I think there's lots more.'

Reporter - 'But you don't need that?'

George - 'No, the thing is, the main, the obvious thing, you see with their music they have to learn how to handle the instrument, they have to learn all the scales, all the exercises, it's all really disciplined. And I think actually years and years of strict exercises, then they don't start the improvising until maybe eight years later. And then they sort of absorb the music into themselves. I mean, this is the thing really, Ravi Shankar is the music, really, himself. Because he's absorbed it all into him so, and he sits to play it, anything can come out, you know, anything, it depends entirely how he feels.'

Reporter - 'Mr. Shankar and Indian music have meant more to you than just simply a new mold of music, I mean it's been a whole. . .'

George - 'I think it's the discipline, really. I mean, being in my position, they were the things really I liked about Ravi Shankar. I'd met in my career, I'd met all sorts of people, film stars and all this sort of thing, and yet there wasn't really one person that I had a lot of respect, that much respect for. Because there wasn't one person I'd met who was that good in my estimation, until I met Ravi Shankar. Because he really is, you have to meet him to know, the discipline and just the respect that he just has for all that music and the culture. And he just, he knocked me out, really. And the whole thing of, for him to sit and show me the very first exercise on sitar, and he enjoyed doing it himself. It's really amazing that somebody that great can come down to a low level and do it completely.'

Reporter - 'Do you feel that this Indian music and this Eastern music is going to be more and more a part of what you're playing and writing?'

George - 'I hope so. In fact, since my interest in Indian music, I've had trouble with chords actually, with modulation. I didn't realise this for some time, but I got completely into the Indian music and just practiced sitar as much as I could. And now I realise I was neglecting the guitar and all that thing, so then I became a Beatle again, and then I found I'm neglecting this. And it's very hard, you know, because obviously I can't become an Indian musician, can't become a sitar player. And if I stop doing everything else and just concentrate on that which I can't do, because I'm a Beatle and I've got to be a Beatle.'

Reporter - 'Is it affecting their music?'

George - 'Yeah, well maybe. Yes, I think it is a lot. They've all seen Ravi perform and you know, I tried to get Ringo interested in playing tabla. I think now he's ready, you know, to learn a little bit. About two years ago when he first saw it, it was so far out for him, you know, it was just too much, he couldn't, you know I think he got scared by it because it's so deep and so involved.'

Reporter - 'But you think that there's a particular reason why people are ready for Ravi Shankar now, where they wouldn't have been fifteen or twenty years ago.'

George - 'Yeah. I think the reason is because the evolution, you know, obviously like one generation, a struggle against the older generation, and then the younger generation become the old generation and the generation then has that struggle again. Most of all the time, it's changing and slowly getting better and better all the time. I think we've reached a state now where all these influences have all got to, they've manifested themselves onto this level of life. Not just with the music, with the spiritual thing like in New York in particular, there's so many swamis and people. I think there's so many people now, doing, going in for all this, for yoga, meditation and things like that. I think it's just got to a time now when people want something a bit more solid in their life. Something they can rely on, and they found most of the things . . . there's nothing in it, you've got to go a bit beneath the surface to get something real out of life. And I think the younger generation are more aware of this than say the old people. I think that the next generation will be even more aware of it.'

Reporter - 'Do you think this is what Shankar and his music and his world is offering?'

George - 'Well, I think it's all part of the big plot, the music and the spiritual thing. And all they are, among the younger generation that want something more out of life, it's all part of the big thing that's going to change the world eventually. It may take two thousand years more, I don't know. But the climax of it all will be the golden age and everybody will be very spiritual and very friendly, there'll be no wars, and in actual fact, earth will be heaven, as it were.'[96]

Chapter Fourteen
Wonderwall

Prior to his death, Brian Epstein had been attempting to create a situation whereby The Beatles would derive greater income from their work. To that end, in April 1967, he set up Beatles & Co, so that each individual member of The Beatles would be taxed at a lower rate. After Brian's death John, Paul, George and Ringo decided to continue this initiative and in September 1967, Apple Publishing was formed. Then came Apple Films, which is now set to release their *'Magical Mystery Tour'* movie. Another of Brian's plans was to branch out into retailing - selling cards, posters and clothes, creating a chain of boutiques even. In order to get things started, John Lennon wants to get his school buddy, Pete Shotton, involved, even though Peter's retail experience to date has been limited to running a small supermarket in the Isle of Wight.

John - 'Now listen, Pete. In a nutshell, what's going on is this: The Beatles have been told that we have three million pounds, which will have to be paid off in tax if we don't put it into a business. All we've got to do, then, is just fucking spend it! So why not have a go at a business, and have a few laughs while we're at it? If it works out - great; then we'll have even more millions to play with. If it doesn't - well, what's the fucking difference; it's only money the taxman would have taken anyway.'[34]

Peter is tasked with the setting up and running of a unisex boutique, selling clothes designed by The Fool, and with Jenny Boyd to be in charge of the day-to-day supervision of the shop staff. A three-storey shop property on the corner of Baker Street and Paddington Street is leased, and on Tuesday, 5th December 1967, John Lennon and George Harrison host a party and fashion show to celebrate the launching of the Apple shop. Guests, including director Richard Lester, and pop stars Eric Clapton, Jack Bruce and Keith Moon, are given apples to eat and apple juice to drink (but no alcohol). The Fool is also in attendance, attired in outlandish mediaeval style costumes and playing their own brand of psychedelic Eastern music. Unfortunately, Ringo can't be at the launch, as he is currently in Rome involved with the filming of *Candy*, a movie he is appearing in alongside acclaimed actor Marlon Brando.

The shop's official opening is planned for Thursday, 7th December 1967, and over the next few days the outer walls of the shop become adorned with a vast, extravagant and very colourful mural. Pathé News tell cinema audiences that according to John and George the boutique is; *'A kind of Garden of Eden for lovers of Hippie gear with all the trappings of beautiful living.'*

❈ ❈ ❈

Paul McCartney and John Lennon meet up for lunch with Ray Coleman of *Disc and Echo,* and chat about a whole range of things, including Beatlemania, recording, vegetarianism and meditation; the latter being a topic both John and Paul both get very defensive about.

John - 'It's not opting-out - it's opting-IN!'
'You don't have to go to Wales and do it, or even cut yourself off from society or reality. And you don't have to get so hung up about it that you go round in a trance. I can't understand why people are so stubborn, and why they're not open-minded. I do my meditation in the car on the way back home from work'
Paul - 'People who put these things down, like meditation, don't listen to anything. They have closed minds. They always advance some argument against it - and that's easy to do.
'It's so stupid, you see, because they're not allowing anything fresh or different to get inside their heads. Even if it could possibly be right, or good.
'THEY'RE the cranks - we're not trying to force any issues or say we're right, even. We're just trying, while other people fight against a natural enthusiasm for something.'
John - 'If the Maharishi was asking people to devote their lives to meditation, that would be different. But what possible harm can it do anyone to TRY for a half-an-hour a day something that could be good?'
Paul - 'We're just trying to find out about things instead of putting them down as a lot of rubbish. Instead of doing what a lot of others do - go naturally against things, all suspicious-like, we're giving it the benefit of the doubt.
'Meditation might be a big "con". That doesn't matter either. I don't think it is a "con" but if it is, I want to find

out why. I don't believe the Maharishi is a "con".
'I BELIEVE HE'S TELLING THE TRUTH.'[97]

> "The Beatles?" said the Maharishi, poking his bare feet into the sandals. "If they continue with the system, they could be youthful together for a long time."
>
> - *New York Times* 17th December 1967.

It seems, from another interview, that George too is niggled by the criticism levelled at Maharishi.
George - 'It's easier to criticise somebody than to see yourself. We had got to the point where we were looking for somebody like the Maharishi, and then there he was. Most other people had never thought about this before and suddenly there he is being thrust down their necks.
'The Maharishi is a monk and he hasn't got a penny and he doesn't want to have a penny. He doesn't want any money and obviously you get the Press saying he's staying in the Hilton and he does this and he does that - but in actual fact he didn't stay in the Hilton but in a meditator's house.'[98]
The Beatles are definitely the most successful British pop group and are wildly popular elsewhere too, but the most successful American pop group might be said to be The Beach Boys, comprising of brothers Brian Wilson, Carl Wilson, Dennis Wilson, cousin Mike Love and friend Al Jardine.
Al Jardine - 'We were invited to perform for UNICEF - the United Nations Children's Emergency Fund.
'And so we were engaged to go over there [to Paris], we did a concert I believe on the way over, in London, England and for some reason I heard a tap at my door, you know, a little mystical rap on the door, and I opened it up and there were two Beatles standing there. This is the London Hilton about 1966.. 1967 as I recall. And it was George and John, and they asked if they could come in, so I said, "Well, sure come on in", you know. And they wanted to talk to me about something called TM, which is another.. a short acronym for Transcendental Meditation.
'So they proceeded to inform me about this new.. meditation and this fella called Maharishi who - by then people knew who Maharishi was, he was the guru who was the "Guru To The Stars", err I guess. He'd already taught The Beatles in that regard.
'He'd taught it to The Beatles and he said; "Hey guys. Hey Beatles," he said, "who do you know in America that can get a whole.. can get a lot of attention and get the kids together, whatever, the young adults, and I can get the word out to America, because it's not taking hold there very well?" So their immediate response was to get The Beach Boys to do what they did, in.. all over the world, you know, basically - well in the western world anyway - to bring light on this very important subject.'[99]

As it happens, John and George decide to go to Paris to meet up with Maharishi.
By an unexpected coincidence, John's friend Pete Shotton is also in town, and at a private audience with the Maharishi, he hears John ask his teacher what can be done to bring a halt to the American war in Vietnam.
Peter Shotton - 'He delivered his reply in the soothing tone of an over-indulgent parent to a wayward child. "You're all very fortunate," he said, "to be living under a democratically elected government. You have every right to voice your own opinion, but in the end you must uphold your country's democratic system by supporting your government, which represents the will of the people."'[34]
Also at the meeting is Alexis Mardas, whose father is alleged to have worked for the Greek secret police.
Peter Shotton - '"I know you!" he exclaimed suddenly. "Didn't I meet you in Greece, many years ago?"'
"No, no," the monk tittered. "I've never even been to Greece."
"I *know* I've met you," Alex persisted. "Only you didn't call yourself the Maharishi then. You were travelling under another name, doing something completely different from what you're doing now."'[34]
After the meeting, Mardas continues with his accusations.
Alexis Mardas - 'I'm *positive* I've met him, John. He's *not* what you think he is. He's just an ordinary hustler. The man's only in it for the money.'[34]

✺ ✺ ✺

On Monday, 18th December 1967, Maharishi attends rehearsals for a concert at the Palais De Chaillot, in aid of UNICEF, at which *sitarist* Ravi Shankar is due to appear. The Beach Boys are also due to perform, and their drummer, Dennis Wilson, arrives in time to see John and George in the company of their Indian teacher,

watching Ravi Shankar's recital.
Dennis Wilson, when he shook Maharishi by the hand - 'All of a sudden, I felt this weirdness, this presence this guy had. Like out of left field. First thing he ever said to me [was] "Live your life to the fullest."'[100]

Dennis Wilson and Al Jardine are both invited by Maharishi for an introductory talk at a hotel in Paris, and it is not long before The Beach Boys are all ready to get initiated into meditation.
Dennis Wilson - 'And then I got my mantra, and as the Maharishi was giving them to us he said, "What do you want?" I said, "I want everything. Everything." And he laughed and we meditated together. It was so wild.'[100]

❀ ❀ ❀

On Monday, 18th December 1967, George Harrison's passion for eastern classical music inspires him to go and enjoy the last night of *'Ragas and Talas - Four Concerts of Indian Music'*, at the Queen Elizabeth Hall and Purcell Room in London - and tonight there is a performance by two virtuoso instrumentalists, Ali Akbar Khan, playing *sarod*, a fretless stringed instrument, and Nikhil Ranjan Banerjee on *sitar*.
'Ragas' and 'Talas' are Indian musical terms, which roughly translated mean 'Melodies' and 'Rhythms'.

❀ ❀ ❀

George has been getting on with the *Wonderwall* score and setting down the basic tracks with a little help from his friends, notably 'Richie Snares' (Ringo Starr) and 'Eddie Clayton' (Eric Clapton), and some old mates from Liverpool, The Remo Four; guitarist Colin Manley, bassist Philip Rogers, pianist Tony Ashton and drummer Roy Dyke. At the suggestion of George Martin he also calls on the help of legendary harmonica player, Tommy Reilly. John Barham, a classical pianist and orchestral arranger, whom he met when John was working with Ravi, now assists George.

John Barham - 'A few months before recording began on *Wonderwall*, he [George] asked me if I wanted to do some arranging, and so of course I agreed.'[92]

Colin Manley - 'The chance to work on *Wonderwall* certainly came as a bolt out of the blue!'
'Needless to say we jumped at the chance!'
'George had a friend from the London Symphony Orchestra who followed him around taking notes because George couldn't read or write music. He had a car with a big eye painted on the door [The doors of George's Mini Cooper are painted with *yantras*, which might be mistaken for eyes.] - this kind of set the tone for the whole event, it was all very laissez-faire and creative. I remember a guy called Tommy Reilly who played the harmonica. He was incredible, he used to play excerpts from Grieg's Piano Concerto. George had a great attitude, he just called up whoever was in town and invited them to play. One day a pedal steel guitar was hired and neither George nor I had played one before. I was trying to figure it out, but George just picked it up and played it, he had way of getting the best out of everyone - including himself.'
'I for one, not to mention Eric Clapton and Ravi Shankar, am in debt to him for the invaluable insights into what was a total revolution in music recording during those priceless sessions.'[102]

Roy Dyke - 'We would sit in a circle and listen to George explaining what he wanted, sometimes on a guitar. Then we'd jam a little bit, come up with something, and he'd say, "Yeah, I like that," and we'd record. It was all improvised, nothing written down, all very quick. And it was such a warm atmosphere.'
'George had all kinds of instruments there. Tony was a good keyboard player, particularly organ.'[92]

John Barham - 'I went down to Twickenham studios with George, we saw the film and met the director, Joe Massot. I noticed that he liked big cigars, exactly what I imagined from an American film director. He had a wicked sense of humour - I liked his style.

I was fortunate to meet the Indian sarodist Aashish Khan when he played on the Abbey Road sessions. I owned thirty LPs of his father, the great Ali Akbar Khan; when I heard Aashish play it sounded so much like his fathers music - it was uncanny.
Another musician who impressed me was Eric Clapton who came in for just one session. He played on a track called *Skiing*. I have never heard anyone play the guitar quite like Eric did on this track.'[102]

For *'Love Scene'*, Barham suggests to Aashish Khan, the *sarod* player, that he plays a *raga* called *'Mauj-Khamaj'*, originally created by Aashish's grandfather, Allauddin Khan. After Khan performs several takes, George reckons the result would sound even better if it were 'double-tracked'.
George, suggesting this idea to Khan - 'Why don't you play something along with it?'
Aashish Khan - 'At first I was very confused, but then I started listening and found some spaces in between and started filling them, and he liked it very much.'[92]

Over the last weeks The Beatles have put in a lot of work editing all the *Magical Mystery Tour* film footage they have taken, and making a decent soundtrack. When it is completed they decide to preview their work on Thursday, 21st December 1967, before an invited audience of fellow pop stars, friends and employees, at a party to be held at London's Royal Lancaster Hotel. And John Lennon wants his old pal Peter Shotton to be there with him for the occasion.
John - 'Let's just go as Teddy Boys, and dress the way we always wished we could when we were at school! Let's do it properly this time!'[34]

Cynthia - 'It was an extravagant fancy-dress affair and I wore a crinoline dress, like something on a chocolate box, while John went as a greased-up, leather-clad Teddy-boy. He had invited his father, Alf, to come and they got very drunk together.'[10]

Peter Shotton - 'By the time we were seated for the screening, John had, in best Teddy Boy style, got himself smashed on good old fashioned booze. Just as in the good old days, moreover, the alcohol seemed to accentuate the more aggressive aspects of John's personality. When he found that the two of us had been placed at different tables, he made a nasty little scene…..'
'Another unpleasant scene developed toward the end of the party, when a band took the stage and most of the guests paired off to dance. Totally ignoring Cyn (who was decked out for the occasion as a fairy princess), John instead lavished all his attentions on Pattie Harrison - with whom he actually went so far as to "dance," probably for the first time in about five years. Though Pattie had undeniably made herself especially desirable as a scantily clad belly dancer, neither Cyn nor George were the least bit amused by John's open flirtation with her. In the end, however, it was Cyn's close friend, the diminutive pop singer Lulu - impersonating Shirley Temple, complete with an oversized lollipop - who elected herself to give the inebriated Beatle-cum-Teddy Boy a good talking to.'[34]

Cynthia - It was such a lovely sight, Lulu cornering John and giving him what for. John was very much taken aback by Shirley Temple's serious lecture on how to treat his wife.'[7]

Chapter Fifteen
Inner Light

The *'Magical Mystery Tour'*, The Beatles' film, which has a running time of 52-minute is due to air on BBC television on Boxing Day, Tuesday, 26th December 1967, in the evening at 8-35pm.

There has been such a big build up to the showing of this latest movie of The Beatles, that for some this is seen to be the most important programme being shown this Christmas holiday. In this week's *Radio Times*, the BBC television and radio guide, is a caption which gives an indication as to just how important this film is: *'Probably the most talked-about TV film of the year. It is by the Beatles and about the Beatles. The Story? A coach trip around the West country reflecting the Beatles' moods, and also launching a handful of new songs. This is the first time the Beatles have produced and directed their own film. How has it turned out?*

Tonight you can find out by joining the Magical Mystery Tour.'

Magical Mystery Tour has some great new music and lots of crazy carrying on! Viewers get to see The Beatles in wizards' get ups, working out their spells, but importantly, the hour-long film is a bit of an adventure, and seems to be all about The Beatles having FUN!!!

It would have been nice to be able to watch it on the big screen in a cinema, for that way it could be seen in colour instead of black and white, but it is, nevertheless, still a very entertaining film. The wonderful musical sequences of *'I Am the Walrus'* and *'Fool On the Hill'*, the dazzling dance routines of *'Your Mother Should Know'*, and the intriguing mysterious *'Blue Jay Way'*, are undoubtedly the highlights which provide thought provoking images and scenes that linger in the memory.

However, when the papers come out the next day, it appears the critics must be looking at quite a different film and have watched against their wishes!

Peter Shotton - '… the critics instantly pronounced it the Beatles first unqualified flop. Vindictive though the notices may have been - "chaotic," "appalling," "a colossal conceit," and "blatant rubbish" were just a few of the barbs that were hurled at the Beatles in the next morning's papers - they nonetheless constituted quite a rude awakening for John, Paul, George and Ringo. For the first time in years, the Beatles were reminded that they might not, after all, be supermen.'[34]

The following day Paul McCartney appears on ITV, on the *David Frost Programme*.

Frost - 'The Beatles' music brings unanimous enthusiasm and approval pretty well. Last night their television show did not bring unanimous enthusiasm and approval, and everyone seems to be discussing it today. Here is the man most responsible, Mr. Paul McCartney.' (applause)

Paul - 'Good evening, Mr. Frost.'

Frost - 'Good evening, Mr. McCartney. Why don't you think that the critics liked this film?'

Paul - 'I don't know, you know. They just didn't seem to like it. I quite liked it myself.'

Frost - 'Well, I liked it. I didn't see it last night because I was busy, but I saw it today, and I liked it... I mean, with reservations and so on. But why were people so puzzled by it?'

Paul - 'I think they thought it was "bitty," which it was a bit. You know, but it was supposed to be like that. I think a lot of people were looking for a plot, and there wasn't one.' (laughter)

Frost - 'Would you call it a success or a failure today?'

Paul - 'Uhh, it's both. You know, it's a Success Failure.' (laughter)

'You can't say it was a success, you know, 'cuz the papers didn't like it. And that seems to be what people read to find out what's a success. But I think it's alright.'[103]

❀ ⌘ ❀

George - 'Now we've got another movie to do, but we don't have to do it any special time, so we thought maybe we'd just write it ourselves and film it ourselves. Because it's got like *A Day in the Life* was, compared to other things around at that time - it's got to be that much better compared to what else is around. I'd rather not make a film ever - I mean I don't want to be an actor or anything like that, it's bad enough having to act all this out, let alone pretend you're someone else. I don't dig all that. I don't mind just being me and having them film me for a bit. We might just go on holiday and let them film us, and stick a couple of songs in. Or just go and film India, us in India. Maybe teach people something at the same time. Because it's got to be something good, it's got to be worthy of going through all that hassle, not some rubbish like Mickey Mouse. Just think of the potential if we were to go to India, there we are swimming in the Ganges, I expect you're wondering, Beatle people. Or in the Himalayas.'

'I used to want to be back in India, but I don't now, because I know it's everywhere. It's nice there because there are more people vibrating and you pick it up, that's why it's good to be there, that's why I would be there, but it's not necessary, you know. If you can do your own thing, and realize it's everywhere, then it's the same. It's too much.'[29]

George sends a telegram off to Shambu Das, on Friday, 29th December 1967. [104]

SHAMBU DAS VILL MANORAMA SWAMI
VIVEKANANDAROAD   BANDRA BOMBAY 15 -

XF   1622 BR 282 LONDON LG 29 OCS P 1/50   85/84
- WILL YOU BE FREE FROM TUESDAY NIGHT THROUGH TO FRIDAY 12TH
FOR RECORDING WITH   MUSICIANS STOP TWO OR THREE SHANHAI THREE SITAR
AND ONE DHA   SHANHAI   STOP   PLEASE CONFIRM IF THEIS IS POSSIBLE SO I CAN
BOOK EMI STUDIOS THROUGH LONDON OFFICE (((50)))) STOP GRATEFUL IF YOU
WOULD ARRANGE APARTMENT FOR MYSELF AND ONE OTHER FOR PERIOD 7-15TH
INCLUSIVE STOP INFORM IF YOU NEED ANY MONEY AS DEPOSIT STOP PLEASE REPLY
NEMSTAFF   LONDON STOP   REGARDS - - GEORGE HARRISON -

So, on Sunday, 7th January 1968, George, booked as 'Mr Brown', flies out on Air-India flight 112 to Bombay in the company of Neil Aspinall and Alexis Mardas. After he arrives, George explains to *The Times of India* about why he is in Bombay.

George - 'We have a lot of music in the movie and also dream sequences.'

'I thought Indian music, played on Indian instruments, would provide the right type of background.'

And what about his interest in meditation? Might he at some time give up his role of being a pop star?

George - 'I don't want to be a sadhu,' he said with a broad smile, 'Meditation and yoga give me additional strength to pursue my musical activities. Meditation and yoga should be encouraged, for they can do a lot of good to the world.'

He explains that in future The Beatles are likely to make records with the help of an orchestra.

George - 'That way we shall be able to have more concerts and raise a lot of money for charities.'[105]

The recording facilities at HMV, Bombay, are not quite what George is used to in England, but help is at hand.

George - 'Mr. Bhaskar Menon brought a two-track tape machine all the way from Calcutta [over 1000 miles away] on the train for me because all they had in Bombay at that time was a mono machine - the same kind we used in Abbey Road to do the 'Paperback Writer' [tape]-echo. It was fantastic really. The studio is on top of offices, but there's no soundproofing. Every time the offices knocked off at 5.30, we had to stop recording because you could just hear everybody stomping down the steps. I mixed everything there as we did it and that was nice enough because you get spoiled working on [multi]-tracks.'[94]

Bhaskar Menon (Chairman of the Gramophone Company of India) **-** 'He had a serious musician's ear for recognizing a number of major Indian instruments. Each evening, George would return to the Taj Mahal hotel and spend his time making notes about the instrument he had heard and the sounds they were capable of making. He was an incredibly hard worker and took this very seriously. It was a kind of immersion for him into the folk music of India.'[94]

Shambhu Das - 'George would convey to me what mood he needed, and the musicians improvised, and then he okayed for the recording.'[94]

Bhaskar Menon - 'Most of them didn't speak a word of English, so he had to depend on his "HMV friends". But mostly it was just musicians communicating, which was marvelous to watch. They would play a little bit of something, he would say, "No, no, no - like this," and then they would record.'[92]

Whilst working at the HMV studios, Bombay, George is fortunate in being able to call on some of the very top Indian musicians to play on his compositions, including Shiv Kumar Sharma, a *santoor* (hammered dulcimer) player who, with Hariprasad Chaurasia, a remarkably talented *bansuri* (bamboo flute) player, have just completed the astonishingly delightful *'Call of the Valley'* LP, which contains some of the greatest Indian music ever released on record.

Shambhu Das - 'Hariprasad was not there during *Wonderwall* recording in Bombay. As per request from George I arranged all the musicians at the sessions in Bombay.'[38]

Progress on the soundtrack for *Wonderwall* is swift, and after a few days of sessions George is left with more than enough studio time to work on a Beatles track he has been planning. On Saturday, 13th January 1968, he starts work on some backing music for the classic Chinese poem suggested by Juan Mascaró, *'Inner Light'*, on which local musician Vinayak Vora is to play the melody on the *tar shehnai*, a stringed instrument that looks a little like a *sitar*, but more like an *esraj* (also known as *dilruba*) as it is bowed not plucked. The vibration of the strings is amplified through a small horn near the bridge, making it sound less like a stringed instrument and more like a wind instrument. Before the availability of pickups and loudspeakers, some inventive person saw the potential to amplify their *esraj* by affixing a gramophone pickup assembly to it, a really rather ingenious idea, and a unique sounding instrument was created. Of course, since the pickup is detachable, one can choose just to play the *esraj* without amplification.

Animated discussion ensues between George Harrison and the gathered artistes, then Rijram Desad, a classical multi-instrumentalist, starts the tune with a sustained single note on the harmonium.

Sound Engineer, announces **-** '1 - 2 - 3 - 4.'

But, take after take, the recording *'Inner Light'* collapses, before the recording really getting started. Amidst the sound of instruments being tuned George attempts make himself understood as he gives directions.

George - '… the only thing there is.. Can we put the slow piece into the fast piece? It'd be cool for them to come in very quickly, and right on the beat.'

Sound Engineer 1 - 'Abracadabra. Abracadabra.'

Sound Engineer 2 - 'Take 8.'

Shankar Ghosh, the *tabla* player, tunes his drums whilst George gives the musicians further guidance, and repeatedly sings a snatch of the melody.

George - '... And can we *not* have "1 - 2 - 3 - 4" on it? So, you'll have to signal quietly, so we.. so we have a clean err...?'

Sound Engineer - 'Alright.'[3]

From the harmonium comes the sound of a pure single note which fills the air, and the gathered musicians pick up on it and play the entire tune without a hitch. George seems so happy with the result. Realizing he still has unused studio time remaining, he proceeds to record two other instrumental tracks; *'Almost Shankara'* and *'Don's Song'* (a composition by friend Donovan).

Gypsy Dave (Donovan's friend) - 'Know that at this time Dono and George were very close, they had a touching of the creative soul that was quite rare for both of them I think.'[38]

Beatles may come to India by month-end

"The Times of India" News Service

NEW DELHI, January 13: The beatles are expected to arrive here towards the end of this month, according to a message from Mahirishi Mahesh Yogi.

The Mahirishi, who is now in Europe, is flying from Sweden to New York on Sunday. He will reach Bombay on January 23 and Delhi on January 24.

In the capital, he will preside over the ninth world assembly of the spiritual regeneration movement, to be held on January 26, 27 and 28.

Whilst George is in India he faces speculation from reporters as to whether or not The Beatles will actually be visiting Maharishi in India, and even if he is likely to leave The Beatles!

On Saturday, 13th January 1968, a short dispatch is sent by *The Times of India News Service* in New Delhi, which announces:- 'The Beatles are expected to arrive here towards the end of this month, according to a message from Maharishi Mahesh Yogi.
The Maharishi, who is now in Europe, is flying from Sweden to New York on Sunday. He will reach Bombay on January 23 and Delhi January 24.
In the capital, he will preside over the ninth world assembly of the Spiritual Regeneration Movement, to be held on January 26, 27 and 28.'

On Monday, 15th January 1968, after his week's work in Bombay, George prepares himself to fly home to London, but before leaving he answers a few questions from the Press.

George - 'I got the music I wanted. Let me go back home with what I have gained.'
'I am not going to announce to the Press when I will go to Rishikesh.'
'As for me, I am going and that is definite.'[106]

❋ ❋ ❋

Rishikesh

Rishikesh is a small town situated on a plain at the base of the Himalayan foothills on the banks of the River Ganges. Rishikesh is a place of pilgrimage on the way to sacred sites in the upper reaches of the Himalayas, and has for centuries attracted hermits and *yogis* who wish to practice their practices in peace and quiet in the midst of natural surroundings. In fact the area is associated with ancient spiritual stories, tales of the very gods themselves. *Babas* are attracted to Rishikesh, and can often be seen enjoying *ganja* (marijuana). The area is sacred, so animals, birds and fishes are protected, and the river has an abundance of *mahseer* fish (*mahi-sher* being Indo-Persian for 'tiger amongst fish') which are fed small dough balls by visitors.

Guru Dev

Guru Dev is said to have been born on Thursday, 21 December 1871, in the village of Gana close to Ayodhya, and named Rajaram Mishra ('Rajaram' is 'King Rama', said to be an *avataar* of Lord Vishnu). After leaving home at the age of nine years old, Rajaram roamed in the Himalayan hills and eventually found a *guru*, Swami Krishnanand Saraswati, who named the boy Brahmachari Brahma Chaitanya. In 1904, at the age of thirty-three years old, his *guru* initiated him into monkhood as a *sannyasi* (renunciate), and gave him the name Swami Brahmananda Saraswati.

Swami Brahmananda led a solitary life, roaming in forests and jungles, and taking shelter in natural caves. For food and drink he would take what nature offered, and supplemented his fare with the gifts brought to him by well-wishers who sought him out.

In a chance meeting with his *guru*, at the Kumbha Mela in Allahabad in 1930, Swami Brahmananda was told:- *'You have stayed a long time in the jungles and mountains. Remain near the towns now, so that some of the people can benefit.'*

So it was that Swami Brahmananda Saraswati became a little more accessible to the general public and shared some of his spiritual radiance and knowledge. In fact, his spiritual reputation spread to the point where he was nominated to take the most prestigious and powerful position in Indian society, that of the Shankaracharya, the leader of the Hindu religion. At length he accepted and became Shankaracharya of Jyotir Math on Tuesday, 1st April 1941.

Guru Dev's teachings are not only for recluses, for believers, but for non-believers too, including those with active lives and responsibilities. He stated that; *'Every man can be mahatma* [a great *swami*] *in his own home'*.

Shankaracharya Swami Brahmananda Saraswati (Guru Dev)

Guru Dev and a group of disciples (including a young Mahesh)

Maharishi met with Guru Dev whilst still a student, and he soon joined his *ashram* (place of refuge) in Benares (Varanasi), taking on the role of the *guru's* secretary.
The *guru* breathed his last in Calcutta, on Wednesday, 20th May 1953, after which his secretary retired to spend time in solitude, before embarking on a journey to the South of India where he started teaching meditation, and soon thereafter formed the Spiritual Regeneration Movement.

Maharishi's academy
When Maharishi first indicated his desire to create a teaching centre in India, his close aide, Dr John Hislop visited North India to search out a suitable site. Initially he set his sights on an area on outskirts of the Himalayan town of Uttar Kashi, and building work soon commenced, creating accommodation for the impending visit of students. But when the chance came to lease a large area of land, near Rishikesh, from the state Forest Department, the other plans were soon put aside.
Maharishi's first teacher training course, held in 1961 was convened at Ramnagar, just across the river from the newly acquired site, and efforts were put in to ensure construction work progressed so that the next course

could be held in a custom built environment.

The 'academy' is built on an area of about 18 acres of forest land, on a knoll on a hill known locally as Manikoot, set between other hills, known as Brahmakoot and Vishnukoot. The site is known as 'Shankaracharya Nagar' (meaning the town of Shankaracharya), with the teaching centre being formally referred to as *'Dhyan Vidhya Peeth',* 'The Academy for Meditation'. The academy has also acquired the name of *'Chaurasia Kutir'* (84 hermitages) as 84 huts have been built there; 84 is a number which seems to hold special significance for Indians.

At present there is no course running at the academy, but it is intended that the next teacher training course will start at the end of January 1968, and to that end preparations are in full swing with building work in progress, with the aim of improving existing facilities. Work has also been focused on providing residential accommodation for Maharishi, who has been making do with living in a grass hut when he stays in the area. A massive donation by one of his supporters - Doris Duke, the American tobacco heiress - has meant the new buildings can be built to a high standard.

Whilst Maharishi is away on his lecture tours, the academy is run by Brahmachari Shankarlal, a monk who was a student of the same teacher as Maharishi, Guru Dev, Swami Brahmananda Saraswati, the former Shankaracharya of Jyotirmath. Brahmachari Shankarlal is helped by Mr Suresh, who manages the day-to-day work, organising things for when Maharishi and the course members arrive at the end of January. But in the meantime, an uncle of Maharishi, Raj Varma, is in residence overseeing building work. Without invitation, Mike Dolan and half a dozen of his friends arrived.

Mike Dolan - 'I had left England with some old school friends to travel overland to India. It was just after The Beatles had famously visited with Maharishi in Bangor North Wales.'

'I met Paul [Theobald] in a hippy hotel in Istanbul and we travelled to India together for no other reason than to smoke hash. We had quite a bit in common, both having studied the works of the faux mystic T Lobsang Rampa, and *Autobiography of a Yogi,* and that kind of stuff.

When we arrived in India it was just before New Years so we all decided to load up with hash and pineapple whiskey to travel up to Shankaracharyanagar which was in the final stages of being built. To say it was to be the most transformative moment of our lives is an understatement. I can't stress enough how disingenuous our intentions were but we were met by a lovely man called Mr Sureshji, who passed us on to Dr. Varma who said we could stay for a couple of days. We were all initiated into TM in Maharishi's Bungalow by Dr Varma.

A little while later Ragvendra, the wild man from Jabalpur, asked Paul and I if we would stay to help liaise between the Indians and the Westerners on the upcoming course.'[38]

❀ ❀ ❀

On Saturday, 20th January 1968, Maharishi visits New York and meets with U Thant, Secretary-General of the United Nations, the intergovernmental organization set up to promote international co-operation, at the UN headquarters. Whilst in New York Maharishi discovers he has an admirer in actress Mia Farrow, who has stated her desire to be taught Transcendental Meditation by Maharishi, and is now going to travel with him to India. Prudence Farrow, Mia's sister, has been interested in consciousness expansion for quite some time, and has tried drugs and meditation both.

Kate Saunders (a BBC radio presenter) - 'What did Mia think of your meditating?'

Prudence Farrow - 'When I first started meditating in 1966, it didn't interest her at all. But then, when The Beatles began, she became very interested in it, like everybody did, a lot of people did. I gave her the name of the person in charge. And so she was going to India, and I still didn't know, you know, for another month and a half, whether I would be going.'

Kate Saunders - 'Did this annoy you?'

Prudence Farrow - 'Of course.'

Kate Saunders - 'What did her husband, Frank Sinatra, think of her taking off for India like that?'

Prudence - 'Oh he thought the whole thing was Pagan.'[107]

❀ ❀ ❀

Allen Ginsberg, the poet, has heard a lot about Maharishi, enough to make him want to find out more.

Allen Ginsberg - 'I saw Maharishi speak here January 21st and then went up to Plaza Hotel that evening (I'd phoned for tickets to his organisation and on return telephone call they invited me up, saying Maharishi wanted to see me) . . . so surrounded by his disciples I sat at his feet on the floor and listened while he spoke.'

'As he'd put down drugs I said there wouldn't have been anybody to see him if it hadn't been for LSD. Devotees gasped. He said, "well, LSD has done its thing, now forget it. Just let it drop."'

'All in all I thought his political statements not so evil as dim and thoughtless, somewhat sucking up to the establishment so as not to cause opposition and trouble. But judging from voicetone of his business manager -- a sort of business man western square sensitive -- sounds like he is surrounded by a conservative structure and he would come on unsympathetic in relation to social problems.'

'But in as much as he does stray into political generalisations he sounds inexperienced or ignorant and unfamiliarly authoritarian.'

'He was nice to me, didn't know who I was, asked at first what I did. I said Kovie -- poet. There's an element of too much mesmerised politeness at his darshans (public viewings) -- a guru is someone who you should make it with, learn from, listen to, enquire -- otherwise it's mere "religion" which Maharishi himself puts down as a failure.'

'The main burden that everyone should meditate half hour morning and night makes sense.'[108]

❀ ❀ ❀

Maharishi - 'This is my ninth trip around the world, every year I've been coming to all these places and awakening people to the glory of their own inner spiritual being.'

Reporter - 'This is your last tour?'

Maharishi - 'No, sometime in Summer I will be coming too.'

Reporter - 'I see, I understood you were going to retire to India forever, and you would not …'

Maharishi - 'At the end of this month, end of this year, will be the time for retirement.'

Reporter - 'I see.'

Maharishi - 'End of this year.'

Reporter - 'What will you do then?'

Maharishi - 'Just retire from activity, 'cos I have been active enough all over the world, and by now, the acceptance of Transcendental Meditation as a means to permanent peace in the individual and in the world, encourages me to take off some time in silence.'[3]

❀ ❀ ❀

On 25th January 1968, George Harrison sends Juan Mascaró a brief note (on bright red writing paper).[110]

> *25th Jan 1968*
> *Dear MR Mascaro,*
> *I think you will like this recording of Rabindranath Tagore, which I obtained in India. I am pleased to tell you, that I have recorded the music to our song "The Inner Light" and I will let you have a copy later when it has all been completed.*
> *I hope you are well, best wishes,*
> *yours sincerely,*
> *George Harrison.*
> *JAI GURU DEV:*

Maharishi leaves New York and flies via London to Bombay, and then to Delhi, with the plane picking up course participants enroute. Onboard is Mia Farrow, her sister, Prudence, and Jerry Jarvis's wife, Debbie who is acting as 'chaperone' for the Farrow sisters. On the plane are several others also headed for Rishikesh, including Larry Kurland and Rosalyn Bonas, from the U.S.A.

In Paris they also pick up American born Richard Blakely, who has been residing there in order to improve his French and to have a working break. Richard served Maharishi well as translator when he was in Paris, so apparently Maharishi is under the impression that Richard is a Frenchman, and so invites him to attend the course, but his Frenchman is rather short of money.

Maharishi, to his assistant - 'Debbie, you will buy this boy a ticket so he can come with us, yes?'

Debbie Jarvis - 'Whatever you say, Maharishi.'[111]

Richard Blakely - 'Rosalyn was a teacher in Brooklyn, whose school had granted her a three-month sabbatical so she could go to India and learn how to become a better teacher, she hoped, more in tune with her kids. Larry was a photographer who was hoping to learn to take better pictures. Both of them had been afraid they wouldn't be allowed to come on the course because they hadn't been meditating long enough…'

'Rosalyn asked me what it had felt like to sit so close to Maharishi. I had to admit I hadn't felt anything, or didn't know it if I had. Rosalyn said that was one of the things she was looking forward to on the course - being so close to Maharishi all the time so she could absorb his vibrations. She had felt them once before, at a lecture in New York, from twenty feet away, and she said they had affected her meditations for days afterwards, making them a lot deeper. She was surprised she couldn't feel them now on the plane, but Larry said that was because of the vibrations of the engines, which were too gross and blocked out everything else.'[111]

Once the party has landed there's some adjusting to do; Mia experiences extreme culture shock.

Mia Farrow - 'A world away from the leafy stillness of Bel Air, I groped numbly through New Delhi's anarchic streets. A swirling cacophony of Indian pop songs blared tinny out of countless unseen radios, as cars driving crazily played on horns; smells of spices, sewers, and piles of rotting garbage. There were cows with red spots painted on their foreheads and bells on their feet traipsing right through the middle of everything, and everybody swarmed in all directions, shoving and spilling out of buses and rickshaws. Vivid saris fluttering, purple sapphire, turquoise, and gold, unreadable watchful dusky faces, vendors of all kinds, fortune-tellers, snake charmers, magicians, flies, and flows of ragged children begging.'[112]

Whilst Maharishi's supporters get acclimatized to being in India they set about preparing speeches in order that they are all ready to speak at a major event to promote meditation in the capital. Maharishi's closest aides, Jerry Jarvis and Charlie Lutes, are in attendance, listening to Maharishi's opening speech.

Maharishi - 'I take delight in inaugurating this 9th World Assembly of the Spiritual Regeneration Movement, which was founded in 1958 with the single aim of spiritually regenerating every man everywhere in the world and creating a natural situation in every society, that life is free from suffering, free from stress and strain, and is in fullness of happiness, harmony and peace.'[3]

Richard Blakely (one of the selected speakers) - 'Soon it was obvious to everyone in the audience that all the speeches were canned. It was also clear that they were designed to convince everyone who had not yet started Transcendental Meditation to do so just as soon as possible.'[111]

The audience gradually becomes boisterous and someone shouts *"How dare you lecture us about Mother India!"*, whilst others join, shouting *"Give your millions to the poor"* and *"Stay at home and help feed the hungry!"* Charlie Lutes rises to his feet and attempts to quell the disruption, but it only seemed to make things worse. So, perhaps the interruptions are organised! Who knows?

Anyway, Maharishi calls to Charlie, and encourages him to sit down again.

✿ ✿ ✿

From Delhi, a caravan of taxis is organised to transport all new students northwest to the meditation academy. The distance to Rishikesh is about 250km (just over 150 miles).

Mia Farrow - 'We journeyed north. Winds howled raw at the foot of the Himalayas, where saffron-swathed monks were wading serenely in the icy Ganges. By the bridge at Rishikesh, lepers begged with fingerless hands.'

'The ashram was a fenced compound consisting of six *puri* - single storey, concrete, barracks-style structures, each with ten [twelve] simple rooms facing a single wan sapling in a sandy courtyard. A gravel path connected the buildings, then wound beneath tall eucalyptus trees toward the kitchen and dining area and beyond to the lecture hall where Maharishi addressed the meditators and responded to questions every evening. All these buildings stood on a hillside that descended steeply to the Ganges.

Patches of snow lay on the ground and the rooms had no heat. Each morning a bucket of steaming water was placed inside my door by a young Indian man with large, mistrustful eyes. I liked the austere little room - its hard bed, chest of drawers, and dim lamp met my needs perfectly.'[112]

✿ ✿ ✿

Maharishi's students gradually settle into their new environment - and for those who can't get their bearings there is a little picture postcard map, available at the little shop on site.

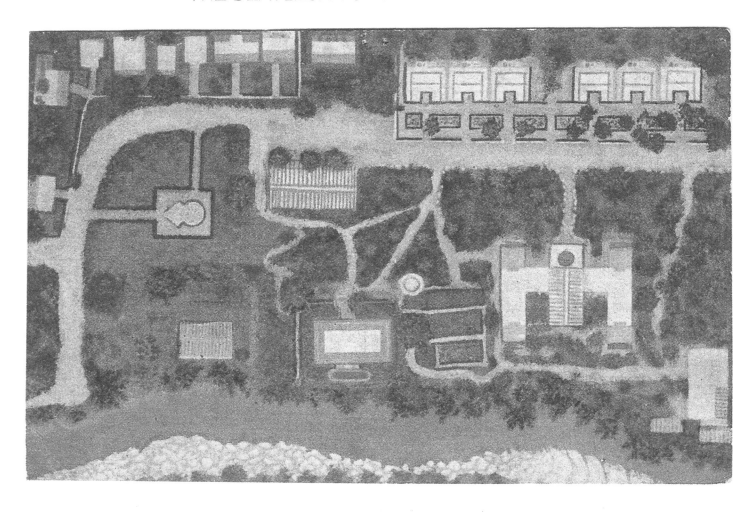

POST-CARD

An arial view of the Academy of Meditation on the Ganges bank.

The main road divides the forest with residential quarters on one side and on the other side from right to left—dining terrace on the Ganges bank, 84 caves in two wings with the lecture hall in the centre, Maharishi's residence in the middle of the site near the Ganges and the cowshed with a red tin roof, the site of the temple at the turning of the road with a press building and stores. On the other side of the Ganges is seen some of the greenery of the small forest area beyond which is the town of Rishikesh.

ACADEMY OF MEDITATION,
SHANKARACHARYA NAGAR, RISHIKESH
U.P. INDIA

TO,

....•

......................................•.........•

....•..•....

...................................•

Following the establishment of Apple Boutique, The Beatles plan to follow it with other Apple initiatives. It is envisaged to set up Apple Electronics, with Alexis Mardas, at the helm.

Peter Shotton - 'We also set Alex up with his own laboratory in a Boston Street warehouse, where he claimed to be putting the final touches on - among other things - his flying saucer and a new kind of paint that would render objects invisible. A few nights before their promised unveiling, however, Alex's lab mysteriously caught fire and all his inventions went up in smoke.'[34]

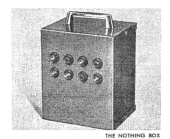

THE NOTHING BOX

Alexis Mardas and Yoko Ono have as a mutual friend John Dunbar, who first met Mardas long ago in 1965 and hosted his *Kinetic Light Sculptures,* one-man exhibition. Several 'Nothing Box' devices, sealed boxes said to have been designed by Mardas each with a panel of six neon lights which flash in apparently random patterns, are obtained by John Lennon. The design is very simple being just a few electronic components (a resistor and half a dozen capacitors) and a hefty battery. It is also available in Britain, sold as the 'What? Box'.

John Dunbar - 'He was quite cunning in the way he pitched his thing, because he knew all that kind of stuff. He wasn't a complete charlatan in the sense that he didn't know anything. He did. And he knew enough to know how to wind people up, and to what extent. He was a fucking TV repairman: Yanni Mardas, none of the "Magic Alex" shit!'[6]

❈ ❉ ❈

The Beatles are now back in the studios again, and there's a run-through of one of John's compositions.

> *'At twelve o'clock a meeting round the table for a séance in the dark*
> *With voices out of nowhere put on specially by the children for a lark'*
> - Excerpt from *'Cry Baby Cry'* by John Lennon & Paul McCartney

Sunday, 4th February 1968

Of several songs The Beatles wish to record, one of them will be chosen for their next single. One is a John Lennon number entitled *'Across the Universe'*, the lyrics of which came to him as he was about to go to sleep one night.

John - 'I was lying next to my first wife in bed, you know, and I was irritated, and I was thinking. She must have been going on and on about something and she'd gone to sleep and I kept hearing these words over and over, flowing like an endless stream. I went downstairs and it turned into sort of a cosmic song rather than an irritated song; rather than a "Why are you always mouthing off at me?" or whatever, right?'[15]

> *'Limitless undying love, which shines around me like a million suns,*
> *It calls me on and on, across the universe.'*
> - Excerpt from *'Across the Universe'* by John Lennon & Paul McCartney

And by adding the words, 'Jai Guru Deva', the spiritual significance of the song is greatly emphasised, for this is the phrase repeatedly used by practitioners of Transcendental Meditation to acknowledge and signal their gratitude to Maharishi's teacher, Guru Dev, who revived the idea of teaching meditation to everyday folks, rather than just monks. Meditation teachers advise that *'Jai Guru Dev'* means 'Glory to Guru Dev'.

JAI GURU DEVA OM

जय गुरुदेव ॐ

After the basic track of *'Across the Universe'* is recorded, at EMI Abbey Road, with acoustic guitar, percussion and *tamboura*, then George overdubs a *sitar* introduction. Later in the session someone comes up with the idea of adding a falsetto-vocal backing to the chorus, so Paul goes out to the fans outside to see if any of them can be of any help.

Paul - 'Can any of you girls hold a high note?'

Gayleen Pease - 'Straight away, Lizzie (Bravo) and myself said; "**Yes, yes, we can, we can**!"'[113]
Mal Evans escorts the girls into the studio where they are given their instructions. After learning the words, John Lennon directs the admiring 16-year-olds to join him close up to the microphone.
John - 'Closer…. Closer…'[113]

Over the next two hours they repeatedly sing the refrain - *'Nothing's gonna change my world'*, stopping only for a short break during which Gayleen phones her parents, to tell them she might be back late. Her parents are not impressed, and insist she return home punctually.
After the girls depart, The Beatles experiment with further ideas, but John is left unsatisfied with the overall result.
John - 'I was singing out of tune, and instead of getting a decent choir, we got fans from outside... They came in and they were singing all off-key. Nobody was interested in doing the tune, originally…'[114]

John - '… we did it all right in the end. The thing I don't like about the version we did, is we didn't dig it the time we did it. All that tamboura was great.'
George - 'I liked those girls singing as well, which you didn't like. The whole record is great, really.'[115]

Comedian Spike Milligan, leading light of 'The Goons', drops by to chat with George Martin who he has known since they worked together on various records. The Beatles famously sang that *'Money can't buy me love'*, and Spike less famously quipped:- *'Money can't buy you happiness but it does bring you a more pleasant form of misery.'* Spike is a staunch supporter of the World Wildlife Fund - the WWF - and sees in *'Across the Universe'*, with its repeated line of *'Nothing's gonna change my world'*, an appropriate song for the WWF, and says as much.

❀ ❀ ❀

Thursday, 8th February 1968
Work is progressing on *'Inner Light'*, the backing track that George produced in Bombay, using Indian musicians playing harmonium, *tabla*, *pakavaj* (a barrel shaped two-headed drum), *sarod*, *bansuri* (flute) and *shehnai* (Indian clarinet). George now lays down the vocals, and on the *'do all without doing'* line, Paul and John join in.
There is also a photo shoot in the studio, and unusually, today all four Beatles are clean-shaven.

❀ ❀ ❀

The *Rolling Stone* magazine has only been running for a few issues when in February 1968 it publishes an interview between Nick Jones and Beatle George Harrison. Naturally, questions George about his association with Maharishi Mahesh Yogi.
Nick Jones - 'The Maharishi Mahesh Yogi is already being criticized, as are the Beatles, in connection with your studies in transcendental meditation.'
George - 'It's easier to criticize somebody than to see yourself. We had got to the point where we're looking for somebody like the Maharishi, and then there he was. It's been about three years of thinking, looking for why we're here - the purpose of what we're doing here in this world, getting born and dying. And I've found out the reason we come here is to get back to that thing God had, whatever you might call God, you know, that scene. Then the music, Indian music, just seemed to have something very spiritual for me, and it became a steppingstone for me to find out about a whole lot of other things. Finding out all about Hinduism, and those sort of religions made me realize that every religion is just the same scene really.'
Nick Jones - 'But how important do you think positive music is in this huge evolutionary cycle?'
George - 'Yeah, very important. I think there is spiritual music. This is why I'm so hung up on Indian music, and from the day I got into it till the day I die, I still believe it's the greatest music ever on our level of existence. I've learned a hell of a lot about Hinduism from being in India, things I've read and from Ravi

Shankar who's really too much. So great. Not only in his music but in him as well. This is the thing: he is the music, and the music is him, the whole culture of the Indian philosophy. Mainly it's this thing of discipline. Discipline is something that we don't like, especially young people where they have to go through school and they put you in the army, and that discipline. But in a different way I've found out it's very important, because the only way those musicians are great is because they've been disciplined by their guru or teacher, and they've surrendered themselves to the person they want to be. It's only by complete surrender and doing what that bloke tells you that you're going to get there too. So with their music they do just that. You must practice twelve hours a day for years and years and years. And Shankar has really studied every part of the music until he just improvises the music until it is just him, he is the music.'[116]

⊛ ⊛ ⊛

At his home in Esher, George chats with journalist Michael Thompson.

George - 'You don't need drugs, you see. The first trip you see that you don't need acid; at least, that's how it was for me. There's high and there's high, and to get really high - I mean so high that you can walk on the water, that high - that's where I'm going. The answer's not pot but yoga and meditation and working and discipline, working out your karma.'[29]

So where does Indian music fit in?

George - 'I'd heard a lot about Indian music, but until about two and a half years ago, I'd never sat down and listened to it. The first time I heard it, I felt as though I knew it, I don't know why, I just felt as though I was doing it with my mind. It was everything, everything I could think of, it was like every music I'd ever heard, but twenty times better than everything all put together, it was ridiculous. It was so strong. I don't know, it just buzzed me right out of my brain.'[29]

Having recorded *'Within You, Without You'* and included it on *'Sergeant Peppers'*, is it likely George will be contributing Indian music to future Beatles releases?

George - 'I can see me using more ideas from Indian music, but never performing alone. I've realized that the way to do it for me is through the Beatles. I'm in the Beatles, and that's why it's there. So it'll keep going as it is, winds light to variable. Who knows, we'll just wait and see what they send us, 'cause *we're* not doing it, you know, we just *do* it, like it's part of our everyday lives, it's just what we do, it's really just a gift somebody gave us. And I really believe that the whole thing is being influenced by Great Powers. I don't want to say what Powers at the moment, it's up to you. A Great Spirit.'

'God is a good vibration. God's in so many ways, just in everything and everyone, but particularly, I think, in art forms, things where people just do things. This is being maybe pretentious to some people - saying our music is an art form - but it is if we dig doing it and lots of people dig what we're doing. The more aware I've become, and the more into this Indian thing I get, the more I've realized that all we are doing is acting out this incarnation, and it's just a little bit of time, and it's, you know, very irrelevant and very relevant at the same time, both together, Yin and Yang.'[29]

⊛ ⊛ ⊛

Meanwhile, in Rishikesh, India, about 60 or so participants are gathering at Maharishi's academy, or *'ashram'*. These students range from those in their early twenties to the few who are elderly. They come mainly from Britain, West Germany, Scandinavia, Australia, America and Canada, and there are others who come from such places as Israel, Sri Lanka and Brazil. Responsibility for the students' well being falls to Brahmachari Raghvendra (formerly Thakur Raghvendra Singh Bsc) who deals with the administrative work and has been a *brahmachari* since meeting with Maharishi in Jabalpur when he visited there in 1962. Up to that time Raghuvendra had been working on his undergraduate degree, in law, at Jabalpur University. Actually, Raghu's father has just passed away, hence the delayed arrival on the course, and the reason his head appears customarily shaved. Coincidentally, Brahmachari Satyanand has suffered very similar circumstances with his father, and he too sports a shaven head.

The students are a mixed lot, old and young, poor and wealthy, English speaking and non English speaking, long time meditators and those who have been meditating only a matter of months. Whilst getting to know one another, stories emerge of people's pasts - one lady is said to have been an opera singer, another a healer. One gentleman, a West German, is said to be an atomic physicist and another to have served in the navy.

Richard Blakely - 'Herr Schraff [Rudolf Schramm] was fifty-something and both his hands were shrivelled, as if they'd been badly burned. While still in Delhi the rumour circulated among us SIMSers that at the end of the war Herr Schraff had been on a Nazi U-boat when it was hit by an American torpedo. Immediately, he had grasped the large wheel that opened the valves that let in water so the submarine could submerge. Even though the wheel had been scorching hot, he'd managed to turn it, enabling the U-boat to plunge to safety just in time, and for him to survive the war and twenty-three years later come to Rishikesh.'[111]

Rudolf Schramm hand has clearly been injured at some time resulting in damage to the thumb and index finger of one hand.

lecture hall

Whist it is quite cold in the night, it is really very sunny in the daytime. So, morning and afternoon lectures are given in the open air, with evening lectures held inside in the lecture hall. Most of the students are getting stuck into their routine meditation and study with Maharishi, but, Mia Farrow, who has not long been initiated into meditation, is unable to make much of the course, and has little else to do but kick her heels and play with a stray dog.

Mia Farrow - 'When I brought back an emaciated, flea-ridden stray puppy, Maharishi named him Arjuna, after the warrior [in *Bhagavad Gita*], and said he could stay with me at the compound.'[112]

Actually, Maharishi is seen to be giving Mia quite a lot of attention, singling her out at question sessions, and giving her other special treatment.

Mia Farrow - 'Not only does he send for me every single day, and not the others, but also, he is giving me mangoes. And to the best of my knowledge, he has not given a single mango to anybody else...'[112]

Nancy Jackson, a middle-aged American socialite, is minded to caution Maharishi about his being over solicitous towards Mia.

Nancy Jackson - 'Maharishi, I think it's better not to pay too much attention to Mia. Movie people are spoiled, and you will get better results by treating her no differently than anyone else.'

Maharishi - 'Nancy, an international star like Mia can bring us such good publicity. We must treat her as a special person.'[117]

Nancy receives a visit from Avinash Kohli, an Indian businessman friend of hers from Delhi, and whilst he's there Mia turns up at the door.

Mia Farrow - 'I've had it. I'm glad you are here, Avi. Will you take a cable to New Delhi for me, or could you send it from the office here?'

Avi Kohli - 'Sure, glad to. First write it out, and I'll ask Suresh to get it off.'

[Mia writes the message]

'Holy Krishna, I can't send this! Every telephone operator in India will know about it. The papers will get hold of it in no time.'

'The message read, "FED UP WITH MEDITATION. AM LEAVING ASHRAM. WILL PHONE FROM DELHI." It was addressed to Frank Sinatra, who evidently was in Miami.'[117]

Avi suggests to Mia that she might benefit from an excursion to a game reserve where she can see the local wildlife, and Nancy Jackson is prepared to accompany her on the trip. It turns out they are to join a couple on a *shikar*, a hunting trip.

Mia Farrow - 'But I don't approve of killing.'[117]

Mia is assured that it is highly unlikely that any animal will be shot.

⊛ ⊛ ⊛

Mia and Nancy return to Rishikesh on Friday, 9th February 1968, the day of Mia's 23rd birthday, and according to her, Maharishi invites her to the building where he lives.

Maharishi - 'Now we will meditate in my "cave".'

Mia Farrow - '… and I followed him down steep steps into a dark, humid little cellar room that smelled of sandalwood. It was my first time in his cave: there was a small shrine with flowers and a picture of Guru Dev, Maharishi's dead teacher, and a carpet on which we settled ourselves in the lotus position to meditate. After twenty or so minutes we were getting to our feet, still facing each other, but as I'm usually a little disoriented after meditation, I was blinking at his beard when suddenly I became aware of two surprisingly male, hairy arms going around me. I panicked, and shot up the stairs, apologizing all the way. I flew out into the open air, and ran as fast as I could to Prudy's room, where she was meditating of course. I blurted out something about Maharishi's cave, and arms, and beard, and she said, It's an honor to be touched by a holy man after meditation, a tradition. Furthermore, at my level of consciousness, if Jesus Christ Himself had embraced me, I would have misinterpreted it.'

'Still, I flung the essentials into my faded cloth shoulder-bag, stuffed passport and money into a pouch hung around my neck, and without a plan, and nothing to lose, I dashed out of the guarded gates headlong into the spreading Indian twilight.'[112]

⊛ ⊛ ⊛

From the perspective of others who are there, the evening celebrations are seen to unfold rather differently.

photo: Per Gunnar Fjeld

Everything is done to make Mia's birthday a grand occasion.

Genie MacLean - 'Maharishi had me go to Dehra Dun with Raghvendra to buy little presents for each person to give Mia at the party tonight. It took us all day to select over fifty articles. Then we had a big feast of ice cream and chocolate sauce. My, did that taste good!'[117]

There is even a surprise firework display.

One of the Britishers, a young woman by the name of Viggie Litchfield, is concerned for Mia's puppy, Arjuna, who she fears must be frightened by the noise of the fireworks, and she enlists Richard Blakely, a young American, to help her find the dog. Eventually the poor animal is located and returned to Mia.

Richard Blakely - 'Viggie and I went up to Mia and Maharishi and deposited the shellshocked puppy in Mia's open arms.'

'As Mia was cuddling her puppy there was another off-sounding explosion out by the cliff and someone close by yelled "Watch out!" Viggie and I turned around just in time to see a rocket hurtling three feet off the ground directly at us, as if it had been aimed. Luckily for us, the rocket took a dive for the ground where it veered left and skittered along twisting and hissing like a mad dragon before it finally hit Gunar in the foot and knocked him down.

This basically put an end to the fireworks.'[111]

Later, Mia returns to her room where a get together has been arranged by Nancy Jackson, Avi and his cousin Moni.

Mia Farrow - 'I'm so fucking mad! Have you ever seen anything like it! I felt like an idiot up there on that stage, with everyone bowing down to me. Avi, when you leave tomorrow, I'm going with you. That is final - this time you cannot change my mind!'

Avi Kohli - 'That's fine, Maharishi asked me to send a cable to your brother, Johnny; he will go to Goa with you.'

Apparently this is in response to Mia wanting to go to see a colony of European hippies there. To celebrate Mia's birthday, Moni has brought along a cake and some champagne.

Mia Farrow, raises her glass - 'To the last night in this holy place. Hah, that is a laugh. Maharishi is no saint - he even made a pass at me when I was over at his house before dinner.'

Moni Kohli - 'To more un-holy saints.'

Nancy Jackson - 'Mia, wait a minute. How can you even think such a thing!'

Mia Farrow - Listen, I'm no fucking dumbbell; I know a pass when I see one.'

Nancy Jackson - 'Please explain how it happened.'

Mia Farrow - 'He asked me down into his private *puja* room, saying he would perform a *puja* for me on my birthday.' [Her laugh was derisive.] 'Big deal, but what could I say.'

'He made me kneel on a small carpet in front of an altar-type table and a picture of Guru Dev. He went through some of the *puja* ceremony and then put a wreath of flowers round my neck. That is when he made the pass.'

Nancy Jackson - 'But how so?'

Mia Farrow - 'He started to stroke my hair. Listen, I know a pass from a *puja*.'

Nancy Jackson - 'Oh, Mia, what Maharishi did for you was such an honor. When he ran his hand down your hair. He did it for Helen Lutes, just like that. That is the way he presents you to his beloved master.'[117]

Nancy's explanation seems perfectly reasonable, but, what if Maharishi had taken a shine to Mia? There seems to be presumption that because their teacher is a *'maharishi'*, 'a great sage', that he is above sensual attraction, is wrong? After all, the term 'Maharishi' is not an official title conferred on him, but a name that just came to be applied to him.

Maharishi - 'A North Indian name [Mahesh] is not so easily remembered by the South Indians, like that, like that.'
'I didn't object to it. (audience laughter) Otherwise I have to explain why they should **not** call me "Maharishi", but just call me something else.'[118]

When speaking to Les Crane in September 1967, he described himself as *'life celibate'* (*bal brahmachari)*, but is it possible he has since changed his mind? Though he seldom seems to make physical contact with others; he was earlier in the year photographed with Donovan's hand on his, so he can't be opposed to all physical contact, but on those rare occasions when he shows himself ready to get close physically, it is difficult to read his intentions. But it is unclear what Maharishi thinks about matters of sexual attraction; why, even assuming Maharishi were attracted to any of his students, how likely is it that he would actually try anything on with one of the women here?

 Perhaps it would be good for someone to suggest for Maharishi to give a lecture on sex and sensuality.

Nancy Jackson - 'We arose early to have a group picture the day after Mia's birthday. I tried to dissuade Maharishi from this project, but nothing doing. He loved directing and told each person where to sit. Mia was asked to don the silver crown again and sit dead-center. She went along with the whole thing in a surprisingly good humour. Maybe it was because she was leaving the ashram that day. She promised Maharishi to come back after her trip to Goa. I hoped she would not.'[117]

London, England.
Cynthia - 'A few days before our departure, we had a meeting with the Maharishi's assistant at a house in London to finalise details of the trip. As we entered the main room I saw, seated in a corner armchair, dressed in black, a small Japanese woman. I guessed immediately this was Yoko Ono, but what on earth was she doing there? Had John invited her and, if so, why?
'Yoko introduced herself to the group, then sat silent and motionless throughout, taking no part in the proceedings. John chatted to the other Beatles and the Maharishi's assistant and appeared not to notice her. My mind was racing. Was he in regular contact with this woman? What on earth was going on?
'At the end of the evening Anthony was waiting outside for us. He opened the car door and, to my astonishment, Yoko climbed in ahead of us. John gave me a look that intimated he didn't know what the hell was going on, shrugging, palms upturned, nonplussed. He leant and asked if we could give her a lift somewhere. "Oh, yes, please. Twenty-five Hanover Gate," Yoko replied. We climbed in and not another word was said until we dropped her off, when she said, "Goodbye. Thank you," and got out.
"How bizarre," I said to John. "What was that all about?"
"Search me, Cyn."
'Soon after this, in a pile of fan mail, I came across a typed letter from Yoko to John. In it she talked about wanting her book to be published again right away so that she could take people into the world of surrealism to change the whole world into one big beautiful game. She said she was afraid she might flip out soon if she had to carry on holding her message to herself. She went on to apologise for always talking about herself so much and pushing her goods to him - by which I assumed she meant being pushy about her art. She thanked him for his patience and said that when she didn't see John she was thinking very much about him. She also talked about her fantastic fear, whenever John said goodbye, that she would never see him again because she had been so selfish.
'I tackled John, who told me she'd written many times, both letters and cards, but said, "She's crackers, just a weirdo artist who wants me to sponsor her. Another nutter wanting money for all that avant-garde bullshit. It's not important."'[10]

Chapter Sixteen
You Don't Have to Go to India

John Lennon responds to a letter from designer Christine Marsh.

Dear Christine,

The only way to answer your questions is to meditate yourself and experience it - you can only find out so much by reading.

A guru is a teacher - thats what the word means - he's certainly a teacher. His idea of helping the world is to help <u>everyone</u> - its no good feeding people who are just going to be hungry again in a few months - the point is change the situation which causes starvation disease etc - the cause is people - governments politics-you-me - everything must be changed so that the less fortunate aren't. Theres enough food etc for everyone in the world - so where is it? People destroy it for 'economical reasons'.

I believe Maharishi wants publicity - why shouldn't he? The only way to get a message over to everyone is to publicise it - that is the 20th century. If Jesus was here now don't you think he'd be on T.V.?

You ask me to try God - thats what meditation is about - experiencing God.

'The Kingdom of Heaven is within' said Jesus - and he meant within which is where the mantra takes your mind. Sure the system is scorned in India and elsewhere so is God, so is everything scorned by someone or other - it doesn't mean its bad does it?

Anyway as I said - try it - it won't harm you - you <u>do not</u> have to be rich to do it - you <u>do not have</u> to go to India to do it - you just DO IT.

With love
John Lennon

P.S. excuse paper I don't seem to have anything else.

Chapter Seventeen
Hey Bullfrog

'Friday night arrives without a suitcase
Sunday morning creeping like a nun'
- Excerpt of 'Lady Madonna' by Paul McCartney & John Lennon

Another Beatles song being progressed is one by Paul McCartney, a stomping piano boogie called *'Lady Madonna'*, a nod towards the sort of crowd-pleasing material The Beatles used to produce in their touring days. The song is reminiscent of a hugely successful tune called *'Bad Penny Blues'*, a Trad Jazz number by Humphrey Littleton, produced by Joe Meek and released on Parlophone Records, back in 1956. With it's catchy piano riff, *'Lady Madonna'* is chosen as the next Beatles single.

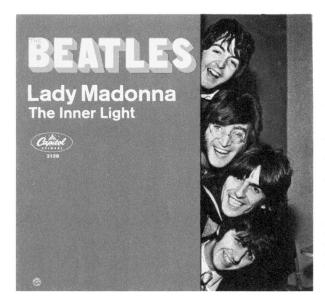

❀ ❀ ❀

'Well, did you ever wake up,
With them bullfrogs on your mind?'
- Excerpt of 'Bullfrog Blues' by William Harris (1928)

On Sunday, 11th February 1968, The Beatles meet together at Studio 3 EMI to make a promo film for *'Lady Madonna',* and whilst they are there, John comes up with a slow tempo tune called *'You Can Talk to Me'*, with the recurrent phrase, *'Hey Bullfrog'*.

Yoko - 'I went to see the Beatles' session in the beginning, and I thought, "Oh well." So I was saying to John, "Well, why do you always use that beat all the time? The same beat. Why don't you do something more complex?"'[119]

The session progresses and Paul contributes his impression of a dog barking, an idea probably inspired by a recording session he was on a few days earlier, produced by his girlfriend's brother, Peter Asher, featuring Jeff Beck (whose inventive guitar solo on The Yardbirds' *'Heart Full of Soul'* successfully emulated the sound of *sitar* some six months before The Beatles' use of the instrument on *'Norwegian Wood'*) and Paul McCartney on drums, playing behind singer Paul Jones on two songs, one of which being *'The Dog Presides'* which has the sound of a dog barking on it.

So, John Lennon's *'Hey Bullfrog'* becomes The Beatle's *'Hey Bulldog'*.

'Some kind of happiness is measured out in miles
What makes you think you're something special when you smile?'
- Excerpt of lyrics of 'Hey Bulldog' by John Lennon & Paul McCartney

Yoko - 'The one time he did try to make a move, it was so sudden, so clumsy, I just rejected it. John had invited me to the record studios. He suddenly said; "You look tired. Would you like to rest?" I thought he was taking me to another room, but instead we went off to this flat - I think it belonged to Neil, the road manager. When we got there, we followed Neil in and he started to unfold this sofa out into a bed. Maybe John thought we were two adults: We didn't have to pretend. But it was so crude that I rejected it. I slept on the divan, I think, and John went into another room.'[120]
Yoko speaks of this situation again.
Yoko - 'Then one day, he kind of expressed his feelings for me. I was a bit scared. So I closed the door on him, almost literally. I went to Paris. In Paris, I thought, "Okay, what did I do? I'm never going to see him again. I messed up, totally!" It was so painful to think about that, so I decided that I would never go back to London. Never. I'm going to start a new life in Paris.'[25]

Chapter Eighteen
Lost Horizon

Mal Evans - 'For me the trip began early. On Wednesday, February 14, I picked up bundles of advance luggage from Weybridge and Esher, suitcases, guitars and trunks belonging to George and Pattie, her sister Jenny, and John and Cyn. Then I caught Qantas flight 754 for Delhi, leaving London at 3.30 in the afternoon. The idea was for me to arrive a day ahead so that I could organise transport at the other end from Delhi to Rishikesh. At London Airport I had to pay £195 19s 6d [roughly two month's pay for an average British worker] in excess baggage charges! So you tell how much stuff I was taking out on behalf of the Lennons and Harrisons.'
'In Delhi on the Thursday one of my first jobs was to buy George a new sitar. I knew where to go - the same shop George had been to on his previous visits. The whole window was full of photographs of George, pictures of him with the shop-owner and notices showing the type of sitar he'd bought there last time.'[121]

❀ ❀ ❀

'I'm thinking of what it would be like if she loved me
How just lately this happy song, it came along'
- Excerpt of lyrics of *'Jennifer Juniper'* by Donovan Leitch

The new single by Donovan entitled *'Jennifer Juniper'*, is released in Britain, it's a love song directed towards Jenny Boyd.

On Thursday, 15th February 1968, George, Pattie, Jenny, John and Cynthia, arrive at London's Heathrow Airport to catch their flight to India. On board the plane there's no sign of Paul or Ringo, nor is there any trace of Yoko either.

John - 'We met around then, but I was going to take her but I backed.., I lost my nerve, because I was going to take me wife and Yoko, and I didn't know how to work it, you know. So I didn't do it, didn't quite do it.'[46]
'I nearly took her to India as I said but I still wasn't sure for what reason….'[5]

And even if Yoko were interested in going, what would Cynthia have to say about it? And what about Yoko's current husband, Tony Cox, and Yoko's four-and-a-half-year-old daughter, Kyoko?

John - 'At the beginning I was just enjoying her company. I mean I didn't know what was happening.'
'Pretty soon after we knew one another I had given up about the one woman thing. It was going to be the holy thing for me. I went to the Maharishi. Yoko stayed here.'[19]

❀ ❀ ❀

Paul - 'John and George were going to Rishikesh with the idea that this might be some huge spiritual lift-off and they might never come back if Maharishi told them some really amazing thing. Well, being a little bit pragmatic, I thought in my own mind, I'll give it a month, then if I really like it, I'll come back and organise to go out there for good, but I won't go on this "I may never come back" thing, I won't burn my bridges. That's very me, to not want to do that. I just see it as being practical, and I think it is.'[6]

Coincidentally, today Mia Farrow is also travelling to Delhi airport, to meet her brother, John Farrow.
Prudence Farrow - 'Maharishi asked me to pick up Mia in New Delhi…'[107]
'Mia arrived in the evening, and we stayed in the Oberoi Hotel. Our room had two single beds, with a nightstand lamp, and phone in between. Maharishi's latest instruction to course participants was that we should meditate as much as we could. I decided this meant I could meditate all night until I fell asleep. I was determined not to miss anything while not in Rishikesh. Late that night, at about three in the morning, the phone rang. Mia picked up and said it was for me. Suspiciously, I took the phone from her. It was Maharishi! He said, "Stop meditating. It's time to rest now."'[32]

The following day the two sisters ready themselves to leave the city.

Prudence Farrow - '... and we were on our way back, and she had found out that The Beatles were arriving that day. And so she had the driver re-route our drive through the airport so she could greet them, pretty much when they were coming out of the airport, because the crowds were there, and she went running off and I got out of the car and was swept away by this crowd of people.'[107]

The Boeing 707 jet - Qantas Airways flight 756 - carrying George, Patti, John and Cynthia, touches down in Delhi at 8.15am. Mal Evans and Brahmachari Raghvendra are there to greet them and garland them with *malas* of fresh bright orange marigolds. Three cars have been organised to take the party on the 150-mile drive to Rishikesh, but before they depart, Mia puts in an appearance and makes a beeline for John, whom she eagerly engages in conversation.

John Lennon, his wife Cynthia and Mia Farrow photographed at Palam on the arrival of the Beatles on Thursday. They dashed off immediately to Rishikesh.

Prudence Farrow - 'Next thing I knew I saw her and The Beatles climbing into her car and another car, and off they went.'[107]

But Mia has no intention of going back to Rishikesh just yet, her plan is to travel with her brother John and go visit Goa, the former Portuguese colony in West India, which these days draws travellers looking to smoke *ganja* (hashish).

Cynthia - 'We collapsed exhausted into the back seat of our allotted cabs surrounded by baggage enough to sink a battleship. Our journey took hours, but what a wonderful opportunity we had to observe the Indian way of life as we drove slowly through villages and towns teeming with turbaned, grinning characters. The colour and simplicity of life was truly fascinating. The market areas were alive with animals; oxen pulled broken-down carts urged on by local peasants. The motor car seemed to be totally out of place, time seemed to be standing still. The noise and excitement and atmosphere of the market place was all-enveloping, Indian delicacies were sizzling deliciously over numerous charcoal grills. The aromas of curry and sweetmeats made our mouths water. Children roamed the roads and side streets, almost naked but always smiling and waving. It was wonderful. What an experience.'[7]

Mal Evans - 'The country is very flat between Delhi and Rishikesh, about 150 miles. We stopped at a Western-style hotel/restaurant situated in the middle of nowhere and known as Polaris. There we had a lunch of egg and chips. Not many Europeans there so we caused quite a stir.'[121]

And then they continue on, northwards, until they are met by the sight of the verdant Himalayan foothills.
They arrive at the Lakshman Jhula suspension bridge across the Ganges at about 3 o/clock in the afternoon.
Cynthia - 'Through an overgrown forest complete with elephants and tigers, we were driven to quite a high altitude. It was cold and wet, just coming to the end of the rainy season. The river Ganges crashed its way through the valleys and ravines below us, full and fast from the rains of the previous months.'
'The Maharishi's meditation centre eventually came into view as our long, tiring journey came to an end.'
'After alighting from the taxis, we were shown to our living quarters. They consisted of a number of stone-built bungalows, set in groups along a rough road. Flowers and shrubs surrounded them and were carefully tended by an Indian gardener whose work speed was dead slow, and stop.'[7]

Reporter Don Short of the Daily Mirror, who has accompanied John and George for the duration of the flight from London to Delhi and shared a taxi to Rishikesh, now readies himself to bid farewell to them.
George - 'I believe I have already extended my life by twenty years. I believe there are bods up here in the Himalayas who have lived for centuries. There is one somewhere around who was born before Jesus Christ and is still living now'

°The way George is going he will be on a magic carpet by the time he is forty°
—JOHN LENNON

John - 'The way George is going he will be flying on a magic carpet by the time he is forty.
'I am here to find out what kind of role I am now to play. I would like to know how far I can progress with it. George is a few inches ahead of us.'
'This is one time in our lives when we refuse to be disturbed by anyone or anything.'

Don Short - 'On his way to the academy George Harrison admitted to me:
"A lot of people think we've gone off our heads. Well, they can think that - or anything they like. We've discovered a new way of living.
"The fact is that since we have been initiated we have moved closer to the people we know.
"We have always been close to our homes and families in Liverpool and its dockers and the people we grew up among. Now we are closer than ever. In the same way with our fans. We hope they have trust in us to know what we are doing. We have always kept our identity with them."
Two years ago, when George started experimenting with Indian music, he reached a point when he nearly quit the Beatles. He yearned for a new life that he felt was awaiting him in India.
He told me: "I felt I wanted to walk out of my home that day and take a one-way ticket to Calcutta. I would have even left Patti behind in that moment and all I would have taken would have been my sitar...
"Anyway, I didn't go and it was just as well for today I realise that the Beatles must never cop out of the scene.
"We have got to prove to people what we believe in, and the only way we can do that is by remaining Beatles and transmitting our message through our music."
"Drugs," said George, "were just a flirtation and nothing more. It served only as an experiment. But we found that through meditation we could reach new horizons."
Nowadays The Beatles adhere to Maharishi's beliefs - including the notion of reincarnation.
George said: "I am sure I was with Paul, John and Ringo before. What were we doing? I've no idea but we couldn't have done all that good because we wouldn't be here now. We didn't make it."
Just before he went into the academy George said to me: "We must go now. I imagine it's going to be something like a school camp." Then he grinned, "Or may be like Billy Butlin's."
And with a wave he shouted back: "We'll see you in a couple of month's time."'[122]

❀ ❀ ❀

Barbara O'Donnell, Brian Epstein's secretary, remembers clearly how anxious Ringo and Maureen were about the trip to India:

Barbara O'Donnell - 'There is a funny story. When they decided to go the Maharishi in India, Maureen was.. Ringo's wife, was petrified of insects so she went to Harrods and bought herself babygrows [all-in-one stretchy fabric outfits for babies], but adult size, so they couldn't get anywhere near her. And Richie, who always had a very squeamish stomach, cos he'd been ill as a kid, said to me; "Can you get me Dr. Collis Brown's, but gallons of it, and baked beans, and fill up a suitcase; baked beans, Collis Brown's" So I did, it was full, this whole suitcase.'[289]

Of course, because some of these preparations, such Dr. Collis Brown's Mixture, contain morphine, or other such ingredients, which in high enough doses can get someone stoned, these preparations are known to sometimes be misused.

Chapter Nineteen
Shangri La

Rishikesh, India, Friday, 16th February 1968.
After having left her sister, Mia, in Delhi, Prudence returns to the academy.

Prudence Farrow - 'As I returned to the haven of my room, I was grateful for the familiar peace. I let the profound silence of meditation settle comfortably over me. I missed being away, even for a day. A knock came at my door. Maharishi had sent a messenger, saying he wanted to see me. When I arrived at his room, his brother monk, Satyanand, told me Maharishi was waiting for me on his roof. Maharishi sat cross-legged, on his deerskin, on a simple straw chair with his back to the Ganges. It was a beautiful afternoon. The sun was soft and warm, and a gentle breeze was blowing. I smelled the exquisite incense drifting from the rooms below. Maharishi greeted me with a warm smile and asked me how my trip was. I told him how happy I was to be back.

He asked how I was feeling with the longer meditations. I told him I loved the longer meditations but felt my heart was still susceptible to flashbacks. He said my heart was filled with stones, which would be dissolved with more meditation. He reminded me fears were not real but stresses, and that when I dissolved and healed those, the fears would no longer exist.

'It was very difficult for me at that time to talk much about Mia. She had gained such fame, and it overshadowed my life. Everyone I met asked about her and Sinatra. As a result, the subject of Mia was a touchy one for me, and Maharishi was aware of this. As I blissfully enjoyed this moment with him, he pushed, asking, "Do you know your sister is a great person?"

Somewhat startled, I said, "No, I don't think she is a great person."

He laughed but continued. "Yes, she is a great person. Doesn't she want to do good?"

"Yes."

"Tell me all about what good she wants to do."'

"What kind of guru are you?" I yelled. "Why don't you just go to Hollywood, where you can meet lots of stars and ask them these questions yourself?"

I was horrified by my brazen response, and yet enjoyed the satisfaction of lashing out. He responded, "Now, go and rest."'[32]

Friday, 16th February 1968. (night time)

John and George arrived today, at least "Mal" - the manager - was sitting opposite me at dinner tonight. The Hilton (Block VI) has been spruced up in recent days. Of course that was quite unpleasant for the adjacent Block V because day and night there has been hammering. I am in Block IV, where it is quieter, but the walls are very damp. When the electricity does not work in Block IV I cannot even light the candle because all the matches are wet. But during the day I can charge the flashlight, and tonight I had one of those crackling wood stoves in my room, so it was quite warm.

- Excerpt from a letter written by Gertrud Soares de Souza to her 19 year-old daughter, Francisca, in West Germany. Translated from German into English.

Compared to the rooms offered to the other students, the facilities in the *'The Hilton'* block are quite luxurious. Each of the half-dozen rooms has a double-bed (a stuffed-cotton mattress on a plyboard base) with mosquito net canopy, a dressing table, chairs and an electric fire, and tiled en-suite facilities which include a bath with attached shower and a flushing W.C. The accommodation is simple and unadorned but not Spartan. Here in the forest the temperature is much colder, so the new visitors take the rugs off the beds and drape them around themselves to keep warm.

George goes off to chat with some of the course members, one of whom is Colin Harrison who they met the day they travelled to Bangor. Colin asks George when his birthday falls; and George tells him *"the twenty-fifth"*.
Colin Harrison - 'Of February?'

George - 'Yeah.'

Terry Gustafson - 'That'll give us time to warn the sanyassis.'

Richard Blakely - 'We all laughed and told George about the birthday party Maharishi had organised for Mia Farrow, with the misfired fireworks, and George laughed too and said, "He's such a child, really."'[111]

❀ ❀ ❀

Saturday, 17th February 1968.

Richard Blakely - 'Down in the kitchen I loaded a plate with singed toast and butter and buffalo cheese and marmalade, poured myself a mug of chai, and moved on to the outside dining area where so far there was only one other person and that person was John Lennon. He was sitting at the far end of the table, looking out over the cliff towards the town in the distance lit by the rising sun beyond a rising curtain of mist. As I sat down a few chairs away we exchanged good mornings and I asked how they'd slept. John said he hadn't slept much himself, but he thought the others were still asleep and would probably keep on sleeping until noon.

It looked like John had been there a while. In front of him on the table was an empty mug and a saucer full of cigarette butts and some loose sheets of paper and a notebook he'd been writing in with a black marker. He looked at the notebook now and read over what he'd written then gazed back out at the horizon and then back down at the notebook and continued writing, leaning into it.'[111]

Saturday, 17th February 1968.

I haven't seen anything yet of the Beatles, but Prudence, Mia's sister, is now back. I thought they were both gone, because Mia told me she would stay just 3 weeks and spend the full moon at the Taj Mahal.

Maharishi is very strict. You cannot leave the area without permission, so I've never been in Rishikesh. It is also quite complicated getting there.
Gerd Hegendörfer is the head of the German delegation.
Yes, Gunnar [Dietrichson] *has now shown up too, Reidun has left him now and Eva* [Rudström] *is happy and radiates.*

- Excerpts from a letter written by Gertrud Soares de Souza to her 19 year-old daughter, Francisca, in West Germany. Translated from German into English.

In the morning John and George attend the outdoor morning lecture, and as usual students have set up their tape recorders to capture Maharishi's words. The cassette tapes also pick up generous helpings of the caw-caw-cawings of the crows. Meanwhile Maharishi explains the theory that Transcendental Meditation is a means to counteract the tension caused by thoughts and actions which are not in harmony with nature.

Maharishi - 'So, when the functioning of the natural laws is disturbed by the life-damaging influence, or negative influence, emitted by man, then stress and strain in nature, and all this outbreak of war, and collective calamities. All that is due to stress and strain outside man, produced by his own way of thinking, way of action.'[3]

He uses an analogy to explain how meditation affects the individual.

Maharishi - 'Watering the root supplies nourishment to whole tree.'

And by extension of this idea; if all the trees about were drawing nourishment through their roots, then all the trees would thrive. Likewise if all individuals were to gain access to the inner nourishment they too would thrive, and communities would be less prone to problems.

Maharishi - 'See the whole possibility? And this is the program that we are to give to the whole world. Incorporate this Transcendental Meditation. The result will be full development of the personality in the integrated state of life and spontaneous support from the almighty nature.'

Student - 'I'm trying to visualise a whole nation meditating and each individual..'

George - 'Don't you think the world's already been at that stage? Like Atlantis..?'

Maharishi - 'Unconsciously.'

George - 'But I mean consciously, like the Atlantis people and all those.. I mean sometime it's been like that, but it's..'

Maharishi - 'Indians see the past of time, of creation, that's called "Sat Yuga" where everyone was very happy and no suffering and life was very long.'[3]

According to Indian history, there are four *yugas* (periods of time), which referred to as Sat, Treta, Dwarpa and Kali Yuga. During these time-periods material life continues in a myriad of species, 84 hundred thousand in number. Individuals are said to progress through many lives, transmigrating from one form to another, through the process of reincarnation. The opportunity to live a human life is believed to provide the greatest opportunity for spiritual growth of an individual, as Maharishi's own master has stated.

Guru Dev (Shankaracharya Swami Brahmananda Saraswati) - 'If having become a human being you do not obtain knowledge of Paramatma [Supreme Self] then understand that it is as if you have sold a diamond for the price of spinach.'[79]

In the cycles of reincarnation, monkeys, elephants and cows are seen to be those species closest to humans.

George - 'What happens if we all reach.. complete the cycle and reach Brahman, don't we have to come back again?'

[*Brahman* is defined a the 'ultimate Reality', 'the Absolute', 'the Divine'.]

Maharishi - 'Then we don't come. We go to the bank, to full the pocket then come back.'

George - 'What happens if we completely evolve to whatever the highest state is?'

Maharishi - 'And then the purpose..'

George - '… keep going, isn't it?'

Maharishi - 'Where is to go? Once the purpose is fulfilled. We are going if we have not reached our destination. And when the destination is there, then we just Be. The Being. And when the fullness of Being comes to be lived, and when it comes to be permanently lived, then one lives a dual state of existence, individual and cosmic.

Indian history records how many millions of years, in this way and this way and this way.'[3]

George - 'Don't you have to take another body if you've attained Cosmic Consciousness for selfish reasons? Don't ..?'

Maharishi - '.. and then that selfish reason is the reason, upheld by the entire cosmic life, it's not isolated selfish, it becomes big.'[3]

A common problem, in terms of understanding the philosophy behind Transcendental Meditation, is that from an early age we are taught not to be selfish, so we tend to check the validity of our actions accordingly. So it is with meditation, which at first appears to be merely self-centred and self-interested, but after consideration it can be understood that until an individual has obtained inner happiness, then he or she only adds to the pool of mass misery. Whereas the idea is that by *'watering the root'*, the individual blossoms, and the community thrives. Only then can the action of meditation be seen for what it is.

George - 'Should the self desire anything?'

Maharishi - 'Then when we are in a state of not desiring anything, then the cosmic desire overtakes. And then it works through us, and then we being selfish individual become universal.

Cosmic force of evolution, and that takes the mind to the maximum level of evolution, to the unboundedness of Being, immediately.'

'So non-desiring is applicable only during the process of meditation. Non-desiring, and that is through a technique, and not just blunt not desiring. And if it's a straightforward blunt not desiring, then it's just peace. Idle, nothing happens. Idle, sitting idle, is not, does not, cultivate a state of no desire.'

George - 'But even no desire, you've got to desire not to have any desire'

Maharishi - 'Not to desire any desire.'

'You see, you know these Quakers? Quaker services? They are very good people - peace-loving people and all that. They just sit and just they don't desire, just sit easy. That makes the mind dull. You don't look to the face of a Quaker. You will, you will find it is a peaceful face but it's not blossoming life, it's not radiating life, what it radiates is some shadow on his face, some, some shadow. Any Quaker who is peace.. peace-loving Quaker. And with practicing Quaker meditation it's just that silent quiet, and quietly they sit. And then some of them take to the tangent of "let God speak through you", and when they let God speak through you, then some spirits overtake. And then they bring out some beautiful messages this way and that way. So either they get subjected to some spirits, spiritual influence, or they become peaceful by way of becoming dull.'

'We want that peace which is the source of all dynamic activity.'

Maharishi often uses analogies to make his points, and when talking of obtaining energy from peace he often uses the example of drawing back the string of the bow before letting the arrow fly. By bringing the string back to a point of stillness the bow becomes capable of shooting the arrow very far.

George - 'There's a Tibetan Lama in… , do you know him?'

Maharishi - 'Tibetan lamas are not much use to the practical world. There are some good talk about this Being and Bodhisattva and all that but.. their meditation is not effective and their whole trend of approach is away from life. They may say that "yes you can meditate and teach in the college" but their mantras are such which tend the whole thing towards going to silence and going out of activity, this trend comes. Not much use.'

The training course has now been going on for over two and a half weeks, Maharishi is curious to hear of his student's experiences.

Maharishi - 'The individual mind expands and expands and expands, takes the state of unboundedness of Being.

Sometimes, maybe some flash one knows, "I am everything" or "I know everything". You have had some such experiences?'

'At some area of meditations, "there, I know everything" or "I am everything?" How many have had such experiences?'[3]

❀ ❀ ❀

After the lecture, Maharishi meets with some of the reporters and photographers who have been making a bit of a nuisance of themselves, trying to get access to John and George. In order to pacify them and accommodate their requests, Maharishi has agreed to meet and brief reporters about The Beatles.

Maharishi - 'The moment they came they met me for about ten minutes

Reporter - 'Do they get any..?'

Maharishi - 'After their breakfast..'

Reporter - 'How long were they together with you?'

Maharishi - '.. and then now they have been with me from about ten o/clock, from 10 until now, about three hours.'

Reporter - 'And what did you do? Did you meditate or did you talk?'

Maharishi - 'Meditation, and some talk, and meditation.'

Maharishi is being asked what each course participant is going to attain.

Reporter - '.. and this person, will they be a graduate meditation guide? What will be their status?'

Maharishi - 'I hope!'

Reporter - 'What do they have to do to attain this?'

Maharishi - 'Attain this.. they have to have deep and clear experience of Being, the Being is the fundamental of life.'[3]

'... leaving me to under.. explain.. to understand the experiences of meditation, and then meeting again, afternoon, and then in the night after their evening meditation. So the whole thing will be.. consolidating their own experience, and understanding about the experiences.'

Reporter - 'You are explaining them to themselves, to some extent?'

Maharishi - 'Yes, that's it, good they experience something, and then I just give an expression to what they have experienced and it's a live connection with the practical field of life in different ways. This is what will make a teacher, a very profound teacher, then he will speak on the basis of his own experience.'[123]

At another lecture outside, later, Maharishi talks to his students of the *'celestial'* and about angels, and he also speaks with them on the more mundane topic of spreading the teaching of meditation.

Maharishi - 'It's, it's not impossible to speak out the *mantra* on television, but the effect won't be there. It will not serve the purpose of giving the *mantra*.'

Student - '.... IBM catalogue everything? ... a machine.' (makes sound of tickertape going through machine)

'Machine can calculate the number and that will be on paper.' (laughter)

'Write down everything about spirituality...'

George - 'You could put all your knowledge into a computer.'

Maharishi - 'And then do what?'

George - 'But then people go to the computer and ask it questions and it gets back the reply. Well you could use the computer to check people's meditation. (laughter) You could do that!'

John - 'We've got one we'd lend you.'

Maharishi - 'Couldn't be possible, err two hundred, two hundred questions about checking, and every time somebody checking.
That the thing will be..'

George - 'But also, the computer, if it's asked a question, and it doesn't have the answer for it, it'll find the answer by checking all the possibilities, around for every answer it knows.'

Maharishi - 'Not difficult to train the checkers - not difficult to train the checkers.'

George - 'You wouldn't even need to do that.'

John - 'You'd have one computer in each capital, in each place where you had it, in case any of the checkers wanted to know more, you know, or forgotten anything. I mean, say, they could replace you in each country. Save you touring.'

'….by telephone. (lots of laughter)
You can do it. It's not funny, you can do it!'[3]

❀ ❀ ❀

Maharishi later decides to talk to his students on the nature of *karma*, about action and its spiritual purpose. Then he moves on to the topic of 'OM' the syllable held sacred by so many.

Maharishi - 'Now just for your information.. hear it and forget about it!'

'OM. Now, that hum is OM. Now, the OM that we say "OM, OM, OM, OM" is.. is NOT that hum. I mean, when we say "OM, OM", .. so sound, and sound. But that hum at the basis of relative creation, at the finest level of crea.. relative creation, that hum is hundred percent OM, and that is life supporting. Life supporting, because it is on the basis of that hum that the entire creation exists. Ermm? That is 100% OM. That OM is only life supporting. It supports creative intelligence, it supports creativity. It's the basis of all evolution, creation and evolution. And this is the glory of OM. Long drawn OM, You have heard sometimes people chanting? Some "OMMMMMMMMMMMMMMMMMM". It's a big huge long drawn OM. That is 75% OM. And a little less long drawn is 60%. And this, when we say, "OM, OM, OM" - this is 25%.

Now, now, now, now. That hum at the basis of relative creation.. because the creation goes on and on and on and on and on, on, on, that hum which is the basis of all this ever going creation, is all, is also almost eternal. Long, long lived eternal. Not as eternal as the Absolute is, but eternal enough for all practical purposes of the relative field. (laughter from audience)

So this.. this OM, 100% OM, is one with eternal life. It supports life, it is life supporting. And when that straight, one long eternal hum, gets broken - OM, OM, OM, OM - when it gets broken, then it loses that quality of life supporting influence, then it beco.. then it starts becoming life damaging. Because when it is continuous it is life supporting, and when it's choppy, then it is quite opposite. It has its opposite value.

Mmm? It is continuous and it is life supporting, and it is choppy, it becomes life damaging. Life damaging.

Therefore, we have nothing to do with OM. Whereas, that completeness of OM, which is full, 100% OM, that is the last reduction of every sound, of any sound. Every *mantra* comes down to this hum and transcends, no matter what. A-B-C-D-E-F, whatever.. eventually it comes to that level.

So, what we are doing is, we are cherishing 100% OM, and we don't want 25%, or 50%. This 100% OM is very rewarding, it's very encouraging, 100%. So in this hum, what we get is, the OM, full, full value as depicted in

119

the Upanishads, and it's something eternal. But every sound, every *mantra*, reduces down to OM and it transcends.

We don't chant anything! Repetition of the.. when we are in the grip of such a beautiful thing which immediately takes us to the omnipresent level of Being, contacts the universal, immediately, then we don't much waste time on the gross.

Because all day long when we are behaving in the outer world, we ARE coming in this field. So, why chant? It's a waste of lungs. (laughter from audience)

"And the word was with God", and this is that word of the beginning of creation - "HUM" - and this is with the omnipresent.'[3]

❀ ❀ ❀

The evening lecture is held inside the lecture hall, where again Maharishi speaks about *karma*, and continues his lecture on the topic of 'OM'.

Maharishi - '... is the first expression of *prana* [life force, breath], the first expression of *prana*. Now. we can take a plate of water, and then strike it.. I mean, disturb it, like that. What do we see.. find.. is the whole water stirs in one curve, a wave goes through the whole, like that, the whole water becomes. And if we keep on stirring like that, like that, like that, like that, then, where they come up, different, different types of waves, here and there and there and there and there.

So, at the start of creation, out of the ocean of Being, a.. a gentle stir comes, a stir, as if you'd stirred a dish full of water. And then one wave goes throughout the whole. That first wave is that hum, finest. And then when we continue to do like that, that means, the process of creation continues, the stir continues. And when the stir continues then that one wave breaks into many, many seg.. segments. And different, different types of waves come up here, like that, like that, like that, like that, like that. These different, different types of waves are the alphabets, 52 alphabets [letters] of the Sanskrit language, and OM is the, not this OM but that hum, that is the basis of all the alphabets. And some the alphabets, some sounds, sounds are be formed, and the combination of one form to the another and all sorts of permutations, it brings out the whole creation. This is the history, the story of how the world was created.

So OM is just the first expression of *prana*, and this is, this is a genuine.. the first expression of the three *gunas* [qualities], because when the three *gunas* are in equilibrium, nothing happens, equilibrium. There has to be a little bit, one less, and one more. Some one has to start predominating. One less, and one more. Then the movement starts, then the whole nature initiates the impulses, and from there the creation begins. So this *prana*, and the hum, this OM, and three *gunas*, have their.. in, in this form of hum, is the first expression of the three *gunas* and the first state of evolution of *prana*.'[3]

❀ ❀ ❀

Saturday, 17th February 1968.

Today it is Richard Blakely's 25th birthday and Gunnar Dietrichson's 35th birthday, and in the evening there are celebrations for them.

Richard Blakely - 'After the lecture that night there was a surprise birthday celebration for Gunar and me. Although it was not on the scale of Mia's - to everyone's relief there were no fireworks, and the two cakes were unassuming mounds of semolina, the kind of cake you'd be happy to have and not eat - my twenty-fifth birthday was one of the best. What better gift, after all, than being sung "Happy Birthday" to by John Lennon and George Harrison - never mind the chorus of spaced out meditators - or sharing my humble cake afterwards down in the dining hall with George, his wife Pattie, and Jenny Boyd?'[111]

❀ ❀ ❀

There is talk that Mike Love of the Beach Boys is planning to join the course in India, and is having outfits tailored specially for the visit. *Melody Maker* reports that all the Beach Boys are set to fly out to India, and also that they plan to tour with Maharishi in May.

Apparently, The Beach Boys are working on a new song, seemingly a meditation related composition, called *'Be Still and Know You Know You Are'*.

Audree Wilson - Brian, Carl and Dennis's mother - has already booked her initiation for the following week.

Brian Wilson - 'If my dad goes to India, I'll know that the Maharishi has done his job.'[124]

BEACH BOYS TO TOUR WITH MAHARISHI

MAHARISHI

NEW York, Monday—The Beach Boys may team up with the Maharishi Mahesh Yogi for a three week American tour.

The tour is taking shape in New York, reports Ren Grevatt. It would be for 20 days at top colleges and universities and is projected to start around May 3.

Beach Boy leader Brian Wilson is currently working at his Hollywood home on new "thoughtful and meditative song material" which the Beach Boys will do to open the evening. The Maharishi will then take over the second half of the programme with a lecture and discussion period.

Bookers and promoters are at work setting up dates for the projected tour. The Beach Boys will leave shortly for India to stay with the Maharishi.

Financial arrangements for the tour are not known but it is expected that the proceeds from the Maharishi's side of the tour will be turned over to America's SRM Foundation of yoga and meditation.

Melody Maker 17th February 1968

Sunday, 18th February 1968.

Yesterday George Harrison and John Lennon with wives, and manager and wife. The others are to arrive next week. George Harrison is my heartthrob. He is my No.1. John was wearing a gorgeous white cape last night, wool, down to the floor, very large. It looked very nice in the night. The women are very pretty and easy, delicate girls, colourfully dressed, but this is what everybody is here.

- Excerpt from a letter written by Gertrud Soares de Souza to her 19 year-old daughter, Francisca, in West Germany. Translated from German into English.

When Maharishi once more talks to his students outside his talk encompasses several topics, the five elements, intuition, the *mantra* in meditation, and the Celestial. The audience is becoming ever more familiar with his characteristic expressions, such as *'And that's the reason why...'* and 'come on, come on' . . . .

He talks about the Indian conception of time, explaining that mankind is currently living in the Kali Yuga, (*'yuga'* meaning 'an age or era'), a period of time spanning 432,000 years.

Maharishi - 'Time is a conception to measure the eternity.'

And he explains that in India, periods of time are even measured in the lives of gods and goddesses.

George - 'What happens after a lifetime of Shiva?'

Maharishi - 'A thousand Shiva's pass away, then one Vishnu!'[3]

❀ ❀ ❀

Speaking from Los Angeles, the man who introduced The Beatles to *yoga* by giving them each a book on *yoga* exercises, speaks out against Maharishi, suggesting that he is offering watered down *yoga* to his students.

Swami Vishnu Devanand - 'He tells young people that it is easy to find inner peace, that you can drink, smoke and eat anything you want and need only meditate 15 minutes a day.'

The short-haired clean-shaven Vishnu Devanand even finds fault with Maharishi's beard, claiming it *'is only for attracting attention'.*[125]

❀ ❀ ❀

Paul McCartney, Jane Asher, Ringo Starr and his wife, Maureen, fly in to India from London Heathrow by BOAC (British Overseas Airways Corporation), touching down at Delhi Airport at 8.15 in the morning, on Monday, 19th February. After the twenty-four hour flight, they all feel jet-lagged and exhausted from crossing five time zones, and having landed now have to endure the attentions of a crowd of reporters.

Mal Evans - 'Everyone was filmed as they came off the 'plane. Raghvendra and I placed garlands of red and yellow flowers around the necks of the newcomers, a traditional token of greeting and welcome.

Maureen Starr (left), Ringo, Jane Asher, and Paul McCartney at Palam on Tuesday.

The yogi's finest hour

When he got the chance Ringo told me he needed a doctor. It wasn't anything serious but his injections were giving him trouble, his arm was swollen and painful and he thought it best to see if any treatment was required.

Our driver lost his way and led us to a dead-end in the middle of a field. The Press came to our rescue - a whole stream of cars had been following us! In the end we accepted the directions of some helpful reporters and found a hospital. We paid a doctor about 11 shillings and he assured Ringo all would be well without treatment.'[121]

Beatles Attracted By Absence of Austerities

RISHIKESH, Feb 20 (UNI)-

Beatle George Harrison is taking to Maharishi Mahesh Yogi's transcendental meditation easier than John Lennon, their Manager, Mr. Evans, told Associated Press yesterday.

Mr. Evans said this was so because Harrison had been a Yoga enthusiast and been visiting India frequently.

The one thing attracting the Beatles to the Maharishi was the absence of austerities, fads and rigidities, Mr. Evans said.

"We can choose the hour, place and posture convenient to us and the diet he prescribes is not must, but only such as will help us in our exercises," Mr. Evans said.

Mr Evans said: "The Beatles keep their public and private lives separate. That is why their wives live private lives and do not mix up with their music programme."

Since the visit to the Yogi's Ashram is private their wives have accompanied them, Mr. Evans explained.

When Paul, Jane, Ringo, Maureen, Raghuvendra and Mal eventually leave Delhi for Rishikesh, on Tuesday, 20th February 1968, they take two cars, one with Paul and Jane in it, the other with Ringo and Maureen.

Meditation won't affect Beatles' career

The cars stop a short way into their journey, at Muradnagar, and a *Hindustan Times* reporter gets the chance to interview Ringo.

Reporter - 'What impressed you in the Maharshi?'

Ringo - 'Oh, that cannot be expressed in words. It was something that came out of our hearts. Here was a man we were looking for. Maharshi is amazing, excellent, marvellous.'

Reporter - 'Was there any particular instance which made you become the disciples of the Maharishi?'

Ringo - 'We became his disciples at first sight. He is man like that. Have you ever met him? Swear he did not impress you?'

Reporter - 'Have you given up smoking and drinking and LSD as the Maharshi does not like them?'

Ringo - 'I have not got rid of these so far but I will certainly do it whenever the Maharishi asks me.'

Reporter - 'Won't you feel any hardship as you may not get these things in the Maharishi's ashram during you stay there?'

Ringo - 'There will be some difficulty if I do not get cigarettes, but it is my duty to obey the ashram rules. Drinks I hardly take even now.'

Reporter - 'If you become a teacher of Transcendental Meditation, will it not affect your musical career?'

Ringo - 'Certainly not. Music has become a part of our life and we can't afford to part with it. Our musical career will continue as usual.'[3]

❀ ❀ ❀

In Rishikesh, whilst Maharishi is speaking to his students, the sound of thunder is heard, but he continues talking.

Maharishi - 'Immediately after meditation we don't take bath.'[3]

He explains that bathing washes away a *'very, very fine layer'* off their skins, of a substance called *'ojah'* - a special lustre secreted during meditation.

This mention of this *ojah* and the explanation as to its meaning leads to a spate of good humoured jokes - of which Rosalyn Bonas's is thought to be the best:-

'Knock, knock'

'Who's there?'

'Ojas.'

'Ojas who?'

'Ojas open the door, you know who it is and what I want.'[111]

Maharishi also tells students about how that in 'Cosmic Consciousness' they will have the ability to experience the full capacity of the Absolute in their lives.

Maharishi - 'Sleeping and remaining awake inside, both at the same time is the state of Cosmic Consciousness.'
'When one is Cosmic Consciousness, one is at times awake, at times dreaming, at times sleeping. Sleep, dream and wakefulness, these continue as ever before. And in the midst of these, the inner awareness prevails.'
'Once it is full then no chance of losing it.'[3]

So, in such a state of consciousness, is there no more room for growth, no capacity to progress?

'Capacity has been reached, now what could remain is; the applied aspect.. applied aspect. Applied in this field, applied in this field, applied in this field, applied.. Applied means, if one wants to fly, one would have to apply that ability to learn how to fly. If one wants to remain underwater.. live in water, then one will have to apply that ability to learn how to live underwater. Everything will be possible, but in some technological training will be needed, some fieldwork will be needed to get on to any field, any desired field. Any questions?

Because what has happened in Cosmic Consciousness, Absolute has been infused in the relative that has become. Now the Absolute has been infused, but the whole relative has not yet been mastered. So, mastery of the.. mastery in the relative field will then need education in different spheres. It will be quick, but it will have to be gained, education, that knowledge will have to be gained. Something there, something there, something there.'

The thunder brings with it rain, and lots of it.

Maharishi - 'Somebody said "When Ringo comes, the storms come in a flash" and clears the passage, the sky's all clear. In that clear air Ringo comes.' (laughter)[3]

❀ ❀ ❀

Ringo, Maureen, Paul and Jane are enduring the long drive.

Paul - 'There was an Indian driver and Raghvendra from the camp in front and me and Jane Asher in the back and it was long and it was dusty and it was not a very good car and it was one of those journeys, but great and exciting. I remember these Indian guys talking in what was obviously an Indian language and I was starting to doze off in the car in the back because once you were two hours into the journey the tourism had worn off a little. It was fascinating seeing naked holy men and the kind of things you just don't see unless it's late-night Soho, and the ones you tend to see in Soho tend to be covered in shit and very drunk. I slipped into sleep, a fitful back-of-the-car sort of sleep. It was quite bumpy, and the guys were chattering away, but in my twilight zone of sleeping it sounded like they were talking Liverpool. If you listened closely, it so nearly slid into it. There was like a little segue into very fast colloquial Liverpool. And I was thinking, Uh, where the fuck am I? What? Oh, it's Bengali, and I would just drop off again. "Yabba yabba, are yer comin' oot then, lad?" It was a strange little twilight experience. It was a long journey.'[6]

When they arrive at the academy Paul and Ringo are shown to 'Hilton' Block 6, where Mia Farrow is also staying. Apparently, Paul sees the starlet as *'a quiet little thing in a sort of Nehru jacket'*.[6]

Nancy Jackson - 'Paul was also accompanied by a slim, willowy red-haired girl he introduced as Jane Asher, a British actress and his fiancée. He made it clear that they would share the same quarters.'

'"Do you mean that Maharishi condones Paul and that actress sharing a room?" asked an indignant Genie [MacLean], who was a supporter of Moral Rearmament, a Christian movement with strict moral values. "Do you feel that is a good example for the rest of the course members?"'[117]

Really! Well wouldn't it be a good idea if someone were to ask Maharishi directly what he feels about sexual intimacy, especially since some members of the course are liaising with one another? Traditionally, *brahmacharya* (sexual abstinence) is considered as a temporary phase, undergone throughout a period of studies prior to marriage. Certainly, some *swamis* have been married, and that is also the case for some *brahmacharis*. Lifelong *brahmacharya* is altogether something much more of a rarity, usually reserved for those who intend to follow the lifestyle of a *swami*, but Maharishi cannot become a *swami*, as such, the rules of caste forbid him. So, what *are* his views on sex, and particularly sex outside of marriage?

Maharishi's lectures continue to fascinate his students, as he describes higher states of consciousness, that he calls 'Cosmic Consciousness' and 'God Consciousness'. They become familiar phrases along with his favourite sayings; *'Now, come on', 'Take it easy'* and *'Such a joy'*. And he re-interprets age-old concepts. He shares with them his definition of sin - that *'Sin is not meditating'*; on the basis that *'non-contact with the inner Being is the basis of all weakness and suffering and sin'*. He suggests that the Biblical tale of Adam, Eve and the snake, is meant for children, in order to impart *'some idea of some supernatural power'*, *'so they don't become completely*

agnostic![3]

As part of his teaching, Maharishi speaks about being able to transcend thought through the medium of *any* of the five senses, but cautions that *yoga asanas,* of themselves, are not a method of transcending, merely exercises so that the body can become normalised.

Maharishi - 'Movement does not produce that state of mind. What the movement does, the movement only makes the body flexible, maintains the flexibility and thereby allows normal function. The system functions normally. That's all that the *Hatha Yoga* does.'[3]

With regard to the body, Maharishi recommends that if there is discomfort during meditation, then the method of *'feeling the body'* should be practiced for a while, a practice whereby one transfers the attention from repetition of the *mantra* to the area of discomfort in the body, and continues to sense it until the discomfort subsides sufficiently enough to return to one's meditation.

❈ ❀ ❈

The recent arrival at the academy of Paul and Ringo seems to have stirred the waiting Press, pushing them to ever greater feats of bravado in order to secure stories and candid photographs of the group. Mal Evans decides it is time to go and have a word with them.

Mal Evans, speaking on behalf of The Beatles to the gathering Press outside the camp - 'They do not want publicity, fans or press. They want to be left alone to meditate and take a holy dip in the Ganges. They will not end up as spiritual dropouts before the course is completed. They are here to meditate for three months and there is no doubt that they will remain here until the end of the course. The boys, I repeat, are keen on meditating.'[12]

In order to further deter photographers from intruding on The Beatles privacy and solitude, site security is being stepped up, with the direct result that course participants now have significantly less freedom to come and go without check. And work on fencing off the extensive perimeter with sheets of corrugated metal is gotten under way.

In addition to the reporters there is also a young Canadian traveller, 24-year old Paul Saltzman, who also wishes to enter the academy, having recently arrived hoping, amongst other things, to solve a philosophical puzzle he has been wresting with - figuring the value of altruism versus the value of ego.

Paul Saltzman - 'I found that I had two main motivating forces when deciding what I wanted to do, whether in my work or in human relationships. One was the desire to be constructive in society, to do good, and the other was my ego - what others thought of what I was doing. I thought that ego was basically a bad thing and the result of the conflict between a "bad" and a "good" motivating force was a lack of direction. I felt that being alone, and learning more about what I wanted, would help resolve this hassle.'[126]

'I went to India to work on a National Film Board of Canada film. I was the sound engineer, and after filming for six weeks across India and up into New Delhi I got mail from home, and I got a letter from my girlfriend and opened it excitedly, and the first line, which is all I remember, was "Dear Paul, I've moved in with Henry".

And I was devastated, it was like a terrible heartbreak, the worst I've ever experienced. And someone said, who I knew for three days in my life, "Why don't you try meditation for the heartbreak?" And I knew nothing about meditation, or anything like that. And he took me to a lecture that night, at New Delhi University where the Maharishi was speaking. And what the Maharishi said, the only part I remember was the part that meant a lot to me, he said that; "meditation takes us beneath and below our daily worries and concerns, to a place of inner rejuvenation, from which we return refreshed and renewed".[127]

'I went to hear him, mostly because I valued The Beatles as artists and people and their involvement with the Maharishi made me curious to see what it was all about. I also heard that The Beatles might be going to Rishikesh, to the ashram, and I wanted to find out if I could go there for a day or two. For a long time I'd wanted to talk with John Lennon about that ego hang-up. I was sure he had gone through it at some stage and that talking with him might help'

'I was met by Raghvendra, a *brahmachari*, or novice monk, who was one of the Maharishi's disciples. After welcoming me with the customary tea and toast, he showed me to a tent I could sleep in, just outside the main area where the people on the course stayed, and told me that I could stay several days at least.'[126]

'… the tent was an old army tent on a wood platform. There were two of them under the trees across from the front gate about 50-60 feet from the gate. One was being used by a tailor who came up from Rishikesh and measured and sewed the Indian clothes for the famous folks and perhaps all the foreign participants on the course, who wanted them. The other tent was not being used and Raghvendra said I was welcome to use it, with my sleeping bag.'[38]

Wednesday, 21st February 1968.

To Francisca
Today Ringo and Paul arrived. Paul is not yet fully developed, tender. Ringo is fairly rough. The two wives don't have the quality of the wives of John and George, both of which are really first class. Tonight we will celebrate the birthday of Mike, 21. He works in the kitchen. Both hippies in the kitchen are sweet and work very hard from morning til night - without pay. Mike has wished for a "Science of Being" [book]*! Paul, the other hippy in the kitchen, gave me pills for my diarrhea and heated the milk for me.*

Yesterday we all got umbrellas because it was raining so hard. Maharishi is bearing everything in mind! Today, the barbed wire fence was again full of photographers who wanted to take a picture of the Beatles. A reporter grabbed me when I went to the tailor. But we mustn't leave the academy. Therefore was not yet in Rishikesh.

- Excerpts from a letter written by Gertrud Soares de Souza to her 19 year-old daughter, Francisca, in West Germany. Translated from German into English.

Mal Evans - 'With a mate of his named Paul, Mike had hitch-hiked to India. In fact they were on their way to Australia but had stopped off at Rishikesh, got themselves initiated as meditating students of the academy and were paying for their keep by working in Maharishi's kitchens! Mike and Paul had been fans of the fellows for years having attended an early ballroom appearance of the Beatles in Southport which is 20 miles to the north of Liverpool. Mike was very pleased with the birthday gift John gave him - a fine set of wooden beads.'[128]

Mike is also presented with a copy of *'Maharishi Mahesh Yogi On The Bhagavad-Gita: A New Translation and Commentary Chapters 1 - 6'*, and most of the course participants have signed their names in the book.

Nancy Jackson - 'When Tim [Mike], one of the English cooks, turned twenty-one, we decided to have a little celebration. We needed to blow off steam. With a bit of foresight, I had smuggled in a bottle of vodka from Delhi on my return to the ashram with Mia and Rik [Nancy's son]. By candlelight it looked like a place you might find if you made a wrong turn in the Casbah, with the heavily-bearded men in Indian shirts and the women in saris.
Raghvendhra joined us. Ascetic looking in his white robes and brown shawl, his black hair cut cowl fashion, he drank two bottles of cider with some alcohol and pronounced the drink quite good.'[117]

Chapter Twenty
Uncoil and Unwind

Back in Britain, Transcendental Meditation is being mentioned on BBC Radio 1.

DJ Brian Matthews - 'I imagine that you've all heard that The Beatles are at present in India studying Transcendental Meditation with the Maharishi. And, Donovan is going out to join them, you can tell us about it Don….'

Donovan - 'Yeah, well. On my recent American tour, three months I was there, Maharishi, who teaches the meditation was doing a tour himself, you might say. And he was onstage somewhere, in Los Angeles, and went down to see him. I've read about philosophies but I've never really got involved with a guru, a teacher, before. So I thought I'd go along and see him, to see what he was like and I found him great, really natural person. And I started meditating, and the meditating helped me all across the tour, erm, because all the planes, the hussles and all the people, and I could just calm myself out. And, so I go out to India to join the rest of the lads out there and have a chat with them.'[3]

But Donovan's trip to India will entail him leaving behind his American girlfriend, Enid Stulberger and son, six-month-old Donovan Junior, in their Hertfordshire cottage.

❀ ❀ ❀

Maharishi's attempts to make all his students feel at home means they are even provided postal facilities and a local shop.

Richard Blakely - 'The little town included a post office, a laundry, and a little store, lemon drops, Cadbury chocolate and Peace cigarettes.'[111]

With the arrival of The Beatles, the Press now congregate around these facilities.

Elsa Dragemark - 'Now one couldn't go to the tailor or the post office without being stopped outside the gates. There were always questions concerning the Beatles. The pop-group used to publicity, took the whole thing quietly and soon melted into the everyday routine within the ashram. They were not regarded as some peculiar creatures within the enclosure of the ashram, but were assimilated in a completely natural way into the community. The boys were rather tired when they came and felt like the rest of us - that it was wonderful to retire for a while from all the stress of the outside world. The Beatles turned out to be very pleasant and natural fellows, sincere in their seeking for the meaning of life, helpful and completely without any grand airs. They carried their laundry bags just like the rest of us and fetched what they needed from the kitchen and had their meals together with all of us.'

'After a few days of zealous waiting outside the gates without any result, the journalists took matters into their own hands and forced down the three gates towards the Ganges and stormed into the area. Without respect for people's integrity, they stormed into the Beatles' rooms, chased by the despairing guards, who were now forced to be a little tougher.'[129]

Richard Blakely - 'The Post Office was a small house with a table inside and a mountain of mail piled up on top of it. Behind the mountain sat a small man reading a copy of Time. As we entered he put down the magazine, stood up, and gave us a joined hands "Namaste!"'[111]

❀ ❀ ❀

George is in contact with Shambhu Das, his *sitar* teacher.

Shambhu Das - '… I was invited by George to visit him then. He made all the special travel arrangement for me since I was busy with Pandit Ravishankarji's *"Raga"* movie production at Bombay during that period. That's the time he introduced me to other members of the Beatles and Maharishi as well. I stayed with them there for 2 days, also played sitar for them.'[38]

'He [Maharishi] made a lovely space for them in his ashram on top of this very beautiful hill. Even the bungalow I was given was fully outfitted by American standards.'

'So I went, but I couldn't stay very long. I was only there about four days, but the Maharishi became very close to me, because George wanted me around, I think. And one day as he was sitting around talking to the Beatles, he suddenly said to me, "We would like you to do some special work for us." But I knew that Ravi Shankar was in a different pot, philosophically, so I was very confused.'[104]

❀ ❀ ❀

Mike Dolan - 'There was a local ordinance, enforced by inspections and fines, forbidding the sale or consumption of meat, fish or eggs in Rishikesh.
It was quite unusual at that time for westerners to be vegan and so most of the people on the course simply did not believe [or] buy into the concept and whilst they understood not eating meat they thought it extreme to not to eat eggs.'[38]

As a child Ringo suffered constant abdominal pains, and was diagnosed with a ruptured appendix, that then led to an inflamed peritoneum. Protracted bouts of ill health left him relatively delicate and so these days he is particularly careful about what he eats.

Mike Dolan - 'Ringo had trouble eating anything and an order came down that we had to buy some illicit eggs, and the shells had to be buried at the side of the kitchen.'[38]

Ringo - 'The food was impossible for me because I'm allergic to so many different things. I took two suitcases with me, one of clothes, and the other full of Heinz beans (there's a plug for you). Then one morning the guys who were dealing with the food said, "Would you like some eggs?" And I said, "Oh yeah, sure," and the next morning they said it again. I thought, "Oh yeah, great - things are looking up."
Then I saw them burying the shells.'
'You weren't supposed to have eggs inside this religious and spiritual ashram. I thought; "What do you mean, you're burying the shells? Can't God see that too?"'[1]

Mal Evans - 'When Ringo arrived… he found some of the curry dishes a bit hot, too many spices. When I went into Delhi again I collected a good supply of eggs so that we would have plenty of alternatives - fried eggs, boiled eggs, poached eggs.'[121]

❀ ❀ ❀

Paul Saltzman - 'In all I waited just over a week. Then one day, in the early morning mist, Raghvendra came through the gate and sat on the ground beside me. He told me I could come in now and learn to meditate. I could spend my days in the ashram, take my meals with them and continue to sleep in the tent at night.'[130]

❀ ❀ ❀

Paul - 'The idea was you'd all wake up at a certain time and you'd all go for breakfast. You'd sit outside all together and chat about this and that, have a bit of breakfast, a communal thing.'[6]

Mal Evans - 'The Maharishi never appeared at meals to eat with this students. He stayed in his own bungalow at these times. We were three weeks behind the rest of the meditators, also he used to give us extra lessons, extra lectures, in the afternoons. We'd all sit in the open air, sometimes on chairs on the grass and sometimes on the flat sun roof. When it was cooler we'd join him in his bungalow, sitting round on cushions. I could never cross my legs comfortably so there was always this big thing about providing me with my own special chair for these sessions!
Basically this was a teacher's course in Transcendental Meditation, a course designed to let the students learn enough to pass on their experiences to others afterwards. We met for 90-minute lectures at 3.30p.m. and 8.30 p.m. Each day people would recount their meditation experiences and Maharishi would explain the causes of sensations and thoughts we'd had. The idea was to build up to longer meditation periods. Gradually tapering off again towards the end of the course so that everyone would come out of Rishikesh more or less feeling down to earth again.'[121]

Cynthia - 'In the first week we settled into a routine, meditating for several hours a day and going to lectures, then spending the rest of the time on our own pursuits. I had taken pens and paper and spent hours drawing and also, for the first time in my life, writing poetry. It was crisply cold in the mornings and, having failed to pack warm clothes, we spent much of our time wrapped in the blankets from our beds. But the simplicity of life at the ashram, with few material goods, was enormously appealing and we all enjoyed slowing down and taking the time to breathe.'[10]

❀ ❀ ❀

Copyright: Avico Ltd.

Nancy Jackson knows some influential people in India, and one couple, the Cambattas, who own Cambatta Aviation Ltd, and offer to fly a helicopter to Maharishi's academy. They keep their word and soon the tranquil peace of the entire area around Rishikesh is devastated by the noise of a Hiller 12E helicopter flown by a highly experienced Parsi pilot, with the curiously apt name of Captain Rustom Captain, a veteran flyer whose previous passengers include the first Prime Minister of India, Jawaharlal Nehru.

Richard Blakely - 'While we all watched, Maharishi stood near the helicopter laughing, just out of range of the still revolving blades. Standing there with a big yellow dahlia in one hand and fingering his beads with the other, he looked like a child waiting for his first ride on a pony. Finally the blades came to a standstill and Maharishi started towards the cockpit, accompanied by two brahmacharis. Despite his dangling dhoti he managed to climb in unassisted on one side, while John Lennon climbed in on the other.'[111]

Amongst the crowd are members of those eager for photos of the event are two new visitors to the area; Vogue fashion model Marisa Berenson and her photographer, Arnauld de Rosney, a French baron whose photojournalism is used by various magazines including *Salut Les Copains,* who decide to run a story by de Rosney as *'Salut Guru'* ('Salvation Guru').[131]

Paul - 'So later I asked John, "Why were you so keen? You really wanted to get in that helicopter." "Yeah," he said, "I thought he might slip me the answer!" Which is very revealing about John. I

Pendant deux mois, les Beatles sont allés rejoindre le maharishi Mahesh dans son centre de méditation de Rishikesh, en Inde, au pied des montagnes de l'Himalaya. Arnaud de Rosnay, envoyé spécial de S.L.C., les a photographiés et vous raconte son séjour.

SALUT GURU

Lorsque John, Paul, George, Ringo arrivèrent à Rishikesh, via New Delhi, le Maharishi n'était pas là. Il inspectait, à bord de son hélicoptère privé, ses terres qui bordent le Gange.

81

suppose everyone is always looking for the Holy Grail. I think John thought he might find it.'[6]

Yet, as all must realise by now, Maharishi states and restates the *'answer'*, over and over and over again; which is, to regularly transcend one's thoughts and experience inner stillness.

Maharishi - 'So, the formula is, meditation and action, meditation and action. Now it is our experience, that when we meditate we completely forget the body, the world, and everything is forgotten, what remains is pure awareness. Inner wakefulness, out of everything forgotten, and inner wakefulness remains.'[3]

So.. how are Beatles getting on these days? Well, John Lennon provides some sort of answer when he says he hopes that by looking at their recent photographs people will notice *"something going on behind the eyes other than guitar boogie"*.[55]

Cynthia - 'Every now and then the Maharishi would arrange an outing for us to a nearby town, where I would marvel at the stalls selling saris and rolls of fabric in every colour under the sun. All of us girls bought saris and learnt to wear them.'[10]

Mal Evans - 'Just before George's birthday I went off into Rishikesh town centre to do a bit of shopping. I remember using this fantastic horse-drawn taxi to take me through the narrow streets. All the local children seemed to think I was an amazing sight. They trooped after me in great crowds wherever I went!

I arranged a special cake for George, with white icing and pink flowers and an Indian greeting - "Jai Guru Deva" - written across the top in gold letters. Then I bought a bundle of fireworks and some streamers, balloons and so forth. Earlier on I had bought an Indian banjo as my own gift to George.'[128]

COLLATION

*Ce jour-là, il y avait au menu :
salade verte, noisettes rôties au curry, champignons chinois,
gâteau au fromage, le tout arrosé de thé.*

Yavar Abbas, a personable independent filmmaker from Britain is here to make a documentary on Maharishi, for a series he is creating entitled *'Faces of India'*. He asks several course participants about their backgrounds. The first is Carole, an attractive young woman from Britain, who tells Yavar how her sister introduced her to the practice. Carole is a teacher, and for her it has not been easy to get the time off work to attend the course.

Carole Hamby - 'Oh, well, I gave up my job to come… I'd been saving, I'll have to get another job when I go back.'[3]

Another of Maharishi's students whom Yavar speaks to is Michael, an intense but amiable young man.

Michael Tyne-Corbold - 'I come from Melbourne, in Australia. …. I teach reading efficiency.'

And then there is Walter, a middle-aged German who has been with Maharishi for about 7 years.

Walter Koch - 'I am an engineer and scientist concerned with outer space.'

It is Walter's intention that when he completes this course, he will likely return to the U.S.A and resume his work on the re-entry of space capsules for the American Government.

The film crew also finds another of Maharishi's students, sitting by a tree. He is actor Jerry Stovin, a 45-year old Canadian who has worked with Sean Connery in *'Hell Drivers'*, and starred in various well known movies, such as Stanley Kubrick's *'Lolita'*, and *'The War Lover'*, with Steve McQueen and Robert Wagner, and also in the television series, *'The Saint'*, alongside Roger Moore. Jerry's acting work has already brought him into contact with the interviewer, but until now Yavar had been unaware that Jerry was a meditator. Now, he expresses curiosity about Jerry's interest in meditation, and asks him why he has come to Rishikesh.

Jerry Stovin - 'Well you can meditate for much longer times here, and one begins to uncoil, and unwind, and goes deeper and deeper into meditation and stays deeper in meditation.'

Jokingly, Yavar suggests that Jerry might *actually* be 'resting', a term used amongst actors to mean *'out of work'*.

Jerry Stovin - (laughing) 'Oh I am resting here always, "its one great big holiday" as Maharishi says.'

'I've just taken 3 months off to come here.'

'Maharishi says that "Nature supports you" when you meditate, so I'm sure it will support me very well. That things will resume as they were before, only better, because one becomes, when one meditates one becomes more intelligent, and one's heart opens up, one's understanding of life and people. And this is a great thing for an actor, to have greater understanding.'

Yavar Abbas also searches out Maharishi and asks him about the meditation course he is running.

Maharishi - 'This is for these three months. I've invited people from the west to train them as meditation guides to work in the west. That's why we don't have any Indians training. When I train Indians then I train only Indians, because, to spread Transcendental Meditation in India it has to have the background of *yoga* and Vedanta and *bhakti* and *karma* and Gita and Koran and Bible. In the west we have to be on the level of systematic, scientific investigation, experimentation. So, the whole language, the whole approach for releasing the society in the west is different, even though, basically, the thing is the same.'

Yavar Abbas - 'Maharishi, The Beatles are in your *ashram* now.'

Maharishi - 'The Beatles are doing very well.'

Yavar Abbas - 'Could you tell us something about their routine, how they're getting on?'

Maharishi - 'They get up very comfortably after good rest of the night, and then they meditate, and then they take their breakfast, and then they meditate. In the meantime they come to me for some little while, for verification of their experiences, and then they take their lunch, and then they have some little rest and reading and writing letters and taking care of their business, and then they take tea in the afternoon about five o'clock, and then they go back to meditation again, and then after supper all the people get together.'

Yavar asks Maharishi what he thinks of The Beatles' music.

Maharishi - 'If the youth of the world appreciates it, I adore it!'[3]

❀ ❀ ❀

Sunday, 25th February 1968.

Donovan arrives in India, and is met in Delhi by Nancy Jackson.

Donovan - 'Luv, have you got a "cough"?' [Cockney rhyming slang; *'cough and drag'* for *'fag'*, cigarette]

A newspaper stand displays the day's papers with some outrageous headlines such as *'Wild Orgies at Ashram'* and *'Beatles Wife Raped at the Ashram'*.

❀ ❀ ❀

George makes a note to himself in his diary:-[94]

'I AM 25'

THE BEATLES, DRUGS, MYSTICISM & INDIA

Mal Evans - 'The weather was good on the day itself so we were able to have an outdoor party. Pattie wore a lovely yellow sari for the occasion. We put decorations up in the trees and everyone had garlands of flowers to put around George's neck. In fact he disappeared beneath a colourful and flowery mountain of garlands before we'd finished. Then there was the special surprise of the evening - at the suggestion of the others I'd organised a band of local Indian musicians and a singer to perform at the party. Maharishi made a nice little speech about George…'[128]

Ringo - 'We had a big party for George's birthday. It was crowded with people and we all got dressed up and had red and yellow paint on our foreheads.'[1]

After a recitation by a local *pandit* [scholar], Maharishi gives a speech in which he makes special mention of The Beatles' contribution to the spread of meditation.

Maharishi - 'The history of the world, that past records a time where it was proclaimed that man is capable of enjoying 200% of life, and with this proclamation comes a wave of world peace. This wave of world peace is brought about by George Harrison, and his blessed friends in the group. I was going around for the last ten years, and what I have was, groups of meditators, here and there in different parts of the world. But when The Beatles came along - I would say headed by George Harrison - the world instantly knew what Transcendental Meditation was. A wave of disciples, wave of hope, in the increasingly stressed world. And this wave of hope has gone back, became more and more intensified. And when they are here, in India today, this place is a focus of attention of the whole world. And everywhere there is that, physical man, or what George Harrison is going to do? Or The Beatles are going to do? And just the thought gives me such great joy and the whole realm in love in my heart. (laughs) That was the day when they came, They met me, Hilton, and the next day was, they saw me at the.. platform, the train. And then the next day was they started meditation. And then the next day was they started to feel near, very near. And today is the day we are celebrating George's birth day. With such great joy, and this is the joy that is then being shared.'[3]

After Maharishi's speech there is a performance of some Indian instrumental music, some *sitar* playing with *tabla* accompaniment, lasting just over twelve minutes. The recital is a *raga*, and passages sound *remarkably* similar to ones occurring in The Beatles' *'Within You Without You'*!

George - 'I had my twenty-fifth birthday in Rishikesh (a lot of people had birthdays while we were there), and they had lots of flowers and garlands and things like that. Maharishi made me play my sitar.'[1]

And now there is a performance of Hindustani vocal music, also accompanied by a *tabla* player - an uplifting presentation lasting about a quarter of an hour. It's quite extraordinary how the human voice can be 'played' as if it were a musical instrument. This Indian vocal style is really quite amazing.

And then it is Mike Love's turn to make a contribution, and for about half a minute he offers up a poetic new composition of his own in which he strings line upon line of lyrical verse, with words swooping and diving, threaded together with the phrase, *'Transcendental Meditation can emancipate a man'*. The song is obviously very new and as yet unfinished, yet unexpectedly beautiful.

The time has now come for Maharishi to presents his gifts; a book (thought to be an old Hindi book on Guru Dev's life and teaching) and a globe, which Maharishi holds upside down and passes to George.

Maharishi - 'This is what the world is like today - upside down.
'It is rotating in tension and agony. The world waits for its release and to be put right. Transcendental meditation can do so. George, this globe I am giving you symbolises the world today. I hope you will help us all in the task of putting it right.'
George, inverting the globe - 'I've done it!'[132]

132

You'd be forgiven for thinking that every day's a birthday for a Beatle, but no Beatle has ever had quite such a birthday party as George Harrison's 25th, which he celebrated during his meditational sessions in India.

Ringo, on his return, described the meditational centre as being "a bit like Butlin's" — which, from all accounts, seems a fair description!

Apparently George hadn't given much thought to his birthday, probably thinking it would be spent meditating. But the Maharishi, a quiet expert in the showmanship field, had some surprises up his sleeve! He had had the assembly hall decked with everything colourful that could be found: flags, curtains, yards of silk, so that it looked more like a theatre setting than a scene for a party.

The timing of the affair was beautiful. When everyone was seated, the Maharishi entered with his priests and sat cross-legged on a deerskin rug beneath the portrait of his Guru. A real Rishikesh rave-up followed, with the chanting of hymns and the waving of a burning oil lamp!

Fashion note for would-be meditators: the shoeless Beatles and their girls were resplendent in rajah coats, saris and silk trousers, all looking very tanned and dressed up for the occasion.

A sort of "say-it-with-flowers" ceremony followed. Firstly the Maharishi garlanded George, then George returned the gesture. Then the whole audience garlanded both George and Patti with floral sprays of yellow marigolds—yellow apparently being an auspicious colour for the event. George carried on from there by garlanding the necks of his fellow Beatles and their wives.

When it came to the turn of Mal Evans, one of the Beatles' personal assistants, chaos developed! The garland around Mal's neck caught on one of George's, leaving them twisting and wriggling around the stage to free themselves, while the whole place roared with laughter!

Mike Love, leader of the Beach Boys, who was in the audience, was then asked up on stage to speak about meditation.

Finally the Maharishi gave George his birthday present. It was a plastic globe of the world. A simple present, but actually full of meaning. The globe had been fitted so that the map of the world was upside down.

"This is what the world is like today—upside down," the Maharishi announced solemnly. "It is rotating in tension and agony. The world waits for its release and to be put right. Transcendental meditation can do so. George, this globe I am giving you symbolises the world today. I hope you will help us all in the task of putting it right."

Accepting the globe from the Maharishi, George immediately turned it over so that the map was the right way up.

"I've done it!" he shouted, and was applauded with laughter for his quick wit.

Finally everyone moved outside for a firework display, and as the Maharishi left, the Beatles bowed and folded their hands, murmuring "Namaste"—good-bye.

A MEDITATION CELEBRATION!

Meditating with the Maharishi had its lighter sides for the Beatles - as these RAVE pictures show!

At the party, the Maharishi, Beatles and wives

George   Patti   Ringo

"A real Rishikesh rave-up"

Ringo looks on as George cuts his cake

A hilarious moment—the garlands of George and Mal Evans become entwined!

photo: Per Gunnar Fjeld

"Beatles are picking up meditation well"
"The Times of India" News Service

RISHIKESH

"TODAY is Mahashivratri, the day of Lord Shiva's wedding," Maharishi Mahesh Yogi told the Beatles yesterday as he sat surrounded by them in his ashram.

Paul McCartney giggled: "Whom is Shiva marrying? - Mrs. Shiva, I believe."

"Parvati," replied the Maharishi seated on a deer skin spread over an armchair and rocked with laughter.

This was the nearest the Beatles and about 65 others, all foreigners undergoing an intensive course in transcendental meditation, came to the legend behind Mahashivratri.

This should not surprise anyone because the Maharishi's ashram is different in preachings and precept from scores of others in its neighbourhood. Rishikesh is, as the Maharishi himself said, "the market place of spiritualism."

WELL-KEPT SANATORIUM

Situated on the Manikoot hillock, at the foot of which the Ganga gurgles as it meanders along, the ashram looks like a well-kept sanatorium.

The Maharishi's own cottage is a modern glass-and-oak structure. Other cottages are impeccably placed, and moderately furnished. They have electric fans, tap water and sanitary fittings.

Towering mountains provide the backdrop for the richly wooded ashram. On the green slopes birds flit and chirp.

The Maharishi has named his hermitage Dhyan Vidyapeeth (meditation school) and its campus Shankaracharyanagar. But the ashram is popularly known as Chaurasi Kutya (84 caves). The Maharishi had originally planned to construct 84 caves in the ashram to honour the memory of his preceptor, who died at the age of 84 as the Shankaracharya of Jyotirmath.

The Maharishi allowed "The Times of India" News Service correspondent to spend a full day at the ashram on Monday. It was first agreed that the correspondent would not use his camera - Beatles do not like to be photographed in the ashram - and would not disturb the meditators.

GROUP PHOTOGRAPH

After crossing the Ganga on a motor launch, the correspondent reached the rear entrance of the ashram about 9.30 a.m. On instructions from the Maharishi's staff, two baton-wielding guards allowed the correspondent in. After a ten-minute ascent, the correspondent reached a plateau and found the Maharishi clad in white, making arrangements for a group photograph of the meditators. The Maharishi got a painting of his guru hung to provide a backdrop for the picture.

The inmates then came out for the group photograph. There were men in multi-coloured bush-shirts, trousers, kurtas and pyjamas and women mostly in saris of Banarasi brocade, printed chiffon and nylon in various shades. Quite a few of them, men and women, smoked. Some ate oranges.

After all the others had trooped in, the Maharishi sent word for the Beatles to come out of their cottages.

George Harrison, whose 25th birthday was celebrated the previous day, led the Beatles, in kurtas and trousers, they came out wearing marigold garlands. George was accompanied by his wife, Patti.

Ringo Starr came hand-in-hand with his wife, Maureen. John Lennon escorted his wife, Cynthia, and Paul McCartney was accompanied by his fiancee, Jane Asher.

Maureen, Cynthia and Pattie were in saris with their foreheads smeared with kumkum.

As the Beatles neared the Maharishi, they folded their hands and chanted: "Jai Gurudev." The Maharishi helped them raise their stooping heads and blessed them.

The Maharishi posed for the photograph sitting beneath his guru's portrait with the Beatles at his feet.

- The Times of India [133]

Note: The term 'kumkum' is Sanskrit and refers to coloured powder, often turmeric, which when mixed with water creates a paste used for making temporary markings on the forehead, and, less commonly, on the arms.

Lewis Lapham, a journalist working for *The Saturday Evening Post*, is being allowed to stay at the academy for a few days, on condition that he merely observes, and makes no attempt to interview The Beatles.

'The restrictions against reporters remained in force, and in the evenings they departed in bitterness to file stories about the congregation of "actors, divorcées and reformed drug addicts." When the more sarcastic accounts reached the ashram, the monks took pains to hide them from the Maharishi.

For people with cameras, however, the restriction to film within the ashram was given to Canadian and Italian television crews, also to a French photographer from *Vogue* magazine. The photographer stayed several days, wearing a series of costumes designed by Pierre Cardin and explaining he'd been diverted from an assignment to take pictures of the milk-white tigers in the Delhi zoo.

The Maharishi posed for long hours, obviously delighting in cameras with the innocent enthusiasm of a child. He even considered himself something of a director, and this assumption was never more apparent than at the times he organized his group photographs.

First he supervised the building of a tier of bleachers, directing two monks where to place the flowers, the potted plants and the painting of Guru Dev.'

'Next the Maharishi drew a diagram indicating where everybody was to sit, and as the meditators appeared (everybody in their best Indian clothes), he hurried them into their places.'

'When everything had been arranged to the Maharishi's satisfaction, the Beatles next to him in the center of the set, he said to the photographer, "You must shout one, two, three before you snap.... Any snap, you must shout."

The photographer, a man from Rishikesh who worked with an old-fashioned camera under a black cloth, planned an angle the Maharishi thought too low.

"Up higher," he said. "You don't get good scenes from there."

The photographer dragged his camera several feet up the hill, and the Maharishi, turning to the assembled meditators, smiled and said, "Now come on, cosmic smiles... and all into the lens."

- *The Saturday Evening Post* [55]

Left Back Row 1. **Ena Mahabir** - Trinidad, 2. **Judy Burwell** - Canada, 3. **Terry Gustafson** - U.S.A.,
4. **Ian Alford** - Australia, 5. **Dr Ute Otter** - West Germany, 6. **Jerry Stovin** - Canada,
7. **Geoffrey Baker** - Great Britain, 8. **Laurence Kurland** - U.S.A.
Left 3rd Row 1. **Gunnar Dietrichson** - Norway, 2. **Elsa Dragemark** - Sweden, 3. **Eva Rudström** - Norway,
4. **Andreas Müller** - West Germany, 5. **Charlotte Peters** - Switzerland, 6. **Per Gunnar Fjeld** - Norway,
7. **Honor Anstruther** - Great Britain, 8. **Gerd Hegendörfer** - West Germany
Left 2nd Row 1. **Viggie Litchfield** - Great Britain, 2. **Millie Drummond** - Great Britain, 3. **Joan Mechim** - Kenya,
4. **Shirley Wilson** - U.S.A., 5. **Georg Meier-Siems** - West Germany, 6. **Michael Tyne-Corbold** - Australia,
7. **Jenny Boyd** - Great Britain, 8. **Ringo Starr** - Great Britain, 9. **Maureen Starkey** - Great Britain,
10. **Jane Asher** - Great Britain, 11. **Paul McCartney** - Great Britain
Left Front Row 1. **Berndt Schrieder** - Sweden, 2. **Benita Glössner** - Sweden, 3. **Sören Askelöf** - Denmark,
4. **Nadine Lewy** - U.S.A., 5. **Debby Jarvis** - U.S.A., 6. **Prudence Farrow** - U.S.A.
Centre Maharishi Mahesh Yogi
Right Back Row 1. **Val Crofts** - Great Britain, 2. **Reuma Rekhav** - Israel, 3. **Traude Leitz** - West Germany,
4. **Dorothie Harrison** - Great Britain, 5. **Anneliese Braun** - West Germany, 6. **Sarah Sadowski** - Canada,
7. **Abe Jehar** - Canada, 8. **Tony Rittendale** - U.S.A., 9. **Tom Simcox** - U.S.A.
Right 3rd Row 1. **Walter L Koch** - West Germany, 2. **Margaret Carroll** - U.S.A., 3. **Della Bernhard** - U.S.A.,
4. **Rudolf Schramm** - West Germany, 5. **Richard Blakely** - U.S.A., 6. **Rosalyn Bonas** - U.S.A.,
7. **Benjamin Lange** - Canada, 8. **Peter Ports** - U.S.A., 9. **Colin Harrison** - Great Britain
Right 2nd Row 1. **George Harrison** - Great Britain, 2. **Pattie Boyd** - Great Britain, 3. **Cynthia Lennon** - Great Britain,
4. **John Lennon** - Great Britain, 5. **Mal Evans** - Great Britain, 6. **Gertrud Soares de Souza** - West Germany,
7. **Hugh Horner** - U.S.A., 8. **Gerda Holzwarth** - West Germany, 9. **Gerlind Eichler** - West Germany,
10. **Carole Hamby** - Great Britain, 11. **Herbert Schulz** - Canada
Right Front Row 1. **Mike Love** - U.S.A., 2. **Genie MacLean** - U.S.A., 3. **Edna Linnell** - Australia,
4. **Katie Plowman** - Great Britain, 5. **Christel Thiele** - West Germany, 6. **Günter Rauchhaus** - West Germany

Cynthia - 'During our stay in Rishikesh, the Maharishi had taken the annual photograph of himself, his disciples and his students. This particular photograph created a great deal of excitement amongst the women of the group. We were all supplied with saris for the occasion (up until then we had been wearing very simple clothes made up for us by our own personal Indian tailors). The photograph of the group was taken in the overpowering heat of the afternoon sun, following a morning of learning how to wrap our saris. I must admit we all looked beautiful when finally we had sorted ourselves out. Our hair was put up and entwined with fresh flowers. Around our necks were hung garlands, also of fresh flowers. We were a sight to behold. The boys wore their Indian style western garb and looked equally impressive. It was quite an occasion, but by the time the session had come to an end our beautiful flowers had wilted; we had wilted; and sunburned bodies needed a great deal of soothing ... The Maharishi sat resplendent on his throne at the centre of his admiring followers. His laughter and good humour were ever present, laughter that rang out above everything like tinkling bells of joy. What a man!'[7]

Missing from the group photograph are various students; Rae Fried, Karin Hegendörfer, Julia and Valentin Schulze from West Germany, Kieran Kilroy from Ireland, and of course Nancy Jackson and Mia Farrow. Then there is also Mike Dolan and Paul Theobold from Great Britain, and the *brahmacharis*, Shankarlal, Satyanand, Dhirendra and Raghvendra, and Maharishi's Uncle, Raj Varma, and the staff, including Mr Suresh, and the kitchen staff, the cooks, John, Lazarus and their helpers; Sundar Singh, Bachan Singh, Jagman Singh, Dabal Singh, Charman Singh, Rhagis and Bhagyanath.

During the afternoon, Maharishi gives a lecture to some 100 extra visitors, amongst whom is a Major-General of the Indian Army. When Maharishi returns to his residence he is met by Ringo and his wife, Maureen.

Ringo - 'Gurudev, may I have two minutes.'

Maharishi takes them to his room and converses with them for a while, and, after a quarter of an hour or so, he leads them to the meditation rooms. When Maharishi emerges he speaks with a waiting reporter.

Maharishi - 'They were beset by some problems. Now they are happily meditating once again.'[133]

'Donovan arrives in late afternoon with a couple of friends.'

- Carole Hamby's diary

And with Donovan is Gyspy Dave, his long time travelling companion for whom he wrote the lyrical *'To Try For the Sun'* and the astonishingly rhythmic *'Hey Gyp, Dig the Slowness'*. Gyp is accompanied by his wife, Yvonne Mills.

Lewis Lapham - 'Donovan arrived... walking up the sandy path to the gate with his guitar over his shoulder and a cigarette drooping from the corner of his mouth. His friend, Gypsy Dave, carried their few belongings in a knapsack. From a distance I saw them confer with the Hindu guards, who at first didn't recognise them, and then a monk came and conducted them up the hill past the charcoal fires burning at the corners of the paths.'[55]

Maharishi - 'Here is Donovan, a great leader of the youth.'[133]

When Donovan gets a chance to meet up with The Beatles he can't resist asking about the *'Beatles wife Raped'* headline.

Donovan - 'Come on, who was the one who got done?'

Nancy Jackson - 'The girls, Patty and Cynthia as the only Beatles' wives, claimed they hadn't had the honor. Cynthia was in a very happy mood.'[117]

❀ ❀ ❀

Lewis Lapham - 'The Beatles arrived toward evening, and Harrison, who was sitting nearest to me at the table, remarked that if he could turn everybody on to transcendental meditation and Indian music, then he could go. Somebody asked him what he meant exactly, and he said, "You know... out... like on a road tour when you leave for the next town."'[55]

❀ ❀ ❀

At the evening lecture, Maharishi speaks to the regular course students about Patanjali, who is believed to have created the *Yoga Sutras*. Maharishi explains that Patanjali did not set out the procedures for *yoga*, but instead gave out concerning the philosophy of various teachings of Lord Shiva, Lord Krishna etc.

Maharishi - 'Patanjali provides a systematic vision of the whole thing, that means he brings out the philosophy of the whole.. principles of *yoga*. This is a clear vision. Our procedure is, we respect Patanjali, but.. and the teachings of the philosophy of *yoga*, but doesn't much do any practical good to us. Theoretically we feel, in our own meditation we experience that the body becomes still, and the *prana* becomes still, and the senses return inwards. And the mind goes in, and the state of being results. All these different phases, which Patanjali describes, we are experiencing. And therefore, there is not much of inspiration from Patanjali. We are in the grip of the direct teachings of Lord Krishna, to rise to Cosmic Consciousness, and then take some of the teachings of Lord Shiva, rise to God consciousness. This is our relation with Lord Shiva, Lord Krishna, Patanjali.'[3]

After a few minutes of explanation about *'the Night of Shiva'* the evening meeting continues with Vedic recitations from a visiting *pandit*. And after the chorus of chanting, Maharishi talks about Lord Shiva as being 'Yogeshwara', the 'Lord of Yoga'.

Lewis Lapham - 'During the evening a visiting pandit gave a short talk and then conducted a chant. Afterwards, seated around around a table at the ashram cafe, other students awaited the verdicts of George and Donovan.

'At last Donovan said, "It built."

Harrison nodded approvingly.

"It's rock," he said. "That's what it is."

Everybody smiled, and there followed a general agreement that the chant had been a groove. Harrison briefly mentioned his idea about ear plugs replacing record players (so that people could hear the music better) and also his conception of the academy the Beatles hoped to build in London. The Maharishi had great hopes for the academy, and Harrison assumed the group could raise enough money to build it by giving a single concert. "Figuring the tax deductions for that sort of thing," he said. He envisioned a large and colorful place where the kids could dance, and I sadly remembered the proposals of some of the other meditators who had spoken to me of remote sanitariums surrounded by neat lawns.'[55]

❀ ❀ ❀

Tuesday, 27th February 1968.

Maharishi is intent on finding out how people's meditations are going, and asks how long they are meditating, getting various answers, 5, 14, 20, 25, 29 hours….

He explains further about the mechanics of meditation, about how thoughts in meditation are the result of the settling of the body, so we should rejoice at all thoughts in meditation. He explains that the abundance of deep stresses can be likened to 'icebergs', of which we see only a small portion of their actual size, and that in long periods of meditation these icebergs are likely to get cleared. To assist in clearing them he suggests drinking the clear Ganga river water, which is said to purify the system. He also wishes to see his students using simple *yoga asanas,* exercises and postures designed to relax the body.

Maharishi - 'Flexibility of the body. Someone should demonstrate all these *asanas* tomorrow. Meet here sometime. What time? You set some time in the morning, and then those who are not doing should try to do. They are all simple things.'

Student - 'Brilliant idea.'

John - '[We're] meditating all day.' (laughter)

George - 'Isn't it important that each person does *asanas*, err, depending on their physical body? Like different people should do different postures and that not every one may work for everybody?'

Maharishi - 'They, they'll work it, they are very standard something - leaning forward, bending backwards - they are very set and standards, or something.'

'Some experience, some indication that the being is not lost even when the *mantra* is very subtle. The being is not lost even when one is in deep sleep, one experiences deep sleep and experiences awareness.'

John - 'But some of them have been doing it for 8 years.'

Maharishi - 'Yes. What is necessary is some consistency of this experience. …… consistency? Consistency, that is permanency of this experience.'

John - 'But you don't advise doing long sessions at home? Is there no gain, not even at the weekend.'

Maharishi - '2, 3 hours maybe, more than this people don't get time.'

George - 'But if we get time, if we make time, would we be allowed to do it?'

Then, after a long delay, Maharishi answers.

Maharishi - 'It'll be good to have someone around to check, to talk about the experiences, because now we have seen some *kundalini* shaking here and there, starts taking place. And that time someone is needed just to say; "Oh, take it easy", just that.' (laughter)

George - 'Say we're doin' it?'

Maharishi - 'Yes, yes, yes, yes, yes, just that much is needed and then everything is fine. Someone, even 2, 3, any.'

George - 'Millie from Great Britain said, that there's a negro who picks people up and shakes them and makes their *kundalini* rise.' (laughter)

John - 'Has he got a goal post?'

Maharishi - 'Out of fear! (laughter) Fear of life, fear for death or life, that makes, wakes *kundalini* up.' (laughter)

'Nothing practically dangerous but the psychology maybe upset. Just, psychology maybe upset. Because none of the experiences are practically harmful, but if one does not understand, and tries to resist, that might upset the whole system.'

MAHARISHI MAHESH YOGI - TRANSCENDENTAL MEDITATION - JAI GURU DEVA OM ॐ

'If the shakes are of the type that would make it rise then it could.
Yeah, but you don't know what shake will suit whom.'
George - 'If you work out which shake…' (laughter)
Maharishi - 'I think the shake that this *prana* gets during meditation, it becomes less, less, less, then more, more, more and then less, less, less. This shake of *prana* is good enough.
We actually don't need the shaking, and violent shake of the body. It is only just to clear the passage.'[3]

Millie Drummond - 'I don't remember telling George about him… He threw/shook people over his curved back in London! Spine to spine... I remember enjoying it very much, it was a beautiful experience, but not much more than that! ... Actually the guy was more about spinal adjustments… I guess one thing leads to the other…. A bit of Chinese whispers regarding the shaking & *kundalini* rising!?'[38]

The lecture becomes interrupted as a group of Indian musicians come to entertain.

✿ ✿ ✿

Ringo - 'One of my favourite stories; we were all in India, and there was a lot of people there, and we were living at the ashram, you know, you had to fight the monkeys off for your breakfast, and God forbid you wanted a bath, you'd have to get the scorpions out the way. Ahh, there was all that side too, but err, you know it was err this guy's there, 'cos the Maharishi was saying, [Ringo now imitates Maharishi Indian accent] "Oh yes and the *kund.. kundalini* shocks" and the guy says [again imitating an Australian accent] "Excuse me Maharishi, what are these *kundalini* sharks?"'[134]

✿ ✿ ✿

Donovan's arrival stimulates a considerable amount of interest, especially among the younger members of the course, after all, he is well known and his records have sold in millions. And he is only too happy to perform for some of the students, and even to be filmed playing. To a handful of students in Maharishi's garden, one tune *'Maharishi'*, is one dedicated to the teacher.

'When the sun is tucked away in bed
You worry about the life you've led
There's only one thing to do
Let the Maharishi straighten you

Maharishi, Maharishi, Maha-rishi, Ma-ha-rishi
Maharishi, Maharishi, Maha-rishi, Ma-ha-rishi

When the sun is tucked away in bed
On the pillow, fluffy red
There's only one thing to do
Let the Maharishi wizen you

Maharishi, Maharishi, Maha-rishi, Ma-ha-rishi
Maharishi, Maharishi, Maha-rishi, Ma-ha-rishi
Maharishi, Maharishi, Maha-rishi, Ma-ha-rishi
Maharishi, Maharishi, Maha-rishi, Ma-ha-'

Lyrics of *'Maharishi'* by Donovan Leitch

Mia looks on in silent appreciation whilst Donovan performs.

Mia Farrow confides to Richard Blakely - 'Good to be back, believe me.'[38]

Wednesday, 28th February 1968.

Maharishi, his *brahmacharis*, Satyanand and Dhirendra, and a crowd of students including Donovan, John, Cynthia, Paul, Jane, George, Pattie, Jenny, Mike Love and Mia Farrow, all traipse down the hill to sit on the sandy shore beside the river to have a singsong in the sunshine. John and Paul bring along their blond Martin D-28 acoustic guitars, and Donovan his Gibson J-45 sunburst - professional 'workhorse' instruments. Amongst the students gathering for the singlong are a couple of dozen other students, amongst them Carole Hamby, Millie Drummond, Geoffrey Baker, Edna Linnell, Gertrud Soares de Souza, Ian Alford, Michael Tyne-Corbold, Benjamin Lange, Jerry Stovin, Abe Jehar, Richard Blakely, Terry Gustafson, Georg Meier-Siems and Andreas Müller. And inevitably there are the journalists too, who settle down beside them. There is also the film crew from Italian television who have come in search of an interview with Maharishi.

Everyone joins in with the well known gospel standard *'When the Saints Go Marching In'*, adding a few new lyrics; *'Jai Guru Deva, Jai Guru Deva, Jai Guru Deva when she comes'*. They also try an old country song, *'You Are My Sunshine'*, and a Christmas favourite, *'Jingle Bells'*, and a traditional campfire folk number *'She'll Be Coming 'Round the Mountain'*. And Donovan gives a rendition of one of his own compositions, *'Happiness Runs'*, a song written since he learned to meditate.

> ***'Everybody is a part of everything anyway***
> ***You can have everything if you let yourself be.'***
>
> - Excerpt of *'Happiness Runs'* by Donovan Leitch

Using Donovan's guitar, George plays some instrumental music for a while, then there's a group rendition of Bob Dylan's *'Blowin' in the Wind'*, and some chanting, in the form of the *'Hare Krishna Mantra'*.

Maharishi urges everyone - 'Enjoy… fathom the infinity, dive in the Ganges. Fathom the ocean! ….'
George - 'Hey, we don't really exist!'
Maharishi, laughing - 'Right, right.'[3]

A brief but pleasant version of *'O Sole Mio'* (probably played for benefit of the Italian film crew) soon morphs into Elvis's take of this classic, *'It's Now or Never'*. Then it's time for Donovan to play another song, and he launches into *'Catch the Wind'* which Mia mistakes for another song.
Mia Farrow - '*100 Miles*!'[3]
Donovan continues, aided by the vocal talents of John and the others. All the while, Jerry Stovin sits attending to a portable reel-to-reel tape recorder, usually used to record Maharishi. Donovan has a small microphone around his neck; whilst larger mikes are placed between John and Paul, and near George.

After the sing along, Maharishi and his students wander over and stand on the pebbles and boulders at the river's edge then cautiously venture in, cooling their feet and splashing their faces with water.

❀ ❁ ❀

Donovan - 'It's part of the job to be a poet, folk singer -- children's songs, rounds, circular songs. And so I made this circular song "Happiness Runs" and it directly references meditation because it says "happiness runs in a circular motion/thought is like a little boat upon the sea." Simple words, but profound.'[135]

Early in his career, Donovan learned so much of his art from fellow guitarists such as Keith 'Mac' MacLeod, who is nowadays working as a bassist with a group called 'Hurdy Gurdy', and Mac has written to Donovan asking if he might write a song for them, so Donovan now has a chance to repay a favour.

Donovan - 'We were gathered together one day in Maharishi's bungalow, the four Beatles, one Beach Boy and Mia Farrow. There was an embarrassed silence in the room. Maharishi he sat cross legged upon the floor, on his deerskin, as was his want and John Lennon, the wit and the humorist, he decided to break the silence. So he walked up to Maharishi, as he sat on the floor, and he patted him on the head and said, "There's a good guru." We all laughed, and Maharishi laughed the loudest. later that night as we were gathered together on the roofs of our bungalows Under the tropical Indian stars we broke out the guitars… and I started to write this song...'[136]

Donovan - 'In the 18th century the hurdy gurdy man played the instrument the hurdy gurdy and he traveled from town to town and he brought the news. So I related the hurdy gurdy man in the song to the teacher, the Maharishi, who brings us songs of love.'[135]

Hurdy-Gurdy Man

Donovan - '… and George Harrison he turned to me and he said, 'I could write a verse for that song, Don.'[109]

'When the truth gets buried deep beneath a thousand years of sleep
Time demands a turnaround and once again the truth is found.'

- the verse written by George Harrison for *'Hurdy Gurdy Man'* by Donovan Leitch

Having friends like John, Paul, George and Don, Ringo must feel as though he's the only one who doesn't play guitar.

Jane Asher also plays guitar and has brought along her classical Spanish style acoustic. Whilst on the course, she dabbles with other instruments too, such as the *sitar* and the *dilruba* (*'dilruba'* literally means 'robber of the heart'). But without a doubt, Donovan seems the keenest guitarist there.

Ringo - 'Don, you never stop playing guitar!'[137]

With so much time on their hands, it is only natural the musicians find themselves wanting to create new material. All The Beatles are working on new compositions. Even Ringo, who is not really known for being a songwriter, cannot resist attempting putting the finishing touches to a part-finished song he has written, *'Don't Pass Me By'*.

Jenny Boyd - 'That really was an opportunity to see creativity in action. They'd be talking about something, start playing and it would just develop into a song. I remember John once saying that he hadn't been able to sleep the night before. He found it quite difficult to adjust at first. That became *So Tired.'*[138]

John - 'I couldn't sleep, I'm meditating all day and couldn't sleep at night.'[15]

To ensure that students maintain contact with the outside world Maharishi organises trips to the town of Dehra Dun, some 30 miles or so northwest of Rishikesh,, where his students can go shopping and visit Nagoli's Restaurant. On one such outing The Beatles look in at Pratap Music House at Astley Hall, who are the local musical instrument suppliers.

Copyright: Avico Ltd.

Ajit Singh - 'They had visited our store and ordered a customized pedal harmonium. It was white with flowers painted on its sides and had to be played sitting on a chair since we had made it a bit elevated. In fact, I also gave a recital of the "vichitra veena" on George Harrison's 25-th birthday which was celebrated while they were here.'[139]

George composes a tune on his keyboard - and puts a song together around it, entitled *'Circles'*.

'He who knows does not speak, he who speaks does not know and I go round in circles'

- Excerpt of *'Circles'* by George Harrison

Richard Blakely - 'Soon after arriving George had set up a little organ on the roof of the lecture hall and that soon became a popular hangout, before or after lectures or in between long meditations, where some of us SIMSers would gather to socialize and listen to George play the organ or strum on his guitar and sing along with him and in between songs, talk about the future of the world.'[111]

Whilst the SIMSers chat, they busy themselves evolving ideas that might improve the chances of spreading the technique of Transcendental Meditation. They talk about various ways that things might be improved, including doing away with the initiation fee.

Richard Blakely - 'We thought about it, seriously, and talked about it intently. Berndt, Rosalyn, Larry, Jenny, George. Us youthful plotters up on the roof, with the sun going down across the river, the monkeys looking on, the crows cawing, and the music playing.'[111]

And there was a rule whereby meditation would not be taught to anyone who had taken any drugs within the last three days, and recently this rule has been extended to three weeks. But there is still no similar mention about abstaining from alcohol for a prolonged period.

These folks who see themselves as 'SIMSers', conclude that it's a plot by the 'old guard SRMers' to discourage young people from learning to meditate, and they decide to confront Maharishi with their concerns!

Richard Blakely - 'Sitting at his feet, we explained to him, George explained to him, that the three-week ban on drugs were turning off a lot of people who would otherwise love to start meditating right away. Maharishi listened politely and tilted his head sideways and laughed, and we said our Jai Guru Devas and got up to leave and regrouped outside before returning to our rooms to continue our long meditations we all agreed with George that it had been a good meeting and Maharishi had taken us seriously and listened carefully to what we had to tell him and we had taken the first step on the pathless path towards a world without war.'[111]

❀ ✿ ❀

Donovan - 'One night I was awakened in the wee hours by a weird rustling of leaves outside my window. I sat up, the moonlight streaming in through the open casement. After so many long and silent sessions of meditation, I followed the Maharishi's instruction and fell into a waking reverie. An exquisite stillness pervaded the gleaming room and I began to compose. Lighting a candle I focused my half-closed eyes on the space between the worlds.'[84]

❀ ✿ ❀

Another musician who pops in and out of the academy is American musician Paul Horn, a flautist who generally plays Jazz, but also appeared in a couple films. In fact he taught Tony Curtis to play the flute for *'Sweet Smell of Success'*.

Ever since he learned to practice Transcendental Meditation, Paul has also explored and worked with Indian music, which led him to produce the record *'Paul Horn in India'*. Last year, he attended the teacher-training programme in Rishikesh and became an initiator. Towards the end of the course he also got a chance to play with some Kashmiri musicians, a meeting which culminated in the release of an LP, *'Paul Horn in Kashmir'*.

Paul Horn - 'In early 1967 there were only 50 people at the Ashram. I was always thinking how great it would be to have a documentary made of those special days for all the world to see. I returned to Los Angeles in June and by the end of that year my wish became a realization.'[140]

'The Beatles happened to come on the scene, and that whole world about Maharishi, and meditating, and the Beatles were going to India.

And I had already a documentary idea, I had, of filming Maharishi and doing a documentary on meditation and his presentation; going back to India. So that was already set in motion, and I had a film crew and everything going over there.

And it just happened to coincide that the Beatles were there.'[141]

⊛ ⊛ ⊛

In the forested jungle around Maharishi's academy, it gets a bit noisy at times.

Mike Dolan - 'During the course people were complaining about monkeys and blackbirds scuffling about on the roof disturbing meditation. So Maharishi dispensed some young Indian boys to the roofs which of course just caused a different scuffle. In an amazing display of species bias, though nobody complained so I guess we can chalk one up for creative intelligence.'[38]

⊛ ⊛ ⊛

Gradually, the newsmen and photographers at the academy gates seem to get the message and drift away, leaving The Beatles fairly free from unwarranted intrusion. Fortunately they don't seem to mind other students snapping photographs for their own enjoyment. A fair few of them have good quality cameras.

Paul Saltzman - 'Having been photographed so often, and in the completely informal ashram setting, they paid no particular attention to the camera. They paused for a moment as I approached. John scratched the inside of his ear with a slightly far away look in his eyes. I snapped a picture. Then Paul started strumming again and John joined in. Paul had a pad of paper sitting on the step beneath him and he started to sing the words that he had scribbled down. It was the chorus to "Ob-La-Di, Ob-La-Da." They repeated it over and over again, and when they stopped Paul looked up at me with a twinkle in his eyes and said, "That's all there is so far. We've got the chorus but no words yet."'[130]

'Ob-la-di ob-la-da life goes on bra
La-la how the life goes on'

- Excerpt of *'Ob-la-di Ob-la-da'* by Paul McCartney & John Lennon

Paul - 'We went down to the village one evening when they were showing a film; the travelling cinema came around with a lorry and put up a screen. It was a very pleasant Indian evening so Maharishi came, everyone came, and we all walked down as a procession. And it was very very pleasant; walking along in the dust slightly downhill through a path in the jungle from the meditation camp with my guitar and singing "Ob-La-Di Ob-La-Da", which I was writing, accompanying the procession on the way.'

'In actual fact, I think they quite enjoyed it. Maharishi quite liked someone strolling along singing.'

'I had a friend called Jimmy Scott who was a Nigerian conga player, who I used to meet in the clubs in London. He had a few expressions, one of which was, "Ob la di ob la da, life goes on, bra." I used to love this expression. Every time we met he'd say, "Ob la di ob la da, life goes on, bra." Or somebody would say "Too much" and he'd say, "Nothing's too much, just outta sight."'[6]

Prudence Farrow - 'At one lecture, John sat in the front row. He turned his chair around and, instead of watching Maharishi talk, he observed our reactions. I didn't exactly know why he was doing that. During another quite long lecture, George stood up and politely told Maharishi his talk was unbearably boring. Everyone laughed, Maharishi laughing hardest. One lovely thing George did was play music for people going through particularly rough moments.'[32]

'… My wire-frame eyeglasses finally broke for good. I had managed to patch them temporarily for weeks, but they always broke again. Paul managed to do an almost impossible job of piecing them together, but it did not last.'

'One evening, John and George jaunted happily into my room, playing "Sergeant Pepper's Lonely Hearts Club Band." Instead of cheering up, I felt worse, for I was terribly lonely in certain ways. Their coming into my room as *the* Lonely Hearts Club Band represented a cosmic irony. Another time, they burst into the room with their new song "Obl-La-Di, Ob-La-Da." I had been quiet all day, and although I loved it, it just felt unfitting.'[32]

Rudolf Schramm - 'The music of guitar playing by the Beatles during meditations session was disturbing the meditation not only of me.'[142]

Millie Drummond - 'It was actually mostly a big intrusion as we had been mostly in silence since early January! They seemed very superficial & I remember telling John as he walked past, that "I'd have thought more of them"! But I did enjoy the beach sessions.'

'I didn't socialise at all, and didn't spend time with them except for Ganges *satsangs* but when our paths crossed either John or George (can't remember which) called out "it's Transcendental Millie…!".'[38]

Mal Evans - 'To make sure we could meditate in peace we had little printed cards saying "MEDITATING, PLEASE DO NOT DISTURB", and we stuck these on the doors of our bedrooms. One night I thought my meditating was reaching a very special new depth. I could see flashing lights around me in the darkness although my eyes were closed. THEN, when I opened one eye to peep, I realised I'd been fooled. One of Maharishi's closest disciples, a friendly young fellow named Raghvendra, was flashing a torch at me through the window. He'd read the PLEASE DO NOT DISTURB sign on my door and thought this would be the most polite way of drawing my attention!'[121]

THE BEATLES, DRUGS, MYSTICISM & INDIA

According to Prudence, whilst she was sitting in meditation one morning she experienced an intense pain in her spine, and soon after receives a visitor to her room.

Prudence Farrow - 'I looked up in surprise. A sadhu, an ascetic, wearing a thin jockstrap and dreadlocks rolled high on the top of his head, stood at my door. He grabbed me from behind, lifted me up onto my feet, and aggressively escorted me into the open courtyard outside.
Pushing me back down into a seated position on the ground, he hit the center of my spine with the palm of his hand. I exploded. The energy in my spine was released in such a way that I felt air pass through every pore of my body. I was bodiless, one with space, infinitely expanded. It was glorious. He pulled me back up, returned me to my room, pushed me back into my seated position, closed the doors, and left.'

Prudence tells Maharishi about the visitation.
Prudence Farrow - 'I told Maharishi I was embarrassed and a little unsettled that sadhus, and even he, could know my feelings and thoughts. Maharishi responded that this was very good. I said I didn't understand. He said neither the sadhus, nor he, caused this phenomenon - I was the cause, and it was a sign of my growth.'[32]

Paul Saltzman - 'One afternoon, Paul McCartney, his girlfriend Jane Asher and I talked about the Maharishi as we sat having tea at one of the long tables overlooking the river. Both of them had been meditating five months and felt it was a valuable thing; that through meditation they were accomplishing good things in their heads and finding great contentment. They liked the Maharishi and respected his intelligence and were enthused by his love for life. But they had a down-to-earth view of him.
Jane Asher was especially put off by his evasiveness; and McCartney was worried that this, and some of his political statements, would be emphasized by the press and people might miss the essential good the Maharishi was trying to pass on. The Beatles, McCartney said, were upset by the comments the Maharishi made about draft dodgers when he was last in the United States. They felt he lost many American young people when he said that young men should obey the law and not evade the draft. "Any fool can make a law," McCartney went on; "that doesn't mean it's right. The Maharishi doesn't know much about world affairs and we've been telling him about Vietnam, and what's happening there, so he'd understand why some of the young men won't fight. The Maharishi just laughs when he can't answer a question, and it alienates people. He really must learn to just say, *'I don't know,'* when he does not. He'll be more respected for it."
They both spoke warmly about the Maharishi and it was in no way a put-down. They felt, as I did, that the Maharishi was human; that he couldn't walk on water. But neither was he a charlatan.'[126]

❀ ❀ ❀

Elsa Dragemark - 'One day, when I was on my way to Maharishi's house, I saw a bathtub and a toilet stool standing on a cement slab at the edge of the garden. It looked rather amusing with these white objects placed right out in nature with magnificent flowerbeds in the foreground. Next day, when I went the same way, there was suddenly a house, where the day before, I had seen the bathtub and the toilet stool. Apparently the bathroom had been installed first and then the house had been built. I took the liberty of inspecting the building more carefully and found it both nice and comfortable with outer walls of thick raffia mats. The house consisted of a bathroom, a large room with flowery curtains and a grey fitted carpet on the floor. Two beds made up the furnishing. A painter was just painting the doorpost and the window-sills in a green colour.'
'For a couple of weeks we could rejoice in having two famous musicians from Kashmir at the ashram - Shri Wachas Pati Sharma, who played sitar, and Shri Rajinder Kumar Raina, who played the tabla.'
'When I looked into the room, Mr. Kumar Raina was curled up on one of the beds playing his tabla, while Mr. Sharma was sitting on the floor playing his sitar. Through the large windows towards the south I could look down into the Ganges and out over the plains towards Rishikesh - a view that I really envied these charming gentlemen.'[129]

Richard Blakely - 'Down along the cliff not far from Maharishi's bungalow was a small one-room house with lots of windows. Within a few days after his arrival George had converted it to a music room, or to be precise, an Indian music room. After lining the floor with thick carpets and placing a bunch of cushions and pillows around, George filled the room with various Indian instruments and invited people to come and listen to him or others practice and play, or even learn to play the instruments themselves.'[111]
'Which is how I learned to play the sitar. Or at least to sit on the floor with one leg up to hold it steady while George guided me through the first few rudiments of fingering.
In the end though I decided to learn the veena.'[111]
'One reason I decided to try learning that instrument was that it looked that I just might be able to. A better reason was that Pattie and Jenny said I should. Both of them were learning to play Indian instruments of their own. Pattie had in fact been taking lessons for some time on a sitar-like instrument called a dilrubha and was already pretty good at it. Jenny's instrument was another kind of veena that looked a little like a zither supported on two gourds that rested on the floor at either end. The plan was for me to become proficient enough on my little box with two strings so that at the end of the course the three of us could give a little concert to a select group of tone-deaf friends.'[111]

Saeed Naqvi (a reporter) - 'A "dream house", with glass walls, jutting out on a rock, with the river a few feet below was the music room. Vachaspati Sharma, the sitar player from Jammu, was always strumming something or other. George Harrison would join him with his favourite raga "Desh" or "Puriya Dhanashri". His sister-in-law would play the dilruba. Often Donovan would end up the recitals with his Hymn to the Guru, with Paul Horn providing the flute accompaniment.'[143]

Paul Horn - 'The Beatles themselves attended because they were sincerely interested in meditation. They didn't expect any preferential treatment, they ate in the dining hall with everybody else; they went to the same lectures. We hung out together in a relaxed way, and pretty soon it was "Hi, George," "Hi Paul," just normal daily life, which is the way we all wanted it to be.
During this time, I had the opportunity to renew my acquaintance with George Harrison. We had met through Dick Bock of World Pacific Records a year or two before. George and I became friends at the ashram and played some music together in a special little music hut that Maharishi had set aside for the Beatles and Donovan and anyone else who wanted to play there.'[144]

✵ ✵ ✵

John Lennon plays flute

Paul McCartney finds himself working on some lyrics for a tune he has written.

'Who knows how long I've loved you?
You know I love you still.'

- Excerpt from *'I Will'* by Paul McCartney & John Lennon

Paul - 'I remember sitting around with Donovan, and maybe a couple of other people. We were just sitting around one evening after our day of meditation and I played him this one and he liked it, and we were trying to write some words. We kicked around a few lyrics, something about the moon, but they weren't very satisfactory and I thought the melody was better than the words so I didn't use them.'[145]

Donovan - 'I don't think I helped with the lyrics. He is very productive and will always take over the writing in a jam.'
'I may have helped with the shape of the chords and encouraged the imagery from tunes I wrote then in India. The descending movements of my songs may have encouraged Paul to write differently.'[6]

⊛ ⊛ ⊛

Per Fjeld is a Norwegian meditator of about 40 years of age, who learned to meditate back in 1964. Per is married to fellow meditator Kari, who is back home in Norway.
Per Gunnar Fjeld - 'I had not heard much of their [Beatles] music before, so I did not know very much about them, other than that they were popular musicians. But when I heard them play "Help!", I realized that they had a message and something to offer.'
'Once they lacked some equipment for a recording they wanted to do, and I had a small Philips tape recorder with me so they got the part that they needed from me.'
'The Beatles behaved totally as "*vanlige folk*" ("normal people") during their stay in Rishikesh. They were with us and ate their meals with us. I remember one time there was a lady who was a little older who came to the table after we had sat ourselves down, and there were no seats free. Then John Lennon moved and gave his place to her. There is one thing I wonder: What does one really say to John Lennon when being seated at table with him?'
'I did not talk much with the members of The Beatles. But I spoke a bit with Mike Love of the Beach Boys. He was smart dressed in specially designed travel clothing; one coat for "*halvsid*", "halftime" with contrasting colors on the inside and outside. This enabled it to be reversed according to the needs - two garments in one! But I had the no idea who he was...'[146]

Mike Love also talks to Richard Blakely and tells him about his vision of progress concerning the area around the academy.
Mike Love - 'Maharishiville!' he shouted. 'Can you dig it?'
'Maharishiville!'
Richard Blakely - 'He took off his cape and laid it over the back of my chair and sat down on the rock beside me. "It's gonna be so bitchin!"'
Mike explained that he and some other people he knew, people with a lot of money, were going to start a

foundation that would one day, "and I mean soon, man - two, three years," finance the construction of the World Capital of Transcendental Meditation. In place of the huts and shacks of Rishikesh, they were going to build a regular little city, with skyscrapers and parks and freeways. There'd be an airport, a modern train station, helicopters flying all over the place. He pointed to a spot beneath us and across the river where a couple of sadhus in loincloths were washing their orange robes. "Right there we're going to build the stadium."
"The stadium?"
"Yeah, man! It's gonna be fan-fucking-tastic!" Mike explained that Maharishi would have to have someplace to welcome the millions of pilgrims who would flock there every year.
"But how about this place?" I said. "The ashram."
"This place?" He glanced over his shoulder at the lecture hall and gave a disparaging snort. "This place'll be a museum by then."
I too looked back at the lecture hall through the trees and had to admit it looked a little quaint all of a sudden. I asked Mike if he'd talked to Maharishi about all this and he said he had and Maharishi was all for it.[111]
Clearly, before proceeding with his plans, Mike Love would first need to convince all of the many charities that own the land and buildings hereabouts, that protect the needs of ascetics who come to this area to spend their time in contemplation and prayer. He would also need to help regenerate the Northern Railway service which runs the trains to and from Delhi, the capital, if the railway terminus is to have any chance at all of functioning. But clearly, Mike has not thought things through at all, he surely doesn't realise how difficult it is to obtain land here? Why, even the area on which the academy stands is only on a short-term lease.
But one thing is clear, if Mike is anything to go by, Maharishi has attracted a very different sort of devotee than did his *guru,* who was responsible for the spiritual welfare of millions, and whose operations were handled from just a handful of buildings sited across northern India, in Benares, Allahabad, and in the Himalayas at Joshimath.

❀ ❀ ❀

Apart from the famous musicians, the course has also attracted the interest of at least one well known artist.
Per Gunnar Fjeld - 'Other more locally known artists attended meditation course. Painter Gunnar Dietrichson… … he has painted many scenes from Lillehammer districts [in Norway], and I knew him from earlier. Among other things we had been in the Scouts together. He was a real bohemian and had hitchhiked large parts of the road from Norway to India to attend the meditation course. He managed to get through Afghanistan without being robbed, and it speaks volumes how scruffy he looked!'[146]

❀ ❀ ❀

Paul Saltzman - 'It was getting towards evening, the sky turning a lovely pale pink, and across the Ganges the sounds of Rishikesh were fading into dusk. A flight of forty or fifty beautiful emerald-green parrots landed dramatically in a nearby tree and glimmered like jewels in the evening light. Gradually, people got up to leave our gathering spot near the cliff's edge until everyone left, except John and me. He was quiet, even a bit sullen, and I got the sense he wasn't happy. I asked him how long he was staying. "We're all taking the Maharishi's course for three months, including Mal, and who knows after that." He looked at me very warmly and smiled, "What about you?"
I thought for a moment, about my ex-girlfriend and the gift of meditation I'd already received, and wondered if he'd even care to hear about it all.'
'I told him about my trip, the heartbreak and how I felt about meditation. That I'd probably hang around for just a few more days. He picked up a glass of water and, after almost finishing it, said that meditation had certainly been good for him, so far. After a moment he looked at me and gently added, "Yeah, love can be pretty tough on us sometimes, can't it?" We both sat quietly. It felt like a moment suspended in time. A lone hawk circled in the sky just above us and out over the river, so close we could see its talons. I looked at John and our eyes met, and he smiled and said, almost mischievously, "But then, eventually, you get another chance, don't you?" "For sure," I said. We were silent again, and after a while John said, "Off to write me music, then."'[130]

Prudence Farrow - 'One evening, while walking from our puri to the lecture hall, John, who was wrapped like the rest of us in a blanket, peered out enthusiastically and asked if Maharishi would do mystical wizardry that night. Of course, I felt Maharishi was doing that all the time.'[32]

165

Chapter Twenty-Two
Spiritual Regeneration Worldwide Foundation of India

'We touched ground on an international runway
Jet propelled back home, from over the seas to the U. S. A.'
- Excerpt from *'Back in the U.S.A.'* by Chuck Berry

'Flew in from Miami Beach BOAC
Didn't get to bed last night'
- Excerpt from *'Back in the U.S.S.R'* by Paul McCartney & John Lennon

Mike Love - 'It was actually a teacher-training course, a gathering to train teachers of Transcendental Meditation. I didn't really realise that that was the case when I first went there, I was so new to meditation. I had only been meditating a month or two and yet I was invited to India by Maharishi, and I said "I don't know about the other guys but I'll be there" and it was really the most fascinating time of my life.
I was there at the breakfast table one morning when Paul McCartney came to the table with his acoustic guitar saying hey Michael, will you listen to this: "I flew in from Miami Beach, BOAC" and he sang me the original version of *Back in the USSR* and I told Paul: "well you ought to talk about all the girls around Russia like we talked about all the girls around the world in *California Girls*" and he did. We had a couple of nice conversations there and listened to Maharishi lecture in the afternoon and evening. It was really, really a fascinating time.'[147]

Paul - 'Mike Love sat in his place and did meditation, but what I found amusing there was that I saw him rather as the quartermaster of the camp. Because we'd all brought our cameras and film cameras and little tape recorders, and we were using a lot of movie film and we'd run out. He was to my mind the resourceful American who decided he'd hire a taxi and go to New Delhi, he'd buy up lots of the Kodak film that everyone needed, so he became like the quartermaster's stores to me. You'd go to his place and say, "You got any Kodak, Mike?" He'd say, "What do you want, Kodak II or Kodacolor?" And behind one of the curtains and in one of the wardrobes of his little Butlins chalet, he had a lot of movie film. He reminded me of a dealer. He had film and batteries and things like that, all the requirements. There wasn't a camp shop so he became the camp shop. It's like when the American army goes anywhere, there's always one guy who can get you stuff.'[6]

❀ ❀ ❀

It is lecture time and the topic this time is the nature of life. Maharishi is telling his students of a venerated statement, to be found in the ancient Vedanta texts, which states that, essentially, all is *'ananda'*, 'bliss'.
Maharishi - 'Upanishads are clear about this expression of happiness. They say.. I'll decipher for you, this..'

आनन्दाद्धयेव खल्विमानि भूतानि जायन्ते ।

आनन्देन जातानि जिवन्ति ।

आनन्दम् प्रयन्त्याभिसम्विशन्तिति ।

सैषा भार्गवी वारुणी विद्या

परमे व्योमन्प्रतिष्ठिता

'aanandaaddhayeva khalvimaani bhuutaani jaayante.
aanandena jaataani jivanti.
aanandam prayantyaabhisamvishantiti.
saishaa bhaargavii vaarunii vidyaa
parame vyomanpratishhthitaa'
[*Taittiriya Upanishad* 3:6]

'Out of *ananda* [bliss] alone, is this creation born.'
'In *ananda* alone, in reality, the whole universe is sustained.'
'In *ananda* alone, in reality, this whole creation, will eventually merge.'
'This knowledge, this reality, this realisation is established in the area beyond *akasha* [space].'[3]

Later, inside the lecture hall, Maharishi again explains the mechanics of thought in meditation.
Maharishi - 'Each thought that comes in meditation provides release of a deep-rooted stress. One thought means one stress gone, one thought means one stress gone. Many thoughts coming and going means many stresses going. So at every thought we have a reason to be happy. You see? Because, it's not a thought, it's the release of a stress. Many thoughts mean many releases have taken place. And at every release we have only reason to enjoy. Therefore, never do we feel agonised when many thoughts are coming, particularly during long meditations. Because, as the practice is growing, what is happening? The mind is becoming familiar to experience these finer states of thought. Finer states of thought are becoming clearer, clear.'[3]

Maharishi's audience is a mix, a mixture of nationalities, ages, and attitudes, but the big divide seems to be to do with drugs - between those that have taken recreational drugs and those that have not.
John - 'Without having LSD I don't think we would have understood half the things you talk about. But.. but having it, and then reading it, we knew a lot about what you were talking about... from there, we recognised it, that it had happened...'
Maharishi - 'There was that experience, some background..'
John - 'It'll change now.' (laughter)
Maharishi - 'And one dose of it, produces? Or do you have to take many doses?'
George - 'Only one.'
John - 'Depends, [if] you have a guide with you, or *guru*, or what. Someone else who has taken it, to tell you what you're experiencing, then one dose might be enough.'[3]

Bearing in mind that meditation promises none of the 'far-out' experiences of drugs, the fact that avid users of LSD are now expressing satisfaction with the effects of meditation suggests that meditation might actually alter the body's chemistry for the better.
Jenny Boyd - 'It was amazing. Just what I needed. I'd been in San Francisco taking acid and all that stuff and it had made me question a lot of things. I was very confused at the time so going to India was absolutely right for me at the time. George knew I'd had some kind of spiritual awakening and invited me. It was wonderful because there was nothing, just meditation and it was so beautiful. I loved it there.'[138]

❀ ❀ ❀

Maharishi contends that the chances of war occurring reduce significantly as the number of meditators increase, and Paul McCartney wants further explanation, he is concerned with the morality of warfare.
Maharishi - 'Yeah.'
Paul - 'Because you can't ever say "that's good"'
George - 'Highly individual.'
John - 'Paul would be coming out of it, 'cos he's an atheist.' (laughter)
Maharishi - 'War..'
Walter Koch - 'Consider just the individual, he can be considered a complex organism, whereas...'
Maharishi - 'No wars, in the sense of wars, and then, wars will not be possible..'
Paul - 'Right, well you know, what I mean is, if you've got peace and war, you know, that would feel, going together, because they are the opposites of each other. And you've got good and bad, then how's it ever going to be.. unless you do away with one of them, that bad become good?'
Maharishi - 'No, no. The war, like that international conflict, or national conflict, they are not an inevitable factor of life. They are just the accumulated tens[ions].. effects of the individual homicidal tendencies. And when the individual homicidal tendencies are missing from the individual life, then, that cloud of war will simply not be, will not rise.'
Paul - 'So, what, what, you were talking before about, the destructive thing, which will be helpful to evolution, right?'

Donovan - 'He's like a pastor.'

Maharishi - 'See the process of evolution, process of evolution is carried out by two forces. The buds gets destroyed at the same time the flowers spring out. So creation and destruction, some *tamo guna* and *sattva guna* [impure and pure qualities] that they are the fundamentals of.. of life. Even though the tendency is destructive and creative, but when they work simultaneously then the effect is evolution, evolution, evolution. The change is there, but the change is **for** evolution, evolution, evolution.'

Paul - 'Yeah.'

Maharishi - 'And that is a natural phenomenon.'

Paul - 'Yeah, so it.. there wouldn't be anything that's bad then?'

Maharishi - 'Yes.'

Paul - 'And there wouldn't be things like killing?'

Maharishi - 'Yeah, wouldn't be, Life destructs.. life supporting influence will be produced by the people. Life supporting.'

Paul - 'You don't mean that, err, you know like, there'd still be killing and there'd still be bad, but it would be good?'

Maharishi - 'No. Killing is just out of frustration, and when the frustration is missing the basis of killing will no more come. We'll be curing all ills of human society, at their source, at their basis, at their cause. Completely.'[3]

❀ ❀ ❀

Paul Saltzman - 'Early one morning I found John sitting alone at the table by the cliff, writing. We both asked for chai, and when we had finished our tea and he had stopped writing we got into a discussion about ego and altruism. I explained that at times I felt torn between these two opposing inclinations—to be constructive in society and to be self-serving. He laughed heartily.'

John - '"Good one, mate! Here's one of the great puzzles in life: How to do good for others and at the same time for yourself. And where's the line between? I still have that in me head, too," he chuckled. "I asked the Maharishi about it the other day and he said ego is not a bad thing. Actually, it's a good thing. The important thing, he said, was whether our ego manifestations result in good for others or in hurt for others. That's where you draw the line, mate. That's how you tell. Then we're doing good for others while we're doing good for ourselves." He paused and smiled. "You know, Paul, it's like the civil rights work you did. Someone said you were in the American South registering blacks for the vote a few years ago. Your civil rights work is a bloody good example of your ego doing something good for others and also feeling good about yourself at the same time."'[130]

❀ ❀ ❀

Richard Blakely - 'One afternoon, while taking the path from my room down to the kitchen, I saw Paul coming the other way. Like George, Paul was affable and friendly and eager to talk with the rest of us who had been at the ashram from the beginning. But now, picking out chords on his guitar and obviously working on a tune, he just nodded and smiled as he went by, the words that trailed behind him having something to do with revolution, well, you know…

The next day at teatime I was sitting with Paul and John and a few other SIMSers at one of the tables lining the cliff. Paul sat directly across from me, with John to his left, at the end of the table, picking out notes on his guitar and every now and then jotting things down in a little notebook with blank pages. I too had brought along a notebook, one of the small ones they had a surplus of down at the printshop and gave out free for the asking. It was a little six-by-eight inch booklet with the words "NOTE BOOK" on the cover and above that a picture of a candle and superimposed over that the enigmatic word "Manjeet" in red letters. While humming along with John, Paul picked up my notebook and began to doodle on the cover. As Paul sketched, John's strumming started turning into the song I had heard Paul practicing the day before. There were a few more stops and starts, while John took time to jot down more words and cross out others, then they both ran through the first verse of "Revolution 1."'[111]

'You say you want a revolution?
Well, you know, we all want to change the world'

- Excerpt of the lyrics of 'Revolution 1' by John Lennon and Paul McCartney

Richard Blakely - 'After the song John set down his guitar on the chair beside him and went back to jotting down notes. Paul put the finishing touches on whatever he'd been drawing on my notebook, gave it an approving nod, and leaned forward to hand it back. On one half of the cover was now a sketch of a man dressed as if he had stepped out of the eighteenth century, wearing a lace collar and a long unbuttoned coat. The man had a lot of hair and a full moustache and beard and looked a little like a cross between Paul and Maharishi, with sad eyes staring out through large round spectacles. From his right hand a bottle had just escaped, and his index finger was still pointing at it, on its way to the ground.

I studied the sketch, then looked up at Paul and said, "So you're an artist too." He gave a modest shrug. "And that song," I said. "Yesterday it was nothing. How can you guys just pull stuff out of the air like that?"

Still tuning his guitar, John peered over his glasses at me and then at Paul and said, "How do we do it, Paul?"

Paul smiled at me, the smile saying "Don't mind John, he's just that way." Then he shrugged and said, "I dunno John. How do we?"

"We just do, don't we?"

"I dare say we do."

At that point John started it on his guitar again and Paul picked up a couple of spoons and started clicking them together and they started putting to music what Paul had just said. Soon this turned into a kind of melodious chant, using a singing mantra the name of a town up the river they had recently visited, "Do-do, Dare-a-dare-a-do, Dehra-Dehra Dun, Dehra Dun-Dun…"

The little ditty took hold and gathered momentum and must have gone on for a quarter of an hour, with John on guitar and Paul on spoons and the rest of us clapping and laughing and singing along.'[111]

✿ ✿ ✿

Pattie - 'Maharishi's lectures were fascinating. He talked about the ideas behind meditation and what we should be trying to achieve, about life and astral travelling, how this can happen when you're meditating.'[21]

Per Gunnar Fjeld - 'There were regular meditation classes, and then it was extended meditations, up to several days, and some lectures. Moreover, there was some entertainment, of course. The Beatles guys performed part, and Donovan, he was very clever. The Beatles recorded songs on a tape recorder in the room, and then we got a hearing of them in the evenings. So they did not play live. But Donovan appeared several times for us, and George Harrison was very keen to learn how to play the sitar, so he played a portion for us.'[146]

> *'Can fool-around with every different cult, there's only one way brings result*
> *Get out of Sour Milk Sea, you don't belong there, get back to where you should be.'*
> - Excerpt of *'Sour Milk Sea'* by George Harrison

George - 'Anyway, it's based on Vishvasara Tantra, from Tantric art ('what is here is elsewhere, what is not here is nowhere'): it's a picture, and the picture is called *Sour Milk Sea* - Kalladadi Samudra in Sanskrit - 'the origin and growth of Jambudvita, the central continent, surrounded by fish symbols, according to the geological theory of the evolution of organic life on earth. The appearance of fishes marks the second stage.

Well, that's the origin of the song title - but it's really about meditation".

'I used *Sour Milk Sea* as the idea of - if you're in the shit, don't go around moaning about it; do something about it.'[148]

'It's a funny thing, but I wrote 'Sour Milk Sea' in Rishikesh in ten minutes. I didn't have a guitar in India, and John had a guitar, but was always playing it and there was only about ten minutes or half an hour, say, of an evening when I borrowed his guitar and wrote that song.

'Even though I was in India, I always imagined the song as rock 'n' roll. That was the intention.'[149]

Jerry Stovin is impressed with George's grasp of spiritual matters, and his ability to be able to describe the various different states of consciousness. Jerry gets on with Paul too, and suggests to him that, should he ever have a daughter, he might think of naming her Beatrice.

✿ ✿ ✿

Meanwhile, back in Europe, Yoko is living in Paris.

Yoko - 'After we first met at that gallery [the 'Indica' in 1966], we were circling round each other for about two years. I wouldn't make a move. I never did. I had left London for Paris, and John was in India. At that point, I thought we'd probably never get started.'[150]

Yoko puts on a show in Paris, and in so doing gets an introduction to a great jazz musician.
Yoko - 'Ornette [Coleman] was already very, very established and famous and respected guy as a musician. And I met him in Paris. The way I met was, I was doing a show and after the show, somebody said, Oh, Ornette Coleman is here and he would like to - okay. Well, hello. Thank you for coming. That kind of thing. And he was saying, Well, okay. So he said that he was going to go and do a concert in Albert Hall and would I come and do it with him because he thought it was kind of interesting what I do.'
'So that was London, Albert Hall. And I felt that I just kind of said goodbye to London at the time, for many reasons. But mainly because I met John. It had a lot to do with that. And I thought, Okay. I'll go back and do that because it sounds very special. So I went back to London just to do that, in a way, and also to see my daughter, who's still in London.'[151]
So, the invitation to appear in London is accepted.
Yoko - 'Fate would have it that soon, I was invited to go back to London for a performance at the Albert Hall. Of course, I took it, and went back. I opened the door to my apartment, and there were piles of letters from John, just on the floor.'[25]

On Thursday, 29th February 1968, Yoko Ono appears onstage with American jazz saxophonist, Ornette Coleman, at London's Albert Hall. The material is improvised, based on a set of instructions from Yoko Ono who handles vocals. She sings, screams, shouts and moans. The performance and the afternoon rehearsal are both recorded.

Whilst in London, Yoko Ono gravitates to The Beatles' offices, as does associate Alexis Mardas.
Tony Bramwell (Beatles' friend and employee) **-** 'They both used to hang out at the Apple Wigmore St. office in early 68! Both pains in the arse!'[38]

❂ ❀ ❂

John - '…"I'm So Tired" and "Yer Blues." They're pretty realistic, they were about me. They always struck me as - what is the word? Funny? Ironic? - that I was writing them supposedly in the presence of guru and meditating so many hours a day, writing "I'm So Tired" and songs of such pain as "Yer Blues" which I meant. I was right in the Maharishi's camp writing "I wanna die . . . "'[5]

'Yes I'm lonely, want to die
If I ain't dead already, oh girl you know the reason why'
- Excerpt of *'Yer Blues'* by John Lennon & Paul McCartney

❂ ❀ ❂

Mike Dolan - 'I was always too poor to afford a camera and somehow managed to avoid being photographed. It used to blow me away in Rishikesh how George H would take photo after photo of just about anything you put in front of him. The cost of film and processing was prohibitive never mind the camera.
Paul T and I were just about the only ones leaving the ashram on a regular basis, one of us would walk down to the village to purchase bits and pieces for the people on the course. The place was surrounded by hundreds of press people and one enterprising photographer who was working for one of the big American Mags offered me £1000 and a Hasselblad camera to expose one roll of film inside of Shankaracharyanagar. I of course said no. Weeks later when I told George the story his reaction was "you must be daft, people take pictures of us all the time, Malcolm sells his pictures of us every day."'[38]

Pattie - 'The cooks were a couple of twenty-one-year-old Australian boys, who were on their way round the world and had heard the academy needed help. Everything they cooked was vegetarian and delicious.
They produced porridge and toast for breakfast, which we would eat watched by hundreds of big black crows in the trees - they were waiting for us to leave so that they could swoop down and peck at our leftovers. Sometimes monkeys jumped on to the tables, grabbed a handful of food and bounded off.'[21]
Mike Dolan - 'I should point out that although I am a chef I never was allowed by the caste gods to actually

cook anything, that thankless task was performed by John and Lazarus in a dark hell of an unventilated room, over the one piece of equipment which was a mud fire pit that burnt logs of dried cow dung. There was no oven so if there was a cake it wouldn't hold a candle.'

'....the vegan food at Rishikesh, which was a bit of a novel concept for westerners at the time and was further complicated by Maharishi, who looked at food in terms of creating a digestive response friendly to long meditation. So he had a whole list of further restrictions like no hot spices no eggplant, no okra, no garlic and on and on. I thought under the circumstances John and Lazarus the cooks did a great job in primitive conditions. What still surprises me to this day is that no one got really seriously sick as all of the water for cooking and cleaning was cold and came from one faucet that was on top of a lead pipe that stuck out of the ground to the side of the kitchen no drainage or anything. But as Maharishi would say "Nature Supports".'[38]

'Born a poor young country boy - Mother Nature's son
All day long I'm sitting singing songs for everyone.'
- Excerpt of *'Mother Nature's Son'* by Paul McCartney & John Lennon

John - 'Paul. That was from a lecture of Maharishi where he was talking about nature, and I had a piece called I'm Just A Child Of Nature…'[15]

'On the road to Rishikesh, I was dreaming more or less
And the dream I had was true, yes, the dream I had was true'
- Excerpt of *'I'm Just a Child of Nature'* by John Lennon

Maharishi is always on call to hear about meditator's experiences and give his responses.
John - 'Whenever I meditate, there's a big brass band in me head.'
Maharishi - 'Write it down, write it down.'[112]

Mia Farrow - 'I think of John, so off-center and quick, peering out from behind his glasses; he made me laugh, which I hadn't done in a while. And at evening assembly he used to turn his chair completely around, and look at everyone. John seemed to see everything on a mystical plane and he thought of Maharishi as a kind of wizard.'[112]

Many of the songs being written evolve during rooftop sing-alongs. Paul has several ideas he is working on; there is *'Martha my dear'* and *'Silly Girl'*, and there is also *'Rocky Sassoon'*.
Paul - 'I was sitting on the roof in India with a guitar-- John and I were sitting 'round playing guitar, and we were with Donovan. And we were just sitting around enjoying ourselves, and I started playing the chords of "Rocky Raccoon," you know, just messing around. And, oh, originally it was Rocky Sassoon, and we just started making up the words, you know, the three of us-- and started just to write them down. They came very quickly. And eventually I changed it from Sassoon to Raccoon, because it sounded more like a cowboy. So there it is. These kind of things-- you can't really talk about how they come 'cuz they just come into your head, you know. They really do. And it's like John writing his books. There's no... I don't know how he does it, and he doesn't know how he does it, but he just writes. It's like any writer, you know. I think people who actually do create and write... you tend to think, "Oh, how did he do that," but it actually does flow... just flows from into their head, into their hand, and they write it down, you know. And that's what happened with this. I don't know anything about the Appalachian mountains or cowboys and indians or anything. But I just made it up, you know. And the doctor came in stinking of gin and proceeded to lie on the table. So, there you are.'[152]

'And now Rocky Raccoon, he fell back in his room only to find Gideon's Bible
Gideon checked out and he left it no doubt to help with good Rocky's revival.
Story of Rocky'
- Excerpt of *'Rocky Raccoon'* by Paul McCartney & John Lennon

Donovan - 'The press arrived *en mass*, asking, "Where's our Beatles. Where's our Donovan." After camping out for days, the press went away and we were left on our own and for the first time in probably a decade, for the Beatles, they were on their own. They were singer-songwriters again. They were free from this extraordinary celebrity and we all had the freedom and the rediscovery of one's own bohemian self, and the path was followed.'[153]

But Donovan's companion, Gypsy Dave, is less keen to stay at the academy, for though he likes the idea of meditation, and believes he knows it works, he considers he already has a spiritual life and therefore doesn't need any help from Maharishi.

Gypsy Dave - 'Anyway, another reason why I left so early was the rather stupid reason that we had forgot that Yvonne would need a visa, the fact that she was Swedish slipped our minds. In the VIP lounge a helper from the airline said, "O K so everyone is English right?" to which we replied, "Yes". Then Yvonne chirped up, "But I am Swedish", this was half an hour before the flight (we all had First Class tickets, including Don's guitar), which set the poor man into running to Indian office at the airport to do something about it. He managed to get a one or two week waiver with the proviso we must get a proper visa for her when there.[38]

bottom two photos: Paul Saltzman, All Rights Reserved

173

Gypsy Dave, Yvonne & Mal Evans, readying to leave - both photos: Paul Saltzman, All Rights Reserved

Gypsy Dave - '... I left before anyone else and at the last moment Ringo and Maureen came with us in our taxi after Maureen had come to our bungalow to ask if she could come with us to New Delhi. Ringo joined us at the last minute saying he felt the place "Rishikesh was like an Indian Butlins Holiday Camp".'[154]

Ringo - 'I didn't leave India because I've had enough of meditation, or anything like that,'
I still think the whole thing is good.'[155]

Do John, Paul or George mind that Ringo is leaving?
Ringo - 'No, we just said we're going home, and they said all right. Not one of us holds the other.'[156]

Does Maharishi know about Ringo's departure?
Ringo - 'We went to see him and he wanted us to stay because he's helping us. If you're going to learn something you might as well learn it from the boss man and he's the guv'nor.'[156]
'The Maharishi didn't really want us to leave and kept asking us if everything was all right'
'He suggested that perhaps we should go off somewhere and take a holiday and then go back to the meditation centre, but we wanted to come home.
'Really, his meditation centre is a bit like a Butlin's holiday camp. We'd been sent lists of what to take with us - like blankets and camping things - but we didn't need any of them. It's all very luxurious.
It wasn't what you'd call a hard life. We all lived in chalets and we used to get up in the morning - not particularly early - then all go down to the canteen for breakfast, then perhaps walk about a bit and meditate or bathe.
Of course, there were lectures or things all the time, but it was very much like a holiday. The Maharishi did everything he could to make us comfortable. I suppose there is a possibility we may go to his other centre in Kashmir, but I don't know yet.'[157]

photo: Per Gunnar Fjeld

Chapter Twenty-Three
Don't Care What Maha Don't Allow

Ringo - 'It was a lot of fun. Anyway, I have great memories of it. I wasn't there long. Ah, we just had a kid, so we came back. Two weeks I was there, we had life to deal with as well.'[158]

Paul - 'Ringo didn't like the flies, but it doesn't bother me too much. Maureen, Ringo's wife, apparently had every fly spotted. She knew the six flies that were in the room. There would be one above the door lintel; she knew that one was going to get her. And then there was one just by the window. She knew it and she hated it. Whereas I would just tend to take a broader view, "Ah yes, it's India, innit? They got flies here."'[6]

Flies are not the only bother though, there are the crows too.
Paul - 'People would complain, saying, "Anything we can do about the crows? They aren't 'alf distracting." And he'd say, "Well, we can only shoot them." And we'd say, "Oh no, maybe not; you know, leave 'em." So you had to deal with it yourself. I didn't mind, I figured it's got to be part of the deal, you can't shoot everything that breathes and makes a noise just because you want to meditate. I thought, I'm not sure they've got the spirit of this here. Really. Then it was "Maharishi, it's too noisy where I am to meditate," and he'd say, "Ah, don't worry about it. If you meditate well it'll go away anyway."
Then we'd meditate and he'd leave us. After one of those sessions, I remember having a great meditation, one of the best I ever had. It was a pleasant afternoon, in the shade of these big tropical trees on the flat roof of this bungalow. It appeared to me that I was like a feather over a hot-air pipe, a warm-air pipe. I was just suspended by this hot air, which was something to do with the meditation. And it was a very very blissful feeling. It took you back to childhood when you were a baby, some of the secure moments when you've just been fed or you were having your nap. It reminded me of those nice, secure feelings. And I thought, Well, hell, that's great, I couldn't buy that anywhere. That was the most pleasant, the most relaxed I ever got, for a few minutes I really felt so light, so floating, so complete.'[6]

Cynthia - '… I was not having the second honeymoon I'd hoped for. John was becoming increasingly cold and aloof towards me. He would get up early and leave our room. He spoke to me very little, and after a week or two he announced that he wanted to move into a separate room to give himself more space. From then on he virtually ignored me, both in private and in public. If the others noticed they didn't say so.
I did my best to understand, begging him to explain what was wrong. He fobbed me off, telling me that it was just the effect of the meditation.'[10]
John - 'I can't feel normal doing all this stuff. I'm trying to get myself together. It's nothing to do with you. Give me a break.'[10]

Pattie - 'Initially George and I shared one [room]. It was sparsely furnished, with two skimpy beds, but we kept disturbing each other in our meditation so we ended up with a room each; John and Cynthia were next door to us to begin with but they were not getting on well - John had met Yoko Ono - and after a week or two he moved into a room on his own.'[21]

✹ ✹ ✹

Maharishi advises his students that meditation brings about a state of mind where the mind is not so easily overshadows by circumstances. He mentions that philosophers such as Krishnamurti, Ouspensky and Gurdjeff all thought that the sense of identification was the problem, and so encouraged followers to 'remember' the Self in order to avoid the overshadowing influence of experience. Maharishi restates his teaching that only it is necessary to meditate and that to try to 'remember' the Self is not recommended.

✹ ✹ ✹

Donovan offers to put on a mini concert in the hall for Maharishi and the students. He is joined in this by a *tabla* player, who, whilst unfamiliar with the material, does his best to keep time. Donovan plays *'Magpie'*,

'First There is a Mountain', *'Pebble & the Man/ Happiness Runs'* and *'Skipalong Sam'*, and then he plays a rendering of his new song, *'Maharishi',* before delivering an enchanting version of the lyrical *'Isle of Islay'*. And when the song is over, the *tabla* player just keeps on playing, readying himself for the next performance where he will be playing accompaniment to some *sitar* playing.

In these days Donovan is working on various songs, including, *'The Sun is a Very Magic Fellow'*.
Donovan - 'Big Mal Evans, The Beatles' famous road manager, was my mate also in that holiday camp of an ashram, working together on my song "The Sun is a Very Magic Fellow". He had previously added lines to many a Beatles song.'[84]

> **'The sun is a very magic fellow he shines down on me each day.'**
> **'The moon is a very old man, livin' on the National Health'**
> - Excerpts of *'Sun Magic'* by Donovan Leitch

Donovan is also working on *'West Indian Lady'*.
'Donovan wrote West Indian Lady when he was in India studying Meditation, he actually had a poster of an Indian girl on his bedroom's wall.'[159]

> **'But he love her drawing pins and all**
> **But he love her printer's name and all'**
> - Excerpt of *'West Indian Lady'* by Donovan Leitch

Donovan - 'The yogi moved me to one of the new bungalows he had recently completed, overlooking the Ganges. The bungalow smelled of fresh wood and paint. I moved in, delighted. Next door, I discovered, was Mia Farrow. She also had just moved into one of the new bungalows. That night, beautiful Mia and I got to know each other and my obsession with Jenny ended. I found her to be an innocent and charming girl.'[84]

Coincidentally, both Donovan and Mia share a childhood problem, that of polio, a condition also known as infantile paralysis, a common ailment they suffered in common with other course members; Michael Tyne-Corbold and Ian Alford, sometimes referred to as the 'gimpy Aussies'.[38]

❀ ❀ ❀

Mia's brother, John Farrow, is also at the academy.
Donovan - 'He took me aside and showed me a great lump of hashish he had brought with him. My eyes widened as I thought of the press getting wind of it - after all, we were officially off the herb and the juice. I took it from him and flung it far into the swirling waters of the Ganges. He just stared at me.'[84]

> Among the new entrants to the ashram is Mr. Russel D. Briends of the U.S. Secret Service. He entered the ashram yesterday. Mr. Briends is staying in the inner camp of the ashram. An inmate of the ashram said he was a casual visitor.
>
> - *Times of India News Service*, Rishikesh, Sunday, 3rd March 1968

It is clear that The Beatles have been taking a lot of film footage on the course, and naturally it is conjectured that they are eventually intending to utilize it as a part of a movie. Actually it is very likely, after all it was something George Harrison appeared to be planning even from before they all left for India. And why not? Clearly, they are in a good position to make such a film, but on the basis of the lack of critical success they had with *'Magical Mystery Tour'*, would The Beatles take the risk of producing another home movie? But even if there were no other considerations, surely they must by now be aware of the long-standing plans of Paul Horn to make a documentary of the course? It is unlikely there would be interest enough in making two movies, so perhaps The Beatles and Paul Horn are joining forces? Obviously, there would be an incredible amount of interest for such a film, even if just on the basis The Beatles are in it, let alone that it is shot in the verdant Himalayas in an area of outstanding beauty with wild animals about! An Indian newspaper leaks the story, though it warns, *'Neither the Maharishi nor the Beatles were willing to confirm reports that the latter wanted to make a film on the Maharishi, the ashram and themselves.'*[160]

Tuesday, 5th March 1968.
In Squaw Valley, Calif, where the Winter Olympics were, will be an international SIMS course from 4 to 30.08.68, for students, under Maharishi's guidance.
The student leader of the United States will come next week, Jerry Jarvis. His wife is already here since the beginning of the course. They are all so natural (artless). A croupier from a casino of Las Vegas is also here. The course in Holsby [Sweden] *is from 28.7. to 10.8. In March another little Kumbha Mela will be held in Hardwar, which is nearby. I wonder whether we can go there?*

- Excerpts from a letter written by Gertrud Soares de Souza to her 19 year-old daughter, Francisca, in West Germany. Translated from German into English.

Maharishi denies Ringo disillusioned

Hindustan Times Correspondent
Lachhmanjhula, Rishikesh, March 4—Maharishi Mahesh Yogi yesterday discounted reports that Beatle Ringo Starr had quit his ashram after some disillusionment.

The Maharishi said Ringo Starr had to leave because of some urgent work and he would return to the ashram soon. Mr Malcolm Evans, manager of the Beatles, said Ringo had to leave "under pressure of his wife Maureen, who was longing to see here tiny daughter." The child could not be brought to the ashram as it was against ashram rules to admit children. Mr Evans said the Beatles were taking keen interest in meditation. Mr George Harrison have done extremely well. Mr John Lennon is also picking up meditation and would stick to complete the course. Mr Paul Macarthey might return to London for short while to fulfil some important assignment, but would be back here to complete his course."

Mr Evans, said there was no truth in the reports that the Beatles were making a commercial film on the Maharishi. "They are filming the various activities in the ashram and would produce a documentary on meditation," he added.

Hhe Maharishi said India had earned about $28,000 from 70 foreigners participating in the current course at his ashram. Each participant was required to contribute $400.

He clarified that at time of initiation every follower of transcendental movement has to contribute one week's wages "once in his or hers life time and not annually as reported." He had 150,000 regular members all over the world.

The Maharishi said he has invited 500 youngmen various parts of the country to take part an all-India convention beginning on March 17 at his ashram.

Ardh Kumbha Mela

Elsa Dragemark - 'A rumour had begun to spread within the ashram - a rumour which said that we were to go with Maharishi to Hardwar and participate in the Ardh Kumbha Mela - a religious festival celebrated every sixth year and a smaller version of the main Kumbha Mela, which is celebrated every twelfth year.'[129]

Hardwar, some 23 miles down river, is thought by some to be the greatest of all holy places, and a particularly auspicious place to bathe, especially when the sun enters the sign of Aries - a day known as Vaisakhi or Baisakhi. The 'Ardha Kumba', the occasion when Jupiter enters the sign of Aquarius, an event which occurs only once every 12 years, is regarded as highly auspicious.

In India, the equivalent to the sign of Aquarius, the water carrier, is 'Kumbha', 'the water pot'; and Ardh Kumbha means 'half pot'. And further downstream, at Allahabad, another *'mela'* (festival) is celebrated, held six years after each Ardh Kumbha, and called Kumbha Mela. Both the Ardh Kumbha Mela and the Kumbha Mela are massive events, drawing celebrants from across India and beyond.

Interestingly, all twelve signs of the zodiac are identical with their ancient Indian counterparts, with the exception of Gemini, the twins, the comparable sun sign (*rashi*) if which is Mithuna, which means 'united', 'couple' 'sexual congress' or 'a pair'.

Nancy Jackson - 'One day George Harrison wandered over to our rooms. We sat with him often at lunch and talked about life. This day he had a particular request.

In his gentle way he asked a favor of me: "Nancy, this means a lot to me; please convince Maharishi to let us go to the *Kumbha Mela* on our own." (This is a special religious gathering of holy men in Rishikesh and Hardwar that takes place every six years.) "He insists that we go on elephants."

His brown eyes were earnest, "Being a Beatle is already seeing life from the back of an elephant; we want to mix with the crowds. Maybe I'll find Babaji (a famous Indian saint) sitting under a tree."'[117]

But Donovan's mind is evidently on other matters.
Donovan - 'I didn't miss the alcohol, didn't miss the street, didn't miss the hashish. I missed a lover's bleat, I missed a lover's bleat. Yes, in all this meditation I still felt sexual desire. Surely this was a sin in an ashram? But then again, lovely young women were walking about the place in the most scanty apparel.'[84]

According to Donovan, Pattie Boyd's request to go into town is refused by Maharishi.

Donovan - 'When pressured for a reason why the girls could not visit the vicinity of the Ganges that day, Maharishi gave in and explained.'

Maharishi - 'If you walk today by the caves of the Swamis in your miniskirts you will become a great temptation. Today, the Swamis who have been meditating for many years in their caves will be coming out, and I cannot be responsible for their actions.'[84]

So it seems that today is a particularly significant day amongst local holymen. In all probability the *sadhus* are getting ready to attend the Ardh Kumbh Mela festival in Hardwar.

When night comes there is a surprise, for it seems there is to be a moonlit outing on the river. The students climb into boats which float off onto the river; Donovan and The Beatles sing *'Happiness', 'Maharishi'* and *'Such a Joy'*.

Monday, 4th March 1968, 11pm.

Dear Francisca, before the experience of that night will be blurred by other experiences, I must tell thee: We were sitting at dinner when Mike Love (Beach Boy) arrived and said: We take the boat on the Ganges and those who are not just meditating, can come. He beamed at us with his blue eyes, so that we did not know really whether we should believe him or not. But I quickly ran to my room and took my scarf, just in case.
At the gate that leads into the forest, we met, and there was the truck, on the floor cloths and a few pillows. Maharishi stood by: "Get in quick". Over a chair I climbed up. Inside we sat there packed like sardines and then it shook and bounced on the dirt road through the jungle.
When getting out, I was glad about the flashlight, because it was quite steep down to Ganges, the stairs often irregular and high.
We went with Maharishi on the boat, Mia Farrow was there, Donovan had his guitar. Maharishi had brought some singing monks who came here from Benares. They were now singing their sacred songs in the

night. Donovan sang and played guitar and the Beatles and we sang with him - the engine was turned off and we glided in the flow - the crescent lying over us and countless stars. On the riverside the lights of Rishikesh. We got sweets offered on large trays - great tasting, sugar, milk and coconut.

Meanwhile, the truck was driven back and had brought more people who came in our direction in a second boat from shore. Mike Love was at the front of the boat in his bright red bathrobe, the white pith helmet and white wide Indian trousers. He is really worth seeing with his red full beard! He played on an Indian flute. The joy was great when both boats were together. A couple was separated, Rai sat with us, so we called to Walter and he went over in our boat.

Donovan sang with his enchanting voice and Mia and the Beatles joined in. Moon, stars and the gentle gurgling of the Ganges. Christel next to me said, "It's like a dream!" Mia gave me her blanket because my scarf was not warm enough, she said. Everybody cares for everybody. All these young brilliant people in the academy! The heart is full to overflowing. Maharishi speaks to us: "It is such a joy!" The Beatles made a song about it. The time is so precious here, and I do not want to waste it by writing.

- Excerpts from a letter written by Gertrud Soares de Souza to her 19 year-old daughter, Francisca, in West Germany. Translated from German into English.

'After dark to Ganges with Maharishi and pandits - Beatles with ashram songs "Such a joy, such a joy, joy"'
- Carole Hamby's diary

Pattie - 'Every so often a tailor would appear and we would get him to make clothes for us. We all wore pyjama trousers and big baggy shirts, and the boys grew beards. It was baking hot during the day so you had to wear loose, flowing Indian clothes. After four in the afternoon it could get quite cold, and when it rained there was no hot water. One evening Maharishi organised boats to take everyone on a trip down the river while two holy men chanted. Then George and Donovan started to sing, and we all joined in with a mixture of English and German songs. It was so beautiful, with mountains on three sides of us. In the setting sun the one to the west turned a deep, deep pink.'[21]

❀ ❀ ❀

Lewis Lapham - 'Walking through the vegetable garden, I encountered Mia Farrow playing with a flower and smiling at her own secrets. She thought she'd heard the scream of a wild peacock in the woods, she said, and George Harrison had promised to teach her the guitar. Unhappily, she had to go to London next week, to do a movie with Elizabeth Taylor, but she knew she would come back to India, and maybe she would buy a place near Bombay.'[55]

Nancy Jackson - 'As for Mia, she soon had to leave to make a film in England with Richard Burton, and was in the process of getting ready for her departure. The tailor was busy for days making a gown out of Kashmir shawls for her to wear on the trip to London.'[117]

Cynthia Lennon and Donovan, both former art students, are particularly keen to create carefully thought out ideas for new clothes. Customers of the tailor use a hardback notebook in which to draw designs of the clothes they want him to make, and the book slowly fills with curious and beautiful designs.

❀ ❀ ❀

Thursday, 7th March 1968 - London Airport.
Reporter - 'Miss Farrow, could you tell us how you found the Maharishi place? What was it like?'
Mia Farrow - "Erm? It's been the most rewarding experience of my life, I think.'
Reporter - 'Ringo, Beatle Ringo said it was a bit like a holiday camp.'
Mia Farrow - 'Yeah, he said he didn't like the food, I loved the food. "Holiday camp"? In what way?'
Reporter - 'Well, he said it was a bit too much organised, perhaps.'
Mia Farrow - 'No. No, no, not at all. No, it was a very happy place.'
Reporter - 'People seem to get the impression that the Maharishi is in business rather than meditation, flying around in a helicopter, this sort of thing.'

Mia Farrow - 'No, He's getting planes and helicopter because he has to cover a lot of territory in India, which, by road would take him many, many more years than he has to spare. Erm.. he's going back into seclusion, as I suppose you know, er.. very soon, like in about a year's time, a year or two. So he has a lot of work to do, you know, what with training everyone, and he plans to visit all, every province in India. So that's the reason for the plane, and if you'd been on Indian roads you'd know what I meant.'
Reporter - 'What can meditation do to help your career?'
Mia Farrow - 'Oh, I don't know, um, it helps your general well-being because you go right to the source of thought, the source of creativity, the source of happiness. And think clearer, act clearer. You have the power of all that is, behind you really. I mean you can't make a mistake...'
Reporter - 'Are you absolutely happy..?'
Mia Farrow - '.. that's when it gets better.'
Reporter - 'Can I ask you? Are you absolutely happy in your own mind that you're not being conned, that you're not being taken in?'
Mia Farrow nods and smiles - 'Yes!' (nods and smiles some more)[3]

❀ ❀ ❀

John writes a postcard to Hunter Davies, who is The Beatles' official biographer. The card is addressed to '*HUNTER + THINGY DAVIES*' and postmarked 'CAMP P.O. 7MAR68'.[75]

Dear Hunters
Thanks for letter. Wish you here there and everywhere. Many blessings on you - may all your children.
Lots of love and maybe see you - its gear world.
John+Cyn x .

John sends lots of cards and letters, and he receives post too, including letters from Yoko Ono.
John - 'Then I went to India with the Maharoonie and we were corresponding. The letters were still formal but they just had a little side to them.'[5]
'… while I was in India she began writing to me: "I am a cloud. Watch for me in the sky."'
'I would get so excited about her letters. There was nothing in them that wives or mothers-in-law could have understood, and from India, I started thinking of her as a woman and not just an intellectual...'
'I kept telling her to meditate too, you know...'[19]

Friday, 8th March 1968.
Paul McCartney writes a postcard to Ringo, addressed to '*MR. & MRS. R. STARKEY*'.[61]

Everything here is still going well, except we miss you both. John and George have each done 7 hours, but we've only managed 2 ½ so far, but we're hoping to do longer ones before we leave. The weather is getting hotter, and there have been complaints about mosquitoes, so Mo isn't the only one. Mia left yesterday and Mal today - latest news is that Maharishi's building a swimming pool! Much love. Paul + Jane.

Many of the course participants, and especially the younger ones, the SIMSers, can't resist the lure of bathing in the refreshing cool water of the Ganges.

Pattie - 'As the days got hotter the cool water in the river was delicious. It moved so fast that you could sit on it, quite literally, and it would take you along as if you were on a chute. George disapproved - he thought it far too frivolous. He never knew that one day when I was in the river I lost my wedding ring. I panicked. George would be so furious. Johnny Farrow was with me and we looked and looked, I was convinced in vain but miraculously, after about twenty minutes, he had it in his hand.'[21]

The Beatles have been shooting vast quantities of 16mm film during their meditation visit to India, and this may subsequently be edited into a documentary feature about the Maharishi Mahesh Yogi. National Press reports, suggesting the group is to produce a professionally directed film of the Maharishi were denied this week.
A spokesman told the NME: "The end product of all this filming may be nothing more than home movies - but if the Beatles consider it worth while, they will make their film available for public viewing."

- New Musical Express - NME[161]

So, if The Beatles really are making a movie about Transcendental Meditation, what about a record too? According to the music press, *'The Beatles are likely to contribute a track to an all-star charity LP now in preparation. Probable choice would be an already-recorded John Lennon composition "Across the Universe".*[161] So it seems that John has decided to let Spike Milligan have a version of the song, after all.

❀ ❀ ❀

Jenny Boyd is not well - '…I was meditating almost all the time, and getting quite hot, like I had a fever. It turned out to be dysentery, but the local doctor diagnosed tonsillitis. I sat with John Lennon a lot, since he didn't feel well either from terrible jet lag and insomnia. He would stay up late, unable to sleep, and write the songs…'
'When I was at my lowest, he made a drawing of a turbaned Sikh genie holding a big snake and intoning, "By the power within, and the power without, I cast your tonsil lighthouse out!"…'[162]

❀ ❀ ❀

Joe Lysowski (a 'psychedelic' artist from Haight-Ashbury) - 'I left for India that first time in 1967. I wanted to go where the Maharishi was and maybe do meditation. I met a man down by the river; and it turned out to be Mike Love of the Beach Boys. He said "Come with me, you can sleep overnight at my place and I'll take you in the morning into the Maharishi's."'[163]

Joe has a travelling companion, his wife Wendy Winkler.
Joe Lysowski - 'Mike took us up to the Maharishi Mahesh Yogi's ashram, where a select group of people were meeting and I thought that these vibrado were going to change the world through meditation. Mike took us up to his cottage where we slept out on the roof together and he introduced us to the Maharishi who gave us jobs to do in return for our mantras, Hindu holy words of vibration. I was to help as a painter on the portraits of his guru, known as Guru Dev, that were being painted by his uncle the Dr. Raj Varma. I believe he was called an old man that talked about Ayervedic medicine and well-being.'
'We were given a large paisley tent to stay in and went to have meals in the small cafe above the Ganges.'
'Often I'd meet with Donovan, a British singer, and he'd tell his tales of Atlantis and the lost lands there to me.'[164]

'All the gods who play in the mythological dramas
In all legends, from all lands, were from far Atlantis'

- Excerpt of *'Atlantis'* by Donovan Leitch

Donovan - 'As the soft evenings descended on the ashram we would slowly gather around the lecture hall and await the arrival of the Maharishi to speak to us and extol the virtues of meditation. One such evening, Paul was finishing a cigarette as I stood by the doors of the lecture hall. The Yogi was approaching. Paul said, "Fags out, boys, 'ere comes the teacher".'[84]
Joe Lysowski - 'So I spent days painting with the doctor and Wendy [Winkler] would be tinting photos for amulet of the Maharishi to be given to the guests of the ashram who were there at that time, the Beatles, George, Paul and John. Ringo had already returned back to London. There were also several British ladies that had been witches in London, as I recall, and a lady opera singer and various other people about. Two young Brits were the cooks for the Western group and meals were very bland, veggies with rice or dal, and later at tea in the afternoons we'd meet for tea and Paul McCartney would often be there with his guitar to sing some of the new songs they'd been writing. I can remember one called *Happy Restaurant* and another called *Jai Guru Deva* which went like this: "We want to thank you, Guru Dev, for being so kind to us. Jai Guru Dev, Jai Guru Dev, we want to thank you Guru Dev." It went on and on! I had a bit of it recorded once, with Bob from George's

birthday party where Paul gave him a tambura? (tanpura) that played a melodic background sound sort of like a droning aum, and looked like a sitar.'[164]

Cynthia Lennon, Pattie Boyd, Joe Lysowski, Wendy Winkler & Richard Blakely

Christel Thiele, John Lennon & Edna Linnell

Back: Sarah Sadowski, Jenny Boyd, Donovan, Wendy Winkler & Joe Lysowski. Front: Edna Linnell, Roz Bonas, John Lennon, Sundar Singh & Mike Dolan.

Donovan - 'One day I was sitting playing my guitar on John's patio, while he was sitting next to me washing his hair. Suddenly he leapt to his feet, effing and blinding as he chased a photographer intent on getting a photo. This incident upset John, who gave the photographer such a chase and a tongue-lashing I guess he'll never forget it. John then stormed off to the Maharishi's bungalow and gave him a piece of his mind also. The Maharishi laughed and the day went on its own inimitable way.'[84]

Joe Lysowski - 'John kept mostly to himself, occasionally sitting out on the stairs to his *pattis*(?) cottage. Brushing his wet hair in the sun and making funny comments.'[164]

Mike Dolan - 'The couple next to Donovan I believe were Americans, I think he designed sound stages, they were only there for a few days.'[38]
And speaking of Donovan..
Mike Dolan - 'Lovely guy, total minstrel saint.'[38]

❀ ❀ ❀

Joe Lysowski - 'Everyone thought I was George in India.'[38]

'No one will be watching us
Why don't we do it in the road?'
- Excerpt from *'Why Don't We Do It In The Road?'* by Paul McCartney & John Lennon

Paul - 'I was up on the flat roof meditating and I'd seen a troupe of monkeys walking along in the jungle and a male just hopped on to the back of this female and gave her one, as they say in the vernacular. Within two or three seconds he hopped off again, and looked around as if to say, "It wasn't me," and she looked around as if there had been some mild disturbance but thought, Huh, I must have imagined it, and she wandered off. And I thought, bloody hell, that puts it all into a cocked hat, that's how simple the act of procreation is, this bloody monkey just hopping on and hopping off. There is an urge, they do it, and it's done with. And it's that simple. We have horrendous problems with it, and yet animals don't. So that was basically it.'[6]

Joe Lysowski - 'Paul had a big crush for Wendy [Winkler].'[38]

❀ ❀ ❀

Richard Blakely - 'During a recent lecture, Maharishi had said that we were all swamis, at least potentially, since "swami" simply meant teacher, which was what we were all in training to become.
Paul and John's little ditty, that they performed at the end of the long outside table, was a variation on "Mama don't allow." Paul introduced it with "A one, and a two, and a…"

    Maha don't allow no swamis swimmin' in here
    Maha don't allow no swamis swimmin' in here
    I don't care what Maha don't allow,
    Swami gonna swim here anyhow!'[111]

Brahmacharis and students gathered on the terrace of Maharishi's residence

Chapter Twenty-Four
Beggars in a Goldmine

Donovan - 'One day we were called to the flat roof of the Maharishi's bungalow. He wanted to know how we were doing with "sitting". John told him that he sometimes found it hard not to write songs when he was in deep meditation and asked what he should do. The yogi laughed and said John should slowly come out of the meditation, write the song down and return to the mantra. This pleased John.'[84]

❀ ❀ ❀

Donovan - 'Some afternoons we would gather at one of our pads and play the acoustic guitars we had all brought with us. Paul Horn, the American flute wizard, was there. John was keen to learn the finger-style guitar I played …'[6]

John - 'How do you do that?'
Donovan - 'It's a pattern. Wanna learn?'
John - 'Yeah, I would. When do we start?'
Donovan - 'Right now if you like. Here, lemme show you. It'll take a few days, though.'
John - 'I've got days.'[84]

Donovan - 'As John was in this period of tuition with me, he told me he wanted to write a song about his mother.'[165]

Mike Dolan - 'So I arrange his [John's] cuppa and go back to the table and he's deep into my book. He was very enthusiastic about the book and asked could he borrow it. What do you say? "Sure take it."' [38]

'Half of what I say is meaningless, but I say it so that the other half may reach you'
'When life does not find a singer to sing her heart she produces a philosopher to speak her mind'.
- Excerpts of *'Sand & Foam'* by Khalil Gibran (1926)

'Half of what I say is meaningless, but I say it just to reach you, Julia'
'When I cannot sing my heart, I can only speak my mind.'
- Excerpts from *'Julia'* by John Lennon & Paul McCartney

Mike Dolan - 'Half of What I say is Meaningless' ('Julia'), that one is borrowed from Gibran, borrowed from Jehar and borrowed from Dolan.'[38]

In the new song, *'Julia'*, John includes the phrase; *"ocean child, calls me"*. So, what or who is an *'ocean child'* then? Intriguingly, 'Ocean child' is precisely what Yoko Ono's Japanese name means in English.

洋子 Yoko; *'yo'* = 'ocean' + *'ko'* = 'child'

Donovan - 'I asked him what exactly it was that he wanted to do. He said, "I want to write a song about the childhood that I never really had with my mother." He asked me to help him with the images that he could use in lyrics for a song about this subject. So I said, "Well, when you think of the song, where do you imagine yourself?" And John said, "I'm at a beach and I'm holding hands with my mother and we're walking together." And I helped him with a couple of lines, "Seashell eyes / windy smile" - for the Lewis Carroll, *Alice in Wonderland* feel that John loved so much.'[165]

Donovan - '... one day in the ashram when we were sitting playing music after our day of meditation, I said, "You four are so famous you don't need to have a photo or a name on your next album, just make it plain white no name, everyone will know its you." George smiled.'[166]

Monday, 11th March 1968.
Dorothy Harrison is Colin's mother. I knew it already from previous courses in Hochgurgl, but did not know that they belong together. Pat Harrison, George's wife is here, all the Beatles' girls are sweet creatures. Another famous person arrived now, but I do not know who he is.

In my block are mostly old ladies: Dorothy Harrison, Reumah from Israel, Anneliese Brown (mother of Ruth the healer), Christel, PH [teachers college] *student from Hamburg, Edna from Australia, Della from Las Vegas, Joan from Kenya, Valerie from Algeria-England, Margret, nurse from Los Angeles, Kiram, a poet from Ireland, Ian, a Hippy, very pleasant and intelligent, from Australia, Benita and I. In Traude's block almost all are men.*

- Excerpts from a letter written by Gertrud Soares de Souza to her 19 year-old daughter, Francisca, in West Germany. Translated from German into English.

On Tuesday, 12th March 1968, Swami Bhaktivedanta, the leader of the 'Hare Krishna' mission, speaks on the radio in San Francisco.

Interviewer - 'The whole world has heard of the Maharishi Mahesh. Is he part of your order?'

Bhaktivedanta - 'No. I have heard so much in the paper.'

Interviewer - 'He is the world's most famous *guru* at the present time.'

Bhaktivedanta - 'He's not *guru*. But he's advertised his name like that (laughs). A guru is different thing. But people are, in your country, in the western part of the country, of the world, people are after some spiritual information. So anyone who comes professing as spiritualist, he is welcome, and if he flatters, then it is very convenient to get followers. So we don't follow exactly in that way. We follow exactly the principles of Vedic ways of life. So in that way, sex life for a sannyasi is strictly prohibited.'

Interviewer - 'So many of the people are going to him for meditation. Is meditation part of your philosophy?'

Bhaktivedanta - 'Yes. But meditation as this Maharishi or any other swami or..., are professing, that is not exactly the process of meditation. The standard meditation is described in Bhagavad-gita. That is very difficult job. You have to select a solitary place, you have to sit in a certain posture, you have to regulate your life, complete celibacy, eating, sleeping... There are so many rules and regulations that that sort of meditation is absolutely impossible for the present way of life. For the present generation, the chanting, vibration of holy name of God, is recommended in the scriptures. It is said that meditation was possible in the Satya-yuga, when people were cent [100] percent pure. And they are... For the present, mostly, people are impure. So they cannot execute meditation as it is described in the standard scriptures.'

Interviewer - 'Is yoga part of meditation?'

Bhaktivedanta - 'Yoga is a very broad term. Yoga means to connect with the Absolute Truth. That is yoga. Yoga means connecting link. So there are different varieties of yoga. Just like one staircase, it is the connecting link to the top floor. So that is, everywhere you can say staircase, but one who has crossed a few steps and one who has crossed a few floors, they are not on the same level.'[167]

'Rishikesh, hot-bed of espionage'
The FPJ News Service

NEW DELHI, March 13: Rishikesh has become a hot-bed of espionage thronged by Beatles yearning for Nirvana and intelligence agents nibbling at India's security, Left Communist member K. Anirudhan complained in the Lok Sabha today.

He urged on the Government to investigate into the reported recovery of a high power transmitter belonging to a foreigner from a hut near the antibiotic factory in Rishikesh.

He referred to the reports of some American intelligence agent staying in the ashram of Mahesh Yogi and said that Rishikesh had become a very sensitive spot now.

On Wednesday, 13th March 1968, a Post Office Overseas Telegram is sent to Denis O'Dell of Apple Films, concerning movie negotiations.[168]

```
                    NNNN

     - MR 13 23 03

     ZCZC LLG2493 NLA445
     SWARGASHRAM 25 13 1440

     DENIS O DELLAPPLE FILMS 95 WIGMORE STLONDON W1 ENGLAND

     COME TO ACADEMY RISHIKESH ASSOON AS POSSIBLE

     FILM DEALS BEING NEGOTIATED URGENT LOVE FROM THE
     BEATLES

     COL 0 95 W1
```

And Paul writes a postcard to his brother, Mike, in Cheshire, England, wishing him well with the new record by his group, The Scaffold. The single *Do You Remember?'* is to be released on 15th March 1968.[169]

Dear Mike, + Ange
As you have heard it's sunny peaceful here and both of us.
We hope record is a record of instant hit beauty for Christ's sake, you know. Here at Skegnes the sky is blue
- we knew just what to do. Love from your bosom buddies Paul + Jane

Donovan and Paul Horn take a short car trip out from Maharishi's academy, in a roomy white Ambassador saloon to Dehra Dun where they intend to drop in at Nanhi Duniya Badhir Vidyalaya - The 'Little World' School for the Deaf, founded in 1946 by Professor Lekh Raj Ulfat and currently run by Phyllis Rodin, an energetic New Yorker in her mid-50's.

Donovan - 'The day arrived for our trip up-country, and John Farrow would join Paul Horn and me to film on his Super-8 camera. I would record the music on my tape machine. We would travel by car to the town of Dehra Dun, there to visit a school for the deaf that was run by an energetic American lady.'
'There, standing in a run-down colonial garden, our hostess introduced us to the smiling students, all Indian boys, all deaf.
Then she took us on a tour of the classrooms and showed us the out-of-date headphones which were used and the simpler balloons which the students would make ba-ba sounds with, pressing their lips to the stretched rubber. The children were also put through their Hatha Yoga postures. The woman shouted to them what to do. It seemed that they could hear *something*, or perhaps it was just the wave of good cheer emanating from their mistress that vibed them. They loved her so.'[84]
'… and then, she turned around to Paul and I and said, "OK, play for the children." And I looked around to Paul, and he looked at me, and said, "They're deaf, right?" So I started playing, and the children started moving to the tempo.'[170]
'The long sonorous notes of his alto flute filled the air and I joined him on guitar, singing one of my little tunes for the kids. Immediately they ran to me and pressed their fingers against the sound box, moving in time to the beat. They could hear (or feel) the music quite well. Marvellous.'[84]

❀ ❀ ❀

Back at the academy, one of the students shares some gossip he has heard.
Terry Gustafson- 'Did you hear that a tiger or leopard ate the kitchen goat outside the compound last night?'[117]

❀ ❀ ❀

Dear Virginia
'... things seem to get weirder and clearer here every day,
'One minute I'm crying and weeping and the next I'm laughing hysterically.
'I'm writing in my little room, with incense burning to keep away the bugs. I have pictures of Maharishi all over my walls, a tea pot empty, honey jars, limes, tangerines, mangoes, paint box, cushions wooden bed, oh dear, oh dear, oh dear, I can't stop laughing. Virginia,
'We can't get away from problems in this relative life of ours, so what is the answer? Get to a field, a level of consciousness, where there are no problems, and when you come back again on a different level, your mind just goes there, straight to the source of the problem, I'm telling you. Anyway, I keep finding the problem has been solved during meditation, either in my own thoughts or if it has lain outside me, kind of it's solved itself.
'M is beyond recognition, one of the several miracles taking place here. The Maharishi is pleased with her progress, her face is so beautiful, she's calm, walks differently, her pain in the shoulder is practically gone and she's beautiful, wow!
'Peoples' faces, relaxed and clear. So many amazing things are worked out during meditation, and it's kind of fun.
'All this fuss and stuff, what is important, the only thing, is to go and get that mantra, that word and repeat morning and evening and find 'heaven' as you put it. That's all it entails.
'It's Mike Love of the Beachboys birthday tomorrow, a nice guy - the Beatles and wives are all so natural and meditate a lot and Donovan is something else, such beautiful songs, he feels he was living as a minstrel in the Arthurian times, is that where I've met him before?
'Mia Farrow cooled down the last few days and was really sweet.
Lots of love
V.

- excerpts of a letter sent by Viggie Litchfield to Virginia Clive-Smith in London (as reprinted in OZ magazine).171

Millie Drummond - 'Wow what a beautiful letter from Viggie, bless her...'
'I think I am the M that Viggie refers to as I've always had a bad shoulder since one of many really bad falls off ponies...'38

Full moon celebration of Holika Dahan (the night before Holi)

14th March - full moon with boat rides on the Ganges. Donovan and George sang then Paul

- Carole Hamby's notes

On Thursday, 15th March 1968, Neil Aspinall, a close assistant of The Beatles, flies out to India.

Holi celebrations
The day after the March full moon is the celebration of the Holi festival, which marks the triumph of righteousness over unrighteousness, of the saving of Prahlad, the youngster who would not give up his faith in the Supreme.

Commonly, Holi is also a day when it is seen to be okay to go out and spray washable colours on other people's clothes and faces. At Shankaracharya Nagar there is a whole lot of colourising going on outside the main dining area, where a group of meditators including Paul McCartney, Jane Asher, Donovan, Mike Love Andreas Müller, Geoffrey Baker, Roz Bonas, Abe Jehar and Sarah Sadowski, along with reporter Saeed Naqvi, dart about daubing one another's faces with red paste.

Guru Dev speaking about 'Holi'

'The coloured powder etc. on the day of Holi is a way of showing happiness. Meeting one another, this causes them to share the good news that today - on this very day - that having given hardship to the devotee of Bhagwan [the Supreme] the demoniacal energy became burned to ashes. The celebration is that the ogress that showed malevolence towards the devout Prahlad was turned to ashes. This is the value of Holi.'[79]

❀ ❀ ❀

Terry Gustafson - 'John Lennon came up to me outside the lecture hall one night. I was dressed like an off-duty park ranger: short hair and khakis. John had his hair dyed five different colors, wore a paisley cape, an Indian shirt, a red sash around his waist, exaggerated white bell-bottom pants and green Egyptian slippers with curled-up toes. With tiny strobe lights built into his eyeglasses, flashing on and off as he entered the semi-dark lecture hall with his cape flowing behind him, he presented quite an image.
"Look at you!" "Look at me!", he exclaimed. "One of us don't belong 'ere." "Get back to the forest! Get back to Tucson Arizona! Get back where you belong!" (I had grown up in Tucson and moved to California.)
He told me to "Get back!" now and then after that, when we happened to meet.'[172]

'Look at me, what am I supposed to be?'
- Excerpt of lyrics of *'Look At Me'* by John Lennon

'Jojo left his home in Tucson, Arizona'
'Get back to where you once belonged'
- Excerpts of lyrics of *'Get Back'* composed by John Lennon and Paul McCartney

Today is Mike Love's 27th birthday, and there is to be a big celebration in the evening, as has become the custom for all birthday boys and girls.

photo: Per Gunnar Fjeld

Donovan and Paul Horn collaborate tonight on a gentle song entitled, *'The Continuing Story of a Shy Little Girl'*; the duo working as though destiny has brought them together, quite a delight. They follow this number with a jazz instrumental, a composition entitled *'Cat Tune'* and then perform a rendering of Donovan's *'Sun is a Very Magic Fellow'*. For another of his new compositions, *'Maharishi'*, Donovan plays alone. But then Paul returns for the finale of *'Happiness Runs'*, and Maharishi even adds an extra verse, which ends with, '.. makes happiness a reality on the day when happiness really runs around you.'[3]

Then it's Paul McCartney's turn to entertain; he plays and sings a new number of his, a meditation song dedicated to Guru Dev called *'Thank You Guru Dev'* which he segues into a rousing *'Happy Birthday Mike'* type song. Both pieces are played in typical Beach Boys style, à la Chuck Berry, and a chorus of stars are on hand to assist Paul.

'We'd like to thank you Guru Dev
Just for being our guiding light
Guru Dev, Guru Dev, Guru Dev
We'd like to thank you Guru Dev
For being up through the night
The Spiritual Regeneration Worldwide Foundation - of India
A-B-C-D E-F-G H-I   Jai Guru Dev.'

This happy song finishes with a flourish of acoustic guitar; da, da, da, da, da, da, da, janggg![3]

And then of course there is cake, and Mike makes a speech, which Carole Hamby takes note of; *'Mike Love's birthday - Indian songs general singing/chanting. Donovan and Paul Horn playing. Mike love said that he wanted "to tour the world on behalf of SRM (the Spiritual Regeneration Movement) and he planned to present a festival of theatre arts of world peace through TM."'*[173]

John has a home made circular card for Mike, a simple pen and ink self-portrait of himself naked with a slightly podgy stomach, and around the edge of the card, in spidery lower case letters, the message:- [75]

'goodbye and see you round the world or somewhere if not england or the disunited states with love to dear mike love from dear john lennon'

The evening finishes with fireworks at the kitchen above the Ganges

And Maharishi invites Mike to his bungalow where he performs *puja* for him.
Mike Love - 'Maharishi reached over with his left hand and patted me on my neck three times, and I'll never forget what he said.'
Maharishi - 'You will always be with me.'[199]

After celebrating his birthday, Mike Love now intends to leave India in order to join The Beach Boys for a forthcoming Stateside tour. But he takes with him at least a couple of ideas for new compositions; the fragments of *'Transcendental Meditation Can Emancipate the Man'* and fond impressions of fellow meditator Anneliese Braun, who he immortalises in the lyrics of *'Anna Lee the Healer'*.

> *'Healer with the healing hands*
> *Makes you well as quick as she can'*
>
> - Excerpt of *'Anna Lee the Healer'* by Brian Wilson & Mike Love

❀ ❀ ❀

On Monday, 17th March 1968, the 'All India Convention' is being convened at the academy, and Maharishi gives four lectures during the day.

In the evening there are two birthdays to celebrate - Pattie Harrison's 24th and Paul Horn's 38th - and the plan is to have a special *puja*, and some entertainment, music and fireworks.

AT A BEATLE BIRTHDAY PARTY By NICHOLAS NUGENT, an English teacher in India

The occasion of Patti Harrison's birthday and that of jazz flautist and meditator Paul Horn, who shared her birthdate (although some 14 years her senior), was one of the outstanding memories the Beatles, Donovan and Mike Love have of their visit to Maharishi's Meditation centre. Here then is my eye witness account of the event.

The party commenced on the Maharishi's arrival with prayers for which the company stood and listened silently to the chantings of their guru (Indian teacher). All formality was after abandoned and the company sang "Happy Birthday" to both Patti and Paul, who sat cross-legged on the stage behind their birthday cake.

Patti was wearing an attractive mauve sari and Paul adorned in an India "kurta" with the words "Paul" painted on the front and "Jai Guru Dev" (long live Guru Dev, the Maharishi's own guru) on the back. The robe was a present from Paul McCartney and Jane Asher, who had painted it for him.

Jane Asher helped Paul cut his cake and distribute it among the assembly. Then Paul presented Patti with a birthday present - a "dilruba" which is a narrow string instrument played with the bow, similar to a cello.

I understand she plays it very well, although we were not able to confirm that. It was George and Paul who demonstrated the method of playing and Paul finally surrendered the instrument declaring "I think I'll give it up!"

'Queen' on sitar

George then sent for his sitar - the most popular of the Indian instruments - and played one or two "ragas" (Indian melodies) and followed this, to the delight of us all, with a rendering of "God Save The Queen." Paul accompanied him by strumming on a tamboura (Donovan's, in fact, the one he had bought that morning). John spent his time discussing his progress in meditation with "Abe" a tall American meditator.

Fireworks

Music finally gave way to fireworks for which we all went outside. This was the third time in three weeks that a firework display had been given in honour of a birthday, George had celebrated his birthday three weeks earlier and Mike Love only two days previous.

The evening finished with a conjuring display from an Indian magician who, like us, had journeyed over that day from Dehra Dun. The Beatles gave a helping hand when an assistant was required but remained as baffled as us all by the "metal hoops" trick and others. Donovan was asked to assist in a turn in which the conjuror's assistant was supposedly hypnotised on stage. He had one of the Maharishi's "sadhus" in fits of laughter. I never thought a monk could laugh so much.

We paid the price of our entertaining evening when we found that we were unable to find transport back to Dehra Dun and as we all spent five hours waiting in a Rishikesh all night tea shop!

The meditators for all their deep concern with their efforts to obtain "Bliss Consciousness" seem to enjoy their seclusion. The only obvious draw-back seems to be food, which, although English style, and prepared by an English chef, they seem to find inadequate judging by the fairly frequent appearances of the Beatles with their wives and girl friends at Nagoli's in Dehra Dun!

- *New Musical Express* - NME, 20th April 1968.

George, Pattie, John, Nicholas Nugent, Ajit Singh, and Steve Browne

lower photo: Per Gunnar Fjeld

195

upper and lower photos: Per Gunnar Fjeld

photo: Per Gunnar Fjeld

Donovan - 'George had brought in Indian instruments to the ashram in Rishikesh and he gave me a tamboura, the Indian bass instrument.'[174]

✹ ✹ ✹

Caste gods of the kitchen
Mike Dolan - 'I should point out that although I am a chef I never was allowed by the Caste gods to actually cook anything, that thankless task was performed by John and Lazarus in a dark hell of an unventilated room, over the one piece of equipment which was a mud fire pit that burnt logs of dried cow dung. There was no oven so if there was a cake it wouldn't hold a candle.'[38]

Cabin fever
Paul - 'Because you weren't allowed to go out, you actually had to ask permission, "Can I go into New Delhi, Maharishi?" "Why?" I was standing there, tending to think, Why not? - you know, I thought, I'm going to sag off. So I got down to the Ganges a few afternoons. I remember playing by the banks of the Ganges, which was rather nice, just like a kid, it was such a nice day. I just thought, I'd rather be on holiday.'[6]

Joe Lysowski - 'I keep thinking about the first time we met Paul. It was after walking down a long path to the river, where we could sit nude and not be seen and swim in the river. I dove down off a rock into the icy Ganges water and saw a rope floating up toward me. "Wow," I thought, "what luck." I can pull myself down to the river's bottom there. And as I went down deeper I saw what I was pulling on. It was fastened to the neck of a cow that must have gotten caught in the river, and as I pulled his head came up to meet me. Bloody hell, what a sight, I thought. Returning to the surface, there was Paul and his wife sitting on the rocks. I didn't know his name or even that he was one of the Beatles, as I didn't pay much attention to any rock stars, thinking that we were all on the same level of being -- except that the only thing that separated them from us was money. He told us all about his farm in Scotland and invited us to come stay with them in London whenever we were out there. It was a fine afternoon in the sun. The meals were so bad we were always hungry and Paul would get out his stash of peanut butter and cookies whenever we'd meet again at the cafe to have *chai* (tea).'

197

'Wendy would wear a *sari* or a piece of cloth around herself or Nehru-style pants and jacket that women wore, while others had to stay at the ashram we were allowed to come and go into town as we pleased.'
'George Harrison and Paul were telling me all about the far-out movie they made with the group called "Help!" and asked what I'd been doing. I told them of the thunder machine made by my partner, Ron Boise -- large musical instruments made to help musicians develop new ways and sounds of music, a way to break traditional habits…'[164]

Jerry Stovin - 'Maharishi was very firm about us not going outside of the camp, so when we heard a gunshot ring out, it was only natural that we wondered, had someone gone out!'[38]

Rik Cooke, Nancy's son, has come to visit his mother, and he makes a good impression on Maharishi - with his clean cut college kid image and his short tidy hair parted to one side.
Nancy Jackson - 'I was requested to go on shopping trips for the celebrities. This was no hardship. On one occasion, Rik (who stayed on and had a small room nearby) and I went to Dehra Dun - an hour and a half by car - and headed straight for a restaurant, where we gorged ourselves on chicken and ice cream sundaes. Our first feast made us both ill. We were no longer used to rich food.
Since other students did not have an opportunity for such outings, I brought back several cartons of hard-boiled eggs and smuggled them into the ashram to distribute. They were like golden apples. Mia's little dog ate all the shells - it was probably his first source of calcium since mother's milk.
One day I was given a long list of Beatles' needs, so I called Avi for assistance, "We need a copy of Swami Yogananda's *Autobiography of a Yogi* for George, a fixture for Paul's tripod, sandals and hair tonic for John." The list went on.'[117]

⊛ ⊛ ⊛

But shopping trips don't hold the same appeal for everyone.
George - 'Although we have this divinity, or creativity, within us, it is covered with material energy, and a lot of the time our actions come from a mundane level. There is an expression "beggars in a goldmine", and that's what we are. We're like beggars in the goldmine, where everything has really enormous potential and perfection, but we're all so ignorant with the dust of desire on our mirrors. While we were in Rishikesh, I wrote a song called "Deradune". I never recorded the song, but it was about seeing people going along the road trying to head for this place called Deradune. Everyone was trying to go there for their day off from the meditation camp. I couldn't see any point in going to this town; I'd gone all the way to Rishikesh to be in meditation and I didn't want to go shopping for eggs in Deradune! The verse of the song said, "See them move along the road/ In search of life divine/ Unaware it's all around them/ Beggars in a goldmine."'[175]

'Many roads can take you there, many different ways
One direction takes you years, another takes you days'

- Excerpt of *'Dehra Dun'* by George Harrison

⊛ ⊛ ⊛

Donovan - 'In the evening there'd be a lecture by the Maharishi, and we'd all go along with a little notebook and take down all the great things he said.
'He'd give us mango juice and listen to our songs. And sometimes he'd go into meditation, when I could *feel* the silence around him. It was very powerful.'
So what does Maharishi *do* for Donovan?
Donovan - 'Not much actually. I think he was more aware of me than I was of him. I wasn't really looking for any answer to a problem. Other people used to ask him for secrets like "Can men really fly?" I asked him if I could have some more mango juice. Meditation doesn't mean you are going to get rid of all your pain so that you'll only feel joy all the time. It's just a way back to God.'[286]

With longer meditations encouraged for course participants, lectures are now suspended.
Richard Blakely - 'To avoid having to go to the dining room for meals during the long meditation phase, we could have them delivered to our rooms, using order forms that were available from the kitchen. The forms

were printed on little quarter page slips of pale purple paper, with boxes to put an X in after "breakfast," "lunch," "tea," or "dinner." Beneath each meal there was a short list of items to check off, and blank lines provided at the bottom for special requests such as extra chapattis, peanut butter, cheese, dried fruit, etc.'[111]

Donovan - '... the Maharishi announced that we would now embark upon an extended period of meditation during which we would not be allowed out of our cabins. Meals would be passed under our doors as we continued to "fathom the infinite". I was moved to a small cottage on the periphery of the compound.'[84]

Richard Blakely - It had been several days since my last veena lesson with Jenny and Pattie down in the music room, which had been converted to a bedroom for Donovan. A few days earlier I had been down there for an impromptu concert with George on sitar and Donovan on guitar, the audience consisting only of Geoffrey, Jenny, Pattie, Cynthia and myself. After a while Maharishi had come to join us and sat down and listened too, this time without continually bursting into laughter. After George and Donovan had stopped playing and put away their instruments everybody went off with Maharishi to his bungalow for tea except for Cynthia and me, the two of us staying on in the little house full of open windows to chat and listen to the river below and watch the sun get lower in the sky.'[111]

Mike Dolan - 'Paul [Theobald] flew back to England with Donovan about 6 weeks into the course.'
'He [Donovan] left with Paul T for March 18th.'
'I think they just became friends, Paul and I were both totally penniless so I imagine Don paid. Mike Love was supposed to go the same day but after being called to Maharishi left for Hong Kong to buy movie cameras and film, very exotic items at the time.'[38]

Donovan - 'As we were leaving the ashram, John gave me the gift of a drawing, to thank me for teaching him. It is a beautiful study of a girl with long dark hair, her hand to her mouth in a secretive gesture. Only later would I recognise this girl as Yoko Ono.'[84]

Tuesday, 19th March 1968.

The birthday parties are getting more gorgeous every time: Pat (George's wife) and Paul Horn shared birthday on Saturday. Paul plays beautifully on a flute. He improvises when Donovan sings and plays, or Paul Horn plays and Donovan plays guitar. These young people are so wonderful. Paul McCartney painted a splendid white shirt colorfully for Paul Horn! Really of artistic value! Paul is left-handed, his guitar is left-handed, and if he gets another one, he turns it around. Jane Asher is also cute and very natural. There is nothing affected about them. Donovan, I think, has flown to a concert in London - but they all come back here, or to Kashmir. Until 17.4. we will stay here, they say.

- Excerpt from a letter written by Gertrud Soares de Souza to her 19 year-old daughter, Francisca, in West Germany. Translated from German into English.

'Dear Prudence, won't you come out to play?
Dear Prudence, greet the brand new day'
- Excerpt of *'Dear Prudence'* by John Lennon & Paul McCartney

John - 'Dear Prudence is me. Written in India. A song about Mia Farrow's sister, who seemed to go slightly barmy, meditating too long, and couldn't come out of the little hut that we were livin' in. They selected me and George to try and bring her out because she would trust us. If she'd been in the West, they would have put her away.
We got her out of the house. She'd been locked in for three weeks and wouldn't come out, trying to reach God quicker than anybody else. That was the competition in Maharishi's camp: who was going to get cosmic first.'[15]

Denis O'Dell - 'I watched as John and George walked over to Prudence's bungalow, sat down outside and John played the song on his acoustic guitar.'[168]

Prudence Farrow - 'Being on that course was more important to me than anything in the world. I was very focused on getting in as much meditation as possible, so that I could gain enough experience to teach it myself.

I knew that I must have stuck out because I would always rush straight back to my room after lectures and meals so that I could meditate. John, George and Paul would all want to sit around jamming and having a good time and I'd be flying into my room. They were all serious about what they were doing but they just weren't as fanatical as me...'[179]

✸✸✸

Richard Blakely outside Block 1

Wednesday, 20th March 1968.

Richard Blakely - 'At the sound of approaching voices I opened my eyes and was surprised to see Maharishi coming down the road towards Block 1. He was accompanied by Tarzan-Devendra [Dhirendra from Bihar, Maharishi's personal aide and cook], who was carrying a furled umbrella, and the bald bramachary who held a large black ledger under one arm.'

'Maharishi seemed glad to see me. Followed by the two brahmacharis, and now Geoffrey, he proceeded around the path until he was standing directly beneath me.

"You will pack up your belongings and move to another room, yes?"

It was one of those questions you could not say no to. Maharishi explained that Devendra [Dhirendra] would wait until I had finished packing then show me to my new lodgings.'[111]

Richard is directed to Block 4, to a room at the back.

Richard Blakely - 'Why had I been moved out of my comfortable little room in Block 1 into this damp little hovel?'

'We found out the answer over lunch, while sitting next to Bernt, Geoffrey and Larry. Berndt said that during the night Prudence had completely flipped out and started shouting and screaming and throwing things around in her room, waking up everybody in Block 6 and a lot of people in Block 5 as well, including Berndt. After a while several people managed to take or carry Prudence down to Maharishi's bungalow. But Berndt said that even Maharishi could not do anything to calm her down, so finally Dr. Gertrude [Dr Ute Otter] was called for and she came and gave Prudence a strong shot of some sort of sedative.'[111]

Timber is taken to Block 1 and alterations made to the room that has until recently been used by Richard.

Richard Blakely - 'Because of what had happened to Prudence there were more people down in the dining area for lunch that afternoon than usual. After lunch a bunch of us proposed to meet again down at the swimming hole. Since we were supposed to start easing out of long meditation that seemed like a good place to do it, especially since it was now starting to get blisteringly hot by mid-afternoon, even on days like today when there were more clouds than sun.'[111]

The Maharishi Movie

Neil Aspinall (assistant to The Beatles) - 'I visited them out in Rishikesh, but only to stop them making a movie, really. There was a suggestion they would make a movie with the Maharishi. I'm not quite sure what it was supposed to consist of, but they have a three-picture deal with United Artists and they'd only made Help! and A Hard Day's Night.'[1]

Denis O'Dell (Head of Apple Films) - 'I understood the Beatles' desire to promote the Maharishi's ideas, but I could not envisage how a subject as inherently introverted, internalised and spiritual as meditation could translate visually into a successful feature film or documentary.'
'Matters were also complicated by the fact that another production company, Bliss Productions, was in the process of arranging a documentary with the Maharishi and, although Bliss wanted the Beatles to appear in the film, they would have second billing to the guru, so there would be a clear clash of interests over control. I also knew that United Artists would never accept such a project as a third film and told them so. I then started to introduce my idea of making a film version of *The Lord of the Rings*. I had brought copies of the books with me and with a little help from Donovan - long an ardent admirer of Tolkien - persuaded John, Paul and George to take a look at the trilogy.'
'John was keen to play Gandalf and was so enthusiastic that he told me it would be no problem to get "at least a double album" of musical material together for the project.'[168]

❀ ❀ ❀

John Lennon sends Ringo a postcard of the Hindu god Lord Shiva seated cross-legged in meditation, postmarked 20th March 1968.[61]

> *Dear Ringo Mo' Zak*
> *Just a little vibration from India. We've got about two L.P.S worth of songs now so get your drums out. Will you ask Dot to get my video tape working (forgot to tell her). It's still the same here. Denis got his mantra and everything is great. We've got a film story too.*
> *Lots of love John & Cyn*
> *and the rest xxx*

Paul - '… I got sunburned in the morning and come lunchtime I was going, "Oh, my God, it's going to be the burning lobster thing." But I meditated for a couple of hours and low and behold, the lobster had gone. I often wondered whether it was just the fact that I'd calmed myself, whereas normally I'd go running around with a shirt on, irritating it, or I'd go to a dance and really rub it, whereas now I was just sitting very quietly with it for three hours. But it certainly didn't bother me.'
'The meditation sessions were increasingly long, they were as long as you could handle. It was a very sensible thing. He basically said, "Your mind is confused with day-to-day stress so I want you to try and do twenty minutes in the morning and twenty minutes in the evening." That's what they start you on. Twenty minutes in the morning is not going to hurt anyone. You sit still, I suppose you regulate your breathing and, if nothing else, you rest your muscles for twenty minutes. It's like a lie-in. That's pretty good. The meditation helps your productivity that day. And then twenty minutes in the evening; I used to liken it to sitting in front of a nice coal fire that's just sort of glowing. That sort of feeling, that very relaxed feeling, a twilight feeling which I quite like. Are you dreaming or are you awake? There's a nice little state that they recognise halfway between it.
My best experience of the whole time, which doesn't sound much but which was very pleasant, came when I was meditating. Some of us were called into little like Bible-study groups, but these were just meditation-study groups, good ones. A few of us would sit around on little chairs on the roof of the building Maharishi lived in and talk to him about meditation.'[6]

Elsa Dragemark - 'There was a pastoral mood over the ashram. Everything was peaceful. I could notice no movement anywhere, not a leaf was rustling, not a fly bussed [sic], not a sound could be heard from the jungle and no workers were making a noise in the park. I stood in the shade of the veranda and tried to catch the roar of the Ganges, but even that seemed dormant today. A crow's raucous croaking suddenly pierced the silence. I saw it sitting in a tree just at the edge of the park. It opened its powerful beak wide, appeared to get set and

croaked louder and louder, just as if it couldn't stand the silence and wanted to cut it to threads.
There were soft steps on the path and a barefoot boy of about nine or ten came padding along with a catapult in his hand. He was one of the small boys, whose task was to hold the crows at a distance, so that they wouldn't disturb our meditation. The boy looked up towards the tree-tops in order to spot the sinner. At last he caught sight of the crow. He bent over, picked up a stone and aimed it with the help of his catapult towards the black lump in the tree-top. The crow lifted, even though unwillingly, and with cries of protest disappeared into the jungle. Again there was silence.'[129]

Paul - 'The difficulty, of course, is keeping your mind clear, because the minute you clear it, a thought comes in and says, "What are we gonna do about our next record?" "Go away!" Meditate, mantra mantra mantra. "I still want to know what we're doing on this next record." "Please go away, I'm meditating, can't you see?" There's inevitably all sorts of little conversations you can't help getting into.
Maharishi used to give some very good advice, things that I suppose tied in with Vedic traditions. He would always translate it into a particular Englishy kind of phrase, like "The heart always goes to the warmer place," which I've ever since always found to be a very reassuring thought. I think at the time I half suspected that, being the perverse spirit that it is, my ego would want go to the thing that's bad for me. You tend to suspect your darker side, I suppose. But he was quite reassuring: "No, your heart always wants to go to the warmer place." Little things like that: the story of the snake which, when you look at it closely, turns out to be a piece of string and your fears were unfounded.
Sometimes Maharishi would ask us questions about how best to advance this system of meditation and we'd try and clue him in on how we thought it would best go down, try and give him some advice. Maharishi was very practical, he liked to know how to do things the simplest Western way. He would ask what kind of car they should use and you'd say, "A Mercedes is a good practical car, not too flash, pretty flash, it'll get you there, it'll tend not to break down." "This is the car we should have!" It was all done like that, it wasn't "Rolls-Royces are very nice, Maharishi. You could have a couple of them on what you're earning." It wasn't that, it was very practical. He wanted to know what was the strongest car that won't break down and that they would get the best wear out of. I never minded that.'[6]

There have been stories circulating, that a CIA man by the name of Mr Russell Dean Brines has paid a visit to the academy.

Mahesh Yogi denies harbouring spies

Rishikesh. March 21 (UNI)
Maharishi Mahesh Yogi, the high priest of transcendental meditation, said here yesterday he was harbouring no spy at his academy of meditation as was being made out by certain people.
He said in an interview that he did not know that a CIA (Central Intelligence Agency of the United States) man had visited the ashram until his manager apprised him of Press reports.
The Maharishi said Mr Brines was introduced to the ashram staff as an author and journalist from the United States by his Indian companion.
Govt. duty
He added it was not his job to take care of spies. It was the duty of the Government - the immigration authorities - to stop such characters from entering India. "Why do they allow spies? I do not investigate the profession or antecedents of the men who come here for meditation. As far as I am concerned all are welcome. But there is no spy at the ashram as far as I know," he said.
The Maharishi, however, added immediately that if the Government tells him not to entertain certain shady persons at the academy, he will go by such advice.
Airstrip soon
It looks like that Maharishi Mahesh Yogi will soon have an airstrip close to his ashram.
The Centre, it appears, has given the green light to the Maharishi's plan to build an airstrip. The U.P. Government has also approved the project in principle.
Maharishi Mahesh Yogi said yesterday that his well-wishers in New Delhi had informed him telephonically that the Centre's permission for the airstrip will be communicated to him shortly.

❋ ❋ ❋

On Thursday, 21ˢᵗ March 1968, Donovan & Tyrannosaurus Rex are booked to play at the Royal Albert Hall, London, in support of the Imperial College charity carnival. When the Press arrive to interview Donovan, his father informs them his son has gone to collect Mia Farrow. When Donovan returns he explains to reporter Bob Dawbarn that the trip to India, to meditate with Maharishi had been 'beautiful'. Further, Donovan mentions that Paul McCartney has recently written a song about *'Army boots, parachutes and sleeping bags for two'*.

> ***'Parachutes, army boots,***
> ***Sleeping bags for you.***
> ***Jhandadara jamboree.'***
>
> - Excerpt from early lyrics of *'Scrap Heap/Junk'* by Paul McCartney

Donovan - 'That's the new Paul McCartney song. Beautiful, isn't it.'
'Lennon and McCartney are so talented. In India they've written between 30 and 40 new songs and they are all great.'[176]

Keith Altham, reporter - 'Mia Farrow (Mrs Sinatra) sat shyly in one corner of the dressing room and looked so young that she might have been fourteen, with her "urchin-cut," no make-up and an Indian shawl (a souvenir from the Meditation Centre on the Ganges) about her shoulders.'[177]
During the interview Donovan is asked whether or not his new song, *'Hurdy Gurdy Man',* will be his next single release?
Donovan - 'I think so. It's a nice happy song. It's the story of the world. Whenever there are bad times and we face some terrible crisis, someone like the "Hurdy Gurdy Man" comes along to make people forget their troubles and be happy. It might be me, the Beatles or the Maharishi. We believe we are heading for a golden age!'[177]

BEATLES PEACE FEST

The Beatles are planning a mammoth Festival of Peace to be staged in Britain in May of next year, according to reports from India. Maharishi Mahesh Yogi would co-operate with the Beatles in organising the event, in which Donovan has already agreed to appear.
Commented their press officer Tony Barrow: "There is nothing official yet - this is something they have been cooking up during their stay in India."

- *New Musical Express - NME.* [177]

Chapter Twenty-Five
Won't You Come Out to Play

Geoffrey Baker (a fellow meditator and art teacher) - 'One morning the Beatles girls produced some colored pens and began drawing at a table under the trees. The Beatles themselves then joined in, I also. Someone asked, "What shall we paint?", to which George answered, "let's do *over the hill came the monster*"', and henceforth began to produce the "two eyes" picture. Paul produced the head and shoulders of some TV personality - I forget who - signed it GB-PM then gave it to me.'[178]

Paul's felt-tip pen artwork appears to be a portrait of BBC television announcer Gordon Honeycombe. The way the face is dealt with is clearly influenced by Pablo Picasso whilst the repeated use of triangles strongly suggests an exposure to Indian *tantric* art.

Geoffrey Baker - 'George's "Balloon Man" is another story. I had written a story (entitled "The Balloon Man") about a balloonist. I thought it might be of interest as a possible movie scenario and gave it to George to look over. The idea of the title must have been an inspiration for <u>his</u> Balloon Man - clearly George himself standing in a field of psychedelic flowers. He presented it to me at dinner.'[178]

On a yellow balloon George draws the ॐ (OM) symbol, and on a blue and white balloon he draws the Taoist *yin-yang* (literally 'dark/light') sign. On another he draws some astrological signs, and on a green and yellow balloon, a swastika, which, whether drawn as 卐 or 卍, is an ancient good luck sign and symbol, a fylflot, seen is many of the pre-history cultures, a symbol of the sun. The Sanskrit word *'Swastika',* means 'Peace', 'Well-being' and 'All is well'.

On Friday, 22nd March 1968, it is Colin Harrison's 26th birthday.

Happy
Birthday
Colin

from
George + Pattie

Best wishes Colin
from.
John + Cyn Lennon.

HAPPY BIRTHDAY COLIN HAPPY BIRTHDAY CO
LIN HAPPY BIRTHDAY COLIN HAPPY BIRTHDAY C
OLIN   HAPPY BIRTHDA
Y COLIN HAPPY BIRTHDAY COLIN HAPPY BIRTHD
AY COLIN HAPPY BIRTHDAY COLIN HAPPY BIRTH
DAY COLIN HAPPY BIRTHDAY COLIN HAPPY BIRT
HDAY COLIN HAPPY BIRTHDAY COLIN HAPPY BIR
THDAY COLIN HAPPY BIRTHDAY COLIN
                    HAPPY BIRTHDAY COLIN HAP
PPY BIRTHDAY COLIN HAPPY BIRTHDAY COLIN HAP
PY BIRTHDAY COLIN HAPPY BIRTHDAY COLIN H
APPY BIRTHDAY COLIN HAPPY BIRTHDAY COLIN
HAPPY BIRTHDAY COLIN
    HAPPY BIRTHDAY COLIN HAPPY BIRTHDAY
COLIN HAPPY BIRTHDAY RALPH HAPPY BIRTHD
AY COLIN HAPPY BIRTHDAY COLIN HAPPY BIRT
HDAY COLIN HAPPY BIRTHDAY COLIN HAPPY
BIRTHDAY COLIN HAPPY BIRTHDAY COLIN
                    HAPPY BIRTHDAY COLIN
HAPPY BIRTHDAY COLIN HAPPY BIRTHDAY CO
LIN HAPPY BIRTHDAY COLIN HAPPY BIRTHDA
Y COLIN HAPPY BIRTHDAY COLIN HAPPY BI
RTHDAY COLIN HAPPY BIRTHDAY COLIN HAPPY
BIRTHDAY COLIN
HAPPY BIRTHDAY COLIN HAPPY BIRTHDAY COL
IN HAPPY BIRTHDAY COLIN HAPPY BIRTHDAY
COLIN HAPPY BIRTHDAY COLIN SPOT THE D
ELIBERATE MISTAKES HAPPY BIRTHDAY COLIN
                    HAPPY BIRTHDAY COL
IN HAPPY BIRTHDAY COLIN HAPPY BIRTHDA

DON'T BE NAUGHTY COLIN DEAR
REMEMBER TO BEHAVE,
YOUR BIRTHDAY COMES BUT ONCE A YEAR
SO THANK YOU GURU DEV.

WITH MUCH LOVE FROM

PAUL
and
JANE.

99
beneath the deep Ambrosia tree
the Subtle Woffell lies.
and he will sing to comfort thee
under the purple skies. 99

happy birthday Colin
with love from John:
Some time in March - Rishikesh
1968.

'Under the greenwood tree
Who loves to lie with me,
And turn his merry note
Unto the sweet bird's throat,'

- *'Under the Greenwood Tree'* (from *As You Like It*) by William Shakespeare

Saturday, 23rd March 1968.

Nancy Jackson - 'George said they had written ten new songs in the five weeks they'd been there, and he was up to twelve hours of meditation at a time. They should have been happy with the treatment they were receiving. When most classes were suspended, they were still having daily sessions with Maharishi - and all of this for free. I hoped they appreciated it.

'One day I asked Maharishi directly what they were being charged. "Nothing, Nancy. Just by being meditators they will bring the world to us. In their own way they will repay for all this happiness they are now experiencing." Love filled his face as he spoke of them.'[117]

❀ ❀ ❀

Mike Dolan - 'I was like the fly on the wall in Rishikesh I was there participating but in a way I was outside. I didn't have the emotional commitment.

It was really very interesting to watch Maharishi say that he was just a simple man and hear him say it in all sorts of different ways then listen to people that I really admired explaining what he really meant. I thought at the time of what Jesus was and what Christianity is. I don't think TM is any different than any other organization with a charismatic leader, we project our own perceptions onto them.

I used to be able to chat with Maharishi when he was walking around the grounds at day break, I would be on my way to the dining area, he was such a charmer. He would ask me the most mundane things, how's your family Mike, sort of things. It was like talking to the postman.'[38]

Sunday, 24th March 1968.

Yesterday I was listening to a long discussion: Geoffrey Baker, John Lennon and George Harrison. Geoffrey is very clear with everything.
In one week, we will come back again to the different reality and lectures will then begin again.
- Excerpts from a letter written by Gertrud Soares de Souza to her 19 year-old daughter, Francisca, in West Germany. Translated from German into English.

Nancy Jackson's son Rik, who is staying at the academy, has brought his rifle with him from the States, and Nancy's friend Avi Kohli arranges for Nancy and Rik to go together on a *shikar* hunt, where Rik and Avi shoot a tiger dead. Rik's mother is full of approval.

Nancy Jackson - 'Rik, I'm so proud of you!

Rik Cooke - 'Mom, I've never shot so fast in my life. That was real luck, I'm sure glad Avi had that big gun, or that animal could have recovered and been up in the machand [hide] with us.'[117]

Nancy Jackson - 'The next day, on returning to the ashram, we went directly to see Maharishi. John Lennon, Paul McCartney, Jane Asher and George Harrison were there with him. Rik was worried about his killing the tiger, "Is that bad karma for me, Maharishi?"
The answer was, "You had a desire, now you have satisfied it and will no longer have the desire."'
'"But wouldn't you call that slightly life-destructive?" sneered John.
"Well, it was the tiger or us," I volunteered, getting into the act.'[117]

Rikki Cooke - 'I was reading the *Bhagavad Gita* at that time and I just said, you know, "Maharishi," I said, that "Am I just a part, an agent, of change, and you know, am I just part of this bigger dance?" and err, John Lennon said something about "destruction" and err, I remember Maharishi, in the coldest way, saying, "Life destruction is, life destruction." End of story!'[180]

'The children asked him if to kill was not a sin
"Not when he looked so fierce", his mummy butted in'
- Excerpt from the lyrics of *'The Continuing Story Of Bungalow Bill'* by John Lennon & Paul McCartney

John - 'Oh that was written about a guy in Maharishi's meditation camp who took a short break to go shoot a few poor tigers, and then came back to commune with God. There used to be a character called Jungle Jim, and I combined him with Buffalo Bill. It's sort of a teenage social-comment song and a bit of a joke.'[15]

Paul - '"Did you have to shoot that tiger?" is its message. "Aren't you a big guy? Aren't you a brave man?" I think John put it very well. Funnily enough, John wasn't an overt animal activist, but I think by writing this song he showed that his sentiments were very much that way.'[6]

❀ ❀ ❀

The Beatles' *'Umbrella'* LP record
Paul - 'John came up with a massive TV scenario! A big TV show. I came up with calling the next album Umbrella, an umbrella over the whole thing. I think this was the point at which George got annoyed at me because we mixed the two things. John and I'd do a lot of chatting.'
'I wrote quite a few songs in Rishikesh and John came up with some creative stuff. George actually once got quite annoyed and told me off because I was trying to think of the next album. He said, "We're not fucking here to do the next album, we're here to meditate!" It was like, "Ohh, excuse me for breathing!" You know. George was quite strict about that, George can still be a little that way, and it's like, "Oh come on, George, you don't have a monopoly on thought in this area. I'm allowed to have my own views on the matter."'[6]

Paul makes a note of his new compositions in a 'Manjeet' note book[1]:-
   1. Obla-dee Obla-da.

2. Scrap heap [Junk (in the yard.)]
3. Ballad
4. Back in the U.S.S.R.
5. Country Boy - Mother Nature's Son.
6. Martha my dear.
7. Silly girl.
8. Rocky Racoon

And Paul is also working on another song.

'This is the story of a boy named Ted
If his mother said, "Ted, be good", he would'

- Excerpt of *'Teddy Boy'* by Paul McCartney

Richard Blakely - '.. Larry had returned from his trip to Japan with Mike Love. Over lunch he'd told me about their return from Tokyo to Delhi. From the airport they had gone directly to the Oberoi to spend the night. When they were told there was no vacancy at the Oberoi, Mike flipped out and demanded to see the manager. When the manager arrived and said the same thing Larry said Mike threw a scene that soon threatened to turn into a brawl. Luckily, Nancy's friend Avi was among the onlookers and since Avi was either part owner of the hotel or knew someone who was, a room was soon found for Larry and Mike and the brawl narrowly averted.'[111]

Mike Dolan - 'I could be wrong but I think it was Hong Kong because Mike's record company had offices there.'
'I do remember Mike brought back lots of vinyl records amongst other things. He was playing Sgt Pepper one day with George and John and they were only listening because the Hong Kong version had been mixed wrongly.'
' At the time and because of the expense in those days movie grade film was not available in India but it was in Hong Kong along with resources of Mike's recording company.'
'They came back with movie cameras, boxes of color film, a portable stereo record player, reel to reels. There was a "spy camera" a little thing about the size of your thumb which was a bit of a novelty.'[138]

Mike Dolan - 'It is the dining room and that's me.'

'The person next to me is Paul Theobald who I had been traveling with and was also helping out with the course.'

'I'm holding a microphone recording a message to the folks back home on a breakthrough technology that was just a precursor to the cassette it was a two inch reel to reel.

I had it at the table and was recording a profound message to my parents when Paul came down and said "Oh I'll help". I had the whole Beatles help me record a funny message to our fellow scouse parents.'

'It actually began with him [John] saying "Hello Mrs Dolan we found your son alive and well and keeping regular...... "'

'I only remember the care free kind of goofy spontaneity of the thing. The made-for-TV Liverpool accents that they put on *"Yer-all-right-der-ar-kid?"* for my parents. They even did a few lines from the folk song about Dirty Maggie Mae. They really were just Liverpool lads, easy going and constantly taking the piss. I remember they were well aware that people who met them just found it almost impossible to act naturally so had this game that was based on how people self-consciously entered or left rooms that they were in. They would mouth to one another imaginary scores; "Five?" "No. Seven", would come the silently mouthed reply. It was really hilarious and cut through the sometimes stifling earnestness that can come about when you have a group of people who are on a crash course to find the answer to everything.'[38]

'Oh dirty Maggie Mae they have taken her away
And she never walk down Lime Street any more'

- Excerpt of lyrics of *'Maggie Mae'* by Lennon, McCartney, Harrison & Starkey

Mike Dolan - 'And I posted to them in the UK. My parents being a bit frugal just taped over it and sent me a message back.'

'God love her, she sent it back with a message saying that I sounded a bit Hindu and three pairs of underpants.'[38]

Chapter Twenty-Six
Indian Rope Trick?

Monday, 25th March 1968.

Today it is 7 years that I have been initiated. I was allowed to celebrate it with Maharishi! Since I told him last night.

We have here a fascinating American, Larry, who is writing an article for "Look". He is photographer and he himself is good-looking.

A scene from lunch:
Richard (a lovely student from Paris - American from California) came to lunch and pulled an egg out of his pocket (eggs we do not get, and that's very hard for Americans) and he tapped it on the table.
I (Gertrud): Richard, you got an egg?!?
R: Yes!
The German next to me furiously: And me, for my health I need eggs and have been asking for it since two months and didn't get any!
Richard begins to crack and peel the egg.
George Harrison discovered the egg.
George: Are you eating an egg?!?
Richard: Yes
G: Where have you got it from?
R: Colin gave it to me this morning.
G: Where has he got it?
R: He took it out of his beggars bag.
G: Is it hard boiled?
R: Yes
G: Oh, then he must have brought it from England! Two months ago!

You should always have a tape recorder with you, because so many things happen that you will forget again. Almost everybody has one of these small Phillips-Recorder, they cost about 200 DM (Deutsche Mark) and work likewise with batteries. Because even in the hall often there is no electricity (bring to mind for the next trip to India)

The boulders, big as an arm, which are painted white, are very nice. Even all the trees are surrounded with two rows of such stones, are planted in between flowers, very touching.

- Excerpts from a letter written by Gertrud Soares de Souza to her 19 year-old daughter, Francisca, in West Germany. Translated from German into English.

Larry Kurland's photojournalism is indeed in this month's issue of *Look*, the main story in fact, entitled *'The Horror of Growing Drug Abuse'*, an inside account on the perils of methamphetamine (speed).

Larry has been practicing meditation for about two years, and was allegedly being thrown out of Maharishi's suite at the Plaza Hotel, New York, whilst on an assignment for *Life* magazine, so he decided to enroll on the Indian course and abandon his role as journalist. Now he is just another student, though he still carries about his trusty camera.

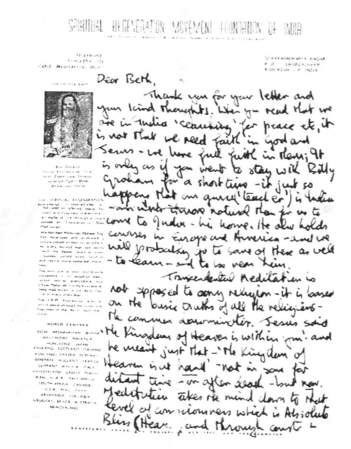

Letter from John Lennon to Beth Dewar, Kenley, Surrey - sent Monday. 25th March 1968.

Dear Beth,

Thank you for your letter and your kind thoughts. When you read that we are in India searching for peace, etc, it is not that we need faith in God or Jesus - we have full faith in them; it is only as if you went to stay with Billy Graham for a short time - it just so happens that our guru ('teacher') is Indian - and what is more natural for us to come to India - his home. He also holds courses in Europe and America - and we will probably go to some of these as well - to learn - and to be near him.

Transcendental meditation is not opposed to any religion - it is based on the basic truths of all religions - the common denominator. Jesus said: "The Kingdom of Heaven is within you" - and he meant just that - "The Kingdom of Heaven is at <u>hand</u>" - not in some far distant time - or after death - but <u>now</u>.
Meditation takes the mind down to that level of consciousness which is Absolute Bliss (Heaven) and through constant contact with that state - 'the peace that surpasses all understanding' - one gradually becomes established in that state even when one is not meditating. All this gives one actual experience of God - not by detachment or renunciation - when Jesus was fasting etc in the desert 40 days & nights he would have been doing some form of meditation - not just sitting in the sand and praying - although meditation is a form of prayer. I hope what I have said makes sense to you - I [am] sure it will to a true Christian - which I try to be with all sincerity - it does not prevent me from acknowledging Buddha - Mohammed - and all the great men of God. God bless you - jai guru dev.

With love, John Lennon

So, what do John and The Beatles make of that side of Maharishi's teachings that seems to suggest that it's really possible to work miracles?

Paul - 'When we were out in Rishikesh, that was one of the things we were interested in ... We were almost throwing in the Indian rope trick too. It was all part of a new thing and we would ask him, "Did they do that? Was that just a magic trick? Do they really levitate, Maharishi? What about levitation, is that actually possible?" and he said, "Yes it is, there are people who do it," but he took it as, "Oh, you wanna see levitation, well there's a fellow down the road, he does it. We can have him up, he'll do a little bit for us if you like," and we said, "Great," but he never actually showed.'[181]

❀ ❀ ❀

Tuesday, 26th March1968.
Preparations are being made for Paul McCartney, Jane Asher, and Neil Aspinall to leave Maharishi's academy.
Neil Aspinall - 'I went in with Denis O'Dell. I stayed for a week, then I came home with Paul and Jane Asher, leaving John and George and their wives in Rishikesh.'[1]

Cynthia - 'John and I, with George and Patti, wanted to stay. Aside from my troubles with John, I got a great deal from being there. I loved the serenity of the place, and still hoped that John would work through his demons and move back to me. In the absence of the true explanation, I put his aloofness down to a bout of intense self-exploration and hoped that it would, ultimately, be good for him and for us.'[10]

Paul and Jane fly back from Delhi via Tehran, and after touching down at London Airport agree to be interviewed.
Reporter - 'So you feel better after your vacation of meditation in India?'
Paul - 'Yes. Yes. Except for the flight. That's quite a long one, so I'm a bit shattered... but the meditation? It's great!
Reporter - 'What exactly have you been doing? How do you meditate?'
Paul - 'You sit down. You relax. And then you repeat a sound to yourself. And it sounds daft... but it's a great system of relaxation. We meditated for about two hours in the morning and three hours in the evening. And then the rest of the time we sun bathed and had fun.'
Reporter - 'Paul, what about the extreme poverty in India? Presumably you saw some of this while you were there.'
Paul - 'Oh yea. The Maharishi's idea is to stop the poverty at its root. You see, if you just give handouts to people, it'll stop the problem for a day or a week, you know. But in India there's so many people that you'd really need all of America's money poured into India to stop it. So you've got to get at the cause of it and persuade all the Indians to start doing things... because their religion is very fatalistic. They just sort of sit down and think, "God said this is it, so it's too bad. We can't do anything about it." The Maharishi is trying to persuade them that they can do something about it.'[182]

Reporter - 'One Indian MP accused this place of being an espionage centre and you, in fact, of being a spy for the West. Well, what happened?'
Paul - 'Don't tell anyone. It's true. We're spies, yes. The four of us have been spies. Actually, I'm a reporter and I joined The Beatles for that very reason, but the story's out next week in a paper that will be nameless.'[43]

But surely, all four Beatles planned to stay with Maharishi for the entire course, why has Paul come back early? Did he fall out with George or with Maharishi, or perhaps he tired of attending lectures?
Paul - 'I came back after four or five weeks knowing that was like my allotted period, thinking, No, well, no, I won't go out and become a monk but it was really very interesting and I will continue to meditate and certainly feel it was a very rewarding experience.'
'No, it is not a gigantic hoax. A lot of people are going to say that I left because I was disillusioned by it all but that just isn't so. The Academy is a great place and I enjoyed it a lot. I still meditate every day for half an hour in the morning and half an hour every evening and I think I'm a better person for it. I'm far more relaxed than I have ever been. You know, if you're working very hard and things are a bit chaotic, you get all tensed up and

screwed up inside. You feel as if you have to break something or hit someone. But if you spend a short while in the mornings and evenings meditating, it completely relaxes you, and it's easier to see your way through problems. If everyone in the world started meditating, then the world would be a much happier place.'[6]

Ringo - 'At the moment I meditate every day. Well, I might skip the odd day if I get up late or arrive in town late or something.'[6]

⊛ ⊛ ⊛

Meanwhile, on a teacher training course somewhere near Rishikesh in India.
Prudence Farrow - 'I heard John practicing and tinkering with different notes and melodies on his guitar every afternoon for a couple of hours or so. I think it was just John and George (and not Paul) that came into my room one evening and played "Ob-La-Di, Ob-La-Da" for me.'
'In the evenings, John and George (and Paul while he was there) would jam with others in the patio outside our front doors.'
'The Beatles being there — I can honestly say — did not mean anything to me. But those two people that I met, John and George, I really liked them, and they were very much up my alley.'[183]

But apparently Prudence's past mental torments are returning, and she seems to need help. One of the course participants volunteers to assist.
'Irma' (Ena) - 'Maharishi, give me the room next to Prudence, I have had training with this type of sickness.'[117]

Paul Horn - 'She was ashen-white and didn't recognize anybody. She didn't even recognize her own brother who was on the course with her. The only person she showed any slight recognition towards was Maharishi. We were all concerned about her and Maharishi assigned her a full-time nurse.'[184]

Richard Blakely - 'In front of my old room thick bamboo poles had been lashed together about two inches apart to form an enclosure resembling all too closely a jail. In the narrow doorway of the enclosure stood one of the staffers with his arms crossed. He was a sturdily built, older man with a turban.'
'One morning while getting a massage I happened to see Prudence escape from her room and run across the road. Seconds later the female nurse came running out after her and was joined by the guard on duty at the gate. Together they managed to corner Prudence behind a tree, then lead her back across the road and into her room.'[111]

⊛ ⊛ ⊛

The prolonged bouts of meditation are taking their toll on some other course members too, who occasionally find themselves suffering unwelcome side effects. Apparently, as Maharishi explains, when the meditator becomes acclimatized to longer periods of silence, unexpected moments of distress can occur, which are explained as being the 'unwinding' of accumulated deep stresses.

Jerry Stovin - 'It's as though in meditation we have been tip-toeing past the "sleeping elephants" of the mind, and then suddenly they are awakened and cause a stir!'[38]
Usually these are personal experiences, and are soon dealt with, but at other times a sort of 'collective calamity' can occur.

Jerry Stovin - ' Maharishi refers to this process as "unstressing", that we're going through a process of inner purification, and Maharishi suggested we go back to our rooms and continue to meditate. But as soon as we settled down in silence, the sound of hammering filled the air. So some of us went out to see where the noise was coming from, and surprisingly it seemed to be coming from the direction of Maharishi's cottage, so we went closer and closer, and then looking up we saw Maharishi on top of the building hammering the roof!'[38]

Wednesday, 27th March 1968
Yesterday I was transferred to one of the back rooms, very narrow. But it is at least dry and after Honor [Anstruther] *will depart next week, I will get her room, facing-forward, next to Katie Plowman (The Queen) in the block III.*

- Excerpt from a letter written by Gertrud Soares de Souza to her 19 year-old daughter, Francisca, in West Germany. Translated from German into English.

Joe Massot (the director of *'Wonderwall'*) - 'Gene Corman, a crazy film producer and brother of Roger, had some arrangement with the Maharishi to make a film with the Beatles.'[185]
'George Harrison sent me a message via Apple from the Himalayan mountains, saying "Come out to Rishikesh. You gotta film it."
By the time I arrived, John and George were the only Beatles around.'
'John was up on a rooftop dressed all in loose white cotton and sandals, playing the melodeon. Later he claimed to have licked the problem of how to meditate and smoke at the same time. He leaned against a tree and closed his eyes in deep inner thought, took a cigarette out of his pocket and lit up, "See? I'm still meditating."'[101]
'John showed me to my room. He saw my Phillips portable cassette and asked what music I'd brought. I told him (Sittin' On) the Dock of the Bay, Otis Redding's last recording - just released - and a small piece of hash. John lowered his voice and told me there was no dope in Rishikesh and not to tell anyone, especially George. George, it seemed, was really very studious in his approach to Eastern religion and was locked into some sort of meditational duel with Lennon to see who was the stronger character.
That night, after dinner, we smoked all the dope and listened to Dock of the Bay at least 20 times.
We got up in the morning and had breakfast in a hall. Prudence Farrow, Mia's sister, was there, literally climbing up the wall with two little Indian guys holding her back, watching her like she's going to kill herself. She was freaked. The Maharishi said she would be cured.'
'I liked the Maharishi. I thought he was a funny man with a very clear vision of the world.'[185]

Mike Dolan - 'I can remember guards outside her door 24 hrs a day and everyone being worried about the hundreds of press people who were camped about 200 yards away finding out that Mia's little sister was broken. I do have to say though that after a week or so a very different Prudence emerged she was very bright and clear. She became beautiful.'[38]

Millie Drummond - 'She looked amazing after whatever she went through, she was really shining & I thought she must have released a LOT of trauma while in the cave which must have been traumatic for her to release (if that makes sense?)'[38]

Joe Massot - 'There was, however, no sign of the film crew, though there was a little silent 16mm camera that everybody would pick up and shoot with; everything - breakfast, lunch, whatever. We'd get up, breakfast, meditate with the morning mantra, lunch, then George would sleep or meditate and John would go up on the roof, play and write. At about five the Maharishi would give a lecture.
George also took an amp to Rishikesh and the melodeon and John had an acoustic guitar. He was writing *'Across the Universe'*, and said he could only play two chords. But that was all he needed. He wrote about four or five different versions of that song. He taped one on my Philips tape recorder, the final version. He'd been fiddling with it since he got there.'[185]

Seemingly on his own initiative, but perhaps at the suggestion of Yoko Ono, Alexis Mardas travels to India and puts in an appearance at Maharishi's academy.

Cynthia - 'In the evenings we got together, occasionally breaking the no-alcohol rule with a glass of hooch, smuggled in by Alex from the village across the river and tasting remarkably like petrol. Giggling like naughty schoolchildren, we'd pass round the bottle, each taking a swig, then contorting as it scorched its way down our throats.'[10]

❀ ❀ ❀

According to Alexis, John records a song about him, and during the song John makes jokes about *'the Alexis Mardas rock'n'roll band'.*[186]

References to Transcendental Meditation, or at least news items connecting pop stars with Maharishi and meditation, continue to appear in the music press.

Donovan's next single has been recorded and the A side will either be "Maharishi", described by his manager, Ashley Kozak, as "a hymn of youth," or "Hirdy Girdy Man."

- Melody Maker [176]

The Beatles are planning a mammoth Festival of Peace, to be staged in Britain in May of next year. Maharishi Mahesh Yogi would co-operate with the Beatles in organising the event, in which Donovan has already agreed to appear.

- New Musical Express - NME [177]

Tony Barrow (The Beatles' Press Officer) - 'There is nothing official yet - this is something they have been cooking up during their stay in India.'[177]

❀ ❀ ❀

But there seems to be some discord in the Maharishi camp.
Nancy Jackson - 'What I didn't like were some of the deprecating remarks Tom, the American actor, had made one night at the dinner table - they were aimed directly at Maharishi. Then, when the Beatles' friend, Magic Alex, arrived, I saw him constantly with Tom and his girlfriend. I felt Alex resented Maharishi's influence on the Beatles. Without his noticing it, I watched his face while Maharishi and John talked one evening. The hostility was so evident I wrote home that night, suggesting that Charlie join us as soon as possible. I felt things were getting out of hand.'
'I'd begun to hear about all sorts of deals involving Maharishi. Mike Love, whom I liked tremendously, was planning a tour for him with the Beach Boys; two other PR men also had a plan - Charlie was needed.'[117]

CHARLES F. LUTES

PRESIDENT S. R. M. FOUNDATION OF AMERICA
WORLD GOVERNOR INTERNATIONAL MEDITATION SOCIETY
3475 W. SIXTH ST. • LOS ANGELES, CALIF. 90005 • 762-1845

Chapter Twenty-Seven
Captain Kundalini

Monday, 1st April 1968.
Charly Lutes is supposed to come, I look forward to meeting him.
- Excerpt from a letter written by Gertrud Soares de Souza to her 19 year-old daughter, Francisca, in West Germany. Translated from German into English.

Joe Massot - 'I'm standing with the Maharishi and John Lennon on an elevated plateau in the Himalayas at the mouth of the Ganges, watching the river below, the whole of India spread before us. In the afternoon to cool off we all went down to the Ganges to swim. The river was a torrent of rushing water carrying whole trees which had been ripped from their roots cascading down river. We gently eased ourselves into the river and were immediately carried hundreds of yards downstream, luckily we reached the shore...'[102]

❀ ❀ ❀

Nancy Jackson - 'One night, the first week in April, the two remaining Beatles and their wives met with Maharishi to discuss the Guru Dev movie. John held Cynthia's hand, the first sign of affection I'd seen him show her.'

John, to Maharishi - 'The only thing is, Maharishi, I miss me little son, Julian. Maybe Cyn and me could go back to England and bring him to Kashmir with us. What do you think?'

Nancy Jackson - 'It might not be wise, Cynthia, to bring such a young child to India. The food situation would be difficult for you, and dysentery is so dangerous for children. If you have him in good hands, leave him where he is.'

John - 'Well, we can make that decision later.'

George - 'Maharishi, what about our doing a big musical event in New Delhi? With all the artists here, we could put on quite a show. Ravi Shankar is keen to do it with us.

'Paul and Donovan both said they'd come back if we got something going. Also, Mike says the rest of the Beach Boys could be counted on.'

Maharishi - 'Yes, yes, we should have an all out effort and proclaim to the world in one big strike that everyone can enjoy life two hundred percent.

We will make enough money to start a TV station here as you suggested and broadcast our messages to the world.'

John - 'Right on, Maharishi.'

Nancy Jackson - 'What is this about a TV station, Maharishi?'

John - 'We're going to build a transmitter powerful enough to broadcast Maharishi's wisdom to all parts of the globe - right here in Rishikesh.'

'This will be done after the picture is finished. We don't have a lot of time to waste, man. We'd better start getting the crew and equipment out here if we're going to shoot the ashram before Kashmir.'

Maharishi - 'Right, it will be too hot here after we return from Kashmir. May is a very bad month - everyone must meditate in the caves.'

John - 'O.K., let's put down on paper what we need and get a cable off to Apple Corp tonight. Can you send this for us, Nancy?'

Maharishi - 'Nancy, call Avi and have him send it straight from Delhi.'[117]

Tuesday, 2nd April 1968.

A strange event! A German was at the ashram with an instrument to measure strength of meditation vibrations, both whilst meditating and when not actually in meditation. The instrument (whatever it was, determined the range of effects). In the evening Maharishi was prompted to talk about the influence of Cosmic Consciousness.

- Carol Hamby's diary

Inevitably, with the weather now getting progressively hotter, Maharishi's students ignore his injunctions about them going down to the river and the shore increasingly becomes a popular *rendez-vous*, a place to socialize and top up the tan. But the area here is quite rocky so, for the benefit of bathers, Andreas Müller sets to work with a shovel leveling some of the riverbed.

Andreas Müller clearing away rocks for the comfort of bathers

Richard Blakely, Geoffrey Baker & Charlie Lutes

Colin Harrison, Richard Blakely, Benita Glössner, Jerry Stovin, Jenny Boyd, Larry Kurland, John Farrow, Geoffrey Baker & Pattie Boyd

Donovan records *'Hurdy Gurdy Man'* at a session at CBS Studios in London, on Wednesday, 3rd April 1968.

❀ ❀ ❀

The topic of 'unstressing' is an ongoing issue, for those who meditate for long periods are aware that there can be interruptions and disruptions to their practice caused by the release of stress. But Maharishi encourages his students not to mind the release and just to bear witness to the process.

Maharishi - 'Once we know the mechanics we are in a position to handle it. At that time what one says doesn't matter, it doesn't matter, it is just the stress that is speaking. And we know to speak it's going to unwound, then it'll be out. So from the physical side we have this understanding that the nervous system of man is capable of reflecting omnipresent pure being.'[3]

❀ ❀ ❀

Richard Blakely - 'Naturally, the arrival of Charlie and his own film crew led to more cancelled lectures and long meetings down at Maharishi's bungalow, during which there were apparently vehement and sometimes violent verbal exchanges between the SIMSers on one hand, represented by the Beatles and their entourage, and the SRMers on the other, represented by Charlie Jackson [Charlie Lutes], whom John Lennon now referred to openly as Captain Kundalini.'[111]

Terry Gustafson - 'I also recall John standing up during one of the arguments inside the satsang hall, after Charlie had finished a diatribe against the 60's culture among young people. He said, simply, "Anyone who believes that has his 'ead up his arse!"'[38]

❀ ❀ ❀

Richard Blakely - 'One night, instead of a lecture, George arranged a concert of traditional Indian music with some friends of his who were visiting from Bombay. There were two sitars - one played by George - a couple of tablas, and several strange string instruments I'd never seen before.'[111]

Maybe recordings of these music recitals will one day appear as part of a record release or as part of a movie soundtrack.

George Harrison, and on his little finger a *mizrab* (a wire plectrum used for playing the *sitar*)

Thursday, 4th April 1968.
Apparently, however, we will go to Kashmir, they say on 14 or 17.4.
Many people will come there [Kashmir], *for example, Donovan and Mia are supposed to come. And Mrs. Gill comes from London. Gualterio Weiss is here. I only saw him once while eating, because we are still in meditation. And Charly Lutes, the chief of the United States, is here.*
Talked to Weiss: the course is said to take place from 15.9. to 15.12.. The first 4 weeks in Kashmir, then the rest here.
    - Excerpt from a letter written by Gertrud Soares de Souza to her 19 year-old daughter, Francisca, in West Germany. Translated from German into English.

Cosmic Consciousness

Maharishi - 'Clear means; you see things through an ordinary glass without colour. You see thing as it is, this is Cosmic Consciousness. (laughter) We see the world as it is, and you find yourself as you are, unconcerned with the field of action. It is transcendental, I, Being, Eternal, Non-changing, Cosmic. The world of activity is changing, change, less change, it is relative, it is absolute. Now this clear vision is the perception of reality. As the world is, and as I am, and as is the natural relationship of I and the world, that there is no relationship. This is like seeing things through a clear glass. Cosmic consciousness is seeing things through golden glass…. God Consciousness. You see things but you see them in much more greater glory. Greater glory, the world is viewed in the celestial light, in a much more ….. quality.'
Student - 'What you're saying that in Cosmic Consciousness I see the world, you see the world as it is?'
Maharishi - 'We see the world as it is but much more glorified.'
Student - 'You mean in Cosmic Consciousness you see it as it is?'
Maharishi - 'As it is. Clear but as it is.'
Student - 'And you're saying in God Consciousness you seeing it more glorified. Isn't that also as it is? Or is it something..?'
Maharishi - 'No! Not as it is but as we can possibly perceive it. As it is has been segregated from us, all this..

the field of the three gunas, and I and this is changeable and variable and I have nothing to do with it. I am a witness to it, and clear, Being, Eternal, Cosmic, Unbounded. I am restricted in time and space, bound into this world of activity. So we see it as it is, but in Cosmic Consciousness we see from our fullest ability to enjoy, so we see it better. As we see something in an ordinary mood and then we see something in a very happy mood, the thing is the same but we enjoy it more. Just if we, God Consciousness means seeing through golden glass, much more, and bliss. Yes?'

John - 'Do we all look like angels to you?' (laughter)

Maharishi - 'And when that is my normal vision then I don't see the contrast. If it was that someday like this and someday like this, then there would be differentiation, and if that is the normal vision, then that is the normal vision.'

Maharishi - 'It is just a mental hallucination, as you said.'

George - 'But if you have experience, then it can no longer be faith. So. ..'

Maharishi - 'So there is a concrete reality.'

George - 'It becomes a belief rather than faith.'

Maharishi - 'Becomes a reality, living reality, then it becomes a living faith. Otherwise a faith that has no life.' 'So faith, without any concrete basis of verification, is not valued in this scientific age.'[3]

❀❀❀

With the constant drip feed of information about Indian thinking there are inevitably some who begin to wonder if there might be a conflict with their Christian upbringing.

Mike Dolan - 'Kieran had a quiet meltdown a bit like Soren it was as if they suddenly realized that just below the surface of TM they were dabbling in Hinduism.'[38]

❀❀❀

Some student's experiences of stress, 'unstressing' and 'unwinding' are much more physical than others.

Mike Dolan - 'The Michael T/C affair was one of the most remarkable things I have ever witnessed in my life. We were in the middle of the nightly lecture and Michael, who had one of those iron leg casts that you saw back then when the world was full of polio survivors, came sobbing and blubbering about a snake that was wrapped around his leg. He was screaming and actually fighting with this imaginary monster. Maharishi told him to sit down and take it easy, which eventually he did. Then it was, take it easy and introduce your mantra. He seemed to calm, then he just fell asleep in the chair. We left him there alone slumped in his chair at Maharishi's insistence.

By the end of the week T/C emerged *sans* leg brace a new man.'[38]

❀❀❀

Thursday, 4th April 1968 - The news of the assassination of Civil Right's leader Martin Luther King sends shock waves throughout the world. The man who spoke out against inequality and unjustness, who told us, *'I have a dream'*, has been murdered. When MLK had visited India back in 1959, he announced, *'To other countries I may go as a tourist, but to India I come as a pilgrim'*, and he referred to Mahatma Gandhi as *'the guiding light of our technique of nonviolent social change'*.[186]

The Beatles made their contribution towards equality and civil rights some years ago, back in September 1964, by refusing to play to play before a segregated audience in Jacksonville, resulting in a policy of them only playing to mixed audiences there and elsewhere in the Southern States, at venues which had formerly only been segregated. This action directly impacted on the problem of racism in the U.S.A.

Mike Love - 'I flew back and (I think) the day before the tour opened we were sitting in Nashville and Martin Luther King, Jr. was assassinated in Memphis. Almost immediately more than half the shows were cancelled, because a lot of those cities were burning and the National Guard came out. We lost a lot of money. I was thinking to myself, "Had I stayed in India we would have rearranged the tour and not been right in the middle of that thing."'[188]

❀❀❀

According to Alan Waite, he learned to meditate from Paul Horn in April 1967, after Paul had been made a teacher of Transcendental Meditation, and in August 1967 he acquired permission from Charlie Lutes to film the next course in Rishikesh, at which time Charlie indicated The Beatles were likely to be involved. Alan strikes an agreement to sell the film rights to David Charnay of Four Star Productions, after which Verite Productions is established as a production company. The documentary is to be based around aspects of life of Maharishi Mahesh Yogi, so the title of the movie is to be *'Maharishi'*, with Paul Horn as the producer (and composer of an original background music score), Alan Waite associate producer and Earl Barton as director.

Four Star International make several initial payments; $80,000 to Charlie Lutes for SRM, $6,000 apiece to Alan, Paul and Earl, and also hand over an American Express cheque for $300,000 to cover production expenses. Gradually, a crew is assembled, a 15-man team, with a cameraman from France, a cameraman and a soundman from Britain, various personnel from the U.S.A., including John Farrow, Mia's brother, who is recruited on site.

Paul Horn - 'The year before, everyone came for the purpose of meditation. This year many people were not meditators. Most of my film crew, for example, had never heard of meditation. Others had heard about it, but they thought it was all nonsense and did not believe in it.

Four Star Productions committed to the film. I was the producer, and Gene Corman was the executive producer, which made him my boss. I had chosen Maharishi to be my master, my guru, my spiritual guide, but Corman created a lot of problems. In fact, he became a total drag.

Meanwhile, I was responsible for a $500,000 budget and for seeing that the film got made. I had a responsibility to Maharishi and a responsibility to the Four Star film company. Corman didn't believe in Maharishi's integrity or authenticity, and yet I had to work with him.

Initially, Corman's arrival was delayed, which meant I was the one who had to get everything rolling. Corman had made many films. I had not made even one - but now I was in charge. It was totally up to me. Following my original idea, I had us film Maharishi as he gave his lectures, and we shot footage of the meditators as they went through their daily routine.'[144]

❀ ❀ ❀

When he's not meditating John devotes time on completing his new material; some are just fragments, snatches of songs yet to be completed; one such song is about *'Mean Mr Mustard'* who has a sister called Shirley.

'His sister Shirley works in a shop
She never stops, she's a go-getter'
- Excerpt from *'Mean Mr Mustard'* by John Lennon & Paul McCartney

John - 'I'd read somewhere in the newspaper about this mean guy who hid five-pound notes, not up his nose but somewhere else.'[15]

Another unfinished fragment of song is about *'Polythene Pam'*.

'Well it's a little absurd but she's a nice class of bird
Yes, you could say she was attractively built'
- Excerpt from *'Polythene Pam'* by John Lennon & Paul McCartney

John - 'That was me, remembering a little event with a woman in Jersey, and a man who was England's answer to Allen Ginsberg... I met him when we were on tour and he took me back to his apartment and I had a girl and he had one he wanted me to meet. He said she dressed up in polythene, which she *did*. She didn't wear jack boots and kilts, I just sort of elaborated. Perverted sex in a polythene bag. Just looking for something to write about.'[15]

Joe Massot - 'In one of our conversations about film I told John I could film anything he wrote. "I don't believe it. I bet you can't film my poetry!" insisted John. "Sure I can. Poetry is the film makers medium." The following day John handed me a sheet of paper with some words he had written that night. "Make a film about that!" he said with a sardonic gleam in his eye.'[101]

> *Constant and intense care for this vital area,*
> *glides quickly and invisibly over,*
> *melting right into the skin to soften expression lines.*
> *Slim as a lipstick,*
> *always at hand for fast convenient application, many times a day.*
> *And, you can work with it; you can play with it,*
> *for people who like to play it both ways.*
> *Hydro-elastic suspension trims uneven surfaces.*
> *Luxury length is only half the story,*
> *it's the deep acting lanolin that does it.*
> *Hmmm yeah ...*
>
> *- 'John's Poem'* [189]

The poem appears to be a collage of copy lines taken from glossy magazine advertisements, for such diverse products as Estée Lauder's *'Wrinkle Stick - Its rich emollients glide easily, invisibly over make-up, melting right into the skin to help soften expression lines'*, to an automotive suspension system produced for the British Motor Corporation (BMC) termed *'Hydrolastic'*.

Perhaps one might have expected something more metaphysical from John after all those many, many hours of meditation, and here he is putting together something sensual, suggestive and even vaguely auto-erotic!

❀ ❀ ❀

Cynthia - 'Just one of Maharishi's acts of kindness was experienced by John and myself when we mentioned it was our son Julian's birthday in the near future.'

Clearly Maharishi made a mental note that it was John and Cynthia's son's birthday soon.
Cynthia - '… we were summoned to his quarters. On entering his rooms we were confronted by the Maharishi beaming with happiness when he saw our expressions of delight at what we saw. For Julian he had had the most beautiful Indian clothes made. They were fit for a little Indian prince, a complete wardrobe. Accompanying the clothes and set out on the floor around him was a complete set of exquisitely hand-painted figures of animals and authentic Indian hunters, John and I were overwhelmed. The Maharishi's kindness and thoughtfulness bowled us over. It was particularly unexpected in the stringent circumstances to which we had become accustomed in Rishikesh. On leaving the Maharishi, John held my hand. He was overjoyed.'
John Lennon - 'Oh, Cyn, won't it be wonderful to be together with Julian again. Everything will be fantastic again, won't it? I can't wait, Cyn, can you?'[7]

❀ ❀ ❀

John replies to a begging letter from a Mr Bulla.

> *Dear MR Bulla,*
> *Thanks for your letter.*
> *- If every request like yours was granted - there would be no 'huge treasure' as you call it. You say 'peace of mind minus all other things on earth is equal to nothing' - this doesn't make sense. To have peace of mind one would have to have all that one desires - otherwise where is the peace of mind?*
> *Even a 'poor' clerk can travel the world - as many people do - including friends of mine some of whom are at this academy now, all equally 'poor'. All you need is initiative - if you don't have this I suggest you try transcendental meditation through which all things are possible.*
>
> *With love*
> *John Lennon.*
> *jai guru dev.*

SPIRITUAL REGENERATION MOVEMENT FOUNDATION OF INDIA

Under the Divine Guidance of His Holiness Maharishi Mahesh Yogi of Uttar Kashi

TELEPHONE:
RISHIKESH 121
CABLE: MEDITATION, DELHI

SHANKARACHARYA NAGAR
P. O.   SWARGASHRAM
RISHIKESH, U.P. INDIA

Our Guiding Light

His Divinity
Swami Brahmananda Saraswati Jagad-Guru Shankaracharya Jyotir-Math Himalayas, India.

THE SPIRITUAL REGENERATION MOVEMENT FOUNDATION is dedicated to offering peace, harmony and happiness to everyone in all walks of life through a simple system of Transcendental Deep Meditation.

His Holiness Maharishi Mahesh Yogi has developed and promoted a simple system of meditation whereby every normal man can easily reach the deeper levels of consciousness, unfold latent faculties and realise more complete happiness.

The main aim of this world-wide movement is to establish meditation centres everywhere and infuse Maharishi's simple system of deep meditation in the daily routine of every individual.

The S.R.M. Foundation aims at world peace through harmony and happiness in the life of each individual.

WORLD CENTRES

INDIA, AFGHANISTAN, BURMA, WEST INDIES, MALAYSIA, HONGKONG, JAPAN, ENGLAND, SCOTLAND, ICELAND, FINLAND, SWEDEN, NORWAY, DENMARK, HOLLAND, FRANCE, GERMANY, AUSTRIA, ITALY, SWITZERLAND, GREECE, TURKEY, IRAN, U.A.R., EAST AFRICA, SOUTH AFRICA, CANADA, U.S.A., PERU, CHILE, ARGENTINA, COLUMBIA, URUGUAY, BRAZIL, AUSTRALIA, NEWZEALAND.

REGISTERED UNDER THE SOCIETIES ACT 1860, AND TAX-EXEMPTED

Dear MR Bulla,

Thanks for your letter. — If every request like yours was granted —there would be no "huge treasure" as you call it. You say 'peace of mind minus all other things on earth is equal to nothing' — this doesn't make sense. To have peace of mind one would have to have all that one desires —otherwise what is the peace of mind?

Even a 'poor' derek can travel the world — as many people do — including friends of mine some of whom are at this academy now, all equally 'poor'. All you need is initiative — if you don't have this I suggest you try transcendental meditation through which all things are possible.

with love

John Lennon.

jai guru dev.

On Saturday, 6th April 1968, George Harrison writes a letter to someone called Ivan, who has evidently been asking *him* for money.

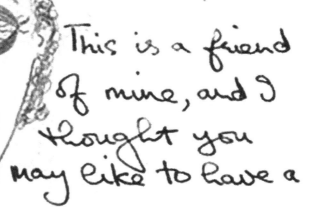

RISHIKESH
HIMALAYAS
INDIA.
6 April.

Dear Ivan,

This is a friend of mine, and I thought you may like to have a look at her. She is called Mary and only comes out during early spring, after the monsoon period.
I have just lent her my last $100. so unfortunately you are out of luck, So You will have to be satisfied with my best wishes.
Keep practising, and the best of luck to your group and yourself.

George Harrison.

RISHIKESH
HIMALAYAS
INDIA.
6 April.

Dear Ivan,
This is a friend of mine, and I thought you may like to have a look at her. She is called Mary and only comes out during early Spring, after the monsoon period.
I have just lent her my last $100. so unfortunately you are out of luck, So You will have to be satisfied with my best wishes.
Keep practising, and the best of luck to your group and yourself.
George Harrison.

George's letter makes mention of a 'Mary'. Curiously, Mia Farrow's name is really Mary and Jenny Boyd's real name is also Mary; Helen Mary Boyd, 'Jenny' having been the name of Pattie's doll. And of course, talking of changed names, Ringo Starr is an assumed name too, the name given by his family being Richard Starkey or even more properly, Richard Parkin (Ringo's great-grandmother having remarried and taken her new husband's surname, Starkey).

John Lennon sends a postcard to his father, the card is postmarked 'CAMP P.O.', 6th April 1968.

Dear Fred + Pauline
It's great here - hope it's great there.
See you when we get back
lots of love
John + Cyn xx
P.S. forgot your address.

Mike Love flies to London, where he talks with Keith Altham of the *New Musical Express* and explains a new initiative to spread Transcendental Meditation.
Mike Love - 'World Peace I is the first in a series of world wide concerts that we are planning this year. We are hoping to open in London and then go on to play most of the major European and Continental countries like Paris and Copenhagen'
'We are hoping to involve as many creative people in all forms of art and entertainment as possible from Picasso to Heffners bunny girls.
'Some of the most famous names in the pop world have guaranteed their assistance. The movement is aligned to the Maharishi Mahesh Yogi's drive for "Permanent World Peace" and the proceeds of the concerts will remain in the countries we play to promote that end.
'In this way we hope to go into phase two which, will be "World Peace II" playing venues as far apart as Moscow and Bangkok.'[190]

❀ ❀ ❀

On Sunday, 7th April 1968, The Beach Boys belatedly start their tour, playing at Township Auditorium, Columbia S.C., where they are supported by Buffalo Springfield, The Strawberry Alarm Clock and The Epics.

❀ ❀ ❀

Monday, 8th April 1968, is Julian Lennon 5th birthday; he was born 8th April 1963 and christened John Charles Julian Lennon.

❀ ❀ ❀

Mike Dolan takes great care of his birthday present, the signed copy of *'Bhagavad-Gita: A New Translation and Commentary'* by Maharishi Mahesh Yogi, which includes signatures from Mia Farrow, Donovan, Charlie Lutes and Paul Horn, who were not there the day it was presented to him.

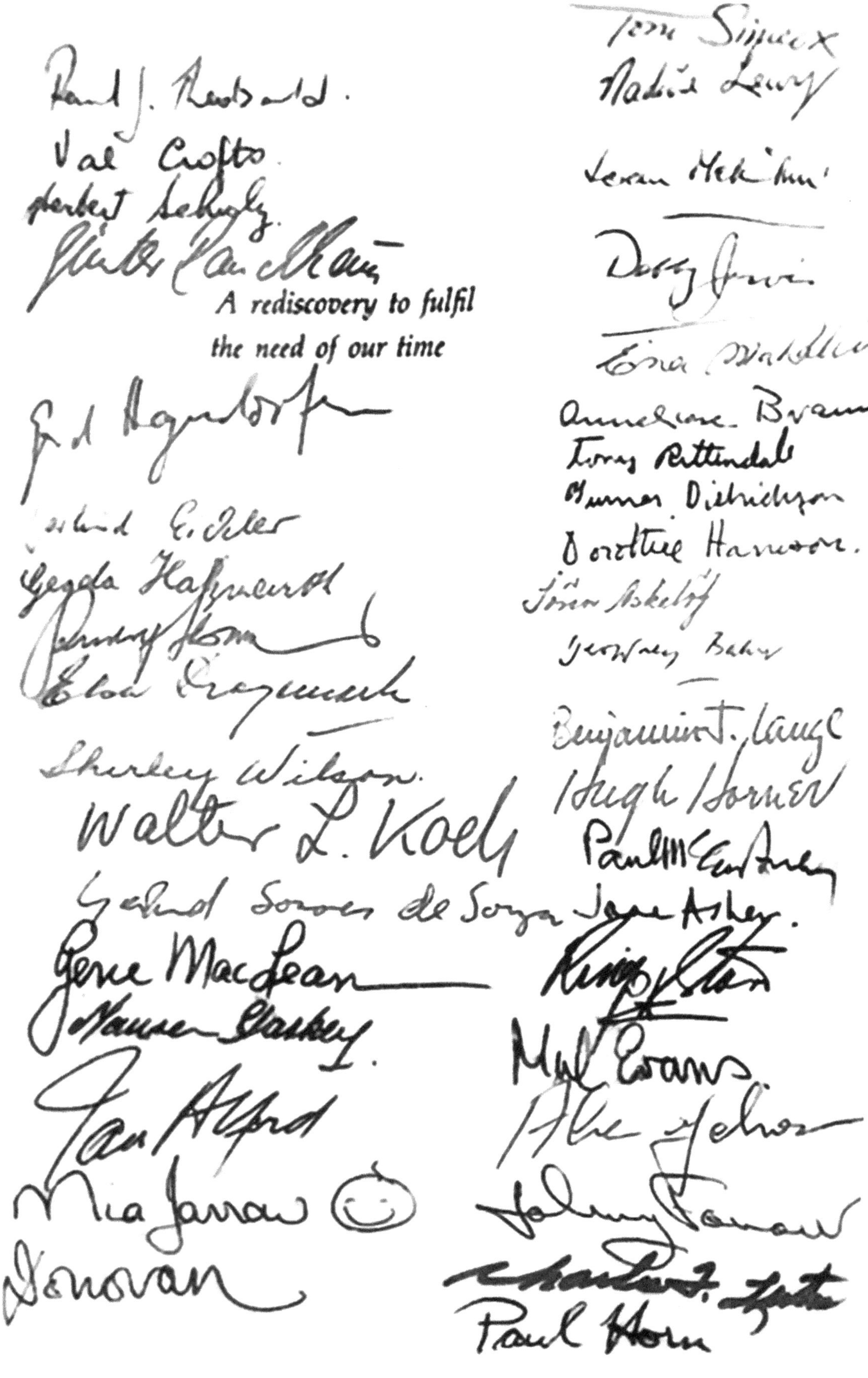
A rediscovery to fulfil
the need of our time
Donovan
Paul Horn

Maharishi announces that he won't be attending the Kumbha Mela, at Hardwar, a decision that disappoints many of his students, why George Harrison had even hoped he might meet with the legendary Babaji there.

Monday, 8th April 1968.

In "Look", February 6, an article was published about Paul Horn. He is one of my favorites here, and the article and the cover-photos apparently are very good.

Probably I will spend the period from 26.4. until May 1st here in the academy, because it is already unbearably hot in Delhi now. At the slightest action the sweat is dripping off my face.

- Excerpt from a letter written by Gertrud Soares de Souza to her 19 year-old daughter, Francisca, in West Germany. Translated from German into English.

'Late in the afternoon I was talking to Cyn and Tom. Tom left and I talked to Cynthia about life and the Ashram. She's a nice lady she poured her heart out. She said she would be glad to leave. She doesn't relate to the people here.'

- Mike Dolan's diary

Tuesday, 9th April 1968.

My dear child, the course is drawing to an end. Saturday we are supposed to go to Kashmir, or Sunday - I do not know, I just let me being drifted...
Maharishi will be in Frankfurt on April 27, large gathering.

Did you get the Easter letter with the little hearts around? Cynthia brought it back to me just when (Gualterio) Weiss was about to leave and I gave the letter to him.

Jemima [Pitman] arrived, and Johannes Olivegren, the professor, who was initiated in Sweden and now is already an initiator!
Already now I am homesick for here and the people we met. At the beginning we were so shy talking to the holy men, but now you're really friends. The few who understand or speak English, are very loving to us. But Dhirendra, the beautiful one, doesn't speak a word in English. Devendra is now in Australia. And I think Maharishi has put Ulla Devi (Gutmann) to Bremen.
Yesterday I spoke with the wife of the man who made a movie here. She also was initiated now.

[There] is the Indian course too. Generally there are very interesting people, but Maharishi kept us disconnected because there he only speaks Hindi.

The base now in Honor's bed is a wooden board with a thick pad on it. My last bed was covered with strings, much softer. But my current room is very nice! The purple carpet looks so elegant. Golden yellow cushion on the chair. A yellow towel as tablecloth.
I'll return to here after Kashmir. You can send the mail to here: "Please await her return"
Have a good time - God bless - Jai Guru Dev

- Excerpt from a letter written by Gertrud Soares de Souza to her 19 year-old daughter, Francisca, in West Germany. Translated from German into English.

Easter card for Francisca

Joe Massot - Then, at last… Gene Corman finally showed up and had a meeting with the Maharishi, George, John and myself. He promptly announced that he had a professional crew in New Delhi and a professional director (a choreographer who'd never made a film before). Unfortunately for me, the cameraman was Nestor Almendros. I worked with Nestor in Cuba. The guy was one of the greatest cameramen in the world.
So, I thought, Uh-oh! Looks like I've lost the job.'
'Next morning I took a cab, the only one in Rishikesh, to the Oberoi Hotel [in Delhi].'[185]

Paul Horn - 'The whole idea was to film things spontaneously, having fun with the documentary, presenting Maharishi and the ashram and the meditators in a loving, natural light - *cinema verité*.
When Corman arrived, he wanted nothing to do with that approach. He wanted everything planned and set up, even though we had no script. As Corman took over, I lost control of the project. He and I clashed on nearly everything.'[144]

⊛ ⊛ ⊛

Mike Dolan - 'My next door neighbor in the Ashram was a feisty New Yorker in her late twenties who I will call RB. She was perkily attractive, very funny and at times combative. She would interrupt Maharishi with pointedly uncosmic questions during his lectures. She was as a lot of people on that course a recent meditator, one of the sudden influx of Beatle fans. It seemed to hit her all of a sudden that this technique was more a part of a greater Hindu Tradition than she expected. She was having trouble as the lectures delved more and more Hindu Philosophy. I believe she felt deceived by the movement.'[191]

Richard Blakely - 'I had talked to Rosalyn while having tea and she'd seemed perfectly happy with the course and with her experience in long meditation. She also seemed just as curious and excited to learn about the mantra and become an initiator as she had been while sitting next to me on the flight to Bombay. She told me about a private meeting she'd recently had with Maharishi, who had advised her to socialize less and meditate more, saying that when she came out of long meditation socializing would be even more enjoyable. And it was true, she said. Now that she was beginning to emerge from long meditation she felt more alive, more in tune with what was going on around her, more in touch. And in fact that day she had looked radiant.'[111]

Mike Dolan - 'She was still friendly but she became very negative toward meditation in general. She wanted so badly to just go home but her plane ticket was dated for the TTC [Teacher Training Course] end so she was forced to stay at the Ashram for weeks until the course ended. RB soon found a friend in Magic Alex, she had stopped attending the lectures weeks before, she stayed in her room with Alex as he made his plans for the revolutionary power pack. I could hear them through the thin wall huffing and puffing as they practiced their asanas late at night. It behooved both RB and Alex to get out of Rishikesh but he couldn't leave without losing face. Magic Alex was under some pressure from his friend/bosses to actually produce something. If he was to stay in Rishikesh he would be exposed as a fraud. The familiar smell of very happy herb would sometimes waft out of the open door, and their behavior was becoming notorious especially with the older establishment meditators like Walter Koch, Nancy Cooke and the newly arrived president of the SRM Charles Lutes.
Charles Lutes had flown to India when Nancy Cooke told him of the plans Maharishi was making with Apple to make a movie with Maharishi as a co-star. Charlie had already a prior arrangement with Maharishi to make his own Maharishi movie with a film company put together by long time meditator Paul Horn. In Charlie's mind the Beatles would take second billing to the Maharishi and he would decide who made the film; it was to be Bliss Productions.
The Beatles of course were the biggest thing since the parting of the Red Sea so this [was] perhaps not the smartest business decision ever made but it certainly put all of those damned hippies in there place. While he was at it he'd clear up the mess with the openly pot smoking whore RB. It mattered not a whit that The Beatles were under contract to make a movie at the time and couldn't appear in Charlie's movie or that RB was kept a captive of circumstance. Charlie had spent too much time with his nose pressed up against Maharishi's window waiting for an audience as the Yogi spent all of his time with the Beatles. A cynical person might think that Charlie was jealous! Charlie was asserting himself running the show again, it was after all his organization.'[191]

❀ ❀ ❀

There's a new visitor in the area, Paul Scrivener, a friendly red haired young Canadian guy, who is staying down by the riverside.

Paul Scrivener - 'In early April 1968, at age 19, I arrived in Rishikesh after travelling overland for four months. I lived alone on the Ganges riverbank south of Maharishi's ashram. One day about 5 o'clock while sitting on a rock in the shade, reading Rabindranath Tagore's *Gitanjali*, I saw in the distance three young women splashing water in the Ganges River. They came walking in contemplation on the white sands toward me. Three muses at the gates of heaven wearing bikinis. I grabbed my backpack hidden behind the rocks and pulled out a women's cotton *kurta* blouse that I had bought to send to my girlfriend in Victoria. I approached and asked the girls if they would mind holding the blouse up to see if it would fit as they were about the same size as my girlfriend. They laughed and liked the blue embroidery. I knew by their accents the girls were from England, and told them, my name is Paul and I've just arrived in Rishikesh, travelling overland from Canada. They introduced themselves to me as Patty, Jenny, and Cynthia and said they were staying in Maharishi's ashram. We wiggled our feet in the sand and before I knew it, they invited me up to the ashram for lemonade. It was late afternoon. They collected their clothes and sandals, and with a warm breeze in the air, we hiked up the steep slope walking single file until we reached an unassuming gate. A commissioner sat quietly at the entrance. The girls told him that I was their guest. I saluted the commissioner and continued up into the ashram with the girls, passing by white canvas tents and makeshift stalls with sewing machines. On the other side was a large canopied tent with a big carpet on the slanting hillside, where Maharishi gave press conferences every day at 3 pm.

Further along the pathway and past the residences, we approached a rectangular dining space overlooking a cliff with a scenic expanse of the Ganges below. Wow. The girls invited me into the dining room where three or four fellows sat at the long table in a serious conversation. They nodded to the girls and said hello. I was introduced as Paul from Canada. I realized in a split second, when they were introduced to me, that two of them were George Harrison and John Lennon from the Beatles, and the girls, Cynthia Lennon, and Pattie and Jenny Boyd. I passed by John to sit at the table and he noticed my peace button. He gave me a pat on the shoulder and turned back to his intense conversation, only quieter. The atmosphere was surreal. The girls poured lemonade from a pitcher and passed me a glass to quench my thirst. We ate almonds and cashew nuts from bowls on the table. The guys ignored us. I took a breath of air and sensed the tension. My mind wondered who were the other fellows who sat at the table with George and John. I knew it wasn't Ringo or Paul.'

'I had a wonderful time chatting with the girls. The sun began setting and the magic hour was fading. I said "Cheerio" as it was time to go down to the riverbank before dusk. George Harrison accompanied me outside and showed me the way to the main path. He offered a cigarette, leaned up against a mango tree, played his guitar, and sang Bob Dylan's *"Don't think twice, it's alright."* I listened. His yearning voice and inspiring guitar stunned me. Without realizing it, I'd made it into the inner sanctum. Three of the most famous girls in the world had invited me into Maharishi's ashram. What an incredible introduction to Shankaracharya Nagar …'[38]

❀ ❀ ❀

Richard Blakely - 'I asked Jenny if she knew how much it would cost to take a taxi down to New Delhi.'
Jenny Boyd - 'You're thinking of leaving us?'
Richard Blakely - 'I would also have to go see Maharishi to tell him I was leaving.'
'Somehow I don't think he'll mind though. He might even be glad to see me go.'
Jenny Boyd - 'You never know about him though, do you? What he really thinks.'
Richard Blakely - 'I let that sink in then asked her if she'd heard anything about the Guru Dev movie. She said she didn't know exactly, meetings had been going on pretty nonstop since the film crew arrived, but she was pretty sure the Beatles' movie was a dead issue and George and John and the others were not happy.'

'The sun was now almost touching the horizon and had begun to turn blood red, its light filtered through all that Oriental dust.'
Jenny Boyd - 'When you think of all that could have been.'
Richard Blakely - 'Yeah, and the worst is that now no one will ever know.'
'She turned to me and said she would miss me if I left and I said I would miss her too.'
'We exchanged addresses and promised to write and headed back up the path to our respective rooms to put in another hour of meditation before dinner.'[111]

Mike Dolan - 'It was getting stiflingly humid both day and night, we could no longer rely on the respite of the cool evenings breeze that came down from the Himalayas along the Ganges gorge. The cool air would bring out the meditators and Shankaracharya Nagar usually silent in the day would fairly bustle from twilight through to Maharishi's seven o'clock Puja and lecture. This particular night was sickeningly hot, the power had gone off toward the end of Maharishi's lecture, perhaps an omen for what was to follow.
'I stayed up late with my friend Sarah and Brahmacharya Rhaghwendra chatting about this and that and watching the reflections of the stars shimmer in the Ganges below us. We both loved Rhaghwendra he was one of Maharishi's top aides and was the liaison between the impatient Westerners and the more dilatory Indians. He was our friend and soul mate, tremendously spiritual yet absolutely outlandish. He was a little saddened because he knew of the move that was going to be made to oust RB from the ashram. He didn't condone her behavior but RB was one of our group of friends, he knew she was having a hard time adjusting, he respected her feelings on [what] was essentially a religious/social issue.
It started to rain. I walked back to our bungalow with Sarah. It was pitch black but RB's door was open I could see RB and Alex in the room their shadows dancing elastic in the candle light. One of the Indian kitchen boys was arriving at the same time. I knew he was coming for RB but I couldn't bring myself to tell her.'[191]

❊ ❈ ❊

Pattie - '… Magic Alex claimed that Maharishi had tried something on with a girl he had befriended. I am not sure how true that was.'[21]

Cynthia - 'I was upset. I had seen Alex with the girl, who was young and impressionable, and I wondered whether he - whom I had never once seen meditating - was being rather mischievous. I was surprised that John and George had both chosen to believe him. It was only when John and I talked later that he told me he had begun to feel disenchanted with the Maharishi's behavior. He felt that, for a spiritual man, the Maharishi had too much interest in public recognition, celebrities and money.'[10]

Could this allegation just be a copycat claim based of Mia's story?
Cynthia - 'To me it was tragic - hearsay, an unproved action and unproved statements. The finger of suspicion was well and truly pointed at the man who had given us all so much in so many ways - the Maharishi. Alexis and a fellow female meditator began to sow seeds of doubt into very open minds.'[7]

Mike Dolan - 'Roz was about 9 years older than me. She was my neighbor in the ashram I liked her a lot, she wore her heart on her sleeve the way New Yorkers do. She was done with the course before Alex arrived and was dying to go home. I don't think she consciously manipulated the situation but she became a player through the collision of circumstances.'[38]
'She was also under the influence of the Svengali-like Magic Alex, would she have made something up if it assured her her plane ride home?'[191]

Tony Bramwell, a friend of The Beatles - '… a few people thought that Alex had latched onto the sexual rumors as a means of escape because the Maharishi - the physics graduate - had taken a keen interest in the proposed radio station. He asked many searching questions that Alex was unable to answer and the young Greek panicked. It was then that he insisted that they all had to leave immediately over the sexual shenanigans.'[192]

Another female student is confused as to how to correctly interpret Maharishi:-
'.. he used to see me after the Beatles!'
'… he did keep asking me to "come closer" one night that I was alone with him in his bedroom. (He often used

to summon me after the evening lecture, no doubt I lacked self confidence & because I used to meditate all day rather than socialise.) Well I refused to go any closer than maybe 2 feet, because I saw him as Divine & felt too impure, so finally he said "OK then we can just sit!" so I moved back against a wall & felt this incredible Love, after which he let me be around him a lot.... '

'I definitely think he only spoke to me as he did that night because I had waited until about 1am to see him.. at the time I was so naive that it absolutely never occurred to me what he might have had in mind! & the Love & Devotion & closeness to him just grew from then on. And he never again repeated that... So in a way I think I passed some test of innocence & purity of intention/mind.

Have to say as far as I'm concerned there was never any question of anything other than a Guru /Disciple relationship apart from that one time, which actually may have been Maharishi testing my intentions, as he had actually forgotten he had called me that evening & it was very late by the time the Beatles left him.'[38]

Very hot today. A film crew arrived at noon. Spent most of the day with Viggie and Sarah. Went to bed late. Must buy Pattie sunglasses.

- Mike Dolan's diary

Wednesday, 10th April 1968.

Cynthia - 'The Maharishi had been accused and sentenced before he had even had a chance to defend himself. All the bad thoughts were flowing back. Lack of faith and trust abounded, and the following morning, almost before any of us had a chance to wake up, Alexis set the ball in motion by ordering taxis to take us to the airport. That was how quickly things got out of hand, with the speed of an arrow.'[7]

Pattie - 'I think Alex wanted to get John away from Rishikesh. - he seemed convinced that Maharishi was evil. He kept saying, "It's black magic". And perhaps John had been waiting for an excuse to leave - he wanted to be with Yoko. Whatever the truth, they left.

We stayed on but the next night I had a horrid dream about Maharishi, and when George woke me the next morning, I said, "Come on, we're leaving".'[21]

Terry Gustafson - 'Colin Harrison, an English meditator, and I left before sunrise to walk up to a tea house on top of the first ridge of Himalayan foothills behind the ashram. The Four Star Productions crew had arrived by taxi from Delhi in the middle of the night. As Colin and I passed the Beatles' quarters on the way out of the ashram, they were already setting up their cameras in the courtyard. A bad omen.

The tea house was just a thatched roof supported by four posts. The owner squatted on the ground, brewing tea on a small grate over a little hole with a twig-fed fire. Colin and I each sipped a glass of tea mixed with rich boiled water buffalo milk as we watched the snow on the distant high peaks change from rosy to white as the hot sun climbed into the sky.'[38]

Terry and Colin return to Shankaracharya Nagar.

Terry Gustafson - 'The story as I heard it is that John Lennon, bleary-eyed and half-awake, with his hair taped back, opened the door of his quarters and stepped out. Without so much as a "Good Morning", the director yelled "Action!", and the cameras began to roll. John exploded in anger, immediately got the other Beatles and wives together and ordered taxis. The Beatles, seething with rage, went together to confront Maharishi.'[38]

Cynthia - 'Meditation practised for long periods renders the meditator truly sensitive to any overt or strong vibrations. His mind becomes very finely tuned. Alexis's statements about how the Maharishi had been indiscreet with a certain lady, and what a blackguard he had turned out to be, gathered momentum. All, may I say, without a single shred of evidence or justification. It was obvious to me that Alexis wanted out and more than anything he wanted the Beatles out as well.'[7]

George - 'Someone started the nasty rumour about Maharishi…

'The story stirred up a situation. John had wanted to leave anyway, so that forced him into the position of thinking: "OK, now we've got a good reason to get out of here."'[1]

Alan Waite and Paul Horn are with Maharishi when John and George suddenly appear and ask to speak with

Maharishi alone.

Alexis Mardas - 'About three to four months after I had arrived at the retreat, we were attending a lecture given by the Maharishi. Also present was an American teacher, whose name I now know to have been Rosalyn Bonas. I remember the Maharishi saying that this lady had an "iceberg" in her brain and was unable to understand what he was saying. In the presence of everyone there, he told her that she should come to his villa after the lecture for private tuition.

On the evening of the following day or the day after (I do not remember which) John Lennon and I were sitting outside John Lennon's little house. The teacher came up to us and told us that the Maharishi had made sexual advances to her while she was in his villa. She also told us that, despite the fact that we were all supposed to be strictly vegetarian, the Maharishi had offered her chicken to eat. She told us that she had been invited back to the Maharishi's villa the next evening.

During the next evening, John Lennon, George Harrison and I were curious and went to the window of the Maharishi's villa at the time that the nurse was supposed to be there. We looked inside and saw that the Maharishi was trying to hug the teacher. Both of them were fully clothed.

All of us were very upset about what [we] had seen. We had complete confidence and trust in the Maharishi and this confidence had now been severely dented.

On the next morning, John Lennon and I went to see the Maharishi about what had happened. John was our spokesman. He asked the Maharishi to explain himself, I remember the exact words that the Maharishi used when answering, namely: "I am only human". John said that he was disgusted with what had happened.'[193]

George - 'The idea of the course was that it lasted however many weeks in Rishikesh and then at the end of that period they shifted the camp up to Kashmir. This was something they did every year. But I'd planned to go just for the Rishikesh trip and then go down to the South of India to do some filming with Ravi Shankar. He was making a movie called *Raga*.

I kept telling Maharishi, "No, I'm not going to Kashmir - I went there last year." I told him I was going south, and that's when John and I left. It was only really John and I who were there from the beginning up until the end of the segment at Rishikesh, and I think John wanted to get back because - you can see it historically now - he had just started his relationship with Yoko before we went to India.'

'We went to Maharishi, and I said, "Look, I told you I was going. I'm going to the South of India." He couldn't really accept that we *were* leaving, and he said, "What's wrong?" That's when John said something like: "Well, you're supposed to be the mystic, you should know."'[1]

Alan Waite - 'John and George were in with Maharishi for about 20-30 minutes, and walked out the meeting moody and quiet. Seeing Paul [Horn] and myself they said to us "Nice to have met with you guys! See you another time" and walked off to get in their cars.'[38]

Cynthia - 'They were confused and bitter at what they had learned, and yet they still didn't give the Maharishi a chance to defend himself. All they could say when asked was: "If you're as cosmically conscious as you claim then you should know why we are leaving."

With that they left him and returned to the dining-area where we were all waiting.'[7]

Jerry Jarvis - 'Maharishi then called me and asked me to find out what's going on with them, he really didn't know why they were leaving.'[38]

It doesn't take Jerry long to discover John and George over in the dining area having breakfast and that they don't wish to talk. So he reports back to Maharishi who then walks towards them but stops short and sits himself down at the 'kiosk', in sight of the Beatles' party.

Cynthia - 'I have never packed my belongings with such a heavy heart. I felt that what we were doing was wrong, very, very wrong. To sit in judgement on a man who had given us nothing but happiness... The real turning of the knife came as we were about to take our leave. While we were seated around the dining-tables waiting for the taxis and conversing in whispers, nerve ends showing, the Maharishi emerged from his quarters and seated himself not a hundred yards from our agitated group of dissidents. One of his ardent followers

walked across to us and asked us to please talk things over properly with the Maharishi. He said he was very sad and wanted desperately to put things right and to convince us that we should stay.'
'I wanted to cry. It was so sad. The Maharishi was sitting alone in a small shelter made of wood with a dried grass roof. He looked very biblical and isolated in his faith.'[7]

Geoffrey Baker - 'After breakfast that day he [George] said, "Come, I've got something for you."
George gave me his copy of Yogananda's *Autobiography Of A Yogi* just prior to his leaving Rishikesh. He inscribed the book "Jai Guru Dev, George".'[178]

Mike Dolan - 'I was woke by Rhaghwendra it was still dark in the very early dawn, I was to go down to the dining area and find the cooks to make tea for some guests who were leaving. It was a little startling to see Cynthia, Patty, Jenny (Patty's sister) and RB standing around in the cool morning air.
Sitting in the open dining area in deep conversation were John, George, Magic Alex and Rhaghwendra, Tom a B-movie cowboy actor and RB's ex-boyfriend sat to the side. It wouldn't have been unusual except that the simple Indian clothes were nowhere to be seen all instead all were dressed in stylish pop star clothes.'[191]

Cynthia - 'The boys were adamant. They had made their minds up, burned their boats and nothing the Maharishi could do or say would budge them. They stood up, filed past him and not a word was said. I will never forget the picture in my mind. It may sound melodramatic but it was a very vivid impression of a scene from the Bible re-enacted in the mountains of India, of Jesus being denied by his disciples. Not that in any way did I believe that the Maharishi was Jesus, but to me he was a man with a quest, a dream for a better world and here were we, a group of people who had the power to influence the youth of the world possibly squashing all the good work he had done. The only person who actually stood up to be counted was the Maharishi, only subsequently to be shunned.'[7]

Mike Dolan - 'I noticed Cynthia had been crying. Nobody looked happy. Patty and Jenny smiled meekly. Rhaghwendra the lovely man wore the gray ashen mask of the defeated. I noticed Maharishi sitting alone on a rock just outside of his garden the rain the night before threw up a light mist giving the scene a theatrical effect. Rhaghwendra told me that something had happened, there had been meetings all through the night, that John and George were upset and that Magic Alex was insisting that they all leave. Which of course they did. Rhaghwendra was given the job of transporting them all to New Delhi, they were very upset when they got into the several taxis the girls were sobbing still trying to persuade them to reconsider, they were fighting back tears as they drove away.'[191]

> *There was a commotion. John and George and the girls along with Roz, Alex and Tom were in a fleet of taxis. I was expecting this but still a bit shocked.*
> - Mike Dolan's diary

Rosalyn Bonas - 'If I wanted to leave the ashram at any time it would have happened. TM did not buy my ticket. I could fly home at a moments notice. Certainly creating a story with Alex as "my ticket out of the ashram" makes no sense at all. I left the ashram the day after I was totally disillusioned with my Guru. Up until that point I believed every word Maharishi said and I was determined to make a difference in the world by teaching his meditation. Yes I might have missed but a few lectures because I found Alex to be quite an interesting character, but other than that I was a devoted student meditating several days at a time, taping every lecture sitting at the feet of Maharishi, studying and reading daily.'[38]

Peter Shotton - '… the Maharishi materialized in the distance as John and the others loaded into a couple of taxis that Alex had commandeered from the nearest village. "John, John," the guru called out mournfully. "Please don't leave me! Come back, come back!"'[34]

Jenny Boyd - 'Poor Maharishi. I remember him standing at the gate of the ashram, under an aide's umbrella, as the Beatles filed by, out of his life. "Wait," he cried. "Talk to me." But no one listened.'[6]

Peter Shotton - '"Even then," John told me, "he sent out so much power that he was like a magnet, drawing me back to him. Suddenly I didn't want to go at all, but I forced meself to carry on before it was too late."'[34]

Nancy Jackson - '…we met a puzzling sight. A taxi stood at the ashram entrance and George Harrison was loading suitcases. His shiny, long hair hung over his flushed face a result of his efforts.

He paused to greet us, "Well, you're just in time to say a fast farewell."

"What do you mean? Where are you going?"

At that moment, a teary-eyed Patty Harrison joined her husband. Patty, delicate and pretty, was usually serene and friendly. At this moment she was obviously distressed. "We have to leave because of a misunderstanding."

'"But only a few nights ago we were discussing all your plans for making the movie of Maharishi's life. You had definitely decided to go to Kashmir with the group and finish the course. Will you still meet us there?"

As I asked this, an angry John Lennon strode up to the car, "We're not going to join Maharishi there or anywhere - we've 'ad it. If you want to know why, ask your fuckin' precious guru!"

His thin face was tight. Behind his granny glasses, his sharp eyes were full of fury.

"Cyn, get your ass out here! I want to get out of this bloody place, *now*, for Christ sakes!"

Cynthia was also in tears. I asked the two girls, who had been so thrilled with Maharishi and his course, "What has happened? I have the things you asked me to buy for you." Taking packages out of my tote bag, I handed them over. "You were all fine this morning. Does Maharishi know you're leaving?" I could not comprehend what was happening.

Before she could answer, John snorted, "Does he know we're leaving? That's the laugh of the day!"

Cynthia spoke with great distress as she was hustled into the taxi after Patty. "We are so unhappy. I can't explain what happened. It is all a big mistake, but the boys insist on leaving."'[117]

George - 'We took some cars that had been driven up there. Loads of film crews kept coming because it was the world-famous 'Beatles in the Himalayas' sketch, and it was one of these film crews' cars we took to get back to Delhi.'[1]

Richard Blakely - 'I had gone down for breakfast, early as usual, and was assembling a tray to take back… when George came running down from Block 6 out of breath and obviously upset. He ran around shaking hands and saying goodbye to the few of us who were down at the kitchen at that hour. He said something had happened. He couldn't explain what. There wasn't time. The taxis were waiting. He said he was sorry to go and he looked it. He also looked a little frantic and I wondered why. What could George Harrison be afraid of? George said it had been a wonderful time and he hoped we would all keep in touch and that maybe somewhere, one day, well who knows. And then he ran back up the path and we heard the taxis start up one by one chug off up the road and they were gone.'[111]

Nancy Jackson - 'Rik helped George fasten down the last bag, and in a few moments the car took off, leaving a cloud of dust to settle over our wet clothes.'
On our way to Maharishi's, I paused, "Wait a minute, Rik; I want to peek in and see how they left the place." We were in front of Block Six. There was nothing much to see, except in John's room. A large photo of Maharishi was torn in half and thrown on the floor.'
'Rick quickly picked it up in dismay, "What bad karma he's tempting!"'[117]

Nancy makes a bee-line for Maharishi.
Nancy Jackson - 'Maharishi was sitting on his bed in his private room when we arrived. He looked sad. We asked him what had happened and told him that we'd seen the group taking off as we returned. He said very little - something about celebrities having fragile nervous systems and icebergs coming to the surface. He suggested we not talk about negative things, that we put our attention on the course.'[117]

Terry Gustafson - 'By the time we returned to the ashram two hours after we had left, the Beatles were already gone.'[172]

Carole Hamby - 'The Beatles left the ashram and Ros and Tom left with them - no fuss just departure.'[38]

Mike Dolan - 'Maharishi got a terrible shafting I thought. John and George were very pissed off about the film crew arriving. Probably rightly so because they were being exploited. A movie with the Beatles in it under the guise of lets record all of this peace and love fest for posterity, ch-Ching ch-Ching.
I always thought myself what's the difference between Maharishi desiring a mango or desiring a woman. He told us every night that there is nothing wrong with desiring. I believed it to be incredibly disappointing and dishonest that the hippest people in the world just then would allow themselves to get hung up because simple man makes pass at beautiful girl. I mean, how earth shaking.
I'll see if I wrote down when the leaders of the *Free Love* movement left.'[38]

Charlie Lutes - 'While I was still at the ashram, I repeated the story I'd heard to him [Maharishi]. His reaction was, "But, Charlie, I am a lifetime celibate; I don't know anything about sensual desires."'[117]

Ironically, one or two of Maharishi's students think that Charlie has eyes for the young ladies, but what they don't know is that, allegedly, Maharishi has given him a special *mantra* to meditate with, one supposed to ensure his celibacy.[195] So, if Maharishi is able to prescribe such a *mantra* for Charlie, surely he is capable of being self-restrained himself?

Nancy Jackson - 'He was saddened by what was happening, but stuck to his guns, "We do not recognize the negative. We just keep on working, putting one foot in front of the other. If we refuse to resist untruth, it will fall on its own. By resisting it, we give it support."'[117]

❀ ❀ ❀

John and Cynthia's journey to Delhi proves unexpectedly difficult.
John - 'God, Cyn, I won't feel safe until we're back in England. I feel as though the Maharishi is going to get his own back in some way.'
Cynthia - 'It was ridiculous, almost as though they were being pursued by some terrible enemy who going to

destroy them. Strangely enough we did have quite a set-back on our journey to Delhi. The taxis… would have been in no condition to pass our MOT test, so it was our luck to break down somewhere in the Indian countryside. Our taxi gave up the struggle and steamed to a halt, flat tyre and no spare. The driver didn't speak English and we didn't understand a word he said but it did dawn on us when he took off down the road that perhaps he was going to get help. We found ourselves parked on a grass verge in the pitch dark without food or drink or any means of light, not a sign of life anywhere. The other taxis had gone on ahead, unaware of our predicament. It wasn't very long before John and I started to get the jitters.

"John, what on earth are we going to do, where are we? We're absolutely stranded without a penny or a friend in a foreign land, and I'm sure we've seen the last of our driver."

John's only solution to the situation was to stand on the edge of the road with his thumb in the air frantically waving it backwards and forwards at the sound of any car approaching. We were about to give up all hope when a saloon car drew up beside us and two very educated Indian men inquired after our health. Were we relieved!

After a great deal of humming and haa-ing we opted for the lift. At least we wouldn't freeze to death and they seemed very amiable and keen to help. The driver of the saloon was a very fast driver. John and I clung onto the front seats like grim death. They could have been maniacs for all we knew. We started to get really worried. Our imagination ran riot and we panicked. We were about to ask them to let us out when one of them made it known that they were aware that John was a Beatle and that they would do all they could to help us get back to Delhi. At that point we put ourselves entirely in their hands and believe me they did us proud. At the nearest village they bought us drinks, and arranged after a great deal of persuasion for another taxi to take us on the remainder of our long journey. They were really marvelous. They also arranged for our luggage to follow us on.'

'Our eventual arrival at the hotel was even more chaotic. The driver took us on a tour of Delhi in order that we might remember where the hotel was. Finally the penny dropped, and the name came to us. We arrived about three hours later than everyone else and the consternation on their faces convinced us that they had all believed we had been "got". Nevertheless, it was a warm, relieved reunion, full of questions and laughter at our story of disaster.'[7]

2 more Beatles quit ashram

Hardwar, April 11 (UNI)—Beatles George Harrison and John Lennon quietly left for home yesterday, two weeks ahead of their scheduled departure date.

According to the previous programme they were to leave at the end of April after visiting Srinagar where they were to conclude their ten-week course as teachers of meditation. The other two Beatles had left Rishikesh a few weeks ago.

The ashram sources did not say why the Beatles left before completing the full course.

Meanwhile, Maharishi Mahesn Yogi is getting ready to leave for Srinagar on April 15 where he will continue the meditation class for another two weeks. Then he leaves for Europe for a week's stay in Holland, and the Scandinavian countries before he flies to the United States for a three-week tour. He will return to India in the last week of May.

Jenny Boyd - 'We went back to the hotel in Delhi and George and John tried to decide what to do. "Should we tell the world that the Beatles made a mistake?" John asked. "He isn't what's happening at all." Everyone was so disappointed.'[6]

Joe Massott - 'I came down to the lobby, and John and George were there.'[185]

'John pretended to be cross with me, "Do you know you took the only cab in Rishikesh. We had to wait a whole day for him to come back and pick us up." George said they were having nothing to do with the movie.'[101]

'Something had gone down between the Beatles and the Maharishi. I was never quite clear what. They did the same as I had: showered, shaved and got rid of the scent of Rishikesh. They were desperate to get back to London. We had dinner in the suite and lunch the following day.'

'While we're having lunch, Corman calls up. He wants to see me now.'

'He came up and he was almost down on his knees to me. His project was dead as a doornail. Would I speak to the Beatles? I knew it was no use, "Well, you know, there's some very beautiful religious festivals around Rishikesh that you can film. And there's the lepers!" The guy left. I told George and John and we were roaring, roaring!'[185]

'That evening I discussed with the two Beatles the plot of my next movie, watching a glorious Indian sunset on the balcony of the hotel, over looking New Delhi.'[101]

'I told them both the plot of Zachariah ….. which I'd come up with watching them dueling together at the meditation centre. Zachariah is the fastest gun in the West but he realizes that being the fastest anything is not the same thing as finding yourself.'[185]

Jenny Boyd - 'And then Pattie, George and I went and met up with Ravi Shankar and then toured with him for a couple more weeks.'[65]

'YOGA SONGS' BY BEATLES

Film producer Joe Massot said John Lennon, having completed the meditation course, left by air for Britain on Thursday.

George Harrison had gone to Madras to see the sitar player Ravi Shankar, who was filming there.

Mr Massot said the Beatles had decided not to join the Maharishi on his visit to Kashmir next week with other foreign disciples as planned.

This was only a holiday trip, and they had been there before.

Lennon and Harrison kept out of sight in Delhi after leaving the centre two weeks earlier than expected.

They checked into Delhi's luxurious Oberoi Hotel.

Reporters were unable to interview Lennon and his wife, Cynthia, before they checked out.

Harrison and his wife, Patti, stayed longer at the hotel but avoided Pressmen.

- The Sun-Herald 14th April 1968

Shambhu Das (Ravi Shankar's assistant) **-** 'Then all of a sudden we got a cable saying that George was coming down to see us in southern India. He was apparently very disturbed for some reason, and I still don't exactly know what happened. He just wanted to talk with Ravi by himself. So Ravi took him off to some isolated place, and they spent a couple of days together, and gradually George started feeling better. Then everyone ran away from us, and I didn't know why?'[104]

Chapter Twenty-Eight
The Visitation

It is Saturday, 13th April 1968, and today is the festival of Vaisakhi, an important day in Indian calendars, being the day preceding the full moon night of April with significance for those visiting the Kumbh Mela. It is also New Year's Day for those of the Sikh religion and Harvest Festival in the Punjab.

Dozens of Indian visitors arrive at Maharishi's academy, and amongst them is an impressive local *sadhu*, the dreadlocked Tat Wale Baba, who arrives with Swami Satchidananda and others.

Carole Hamby - 'The gathering in Maharishi's garden was colourful and quite amazing to see. One extremely elderly sannyasi - said to be 115 years old, many holy men and Tat Wale-Baba. Maharishi said of Tat Wale-Baba that he was 'pure Being, all transcendental'. There were also members of the Indian course and Maharishi spoke about the meaning and significance of "Akanda mundalakaram".[3]

akhanda mandalakaram vyaaptam yena characharam .
tatpadam darshitam yena tasmai shrii gurave namaH ..
gurudevastuti v4 / guru stotram / guru pranam

'The one who has made it possible to realise Him who pervades this entire infinite
universe of animate and inanimate existence, I bow to the blessed *guru*.'

Paul Horn - 'Now this man came to visit us at the Academy. He's just beautiful - 115 years old with pure white hair and very firm skin. He couldn't speak English, only Hindi, but through an interpreter I remember him saying, "the Almighty created only Bliss, man created everything else."'[140]

Mike Dolan - 'He [Tat Wale Baba] came to visit in Rishikesh. He was a very impressive man and there was much speculation about his age most people accepting it to be around 95! A sweet sweet soul.'[38]

The next day those students who have stuck the course now travel to Delhi, after which they will then go on to Srinagar, to spend their time on house boats for the remainder of the course.

Chapter Twenty-Nine
The Big Apple

Cynthia - 'Sad as I was at the way the Indian trip had ended, it was wonderful to hold Julian again. We had brought him back six little Indian outfits and some delicate hand-carved wooden soldiers, gifts from the Maharishi for his fifth birthday a few days earlier. He looked adorable in his Indian clothes and was thrilled to have mum and dad at home.'[196]

✺ ✺ ✺

John is very positive about his experiences in India.
John - 'We meditated for eight hours every day, and then worked on song-writing in our leisure time - it was an ideal place to compose. We now have ample material for a new LP and single.'[197]
'We didn't go there to get certificates. We didn't intend to become teachers. We have more than enough to do as the Beatles without trying to become teachers of meditation.'[198]

Maharishi - 'The Beatles did extremely well in meditation - but they are not amongst the 40 I have selected from the 70 devotees to graduate as guides.
'They are extremely busy people and have to attend to their business at home.'
John - 'I think the course did us a lot of good. We learned a great deal from it. We are all keeping up our daily meditation. Not as a duty but because we find it helpful.'[198]

✺ ✺ ✺

After the rapid departure from Rishikesh, George, Pattie and Jenny decide to stay a few days in Delhi and get their bearings.
George - 'After that I was supposed to have joined Ravi in the South of India where he was making the film "Raga" and I was to have done a short sequence for it. But I caught dysentery and ended up missing the filming ...'[148]

Pattie - 'George didn't want to go straight from two months of meditation into the chaos that was waiting for him in England - the new business, finding a new manager, the fans and the press. Instead we went to see Ravi Shankar and lost ourselves in his music.'[21]

Before leaving South India, George sends a message to Geoffrey Baker, who is in Kashmir with Maharishi. The telegram is stamp dated 20th April 1968.

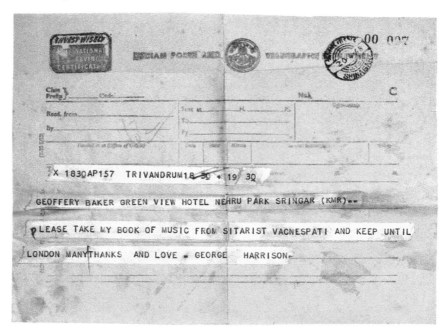

Whilst George is on his way back to England, the weekly music paper, the *New Musical Express,* publishes an update on The Beatles' Indian trip, stating; 'The Lennons and Harrisons cut short their visit when an American camera crew arrived to film the Maharishi.'[197]

Thursday, 25th April 1968.
The course in Kashmir winds up, and Paul Horn is now free of his role as film producer, so with some of his crew he pays a visit to Agra, to the Taj Mahal, in the hope of playing his golden flute in the main dome.

Paul Horn - 'There is always a man there informally standing guard who explains with great pride the inscriptions and magnificent floral inlay work in the marble of the tombs. Quite unexpectedly he bursts forth a vocal "call" every few minutes to demonstrate the remarkable acoustics emanating from the solid marble dome 60 feet in diameter and 80 feet high.'
'From the first I heard his voice I couldn't believe my ears. I had never heard anything so beautiful. Each tone hung suspended in space for 28 seconds and the acoustics are so perfect that you couldn't tell when his voice stopped and the echo took over. Also the individual tone didn't spread as in other great halls, but remained pure and round to the very end.'
'This time I had brought my flute with the very faint hope that I might have a chance to play even one note in that remarkable chamber.'
'I was using my alto flute and the low C just flew out and filled the entire room and just hung there. I couldn't believe it. It was the most beautiful thing I ever heard in my life. The guard stood there transfixed. I played a few more notes. He didn't say anything. I motioned to John [Archer], who had his monitoring headsets on, to "roll it", I just began playing whatever came into my head. I'd let the notes hang there. I could play whole chords and they came back sounding like a chorus of angels. Then I'd play my next phrase on top of that. There was a whole orchestra invisibly suspended in the obscurity of the dome. After a few minutes I stopped. The guard seemed to really enjoy it. He was smiling now and I beckoned him to give his "call". He did, and I signaled to John to keep the tapes rolling.'[200]
So Paul continues recording a series of improvised performances inside the Taj, which are both meditative and stirring. His friends, Earl Barton and Larry Kurland, take photographs of the iconic architecture and of Paul playing flute there.

❀ ❀ ❀

Back in London, John Lennon's early return from India takes Paul McCartney by surprise.
Paul - 'For a week or so there I didn't know if we'd ever see 'em again or if there ever would be any Beatles again. What happened amazed me. They all came storming back and they came round to Cavendish Avenue, it must have been for a recording session, we often used to meet there. It was a big scandal. Maharishi had tried to get off with one of the chicks. I said, "Tell me what happened?" John said, "Remember that blonde American girl with the short hair? Like a Mia Farrow look-alike. She was called Pat or something." I said, "Yeah." He said, "Well, Maharishi made a pass at her." So I said, "Yes? What's wrong with that?" He said, "Well, you know, he's just a bloody old letch just like everybody else. What the fuck, we can't go following that!"
They were scandalised. And I was quite shocked at them; I said, "But he never said he was a god". In fact very much the opposite, he said, "Don't treat me like a god, I'm just a meditation teacher." There was no deal about you mustn't touch women, was there? There was no vow of chastity involved. So I didn't think it was enough cause to leave the whole meditation centre. It might have been enough cause to say, "Hey, excuse me? Are you having it off with a girl? In which case, should we worry about this or is this perfectly normal?" And to tell the truth, I think they may have used it as an excuse to get out of there. And I just said, "Oh yes, okay." But in my mind it was like, well, he never pretended to be anything but a guy, and as far as I'm concerned there's nothing wrong with someone making a pass at someone. Perhaps they had been looking for something more than a guy and found he wasn't a god, whereas I'd been looking at a guy who was saying, "I'm only giving you a system of meditation."'[6]

As planned, The Beach Boys and Maharishi embark on a 25-city tour, with the first appearance being in Washington on Friday, 3rd May 1968.

Richard Duryea (road manager) - 'There was a date at the Spectrum in Philadelphia where quite a few people showed up to see the Beach Boys, but when the Maharishi came on, they all left. No one cared, which is what everyone told Mike would happen. You can't slug your audience around like that and ask them to pay a high-priced ticket to hear this guy talk.'[100]

After just a handful of dates the tour is halted due to poor attendances. The cancellation is estimated to cost The Beach Boys about $250,000.

❋ ❋ ❋

In mid-May, John and Paul fly out to the 'Big Apple' - New York - in order to publicise their plans for Apple, and are ready to describe their vision and their hopes for their new business empire.

First off is a Press conference at 1:30pm on Tuesday, 14th May 1968, at New York's Americana Hotel, but before dealing with Apple they find themselves being asked to explain their current relationship Maharishi.

John - 'We made a mistake.'
Reporter - 'Do you think other people are making a mistake to go see him now?'
John - 'That's up to them.'
Paul - 'We thought..'
John - 'We're human, you know.'
(laughter)
Reporter - 'What do you mean he was a mistake?'
John - 'And that's all, you know.'
Paul - 'We thought there's more to him than there was, you know, but he's human. And for a while we thought he wasn't, you know. We thought he was, uhh...'[3]
Reporter - 'Do you have any other new philosophical leaders?'
John - 'No.'
Paul - 'Nope.'
John - (jokingly) 'Me.'
Reporter - 'Do George and Ringo feel the same way about the Maharishi as both of you?'
John - 'Yes, yeah. We tend to go in and out together. I mean, with a few spaces. So, yeah.'
Reporter - 'Are the Beatles still meditating?'
Paul & John - 'Yeah.'

John - 'Now and then.'

Paul - (giggles) 'At this moment.'

(laughter)

Reporter - 'Why do the Beatles meditate?'

John - 'Because it seems to be nice, like cleaning your teeth, you know. It does have some sort of end product. I think Maharishi was a mistake, but the teachings have got some truth in them.'[201]

In the evening, at the St Regis Hotel, John & Paul meet with Larry Kane, a journalist they have known for a very long time. He asks them about their business plan.

Larry Kane - 'How expansive, how large will this be in America?'

Paul - 'Oh we don't know yet, it'll be big, I think.'

John - 'We're just blowing up a balloon.'

Paul - 'There's lots of things, you know. We've just got a friend of ours whose in electronics.'

John - 'Oh yeah.'

Paul - 'I'll tell you about this gent, he's called Alex. He's great, he's a Greek fella. He's inventing incredible things, you see. So, that'll be big.'

Larry Kane - 'Oh, are the days.. are the days of The Beatles onstage over?'

John - 'Err well, they've been over for the last two years because we've been on land. But, you never know do you? With all these incredible electronics, we might come flying over New York playing one day.'

Larry Kane - 'Do you, err.. did you enjoy the trip over to India?'

Paul - 'Yeah.'

John - 'The journey was terrible but the trip was all right.'

Larry Kane - 'There was a report that, err.. now we, we .... reports.'

John - 'Massive.'

Larry Kane - 'You didn't err, didn't like it? Or you didn't have the patience so you decided to go home?'

John - 'We were there four months, or George and I were. We lost thirteen pounds and didn't look a day older.'

Larry Kane - 'Did you think, err, this man's on the level?'

John - 'I don't know what level he's on but err..'

Paul - 'He's on the level.'

John - 'We had a nice holiday in India and came back rested to play businessman.'[3]

❀ ❀ ❀

The next day John and Paul are interviewed for WNDT, a New York educational TV station.

Mitchell Krause - 'We meet two of the famous Beatles quartet, John Lennon lyricist and Paul McCartney composer, in this country for a brief business visit. John Lennon and Paul McCartney, what do you think is the one single thing that most contributed to your phenomenal, unprecedented success this past eight or nine years? Any single thing?'

John - 'Alright.. God!'

Paul - 'I'll go along with that.'

Mitchell Krause - 'You went to India and spent time with Maharishi who has had great impact, you feel, on your whole outlook. Could you describe how he's changed things for you?'

John - 'Well, we sort of feel that Maharishi for us was a mistake, really. Meditation we don't think was a mistake. But I think we had a false impression of Maharishi, like people do of us, you know. But what we do happens in public, so it's a different scene slightly.'

Mitchell Krause - 'What was your original impression of him?'

John - 'Well, we thought he was something other than he was probably, you know, we were…'

Paul - 'We thought he was magic, you know, because he's got that kind of thing, you know. And he sort of, I don't know, the twinkle in the eye. And you just think he...'

John - 'We were looking for it, and probably superimposed it on him.'

Paul - 'Yeah, it was just the right time anyway. There were we, waiting for someone.. the great magic man to come.'

John - 'Waiting for a *guru*. He came.'

Paul - 'And he came, you know. There he was and he was talking about it all. And he had great answers, 'cos he said "You can sort yourself out," you know, and all that "you can calm yourself down just by doing this very

THE BEATLES, DRUGS, MYSTICISM & INDIA

simple thing" you know. And it works, that bit of it. It really does do it, you know.'

John - 'And the other bit - he's giving out recipes for something that.. he's still creating the same kind of situations which he's giving out recipes to cure.'

Paul - 'But it seems like the system's more important, you know.'

Mitchell Krause - 'Sort of a touch of establishment in the Maharishi?'

John - "Well.. I don't, something, you know. We can't say what..'

Paul - 'He's okay, but the system's more important.

John - 'There's something taken over from that.'

Paul - 'The idea of it, you know.

John - 'Some future virus…'

Paul - 'It always goes by the board, that bit. If people watch Maharishi, or watch us, they don't think about the system - don't think about what it's about, you know.'

Mitchell Krause - 'He got you to stop taking drugs.'

John - 'No he didn't. We'd stopped taking drugs a couple of months before we met him. And that was just sort of... The newspapers said, "Oh! Boop, boop, put it together, we got a title." But it's just not true.'

Mitchell Krause - 'Do you feel that drugs just aren't necessary anymore?'

John - 'I don't know. I'm not making any statements about what I'm going to do for the next sixty years or whatever it is, 'cos I've got no idea, anymore. And you can never ever really know, but just have a vague goal.'

Paul - 'Not at the moment anyway, you know.'

John - 'There's no use saying, "I will never take drugs", or "I will take drugs", because you don't know.'

Mitchell Krause - 'I mean, after the experiences you've had, you think that young people who are your fans, who idolise you, ought to try the same…?'

John - 'We don't give instructions on how to live your life. The only thing we can do because we're in the public eye is to reflect what we do, and they can judge for themselves, what happens to us. With Maharishi, with drugs, and with whatever, we don't want them using us as a guideline, and we can only do what's right for us, and therefore, we hope right for them.'[3]

❀ ❀ ❀

And a little later, in the evening, they appear on NBC-TV Newsfront, on *'The Tonight Show'*, usually hosted by Johnny Carson but tonight hosted by former baseball player Joe Garagiola, with guest announcer Ed McMahon and actress Tellulah Bankhead also present.

Joe Garagiola - 'Listen now; I have something in common with both of you. I met the *guru*, the Maharishi. And I noticed that he went out with an act, The Beach Boys, and it folded.'

John - 'Right.'

Joe Garagiola - 'Would The Beatles go out with a yogi as an act?'

John - 'Well, we found out that we made a mistake there.'

Paul - 'We tried to persuade him against that, you know. I thought it was a terrible idea.'

John - 'We believe in meditation, but not the Maharishi and his scene. But that's a personal mistake we made in public. So, to explain that to these five million and ten people..'

Joe Garagiola - 'When did you find out it was a mistake?'

John - 'Well, uhh, I can't remember the date, you know, but it was in India. And meditation is good, and it does what they say. Like exercise or cleaning your teeth, you know. It works, but err.. We have, we've finished with that bit, for a bit. Da, da, da, da, da-da-da, shhhh.' (John mimics the end of the Looney Tune melody *"That's all Folks!"*, to audience applause and laughter)

Ed McMahon - 'Has he changed? Is that what..?'

John - 'Well, no. I think it's just that we're seeing him a bit more in perspective, you know, 'cos we're as naive as the next person about a lot of things.'

Paul - 'We get carried away with things like that, though, you know, I mean we thought he was.. uhh pheeww.. magic, you know.. just floating around and everything, flying.'

Joe Garagiola - 'Do you think the Americans, the kids in America have turned him off?'

John - 'Well, it could be something to do with it, you know. But I wouldn't say, "Don't meditate" to them, a lot of them would get a great deal from it.'

Paul - 'The system's, you know.. but the system's more important, than Maharishi.'

248

John - 'He's surrounded with.. it seems like the old establishment that we know so well.'

Joe Garagiola - 'Are you saying, "Meditate, but not with the *yogi*"?'

Paul - 'Yeah. I mean, he's good. There's nothing wrong with him. But I, we think the system is more important than all the big personality bit, you know. Cos he's, you know he gets sort of treated like a big star, you know and he's on the road with The Beach Boys, it's all that scene.' (laughter) 'And it's, you know, a bit strange and also it folds you know. That's the silly thing.'

(laughter)

Tellulah Bankhead - 'Does he giggle as much as...?'

John - 'Yes. It's his natural asset.'

Tellulah Bankhead - 'Yes, yes.'

(laughter)

John - 'Well, you see, it depends on what way you're looking at it at the time. If it's not getting on your nerves, well "Oh, what a happy fellow". But it's how.. you know, how you feel when you look at him.'

Joe Garagiola - 'I had him on the show, and he just giggled and giggled the whole time. I figured there was something, maybe my tie was loose, something like that. Who was the first one that met the *yogi*?'

John - 'We all met him at the same time.'

Joe Garagiola - 'Can you tell us the circumstances?'

John - 'Well, he was just doing a lecture in London at the Hilton. And, which is all right, so don't worry about it. But err.. so we all went and we thought, "What a nice man." And we were looking for that. You know, everybody's looking for it, but we were looking for it that day as well. And then we met him and he was good, you know. He's got a good thing in him. And we went along with it.'

Joe Garagiola - 'But now, you just got off the train, huh?'

John - 'Right. Nice trip thank you very much.' (laughter) [3]

✸ ✸ ✸

John - 'We're still a hundred per cent in favour of meditation, but we're not going to go potty and build a golden temple in the Himalayas. We will help where and when we can - we can't do everything overnight. But we're not going to empty the gold out of our pockets, there are other ways of helping.' [1]

✸ ✸ ✸

When the Press catches up with Maharishi, he is asked for his reaction to what The Beatles have been saying.

Maharishi - 'I think I would love them whatever they say.'

Reporter - 'Why do you think they made such a statement?'

Maharishi - 'I'm unaware completely, why.'

Reporter - 'Do you think that ..?'

Maharishi - 'I only extend my love to them.' [202]

Chapter Thirty
Hey Jules

So, how do the rest of The Beatles' party view the time spent in India?
Pattie - 'We had learnt to meditate at the feet of a master - despite the allegations, George and I still regarded Maharishi as a master - we had been shown the way to spiritual enlightenment, we had returned from Rishikesh renewed and refreshed, and yet from the time we left India our lives and our relationship seemed to fall apart.'[21]

George Harrison speaks to Alan Smith of the *New Musical Express*.
George - 'There's about 35 songs we've got already, and a few of them are mine. God knows which one will be the next single. You never know, not till you go right through them. I suppose we've got a vague idea of the overall conception of the kind of album we want to do, but it takes time to work out.
'We could do a double album, I suppose … or maybe a triple album. There's enough stuff there.'
Alan Smith - 'I tell George I hate to bring up the topic, but….'
George - 'Yeah, I know,' he smiles, 'what about the Maharishi?'
'The thing is, we just went off him. I'm not against spreading the word of meditation - I still believe in it as deeply as I ever did - but he started to go about it the wrong way and make the whole thing seem a drag. That Beach Boys things, for instance…'[203]

Ringo - 'I'm still 100 per cent for meditation. But I'm not 100 per cent for the Maharishi. I've nothing against him personally, but, as I say, it is just one of those things.'[204]

George - 'You can't mass produce cosmic consciousness. The Maharishi's main trouble was a tendency to spread something subtle in a gross way.'[205]

Donovan - 'We told the world we're going to India, we're going to do it, and we're stopping taking drugs and alcohol, we don't care what you lot are doing, 'cos that's not what we're about. And so, we went to India, and we studied. But then, when that word came out into the world - meditation, millions of people wanted to know what it was. So then we were promoting another part of the bohemian manifesto, the spiritual path, how to explore your own consciousness without endangering your health. Meditation is the safe way. And we brought it back. And we promoted meditation. And that was a good thing. The natural high.'[206]

❀ ❀ ❀

On John's return from New York, Press Officer Derek Taylor organises a dinner date for John, with his teenage fantasy woman, French actress Brigitte Bardot.
Afterwards, John is met by his personal assistant, his old friend Peter Shotton, and asked about the evening.
Peter Shotton - 'What happened, what happened? I can't bear the suspense another minute!' (he asked breathlessly)
John - '"Fucking *nothing* happened!" He finally snapped. "I was so fucking nervous that I dropped some acid before we went in, and got completely out of me head. The only thing I said to here all night was <Hello>, when we went in to shake hands with her. Then she spent the whole time talking in French with her friends, and I could never think of anything to say. It was a fucking terrible evening…"'[34]

❀ ❀ ❀

John and Peter spend a lot of time together.
Peter Shotton - 'Perhaps the most memorable evening I ever spent with John Lennon began routinely enough in the recording studio at the far end of the attic. We shared a piece of LSD, smoked a few joints, and idly amused ourselves with John's network of Brunell [Brenell] tape recorders.'
'In due course we tired of "messing about with the tapes," and ended up sitting cross-legged on the floor.'
'Our conversation grew increasingly hushed and serious as John spoke of his disillusionment with the Maharishi, and with everyone else to whom he had ever looked for guidance.'
'Suddenly John began waving his arms in the air, making slow, whirling motions with his outstretched hands.

And out of the blue he announced in an awed whisper; "Pete, I think I'm Jesus Christ."
"What was that again, John?"
"Yeah," he said, and I could see he was dead serious, "I think I'm Jesus Christ. I'm . . . back again."'
'"Well then," I finally ventured, "what are you gonna do about it?"
"I've got to tell everyone," he said. "I've got to let the world know . . . who I am."
"They'll fucking kill you," I said. "They won't accept that, John."
"That can't be helped," he said firmly. "How old was Jesus when they killed him?"
"I'm not sure," I said. "I reckon he was about thirty-two."'
'"Hell," he said, "at least I've got about four years."
"Well," I said. "What's brought all this on, then?"
"I just think this is it. This is my reason for being here on this earth."'
'"Don't you think being John Lennon is enough?"
"Why?"
"You could do as much being John Lennon as being Jesus Christ. And look at a the trouble religion's caused. As John Lennon, you've been able to bring together people from all over the world, regardless of their religion, race, or creed"
But John was adamant, absolutely convinced he was Jesus. "First thing tomorrow," he concluded, "we'll go into Apple and tell the others."
The next thing we were aware of was the footsteps of Dot the housekeeper, who had just come in for the day. Somehow John and I had both managed to fall asleep in a heap on the floor, and opened our eyes as one to catch Dot gazing back at us.
Starting into wakefulness, John bounded to his feet. "Oh Christ," he said. "She'll think that we're fucking each other."
"Why on earth," I said groggily, "would she think something like that? We've got our clothes on, for a start."
Far from forgetting the previous night's metamorphis, John quickly got down to business. The so-called inner circle - comprising the Beatles, Derek Taylor, Neil Aspinall, and myself - was summoned to a secret board meeting at Apple.'
'"Right," John began from behind his desk, "I've something very important to tell you all. I am . . . Jesus Christ come back again. This is my thing."'[34]

That evening Pete and John return to Weybridge.
Peter Shotton - 'And he said to me, about 10 o'clock at night, "Do you mind if I get a girl over?", … and when he told me it was Yoko I was most surprised. I said, "Oh, I didn't realised you fancied her." "Well I don't know," he said, "there's something about her I like. But while the wife's away I might as well find out what it is".'[207]

John - 'When we got back from India, we were talking to each other on the phone. I called her over, it was the middle of the night and Cyn was away, and I thought, "Well, now's the time if I'm gonna get to know her anymore."'[5]

Peter Shotton - 'Yoko appeared shy and nervous and mumbled a lot, so I couldn't hear what she was saying. After about half an hour's awkward chat, I went to bed and left them to it.'[34]

John - 'Well, after Yoko and I met, I didn't realize I was in love with her. I was still thinking it was an artistic collaboration, as it were - producer and artist, right?'
'… and Yoko came to visit me and we took some acid. I was always shy with her, and she was shy, so instead of making love, we went upstairs and made tapes. I had this room full of different tapes where I would write and make strange loops and things like that for the Beatles' stuff. So we made a tape all night. She was doing her funny voices and I was pushing all different buttons on my tape recorder and getting sound effects. And then as the sun rose we made love and that was Two Virgins.'[15]

Cynthia returns prematurely from her short break in Greece, only to find John and Yoko wandering about in bathrobes. So she thinks it best to leave, and lets the dust settle, whilst she stays over at Alexis Mardas's flat.

But, according to Cynthia, Alexis slips into bed with her and makes sexual advances, which she repels.

When she returns home, Cynthia and John effect a reconciliation of sorts, but things are not quite right between the two, as soon becomes apparent. John corners her and starts interrogating her about her love life.

Cynthia - 'I haven't been unfaithful to you, I'm sure you know that.'

John - 'Forget all that bullshit, Cyn. You're no innocent little flower… What about that Yankee cowboy?'

Cynthia - 'What Yankee cowboy?'

John - 'In India.'

John - 'You know that when he left Rishikesh that cowboy gave George a letter to pass on to you, but instead he gave it to me. He was being loyal.'

Cynthia - 'So, what was in this mysterious letter, John?'

'He refused to tell me. I suspected he was disappointed I hadn't looked more guilty.

Yoko came back in. John announced, in the same cold, clipped tone he had used throughout, that talking was pointless.

I was feeling more and more distressed. I tried one last time: "John, please, let's discuss things."

"We can do that through the lawyers." Then, to Yoko, "Come on, let's go." He called "Bye", to Julian, and marched out of the house, Yoko at his heels.'[10]

❀ ❀ ❀

In late May The Beatles meet at Kinfauns, George's psychedelic bungalow in Esher, where he lives with Pattie and their two Siamese cats, Rupert and Joss-stick. The Beatles set about recording 'demos', rough cuts of songs which might be used on the new album, including a composition George has recently written, called *'Not Guilty'*.

'Not guilty, for looking like a freak, making friends with every Sikh
Not guilty, for leading you astray on the road to Mandalay.'
- Excerpt of *'Not Guilty'* by George Harrison

George - 'It was me getting pissed off with Lennon and McCartney for the grief I was catching during the making of this White Album. I said I wasn't guilty of getting in the way of their careers. I said I wasn't guilty of leading them astray in our all going to India to see the Maharishi.'[208]

The *'road to Mandalay'* is also referred to in a song from 1956, about 'Nellie the Elephant' who escapes the circus and runs off to Hindustan (India) to live in the jungle.

'The head of the herd was calling Far, far away
They met one night in the silver light on the road to Mandalay'
- Extract of *'Nellie the Elephant'* by Ralph Butler and Peter Hart

But, more importantly, the *'road to Mandalay'* also figures in a much earlier work, a poem called *'Mandalay'*, written in 1890 by Rudyard Kipling, who, having himself returned from spending some seven years in India, tells the plight of a soldier who endures the cold, fog and formality of British culture whilst all the while yearning for the life he experienced out in exotic Asia.

'For the wind is in the palm-trees, and the temple-bells they say:
"Come you back, you British soldier; come you back to Mandalay!"'
- Excerpt from *'Road to Mandalay'* by Rudyard Kipling

And it was, of course, Kipling who in 1889 coined that memorable phrase *'East is East, and West is West'*, a line all too often quoted out of context of the verse to which it belongs.

'Oh, East is East, and West is West, and never the twain shall meet,
Till Earth and Sky stand presently at God's great Judgment Seat;
But there is neither East nor West, Border, nor Breed, nor Birth,
When two strong men stand face to face, though they come from the ends of the earth!'
- Excerpt from *'The Ballad of East and West'* by Rudyard Kipling

❀ ❀ ❀

Tuesday, 28th May 1968.

Michael Herring, a 19-year old art student who is studying in Kensington, London, makes the rather bold decision to turn up at John's house, Kenwood in Weybridge. John opens the door attired in his favourite green and blue floral print shirt and Seville orange trousers.

John - 'Well then, what's it about?'

Michael Herring - 'John, I wish you could be me so that you know what it feels like to meet you.'

On the strength of this remark, he is invited in for breakfast, and there he meets Yoko Ono.

When John realises Michael is quite knowledgeable about Yoko's artwork, he invites him to go along to rehearsals at George Harrison's home. Before they leave, Michael notices that Yoko *'never spoke a word and was just mumbling into a cassette recorder.'*

John drives the short distance to 'Kinfauns', where they find George sitting on the lawn, dressed casually in a light-blue high-necked Indian shirt and pale blue trousers.

Michael Herring - 'George looked up and said, "Who's this, then?" John said, "This is Michael. He's an artist. I found him in me garden."'[209]

Michael gets to meet Pattie Boyd too, and when Ringo arrives Michael gets to take a few photographs of John, George and Ringo against the outer wall of the bungalow, adorned with its psychedelic murals of flowers and *tantric* fantasies; and in the distance a clothes line hung with washing out to dry. Apparently, Paul is unable to make it, and the others say he has quit! The three Beatles rehearse and record, only stopping for lunch; a vegetarian Indian affair.

At the end of the day, John gives Michael a lift back to the station.

Michael clutches a souvenir of his day out, a sheet of paper on which is written; *'To Michael Best Wishes Ringo✪Starr'*, and *'To Michael with a load of wit John Lennon 卍'*.

⊛ ⊛ ⊛

Recording on the new Beatles LP begins at 2:30pm on Thursday, 30th May 1968, at EMI Studios, Abbey Road, in Maida Vale, London. All members are present, as is Yoko Ono.

⊛ ⊛ ⊛

On Friday, 7th June 1968, Pattie, Ringo, Maureen and Mal Evans fly out to California to accompany George who is to make a guest appearance in Ravi Shankar's film *Raga*. Ravi and George are filmed sitting cross-legged atop of the coastal cliff at Big Sur, California, participating in a teach-in of *sitar* players.

George - 'It was the last time I really played sitar. I thought I am never going to be a sitar player, because I've seen a thousand sitar players in India who are better than I'll ever be and, out of them, Ravi only thought one was good. Ravi was more worried for me than I was. He was trying to find my background or some roots and he was saying, "What about Liverpool?" and I said, "No, I feel more at home in Benares, India than I do in Liverpool." Then I thought, "What's my root?" The first thing that I could call a root, musically speaking, was riding down the road on my bike and hearing "Heartbreak Hotel" by Elvis Presley coming out of somebody's house. On my way home (from California) I went to New York. When I checked into the hotel, Jimi Hendrix and Eric Clapton happened to be staying there, which is another little cosmic point. From then on I thought, "Well, maybe I am better off to get back into being a pop singer, guitar player, song writer; whatever I am supposed to be". So it was Ravi really, who helped me get back into being a pop singer and guitar player again.'[94]

⊛ ⊛ ⊛

George - 'I had very little to do with Apple. I was still in India when it started. I think it was basically John and Paul's madness - their egos running away with themselves or with each other. There were a lot of ideas, but when it came down to it, the only thing we could do successfully was write songs, make records, and be Beatles.

By the time I came back, they'd opened the offices in Wigmore Street. I went into the office and there were rooms full of lunatics; people throwing I Ching and all kinds of hangers-on trying to get a gig.'[1]

⊛ ⊛ ⊛

Maharishi is currently in Lake Louise, Alberta, Canada, where Canadian Broadcasting Company (CBC) is making a short documentary. Alan Waite is at Lake Louise too, directing his own film documentary of Maharishi which is being made to replace Four Star project, which has now been abandoned. Rumour has it that Paul Horn offers the Spiritual Regeneration Movement to buy the film, at a fraction of the price it has cost to produce, but that they do not take up the offer. Instead, the project is restarted under the directorship of Alan Waite, a fresh production titled *'Sage for a New Generation'*.

On Wednesday, 12th June 1968, Maharishi's assistant, Jerry Jarvis, takes questions from students on the course, and someone asks him about *'the real truth'* concerning Maharishi's recent tour of the United States and, *'Why are certain rather world famous figures noses currently out of joint?'*

Jerry Jarvis - 'The current, the Beach Boy tour?'

'It was cancelled for several reasons. One was that they found the whole thing was just a little bit too, too heavily committed. It wasn't that; seems there wasn't enough advanced preparation. Second thing, Maharishi was little bit in need of rest at that time. When he came from conducting two courses simultaneously for three-four months in India, one Western course and one Indian course, plus working day and night on other projects - Beach Boys being very sweet, loving devotees of Maharishi clearly saw that it would be advantageous to let him have that time to rest, and also nothing much was lost by it. Just didn't work out, so it was cancelled - there wasn't any kind of mysterious meaning to it or anything like that.'

'… it just, it just happened that way. There were other commitments and so forth and by mutual agreement it was agreed that this wasn't the time to do it. Maybe it'd be better to do it later on. So they're planning for it later on.

What happened to The Beatles? That's what -- I hear that the response has been "What's the matter with The Beatles?" (audience laughter) "By the way, when are you having the next course in meditation, I want to start." This is what we've heard in California.

Actually The Beatles have, if you know exactly what the Beatles have said, it's been misinterpreted what they've said. They've said that they like meditation, they meditate regularly, it's fine, they were -- they didn't like to see Maharishi flying around in jets and doing all these things and making films and all that sort of thing: little disappointed in those things; they maybe had some idea of some saint sitting in a cave all the time, slowly opening his eyes. (Audience laughter, Maharishi laughs) (Audience applause) Maybe they were a little disappointed when they found him to be so practical a man and so eager to, to use any means possible to, to let humanity to come out of their suffering as quickly as possible. It's nothing, it's just that they, they thought that way. But you've heard about it, it's been misinterpreted. If you talk to people who actually saw that television show, within the context of it it was, it wasn't-- they just were, actually out of, I think out of love they were, why would they be bothered unless they were, love and concern.'[210]

❀ ❀ ❀

Saturday, 15th June 1968.
John and Yoko stage their first public appearance together in Coventry, a peace happening,

John - 'This is what happens when two clouds meet.'

Yoko - 'In acorn event we decide to plant two acorns, one in the east and one in the west. So we dug a hole and I put one inside, John immediately put his right next to mine. So I said "OK", I understood what he had done. With our love, or whatever, we had actually shrunk the distance between east and west. John smiled, it was the front yard of a church, and er, by the way they did not want us in the group show. I had John with me, and they did not want us to be in the show because we were not married. We exercised the particular event with great weight and dignity, John stood up, and like a priest, he said "We have now planted two acorns, and this is to show that east is west and west is east." He said it like that, as if there were two hundred people around us, actually it was just us and an assistant.'[211]

❀ ❀ ❀

David Goggin, the American student who got to sit in on The Beatles' *'I Am the Walrus'* recording session nine months before, turns up at the Apple offices in Wigmore Street, and John remembers him.

John, introducing David to Yoko **-** 'I found him in my garden with my face on his back.'

David Goggin - 'I brought up the subject of Tarot cards and John gave me two pounds to buy him a deck. We also spoke of Tibetan Buddhism, as I had recently visited the Samye Ling monastery in Scotland and met with Chogyam Trungpa, Rinpoche…'[86]

John and Yoko give David a picture of themselves, a promo photo for the 'Acorn' event, of them seated behind two flower pots, autographed and dedicated to him by both of them; dated, *'1968. June 17'*. [221]

David asks if John is recording, and so gets invited to visit the studios later. David goes to the studio and finds John, Yoko, Ringo and George at work on an experimental recording, using a repetitive loop; with a voice repeating, *'Number 9, Number 9, Number 9, Number 9, Number 9, Number 9, Number 9, Number 9, Number 9"*.

George - 'Ringo and I compiled that. We went into the tape library and looked through the entire room and pulled main selections and then gave the tapes to John and he cut them together. That whole thing, "number nine, number nine", is because I pulled box number nine. It was some kind of education programme. John sat there and decided what bits to cross-fade together…'[212]

David Goggin - 'In my notebook I wrote down "Black bird flying into the night." George was pumping away on a harmonium, Ringo was banging away on the drums. John called out, "Give us any beat ya got, Ringo!" Tapes were being played at different speeds, going backwards and forwards.'[86]

❀ ❀ ❀

John - 'My marriage to Cyn was not unhappy. But it was just a normal marital state where nothing happened and which we continued to sustain. You sustain it until you meet somebody who suddenly sets you alight.'[213]

Alexis current role is to act as an intermediary between John and Cynthia, attempting to get the best possible separation deal for John.

Alexis Mardas - 'I've come with a message from John. He is going to divorce you, take Julian away from you and send you back to Hoylake.'

Cynthia - 'My knees gave way. I felt drained and ill. All I could think at that moment was how cowardly John was to send his lapdog because he couldn't face me. Far more than simply evasive, it was sinister and cruel.'[10]

Cynthia - 'During the divorce proceedings I was truly surprised when one sunny afternoon Paul arrived on his own. I was touched by his obvious concern for our welfare and even more moved when he presented me with a single red rose accompanied by a jokey remark about our future.'

Paul - 'How's about it, Cyn. How about you and me getting married?'[7]

Cynthia - 'On his journey down to visit Julian and I, Paul composed the beautiful song *Hey Jude* - he said it was for Julian.'[7]

> ***'And anytime you feel the pain, hey Jude, refrain,***
> ***Don't carry the world upon your shoulders'***
>
> - Excerpt of lyrics to *'Hey Jude'* by Paul McCartney & John Lennon

Paul - 'I started with the idea "Hey Jules," which was Julian, don't make it bad, take a sad song and make it better. Hey, try and deal with this terrible thing. I knew it was not going to be easy for him. I always feel sorry for kids in divorces…'[6]

❀ ❀ ❀

Maharishi is asked to comment on The Beatles.

Maharishi - 'They are not a great success for me because they were too unstable - and they weren't prepared to end their Beatledom for meditation.

'Perhaps if they were older, and more stable, they would have been better.'[214]

Maharishi speaks about his efforts to spread the message of Transcendental Meditation worldwide.

Maharishi - 'I set out in 1960 and gave myself nine years to spread the message around the world. But I know I have failed.'

'I shall retire to a quiet place next year. I have been able to reach a lot of people, but my mission is over.'[215]

Monday, 8th July 1968.

Paul, George and Ringo attend a Press screening of *Yellow Submarine* at the Bowater House Cinema in Knightsbridge. This is the first time any of The Beatles have seen the animated movie in its entirety.

Paul - 'We're just in it as drawings, and it's like us animated, goes through it, you know.'

Reporter - 'But did "Mystery Tour" put you off making a film completely yourselves?'

George - (jokingly) 'Yeah, we're only ever gonna be cartoons forever now, because they really put us off... those no good, damn critics.'

Paul - (laughs) 'It's a new career Pete.'

Reporter - 'The film makes, the cartoon makes a bit of fun at the Maharishi. Does this mean you've finished with him now? He's a figure of fun?'

Paul - 'He's not, not FINISHED with, but we're over that phase, it was a bit of a phase. But he's still a nice fella, and everybody's fine... but, we don't go out with him anymore.'[182]

After the preview, journalist David Griffiths of *Record Mirror* gets a chance to speak with George.

David Griffiths - 'Did he still meditate?'

George - 'Yes.'

David Griffiths - 'Any contact with the Maharishi?'

George - 'No.' (Said in a manner that subtly discouraged further probing).

David Griffiths - 'Did George retain his affection for India?'

George - 'Yes, very much so. There's a lot of suffering and poverty but there's so much beauty and the people are very pleasant.'[216]

❀ ❀ ❀

John speaks to Jonathan Cott, for *Rolling Stone* magazine.

Reporter - 'What do you feel about India now?'

John - 'I've got no regrets at all, cause it was a groove and I had some great experiences, meditating eight hours a day - some amazing things, some amazing trips - it was great. And I still meditate off and on. George is doing it regularly. And I believe implicitly in the whole bit. It's just that it's difficult to continue it. I lost the rosy glasses. And I'm like that, I'm very idealistic. So I can't really manage my exercises when I've lost that. I mean I don't want to be a boxer so much. It's just that a few things happened, or didn't happen, I don't know, but something happened. It was sort of like a (click) and we just left and I don't know what went on, it's too near - I don't really know what happened.'[217]

❀ ❀ ❀

On Thursday, 11th July 1968, John and Yoko attend the wedding of close friend Alexis Mardas and his artist bride, Euphrosyne Doxiadis, at a Greek orthodox church in London.

John Lennon and Donovan share best man duties, whilst George and Pattie are also in attendance.

❀ ❀ ❀

And The Beatles go into the recording studios, and John is with Yoko.

Yoko - "After we started living together, it was John who wanted me there all the time. He made me go into the men's room with him. He was afraid that if I stayed out in the studio with a lot of other men, I might run off with one of them.'[120]

Yoko tends to communicate in a whisper, but when she gives some advice to John, about what he is singing, she is overheard.

Tony Barrow - 'The other Beatles looked around, straight-faced, startled, stunned. There was a moment's dead silence that was broken by Paul: "Fuck me! Did somebody speak? Who the fuck was that?" Of course he knew full well who had spoken. The others joined in: "Did you say something George [Martin]? Your lips didn't move!" "Have we got a new producer in?"'[218]

Pete Shotton - 'During my many visits to Abbey Road, all the old fun, laughter and camaraderie seemed conspicuous by their absence. The Beatles' recording sessions had turned into a very serious, dour operation.[12]

John, Yoko and their respective children, Julian and Kyoko, have a car crash in Scotland and receive medical attention. When John and Yoko return to London Yoko continues to have health problems.

George Martin - 'I remember Yoko fell ill and John insisted on bringing Yoko into the studio in her bed while we were recording. That kind of thing doesn't make for an easy relationship with the other Beatles, or with anyone, to have the wife of one of the members lying ill while you're trying to make a record.'[12]

Yoko - 'When he's doing things with The Beatles, I participate by sitting and waiting. But, just being with John is all right; otherwise we miss each other. I like The Beatles and I think that what they're doing is great. I have no intentions of breaking whatever it is they have.'[12]

The Beatles continue recording sessions for their next LP, but things get so tense that on Thursday, 22nd August 1968, Ringo actually quits the group, and afterwards goes straight back home to his wife, Maureen.

Maurice Devereux, a reporter for *Le Chroniqueur* magazine - 'Were you there when Richy walked out?'

Maureen - 'No, but I was surprised when he came home so soon. He told me to pack my bags without giving me much of an explanation; but I could see a look of distress in his eyes. It was just painful. I fought with him for a while, I really did and I told him that it was foolish to go away so soon, but I could tell he didn't really care at that point. I do remember him muttering something about Paul under his breath- something really dirty which made me believe that Paul and Richy had a row.'[219]

Ringo and Maureen take a brief break on Peter Seller's yacht in Sardinia, where he hears from the vessel's captain of how octopuses pick up stones and shiny objects to make gardens for themselves, Ringo feels inspired to write a song.

'It would be nice, paradise
In an octopus's garden in the shade'

- Excerpt of original version of lyrics to *'Octopus's Garden'* by Ringo Starr

Ringo decides to rejoin to The Beatles, and on Wednesday, 4th September 1968, when he turns up at their next recording session he finds his drum kit festooned with flowers; a nice touch by George.

✿ ❀ ✿

Several days later George decides to get his friend Eric Clapton in to play lead guitar on a new song he has written recently.

George - 'I wrote "While My Guitar Gently Weeps" at my mother's house in Warrington. I was thinking about the Chinese *I Ching*, "The Book of Changes". The Eastern concept is that whatever happens is all meant to be, and that there's no such thing as coincidence - every little item that's going down has a purpose.'

'I decided to write a song based on the first thing I saw upon opening any book - as it would be relative to that moment, at *that* time. I picked up a book at random, opened it, saw "gently weeps", then laid the book down again and started the song.'[1]

✿ ❀ ✿

With his romance with Jane Asher having hit the buffers; these days Paul is single and footloose.

Paul - 'I was going through a really difficult time around the autumn of 1968. … I was staying up too late at night, drinking, doing drugs, clubbing, the way a lot of people were at the time.'

'Some nights I'd go to bed and my head would just flop on the pillow; and when I'd wake up I'd have difficulty pulling it off, thinking, "Good job I woke up just then or I might have suffocated."

Then one night, somewhere between deep sleep and insomnia, I had the most comforting dream about my mother who died when I was only 14.'

'So in this dream 12 years later, my mother appeared, and there was her face, completely clear, particularly her eyes; and she said to me very gently, very reassuringly, "Let it be."

It was lovely. I woke up with a great feeling. It was really like she had visited me at this very difficult point in my life and gave me this message: Be gentle, don't fight things, just try and go with the flow and it all will work out.'[220]

'When I find myself in times of trouble, mother Mary comes to me
Speaking words of wisdom; "Let it be, let it be".'

- Excerpt from lyrics to *'Let It Be'* by Paul McCartney & John Lennon

THE BEATLES, DRUGS, MYSTICISM & INDIA

Paul is seeing an increasing amount of Linda Eastman, an American photographer.

❀ ❀ ❀

Judging by media coverage, communications between The Beatles and Maharishi have not resumed yet.
Maharishi, tells newsmen - '(The Beatles) came to become teachers. There was lot to learn ... a lot of devotion to be done in three months. But they were just not ready, being what they were.'[222]

Ringo - 'He never actually used us. We never did anything for him. We never paid him one penny. The only money we ever laid out was our air fare to India. We never gave him anything.'[12]

❀ ❀ ❀

George - 'I've got my "Wonderwall" album coming out in a couple of weeks, and that's very Indian-influenced.'
'But the thing with that is, I recorded it in December of last year and January 1968. I still like it. I think it's very good. But it's not me.'
'I'm back to being a rocker now ... for at bit, at least! You go through so many changes and realisations, and so often you come right back to where you started.'[149]

On Friday, 1st November 1968, Apple Records release George Harrison's *'Wonderwall Music'*, a record filled with Indian music and off-beat rock arrangements. To the outside world, George is fast emerging as an increasingly inspirational force within The Beatles, possibly more so than the other group members.

❀ ❀ ❀

Monday, 4th November 1968
George writes a friendly letter to Art Unger, the editor of *Datebook* magazine, for whom he has given an interview about Transcendental Meditation, in which he recalls his recent visit to India. George uses coloured pens to emphasise his points. [223]

To Art
India was, and no doubt still is, "too much". [Pardon the hip talk man] I couldn't start to tell you about it, but its so beautiful. The religion is everywhere you look and its a pleasure seeing and being with others who believe in something real, instead of a lot of hypocrites, who fear the local vicar, rather than love for their creator. [But who am I to judge others?] I ask myself!
Anyway, it was great, and I expect to be there again soon, or as soon as I get the sign.
If there is a God, we must see Him; if there is a soul, we must perceive it; otherwise it is better not to believe.
It is better to be an outspoken atheist than a hypocrite [by Swami Vivekananda.]

Friday, 22nd November 1968.
A lot of the songs written by The Beatles in India (along with new material) are included on a double-LP release, entitled simply *'The Beatles'*, and packaged in a plain white sleeve, supplied with four portrait colour photographs of the individual Beatles, a foldout poster and a sheet of clean white paper.

George - 'Donovan was all over the White album.'[1]

❀ ❀ ❀

A first year university student, Maurice Hindle, writes to John Lennon hoping to get an interview, but not only is his request granted he is also invited to John's home. John even meets him at the local railway station in his Mini Cooper car.
Maurice practices Transcendental Meditation so it is only natural that when they meet, on Monday, 2nd December 1968, that John should want to talk about his experiences with meditation.
John - 'Well, err.. I was 100% saying meditation could do it, I still believe it you know. People can become aware of this with acid, meditation and macrobiotic diet, you know.'
'So then meditation came along. And that worked all right, you know. And it made.. you could handle each day better than I could handle it before. But then the India thing came and I had some great experience over there cause I was meditating eight hours a day and things like that. And it was really some trip, like acid was nowhere, you know?'
Maurice Hindle - 'Is that a fact?'
John - 'Yeah, just, it.. just… just sitting there muttering some word in a room, and it was the biggest trip I've had in me life, you know. But still when I got home with all the hassle that went out there and we came rushing home, and I still haven't gotten back into it regularly.'
'…you know, the happiest time in my life, one of the happiest times was in India, in some kind of pit. And, happily mentally and physically, because it was just was such a groove. Such a pure thing.'
'And, there's no such thing as just happiness, pure, like that. I think you can reach a state of consciousness, err.. I don't know whether you can make it in this life, you know. I mean, all the Buddhas and the Jesus's, all the great ones that were pretty hip, conscious-wise, I don't think they had complete happiness. But I reckon that you, I get that; I think complete happiness is when you *are* a bit of electricity, when you've made the absolute of the Buddhists or whatever it is they say. And then the concept of what we think of happiness, of just being, which is what happiness will be for all of us, it's not.. and I've had that through meditation, just a state where you are.. not aware of ANYTHING. So there you've been and that's complete happiness, you know, you just ARE. And that is what happiness.. is the bit we're all.. it's the peace, you know, the peace we're looking for. It's just to BE and nothing affects you and you affect nothing, literally. Well, of course you must do in a way cause otherwise... ramble, ramble, ramble. But you just are, you know, and the happiest people, the people that are, that are "BEING" more times a week than anybody else, you know. It's just down to that.'[3]
They talk on many other issues too, mainly political topics, and in this John is very clear about what he thinks will happen to those who become allied to humanitarian concerns.
John - 'Just whoever… the ones who are really doing it get shot, y'know. It's him, the guy who wrote the letter that'll do it. He'll shoot me just for living here.'[3]

❀ ❀ ❀

On Wednesday, 11th December 1968, as part of a filmed appearance for an upcoming movie called *'Rock and Roll Circus'*, John and Yoko join with Rolling Stones Mick Jagger and Keith Richards, Mitch Mitchell (drummer of the Jimi Hendrix Experience), and Eric Clapton. Together they play as Dirty Mac, and perform a version of a track off the newly released *'The Beatles'* double-album, a number called *'Yer Blues'*.

❀ ❀ ❀

'Get Back'
The Beatles decide to hire director Michael Lindsay-Hogg in order to make a television special with the working title of *'Get Back'*, a documentary film of The Beatles, to feature them recording a new album, and rehearsing for a live appearance. But the filming of the *'Get Back'* movie gets quite fraught, and on Friday,10th January 1969, George has an altercation with Paul and walks out of the studio.

George - 'They were filming us having a row. It never came to blows, but I thought, "What's the point of this? I'm quite capable of being relatively happy on my own and I'm not able to be happy in this situation. I'm getting out of here."'

'Everybody had gone through that. Ringo had left at one point. I know John wanted out. It was a very, very difficult, stressful time, and being filmed having a row as well was terrible. I got up and I thought, "I'm not doing this any more. I'm out of here." So I got my guitar and went home and that afternoon wrote *Wah-Wah*.

It became stifling, so that although this new album was supposed to break away from that type of recording (we were going back to playing live) it was still very much that kind of situation where he already had in his mind what he wanted. Paul wanted nobody to play on his songs until he decided how it should go. For me it was like: "What am I doing here? This is painful!"'[1]

George's diary entry for January 10th includes a brief mention of the morning's business:- [94]

> ***'Went to Twickenham, rehearsed until lunchtime - left the Beatles - went home...'***

Michael Lindsay-Hogg - 'At the morning rehearsal, I could tell by his silence and withdrawal that something was simmering inside him, and so in my role as documentarian, I'd asked our soundman to bug the flower pot on the lunch table.

We'd finished the first course when George arrived to stand at the end of the table.

We looked at him as he stood silent for a moment.

"See you 'round the clubs," he said.

That was his good-bye. He left.

John, a person who reacted aggressively to provocation, immediately said, "Let's get in Eric [Clapton]. He's just as good and not such a headache."'[224]

> ***'Now I don't need no wah-wah's***
> ***And I know how sweet life can be'***
>
> - Excerpt of lyrics to *'Wah-Wah'* by George Harrison

But, apparently both Paul and Ringo are both dead set against changing the lineup of the group, and anyway, George eventually agrees to return to work with the group on the proviso that filming is moved from the vast Twickenham Studios over to the much smaller Apple studio in Saville Row, which has a more intimate feel.

✽ ✾ ✽

Michael Lindsay-Hogg - 'Let's make a silent movie, yes - slow and speed it up when we play it back, as they're always funny to watch.'

Paul - 'An 'X' film starring the Maharishi.'[225]

Paul - 'I was looking at the film I did at the Maharishi's. Just to see what we were doing, it's incredible.'

Ringo - 'What were you doing?'

John - 'Yeh, what were we doing?'

Paul - 'I don't really know. But like we totally put our own personalities under for the sake of it, and you can really see that.'

John - 'We were writing all those songs. I filmed the helicopter.'[225]

Paul - 'Yeh, I noticed you taking it, it was incredible, just sort of to see us. We weren't sort of really very truthful there. You know.. I mean we could have.. You know things like sneaking behind his back and sort of saying, "It's a bit like school, isn't it?" But you can see on the film that it was very like school, and that, really, we should have said it. And the reason we should have sort of said, like we needed...'

John - 'We should call it: "What We Did On Our Holidays".'

Paul - 'Well you know. The reason I'm saying that is, there's a long shot of you sort of walking with him, and it's just not you. (Laughing) you know. More a sort of "Tell me, O Master" . . . '

John - 'Tell me old Master.'[226]

Paul - 'I was telling Linda last night about that thing you said the other night, that you went up in the helicopter with him; you just thought he might slip you the answer.' (laughter)

'Linda was saying, "Didn't he ever really, sitting up on his roof and that, and looking at that movie, Didn't you ever really feel like going out in it, you know?"'[226]

George corrects him, reminding him that Maharishi arranged for the students to get out and about, but Paul appears adamant, saying that it would have been nice just to go and explore the locality. Of course this was what the other students had been accustomed to be able to do, before The Beatles arrived, bringing the world's Press with them!

Paul - 'Yeah, yeah, you know, the bits in the villages and stuff, like with all the stuff, the bit that everyone else that 95 per cent of them were doing around there, except for the converts on the hill, you know. Everyone else was digging that place.'

Again George corrects him, pointing out that the visit was to rest not to go *'bollocking about'*. John and George chat together, and George begins to talk to John about an Indian teacher called Sri Aurobindo, until Paul brings the subject back to the film he has been watching.

Paul - 'It opens with Cyn and Pattie, Jane, you know it goes through all, it goes through all different changes and stuff, there's all the people who were there. Geoffrey, err, the little American girl, and it's all of them. And they're just all in the same shot, against the sky. Then that changes to someone else, it's a great opening too, you know… there's a big sort of white blur… because it's a change of reel. It great, that it burns out white and then like, then the sound track should start.'

John - (singing) 'Flew in from Miami BOAC.'

Paul - (laughing) 'Yeah, it is like that, because Mike Love comes in. And he's doing, and he's really, and then he's sitting with Cyn and Jane waving. Like, incredible film, and then, err, then the next thing, it burns out white again and the next scene is just this monkey that comes up and humps this other monkey. (laughter) It's all, it's great. And in a way, oh, it really gets in there, really gets in there, the monkey, really does, stretches out.. it bangs her, and then they just jump off and they start just picking each other and the children…'

'It's great stuff, and, there's a great one of you [John]…, I don't know why it is, it's to do with that thing, like "slipping the answer". When you, once you think it's that, it's great. You know, it's like you come off of a one-to-one on the roof and you walk, and you look like a student of philosophy with your tape recorder.'

John - 'I have all the soundtracks, too, I think.'

Paul - 'It's that thing, we probably should have..'

John - 'Been ourselves.'

Paul - 'Yeah, lots more, yeah.'

George - 'That, that is the, the biggest, err, that is like the joke, to be yourselves, to be yourselves. That was the purpose of going there, to find out what's behind the exterior selves in these years.'

John - 'Yes, well we found out in the end.'

George - 'And if you were really yourselves you wouldn't be any of whom we are now.'

Paul - 'Ermmm.'

John - 'Act naturally, then.'[226]

❀ ❀ ❀

A national newspaper, the *Daily Express*, profiles John and Yoko.

Yoko - 'The only thing about being in love, is that it takes so much time. The work suffers. I am not working enough now.'

John, shouting - 'What do you mean? It's never been *easier* for you to work. If no one will produce what you do, *I* will.

'Whenever I'm not doing my Beatles work I'll do her work completely. There's not much Beatle stuff now, anyway.'[19]

❀ ❀ ❀

On Wednesday, 12th March 1969 Paul McCartney marries Linda Eastman, at Marylebone Register Office in London. Mike McCartney and Mal Evans act as witnesses but other than Paul, there are no Beatles in attendance.

❀ ❀ ❀

In March 1969, Maharishi is asked by one of his followers what to say if he is asked whether The Beatles have stopped meditating.

Maharishi - 'We tell them "We don't take Beatles' diaries, but, they must be meditating, any sensible man would continue to meditate" we just say like that. And if someone says, "They have stopped", fine, every man is free to do what he wants to do. Ha, ha. People go to college and earn their degree and then they stop. they don't learn ahead, or go ahead. And nobody knows about The Beatles, what they doing. When I myself don't know, then who else will know? Ha, ha, ha, ha.

And we tell the people, "This meditation does not depend on any personalities." It's just the natural flow of life to find fulfilment, and it does.'

'Is this Beatle issue an issue in society?'

'Ideal expression to answer Beatles problem....'

'We can tell, oh one thing, we say, what is that? Canterbury? "Archbishop of Canterbury congratulated Beatles when they started, what he says about them now we haven't heard." (laughter) This will be a very beautiful thing to say (laughter) "Archbishop of Canterbury congratulated Beatles when they started to meditate and what he says about them lately we haven't heard" (laughter) and this will put an end to the whole thing. That's something good to say. And one or two more such striking sentences.' (laughter)

Someone informs Maharishi that, according to recent interviews, at least two of The Beatles still meditate.

Maharishi - 'So when they want to be mischievous they don't meditate. (laughter) And then they want to be good boys, then they gather their senses and meditate... "They are trying with their life."'[3]

❀ ❀ ❀

On Thursday, 20th March 1969, John Lennon & Yoko Ono marry in Gibraltar and then honeymoon in Paris where John writes *'The Ballad of John and Yoko'*.

*'The way things are going
They're going to crucify me'*
- Excerpt from the lyrics of *'The Ballad of John and Yoko'* by John Lennon & Paul McCartney

And when John returns home, George is on holiday and Ringo is away filming for a movie, so he and Paul get on and record the new song without them.

John, on guitar - 'Go a bit faster, Ringo!'

Paul, on drums - 'OK, George!'[6]

❀ ❀ ❀

Gill Pritchard (a Beatles fan) - 'One evening during the end of the *Abbey Road* sessions, Paul came racing out of the front door of the studio in tears, went home and didn't come back. The next day he didn't turn up at all even though the studio was booked.'[185]

Wendy Sutcliffe (a Beatles fan) - 'John was *really* angry because they were all waiting and he came storming out of the studio and made off towards Paul's house. We followed and when he got there he stood outside and just banged on the door again and again, calling for Paul to open up. Paul didn't answer so John climbed the gate and hammered on his door. Then they had a screaming match. He was shouting that George and Ringo had both come in from the country and Paul didn't even bother to let anyone know he couldn't make the session.'[227]

❀ ❀ ❀

Raghvendra

Maharishi is allotted 60 acres of land on which to build another academy in India, but someone tries to stir up trouble for Raghvendra complaining that under his supervision a lot of money is being spent. Allegedly, in a full meeting, Maharishi asks Raghuvendra for an explanation, and this hurts him.

Brahmachari Raghvendra, addressing Maharishi - 'The prefix "Maharishi" is only used by seers, the ones who can look into the hearts and truths of people. You clearly are not capable of doing so. This is why I would recommend that you remove the prefix "Maharishi" from your name. And with this I leave your organisation now.'[228]

Raghvendra walks out that very day, and though Maharishi sends several people after him hoping they will persuade him to change his mind, it is of no avail, for as Raghvendra's brother explains; *'by then Raghu's heart had broken and he never returned'*.

Mike Dolan - 'Rhagvendra was more than a nice guy...
He was the most fantastically fearless and interesting person I have ever met.'
'All of the youth faction on the course idolized him.'[38]

❀ ❀ ❀

Allan Kozinn (in the *New York Times*) - 'What is often overlooked… is the influence the maharishi - or at least the experience of going to Rishikesh to meditate for several weeks - had on the group. For one thing, he weaned them from LSD. Harrison had been heading in that direction anyway, and Mr. McCartney and Mr. Starr were only occasional users, but Lennon was a heavy user. Not that they gave up drugs entirely. They continued to smoke marijuana, and a year later Lennon was using heroin.'[229]

Late in the Spring 1969 John strums his guitar and tells Yoko a story of his time in India.
John - 'Well, let me tell you something about the Maharishi camp, in Rishikesh. There were one or two attractive women there, but mainly, looked like, ya know, school teachers or somethin'. And the whole damn camp was spyin' on the ones in the bathing suits. And they're supposed to be meditatin'. And there's this cowboy there called Tom who plays cowboys on T.V. And *my*, did the Beatle-wives go for him in a big way....! I wondered what it was? It was his tight leather belt, his jeans, and his dumb eyes. They seem to love dumb eyes 'cause all they see is dumb eyes.'
Yoko - 'What's wrong with his eyes? You have good sight.'
John - 'Me? I took it for real. I wrote 600 songs about how I feel. I felt like dying, and crying, and committing suicide, but I felt creative and I said: "What the hell's this got to do with what that silly little man's talking about?" But he did charm me in a way because he was funny, sort of cuddly, like a sort of.. you know...'
Yoko - 'Like a teddy bear.'
John - 'Little daddy with a beard telling stories of Heaven, as if he knew. You could never pin him down, but he often spread rumours through his right hand man who used to be with the CIA and told about the planes he saved. How Maharishi came through the storm on a plane, and the pilot was gettin' worried they couldn't land. When Maharishi looked up and with one foul look - according to the man who works for him - everything was OK and they landed! After that I thought; LIES.
But who was that woman who looks like Jean Simmons who keeps going to him for private interviews? She musta been about 40-45. Kept talkin' about her husband 'cause he wasn't there. Always tryin' to get a private audience with the Maharishi and he kept refusing. I knew only one thing. He must of had some of his own. It musta been that little Indian piece. She came with the tailor and could sit at his feet and that was one in 500. The rest had to wait like good American people, in lines, to see the master walking on the petals, who lived in a million dollar staccato house overlookin' the Himalayas. He looked holy.'
Yoko - 'But he was a sex maniac...'
John - 'I couldn't say that, but he certainly wasn't...'
Yoko - 'Holy.'
John - 'In the true sense of the word that is...!'[230]

❀ ❀ ❀

On Thursday, 8th May 1969, John Lennon and Yoko Ono are interviewed at the Apple offices in London.
David Wigg - 'And do you feel that what you did previously, going to India and things like that, were of any help?'
John - 'Yes. That's what I mean, I don't regret anything. Meditation, I still believe in and occasionally I use it. And I don't regret any of that. I don't regret taking drugs, because they helped me. I don't advocate them for everybody, because I don't think I should, you know. But for me it was good and India was good for me. And I met Yoko just before I went to India and had a lot of time to think, and think things out there with three months just meditating and thinking. And I came home and fell in love with Yoko and that was the end of it. And it's beautiful.'
David Wigg - 'What does life mean to you, John. Will it matter to you if it finished tomorrow or do you want to live to an old age?'
John - 'I'd like to live to a ripe old age, with Yoko only, you know. And I'm not afraid of dying. I don't know how it'd feel at the moment. But I'm prepared for death because I don't believe in it. I think it's just getting out

of one car and getting into another.'

David Wigg - 'Do you ever go to church?'

John - 'No, I don't need to go to church, because church.. I respect churches because of the sacredness that's been put on them over the years by people who do believe. I think a lot of bad things have happened in the name of the church and in the name of Christ and therefore I shy away from church. And as Donovan once said, "I go to my own church and my own temple once a day", you know. And I think people who need a church should go, and the others who know the church is in your own head should visit that temple, 'cuz that's where the source is.'[231]

In June, John and Yoko take another honeymoon, this time in Canada, where they stage a bed-in and perform a new song by John, *'Give Peace a Chance',* which is soon released as a single by the Plastic Ono Band.

> ***'Let me tell you now, ev'rybody's talking about revolution, evolution, masturbation, flagellation, regulation, integrations, meditations, United Nations, congratulations.'***
>
> Extract from the lyrics of *'Give Peace a Chance'* by John Lennon

❀ ❀ ❀

In an interview with *International Times,* George talks about meeting Maharishi and about learning to meditate.

George - 'It was very nice and, in fact, we still meditate now, at least I do. I can't speak for any of the others.'

Reporter - 'There was a feeling created by the way it was told that - like it had all come to an end. Is that a true picture of what happened?'

George - 'Personally I wanted all that scene as a personal thing. It goes back to the Beatle days, you know, we were always in the public eye, always being photographed and written about, and even if you went to the bog it was in the papers. And I thought, well at least when I find me yogi it's going to be quiet and in a cave - and it's going to be a personal thing. Because the press always misinterpret things anyway - and they have done right down the line. They never really know what we are or what we think, they give their own image of how they see us. People can only see each other from their own state of consciousness, and the press's state of consciousness is virtually nil. So, they never really get the true essence of anything they write about. The Maharishi was right, because the whole thing is - the physical world is relative, that means right is half of wrong, and yes is half of no, so you can't say what is right and what is wrong. The only thing which Maharishi said which determined what was right and what was wrong was that right or good is something that's life creating - and something is bad is something that's life-destroying. And so you can't say that going on the television and speaking to the press and doing things like that is a bad way to tell people about meditation. On the other hand, after being through all that, it was part of our everyday life. I want it to be quieter, much quieter. Anyway, the main thing was you asked whether it had ended or not - it's just that we physically left Maharishi's camp - but spiritually never moved an inch. In fact, probably I've got even closer now.'[232]

❀ ❀ ❀

Early in their career, John, Paul, George and Ringo, dressed in identical black trench coats, turned up at a Rolling Stones' gig in Richmond, Surrey, and sat huddled together in the front row. Mick Jagger jokingly referred to The Beatles, as the *'Four-headed monster',* and of course they did tend to go about together. Nowadays though, relations between the four are at times strained, but they continue working together and are recording a new LP, to be called *'Everest'* (the name of the brand of cigarettes smoked by engineer Geoff Emerick). Importantly, they each find time to contribute to a collaboration, a song that is intended to be the final track, a composition provisionally titled *'The Ending'.*

> ***'And in the end, the love you take is equal to the love you make.'***
>
> Extract from the lyrics to *'The End'* by Paul McCartney & John Lennon

John - 'That's Paul again … He had a line in it, "And in the end, the love you get is equal to the love you give," which is a very cosmic, philosophical line.'[15]

Chapter Thirty-One
Please Mr Postman

Before meeting Maharishi, George and John both experimented with chanting the *'Hare Krishna' mantra*, then in August 1969, with the help of devotees of the Radha Krishna Temple, London, George Harrison sets about recording the *mantra,* with the intention of issuing it as a single on Apple Records. In fact he records a LP full of Hindu devotional chants, including the hypnotic *'Govinda',* a song based on a very ancient poem.

The head of the International Krishna Consciousness Society is 73-year old Swami A.C. Bhaktivedanta. Born in Calcutta, educated at the local Scottish Church College; 'A.C.' (Abhay Charan) married, had children and became the owner of a small pharmaceutical business. However, on his retirement in 1959, he took the vow of *sannyas* (renunciation) and thus became a *swami* with the *sannyasi* name, 'Bhaktivedanta' - *'bhakti'* meaning 'devotee', and 'Vedanta' being 'the end of the Veda', which refers to the philosophy and understanding of the *Upanishads* and the *Bhagavad Gita.*

Thursday, 11th September 1969.
Swami Bhaktivedanta is staying as a houseguest of John's at his new home at Tittenhurst Park, and this provides John and George with an opportunity to get acquainted with the *swami*, and he with them.
Bhaktivedanta - 'What kind of philosophy you are following? May I ask?'
John - 'Following?'
Yoko - 'We don't follow anything. We are just living.'
George - 'We've done meditation. Or I do my meditation. I have a *mantra* meditation.'
Bhaktivedanta - 'This is also *mantra*.'
John - 'It's not the song, though.'
George - 'No, no. It's chanting.'
John - 'We heard it from Maharishi. A *mantra* each.'
Bhaktivedanta - 'His *mantra* is not public.'
George - 'Not out loud. No.'
John - 'No. It's a secret.' (laughs)[233]

George - 'All people can get the *mantras* that we have, but it's just they must get it from somebody else. We can't give it to them, but it is available for everybody.'
Bhaktivedanta - 'Yes. *Mantra*, if it is valuable, it is valuable for everybody. Why it should be for a particular person?'
John - 'If all *mantras* are... All *mantras* just the name of God. Whether it's a secret *mantra* or an open *mantra*, it's all the name of God. So it doesn't really make much difference, does it, which one you sing?'
Bhaktivedanta - 'No. Just like in drug shop they sell all medicine for disease, curing disease. But still, you have to take doctor's prescription to take a particular type of medicine. They will not supply you. If you go to a drug shop and you say, "I am diseased. You give me any medicine," that is not... He'll ask you, "Where is your prescription?" So similarly, in this age, in Kali-yuga age, this *mantra*, Hare Krishna *mantra*, is recommended in the *shastras*, and great stalwart -- we consider Him the incarnation of Krishna - Chaitanya Mahaprabhu.'

Yoko - 'If the *mantra* itself has such power, does it matter where you receive it, where you take it?'
Bhaktivedanta - 'Yes. Yes. That is a fact. The example is given just like milk. Milk is nutritious. That's a fact. Everyone knows. But if the milk is touched through the tongue of a serpent, it is no more nutritious. It is poison.'
Yoko - 'Well, milk is material.'
Bhaktivedanta - 'No, material. You want to understand through your material senses, we have to give...'
Yoko - 'Well, no. I don't have, you don't have to tell me material senses. I mean *mantra* is not material. It should be something spiritual, and therefore nobody can spoil it, I don't think. I mean, I wonder if anybody can spoil something that is not material.'
Bhaktivedanta - 'But the thing is that if you don't receive the *mantra* through the proper channel, it may not be

mantra.'

John - 'But how would you know, anyway? How are you able to tell, anyway? I mean, for any of your disciples or us or anybody that goes to *any* spiritual master, how are we to tell...'

Bhaktivedanta - 'Not *any* spiritual master.'

John - 'A true master. How are we to tell one from the other?'

Bhaktivedanta - 'It is not that *any* spiritual master. *Sampradaya*. "*Sampradaya*" means a particular line of "disciplic succession".'

John - 'But, you see, Maharishi said exactly the same thing about his *mantras* coming from the Vedic, with seemingly as much authority as you, and he was probably right. So how... It's like having too many fruits on a plate, and you can't only eat two of them.'

Bhaktivedanta - 'No. If *mantra* is coming down in that way, then it is potency; the potency is there.'

John - 'But Hare Krishna is the best one?'

Bhaktivedanta - 'Yes.'

Yoko - 'Well, if Hare Krishna is the best one, what is the reason why we have to bother to even say anything else other than this one?'

Bhaktivedanta - 'You don't require to bother to say anything else. We say that Hare Krishna *mantra* is sufficient for one's perfection.'

George - 'Surely isn't it like flowers? If somebody may prefer roses and somebody may like carnations better... Isn't it really a matter for the devotee, that one person may find Hare Krishna is more beneficial to his spiritual progress, and yet somebody else, some other *mantra* may be more beneficial? Isn't it like just a matter of taste? Like judging a flower. They're all flowers, but some people may like one better than the other.'

John - 'Well, who says who's in the line of descent? You know, I mean, it's just like royalty. Who's who?'

Yoko - 'That's what I was talking about.'

John - 'I mean Yogananda claims...'

George - 'His *guru's, guru's, guru's*...'

John - 'All his *guru's, guru's, guru's, gurus*, like that. Maharishi claimed all his *guru's guru's gurus* went back. I mean, how are we to know? I mean, it's a matter of just deciding, you know.'

Bhaktivedanta - 'But Maharishi does not say anything about Krishna.'

George - 'Doesn't he? No, his *guru* is the Shankaracharya.'

John - 'Which is Shankara's teaching? But they all talk about God, and Krishna's just a name for God, isn't it?'

Bhaktivedanta - 'Anyway, whatever he may be, he does not go up to Krishna.' (chuckles)

George - 'Personality, anyway, of...'

John - 'Well, that's what he used to say in exactly the same way, about anybody else.'

Bhaktivedanta - 'No, no. He cannot be because he does not speak about anything Krishna. A peon comes, he does not know anything about post office -- what kind of peon he is?'

Yoko - 'No, but **his** post office... He was talking about **his** post office'.

Bhaktivedanta - 'No, you cannot create post office. Post office, one. Government post office.'

Yoko - 'Yes, of course. I'm sure there's only one post office.'

Bhaktivedanta - 'You cannot create that he is... Somebody says, "I belong to another post office." Then he is at once unauthorized…'

Yoko - 'No, no. He's saying that **his** post office is the one post office.'

Devotee - 'Then why..? Obviously not satisfied yet with what they found in …. that post office. Why have you come here, then? If you have been satisfied with that... You have to test.'

John - 'Yeah, we've gotta go around. Yoko never met Maharishi. We're asking advice of how to, you know, how to stop. You can go on forever. I know people that have been wandering around for years, seeking *gurus* and spiritual teachers. I mean it's doing them all quite well.'

Bhaktivedanta, to devotee - 'Bring *prasadam*!'

John - 'I mean, we can only judge on a material level by looking at your disciples and looking at other peoples' disciples and looking at ourselves, you know. And, of course, if there's thirty disciples, seven of them look fairly spiritual, another ten look okay, and the others just look as though they're having trouble... You know. So there's no...'

Yoko - 'It's the same thing.'

John - 'We still have to keep sifting through like sand to see whose got the best matter, or...'

Bhaktivedanta - 'Try to understand this, that regarding authority, you say that how to find out the authority. To answer this question, Krishna is authority. There is no doubt. Because if Krishna is an authority, Maharishi takes also Krishna's book and Aurobindo takes Krishna's book, Vivekananda takes Krishna's book, Dr. Radhakrishnan takes Krishna's book. So Krishna is authority. Shankaracharya also takes Krishna's book. You know Shankaracharya's commentary on Krishna? And in that commentary he accepts, *krsnas tu bhagavan svayam* [Srimad Bhagavatam 1.3.28], *sa bhagavan svayam krisnah* "Krishna is the Supreme Personality of Godhead." He accepts. You say that Maharishi accepts Shankaracharya. Shankaracharya accepts Krishna as the Supreme Personality of Godhead.'

George - 'Yes, but it's like the Bible which came...'

Bhaktivedanta - 'Now, don't go to Bible. We're talking of Krishna. (laughter) Just try to understand.'

Yoko - 'Yes, but, you see, the religion is bringing out …'

Bhaktivedanta - 'Just see that Krishna is the authority. He's accepted by everyone. You say Maharishi belongs to the Shankara *sampradaya*. Shankaracharya accepts Krishna. Not as authority... He says, "Krishna is the Supreme Personality of Godhead." He says this very word in his commentary.'

Devotee - *"Bhaja govindam bhaja govindam bhaja govindam."*

Bhaktivedanta - 'So authority means one who has accepted Krishna as the Supreme Lord. Then he is authority.'

Yoko - 'Now, who said that?'

Bhaktivedanta - 'Everyone says. All authorities. Shankaracharya says. Ramanujacharya says. Those who are really authorities, those disciplic succession is going on. In India, there are five sects. Actually two sects. Vaishnava and Shankara. So the Vaishnava accept Krishna as the authority, and Shankara accepted Krishna authority. There are no third sect. Practically, actually, there is one sect, the Vaishnava. Anyway, later on, later ages, Shankaracharya established his sect. But Shankaracharya accepts that *"krishnas tu bhagavan svayam"* [Srimad Bhagavatam 1.3.28] "Krishna is the Supreme Personality of Godhead," in his writing. And at his last stage of his life he said, "You rascal fools, what you are dealing with? That will not save you." *"Bhaja govindam"* "You just worship Krishna." *"Bhaja govindam bhaja govindam bhaja govindam mudha-mate. Mudha-mate"* means "You rascal."' (laughter)

John - 'Means what?'

Devotee - '"You rascal."'

Bhaktivedanta - '"You rascal, just worship Krishna and become devotee of Krishna, Govinda."

'bhaja govindam bhaja govindam
bhaja govindam mudha-mate
sam prapte sannihite kale
na hi na hi rakshati dukrijna-karane'

"When your death will come, all this grammatical jugglery of words will not save you. Krishna can save you. So you *bhaja govindam*." That is instruction of Shankaracharya.'

Yoko - 'But every sect says that...'

Bhaktivedanta - 'No, there is no question, "every sect." Krishna is the centre of every sect. If Krishna is the centre, then there is no question of every sect. Only Krishna sect.'

John - 'Does Krishna mean God?'

Devotee - 'Yes.'

Bhaktivedanta - 'Yes. Krishna means God, and God means Krishna.'

John - 'So for the Bible or any other holy book, they all talk about one God, but they all have many ways of...'

Bhaktivedanta - 'That's all right.'

George - 'Personalities.'

John - 'Yes.'

Bhaktivedanta - 'That's all right.'

John - 'It's still just the one Being everywhere, in all the books. But they all have... Why isn't Hare Krishna or something similar in the Bible, then? I mean, that's the only other one I know because I was brought up with the Bible.'

Devotee - 'It is. In the 150th Psalm it says, "Praise the Lord with every breath. Praise the Lord with drum and flute."'

John - 'But they haven't got very good tunes, you know. I mean, they haven't been passing on any good chants, have they?'[233]

A couple of days later, John Lennon accepts an invitation to appear at a festival in Canada; he recruits Eric Clapton as lead guitarist of the hastily formed Plastic Ono Band, and gets airborne.

George - 'When the Plastic Ono Band went to Toronto in September John actually asked me to be in the band, but I didn't do it. I didn't really want to be in an avant-garde band, and I knew that was what it was going to be.'[1]

'Oh I'll be a good boy
Please make me well'

- Excerpt of *'Cold Turkey'* by John Lennon

John is experiencing problems with heroin addiction, and has just written a song called *'Cold Turkey'*, in which he describes the symptoms of withdrawal. Actually, it seems that John has been taking heroin off and on for over a year.

John - 'We were full of junk too. I just threw up for hours till I went on. I nearly threw up in Cold Turkey.' 'Heroin. It just was not too much fun. I never injected it or anything. We sniffed a little when we were in real pain. I mean we just couldn't - people were giving us such a hard time. And I've had so much shit thrown at me and especially at Yoko. People like Peter Brown in our office, he comes down and shakes my hand and doesn't even say hello to her. Now that's going on all the time. And we get in so much pain that we have to do something about it. And that's what happened to us. We took H because of what The Beatles and their pals were doing to us. And we got out of it.'[5]

Yoko - 'Luckily we never injected because both of us were totally scared about needles. So that probably saved us and the other thing that saved us was our connection was not very good.'[234]

Paul - 'I tried heroin just the once.'
'Even then, I didn't realize I'd taken it. I was just handed something, smoked it, then found out what it was.
'It didn't do anything for me, which was lucky because I wouldn't have fancied heading down that road.'[235]

❀ ❀ ❀

On Saturday, 20th September 1969, at a business meeting, John informs Paul and Ringo that he is leaving the group. George is absent from the meeting as he is off visiting his mother.

John - 'When I finally had the guts to tell the other three that I, quote, wanted a divorce, unquote, they knew it was for real, unlike Ringo and George's previous threats to leave. I must say I felt guilty for springing it on them at such short notice.'[236]

Paul - 'I remember him saying, "It's weird this, telling you I'm leaving the group, but in a way it's very exciting." It was like when he told Cynthia he was getting a divorce. He was quite buoyed up by it, so we couldn't really do anything: "You mean leaving? So that's the group, then…" It was later, as the fact set in, that it got really upsetting.'[1]

Ringo - 'If that had happened in 1965, or 1967 even, it would have been a mighty shock. Now it was just "let's get the divorce over with", really. And John was always the most forward when it came to nailing anything.'[1]

Paul - 'He had told Allen Klein the new manager he and Yoko had picked late one night that he didn't want to continue.'
Linda - 'And Allen said to John, "Don't tell the others." . . . I don't know if we dare tell this.'
Paul - 'Yeah, I don't know how much of this we're allowed to say--but Allen said, "Don't tell them until after we sign your new Capitol Records deal."'
Linda - 'I don't know if we're allowed...'
Paul - 'Even if it can't be said, we'll say it. It's the truth. So it was the very next morning that I was trying to say, "Let's get back together, guys, and play the small clubs and. .. ." That's when John said…'

Linda - 'His exact words were "I think you're daft."'
Paul - 'And he said, "I wasn't going to tell you until after I signed the Capitol thing, but I'm leaving the group." And that was really it. The cat amongst the pigeons.'
Linda - 'But what also happened, after the shock wore off, was that everybody agreed to keep the decision to break up quiet.'
Paul - 'We weren't going to say anything about it for months, for business reasons. But the really hurtful thing to me was that John was really not going to tell us. I think he was heavily under the influence of Allen Klein. And Klein, so I heard, had said to John--the first time anyone had said it--"What does Yoko want?" So since Yoko liked Klein because he was for giving Yoko anything she wanted, he was the man for John. That's my theory on how it happened.'[260]

'Paul and Klein both spent the day persuading me it was better not to say anything - asking me not to say anything because it would "hurt the Beatles" - and "let's just let it petre out"...'

- Letter from John Lennon to Linda McCartney 237

'Something in the way she moves
Attracts me like no other lover'

- Excerpt of *'Something'* by George Harrison

On Monday, 6th October 1969, *'Something'* is released as The Beatles' new single.
George - 'I just wrote it, and then somebody put together a video. And what they did was they went out and got some footage of me and Pattie, Paul and Linda, Ringo and Maureen, it was at that time, and John and Yoko and they just made up a little video to go with it. So then, everybody presumed I wrote it about Pattie, but actually, when I wrote it, I was thinking of Ray Charles.'
'... that's what I was thinking of. I could hear in my head Ray Charles singing it.'[238]

So, if the song is not about Pattie, who is it about?
Pattie - '... there were other women. That really hurt. In India George had become fascinated by the god Krishna, who was always surrounded by young maidens, and came back wanting to be some kind of Krishna figure, a spiritual being with lots of concubines. He actually said so. And no woman was out of bounds.'[21]

❀ ❀ ❀

When the Maharishi is interviewed by the BBC on Tuesday, 14th October 1969, he answers a range of questions, including one which promises to unlock the mystery about his attitude towards sex and sensuality.
Leslie Smith - 'What is the vow you have taken?'
Maharishi - 'To refrain from the, the worldly joys of life - that is a monkish way of life. There are two ways of life, the householder, who takes upon himself the responsibility of society and activity, and someone who goes into the monastery or into the forest and caves, and meditates there.'
Leslie Smith - 'Have you renounced the world?'
Maharishi - 'I did renounce the world, and.. the thing is, for the last many hundreds of years, the idea has been cherished by society in all parts of the world, that if one wants to lead a spiritual life one has to renounce the world. And I... I came out of this same world.
I had the idea that I must renounce the world in order to be really a spiritual man, a *yogi*. But, what I found out is that this spiritual life is not dependent on the renunciation of the world. It's only solely dependant on morning and evening practice of meditation, which can take our mind to the inner being and open to us the great reservoir of intelligence and energy and bliss consciousness'[3]

❀ ❀ ❀

The tapes which John and Yoko's recorded on that momentous night back in May are released on Apple Records as *'Unfinished Music No. 1: Two Virgins'*, the cover of which includes a 'quote' from Paul McCartney, created by selecting words from a newspaper at random,; a process he calls *'found object'* artistry.
Paul - 'When two great saints meet it is a humbling experience. The long battles to prove he was a saint.'

'when two great Saints meet it is a humbling experience. The long battles to prove he was a Saint.' --Paul McCartney
Unfinished Music No. 1. Two Virgins. Yoko Ono/John Lennon.

The cover of _'Two Virgins'_ with self-taken photograph

'Genesis Chapter 2 25 _And they were both naked, the man and his wife, and were not ashamed_.'

George - 'I don't think I actually heard all of _Two Virgins_; just bits of it. I wasn't particularly into that kind of thing. That was his and her affair; their trip. They got involved with each other and were obviously into each other to such a degree that they thought everything they said or did was of world importance, and so they made it into records and films.'[1]

On Monday, 20th October 1969, the Plastic Ono Band release their second single, _'Cold Turkey'_.

❀ ❀ ❀

On Friday, 24th October 1969, BBC Radio's Chris Drake interviews Paul McCartney, confronting him with the rumour, currently circulating, that he is dead. As it happens though, Paul has just been spending an increasing amount of time at High Park Farm, his other home, on Kintyre, a peninsula in Argyll, Scotland, in the company of Linda, her daughter Heather and their new baby, Mary.

Paul - 'I think the locals, the people living in Campbeltown itself, think I'm a bit of a nut, living out in the wilds like this, you know. But all the other people who live out in the wilds think the people who live in Campbeltown are a bit nuts for living in the city when they've got all this beautiful land around them.'
'I've done all my work for this year 'cos The Beatles have.. they've made a film and another album, besides _Abbey Road_, which are unreleased as yet, so I've finished my work 'til about March of next year really, so I'm laughin', so I might not be back in London at all this year, you know.'[3]

John & Yoko take a short holiday in Greece and for 10-days they eat only brown rice, part of the 'macrobiotic' diet designed by Nyoichi 'George' Sakurazawa. But whilst in Athens John meets with a fortune teller who warns him he will 'be shot on an island', so the couple cut their stay, cancelling to a trip to stay on an island with Donovan, and re-route to India where they stay in Bombay, at the luxurious Taj Mahal Palace Hotel. Several days later, John gives a potted description of this trip to reporter Howard Smith.

John - 'We slipped off into the mountains to see some miracle worker [Satya Sai Baba] who didn't do any miracles..'
'We did ten days right, rice, and we got back to Bombay and said, "Right.. **Curry**!" I had three milkshakes, lime, and all that!'[3]

> **'BEATLES ARE ON THE BRINK OF SPLITTING'**
> **John -** 'The Beatles split up? It just depends how much we all want to record together. I don't know if I want to record together again. I go off and on it. I really do.'
> *- New Musical Express - NME,* Saturday, 13th December 1969

In January 1970, John Lennon records *'Instant Karma! (We All Shine On)'* - with George being the only other Beatle appearing on the record - and released as a third single by the Plastic Ono Band.

'Instant Karma's gonna get you
Gonna knock you off your feet'

- Excerpt of lyrics to 'Instant Karma!' by John Lennon

By including the word *'karma'* in the title, and repeatedly suggesting that it will 'get you', John implies that *karma* is a penalty or a judgement, maybe even a form of retribution which occurs instantly, whereas the word *karma* can be equally applied to all actions and reactions, good or bad, originating in the present or the past.

❀ ❀ ❀

On Friday, 10th April 1970, George Harrison is interviewed by Clifford Hanley for a BBC television programme entitled *'Fact Or Fantasy: Prayer And Meditation'*, which also features Pir Vilayat, the Head of a Sufi order, and Archbishop Anthony Bloom.

George - 'I happened to get into meditation through music really, Indian music. I went to India to learn a bit of Indian music and inside I always had a desire to know about *yogis*, and I don't, can't explain that one, it's just something that's been in me from time in the past, and I wanted to know more about that. So I had the opportunity to find out about it in India and consequently that led into meditation, because the goal, there's like a goal in life which is to, really the only reason to be living is to have complete full knowledge, full bliss consciousness, everything else is just mundane and secondary. And so I wanted to know some method of enlarging my own consciousness, and that's meditation, and that's been there millions, millions of years. It's always there, and "Knock and the door will be opened." The thing that really got me interested was after being brought up as a Catholic, until I was about 13, I couldn't take it any longer because it was just full of hypocrisy, and err.. the teachings of an Indian called Vivekananda, which really impressed me, he said "If there's a God we must see him, If there's a soul we must perceive it otherwise its better not to believe. Better to be an outspoken atheist than a hypocrite." Whereas the Catholics were teaching me to be a hypocrite, "just be a hypocrite, believe what we tell you, don't try and have any experience." But the whole basis of religion is to have the experience, have that perception. So, there's these methods of God perception, self-realisation, which is *yoga* and meditation, and the process which you have to get from a spiritual master, somebody who's an authority on this sort of thing.'
Interviewer - 'There is a technique to exercise?'
George - 'Yeah, there's many different techniques, and the technique we did with Maharishi Mahesh Yogi was a form of silent meditation, which, you know, you can transcend. The purpose is to transcend from this relative state of consciousness to the absolute state of consciousness. People think, "this is me", you know, and this isn't me, it's just a bag of bones. Basically everybody is err, spirit, which is really what Christ was here to tell everybody about, "the kingdom of heaven that lies within", which is the state of being, pure consciousness. So, through many years of err, pollution, of consciousness, through material energy and this association, then we've ended up in a fallen state, but really everybody is basically potentially divine. So *yoga*, all these methods are really err, ancient methods just to stop further pollution of your system and consciousness, and to cleanse the system. The whole thing of purity that they talk about in religion is really a mental, physical and spiritual purity, which obtained through discipline and through practice. So the meditation we did with Maharishi Mahesh Yogi was to sit silently and transcend through the sense of sound, like you can transcend with hearing or with touch or vision, like I think some Buddhists meditate by concentrating on an object, like either a garden, Japanese gardens, or on candles, looking at, into the flame, and they transcend that way. But this method was to transcend through sound, so you're given a, a *mantra*, a *mantra* brings all your body to rest, it calms everything down and it, it brings, sort of harmony and err, union to all of your senses, and this way your thoughts become finer and finer and finer until you can arrive at a point which is "transcendental", which means "beyond", it's

beyond the senses, beyond intellect.'

Interviewer - 'And that's George Harrison, the Beatle, and his attitude towards meditation.'
'And I asked George Harrison how much the change has been due, in his case, to meditation.'

George - 'People always say I'm "the Beatle who changed the most", but really that's what I see life is about. The point is, unless you're god conscious then you have to change, because, because it's a waste of time everybody is so limited and so really useless when you come to think of, about the limitation on yourself, and the whole thing is to change and try and make everything better and better, and that's what the physical world is about, it's change. But the change that happens through meditation, I mean it's, it's a gradual sort of thing, but the more you realise, with anything, with just growing old, the more you realise it helps you in some way, with meditation you're able to understand that there is this unity lying beneath everything, there's something there within every atom that holds it all together, and that in actual fact it really is one. But on an intellectual level to say, it is "We are one", then again, you missed the point, it's an experience, you have to really have that perception, that it's one. Maharishi said, "For a forest to be green, each tree must be green." So, if you stand back and criticise the rest of the people, it's again, Christ said, "Put your own house in order". Automatically, if I'm to criticise somebody else I suddenly come back to myself and realise until I'm straight, then I'm in no position to be able to criticise others. So it.. it helps, its, its, it also helps in as much as you can, anytime of the day, any situation you're in, you can get control of yourself just by sitting quietly, and by turning off from the external err, problems we have, noise, and all this society, you can go inside yourselves, where it's always calm and peaceful, it's like being on this level of consciousness, it's like the ocean, it is always changing, and the bottom of the ocean is always calm and still. And if you're not anchored to the bottom of the ocean you're at the mercy of whatever change goes on. Now this process of meditation, or your different types of *yoga*, is all just a way to anchor yourself securely to that pure state of consciousness, to that state of being, so you can still act out your life on the surface but you remain anchored securely.'[239]

❀ ❀ ❀

Without warning, Paul announces he has produced a solo album, entitled simply *'McCartney'*, to be released on Friday, 17th April 1970, and the media are sent advanced promotional material, which takes the form of a questionnaire that Paul has formulated, giving both answers and questions. The questionnaire contains some none-too-subtle references to the way things stand with The Beatles:-

Q: Is your break with the Beatles temporary or permanent, due to personal differences or musical ones?
A: Personal differences, business differences, musical differences, but most of all because I have a better time with my family. Temporary or permanent? I don't really know.

Q: Do you foresee a time when Lennon-McCartney becomes an active songwriting partnership again?
A: No.

❀ ❀ ❀

Daily Mirror Friday, April 10th 1970.

'PAUL IS QUITTING THE BEATLES'

The New York Times Saturday, April 11th 1970.

'McCartney Breaks Off With Beatles'

Chapter Thirty-Two
The Future Is Ours To See

On Friday, 1ˢᵗ May 1970, George is interviewed by Howard Smith for WABC-FM radio in New York City. George chats about his plans for a solo album, and seems very optimistic about the future.

George - 'Yeah, it's alright. All things pass... away... as they say.'

Howard Smith - 'I somewhat detected some kind of animosity between Yoko and Linda. Is that part of what it's about?'

George - 'Ahh, I don't know. I don't think about it, you know. I refuse to be a part of any hassles like that. You know, Hare Krishna, Hare Krishna. Krishna, Krishna, Hare, Hare. And it'll all be okay, you know. Just give 'em time because they do really love each other, you know. I mean, we all do. We've been so close and through so much together that it really... to talk about it like this, you know, we'll never get any nearer to it. But the main thing is, like in anybody's life, they have slight problems. And it's just that our problems are always blown up, and uhh, you know, shown to everybody. But it's not really... it's not a problem. It's only a problem if you think about it.'

Howard Smith - 'So you don't think there's any great anger between Paul and John?'

George - 'No, I think there may be what you'd term a little bitchiness. But, you know, that's all it is. It's just being bitchy to each other, you know. Childish. Childish.'

Howard Smith - 'Hmmm.'

George - 'Well, I get on well with Ringo and John, and I try my best to get on well with Paul. And uhh, there's nothing much more we can... it's just a matter of time, you know, just for everybody to work out their own problems and once they've done that I'm sure we'll get back 'round the cycle again. But if not, you know, it's still alright. Whatever happens, you know, it's gonna be okay. In fact, it's never looked better from my point of view. It's really -- It's very good now -- in very good shape, the companies are in great shape. Apple Films, Apple Records. My song company is in good shape because I've been more productive over the last year or so. It's really good we got back a lot of money that a lot of people had that was ours; a lot of percents that different people had.'[240]

❀ ❀ ❀

After reading a book by psychotherapist Arthur Janov, John Lennon involves himself in Primal Therapy, a therapeutic process based on Janov's view that repressed pain can be brought to the conscious awareness and then resolved through re-experience; and by doing so, one can fully express the resulting pain (during therapy) through spontaneous and unrestrained crying, screaming, hysteria and so forth.

Arthur Janov - 'We had opened him up, and we didn't have time to put him back together again. I told him that he had to finish it, but... I forget what happened then... he moved to New York, so it wasn't possible.'[227]

❀ ❀ ❀

John Lennon agrees to be interviewed by Jann Wenner for *Rolling Stone* magazine, and on Tuesday, 8ᵗʰ December 1970, John faces questions on a wide range of topics, about The Beatles, Yoko Ono, Primal Therapy, God, LSD, and Maharishi.

Jann Wenner - 'When did somebody first come up to you about this thing about John Lennon as God?'

John - 'About what to do and all of that? Like "you tell us Guru"? Probably after acid. Maybe after Rubber Soul. I can't remember it exactly happening. We just took that position. I mean, we started putting out messages. Like "The Word Is Love" and things like that. I write messages, you know. See, when you start putting out messages, people start asking you "what's the message?"'[5]

Jann Wenner - 'How would you characterize George's, Paul's and Ringo's reaction to Yoko?'

John - 'It's the same. You can quote Paul, it's probably in the papers, he said it many times, at first he hated Yoko and then he got to like her. ... and George, shit, insulted her right to her face in the Apple office at the beginning, just being "straight-forward," you know that game of "I'm going to be up front," because this is what we've heard and Dylan and a few people said she'd got a lousy name in New York, and you give off bad vibes. That's what George said to her! And we both sat through it. I didn't hit him, I don't know why.'

'Ringo was all right, so was Maureen, but the other two really gave it to us. I'll never forgive them, I don't care what fuckin' shit about Hare Krishna and God and Paul with his "Well, I've changed me mind." I can't forgive 'em for that, really. Although I can't help still loving them either.'[5]

And John talks about his LSD trips.

John - 'I had many. Jesus Christ. I stopped taking it 'cause of that. I mean I just couldn't stand it. I dropped it for I don't know how long. Then I started taking it just before I met Yoko. I got a message on acid that you should destroy your ego, and I did. I was reading that stupid book of Leary's and all that shit. We were going through a whole game that everybody went through. And I destroyed meself. I was slowly putting meself together after Maharishi, bit by bit, over a two-year period. And then I destroyed me ego and I didn't believe I could do anything. I let Paul do what he wanted and say, them all just do what they wanted. And I just was nothing, I was shit. And then Derek [Taylor] tripped me out at his house after he'd got back from LA. He said, "You're alright." And he pointed out which songs I'd written, and said, "You wrote this, and you said this, and you are intelligent, don't be frightened." The next week I went down with Yoko and we tripped out again, and she freed me completely, to realise that I was me and it's alright. And that was it. I started fighting again and being a loud-mouth again and saying, "Well, I can do this," and "Fuck you, and this is what I want," and "Don't put me down. I did this."'

Jann Wenner - 'Did you have many bad trips?'

John - 'I had many. Jesus Christ, I stopped taking it because of that. I just couldn't stand it.'[5]

And Primal Therapy?

John - 'I still think that Janov's therapy is great, you know, but I don't want to make it into a big Maharishi thing. You were right to tell me to forget the advert, and that is why I don't even want to talk about it too much, if people know what I've been through there, and if they want to find out, they can find out, otherwise it turns into *that* again.'[5]

Jann Wenner - '*"Sexy Sadie"* you wrote about the Maharishi?'

John - 'That's about the Maharishi, yes. I copped out and I wouldn't write "Maharishi, what have you done? You made a fool of everyone." But now it can be told, Fab Listeners.'[5]

> **'Sexy Sadie what have you done**
> **You made a fool of everyone'**
> - Excerpt from lyrics of *'Sexy Sadie'* by John Lennon & Paul McCartney

John - 'Somebody said, you know, "there was a big hullabaloo about him raping Mia Farrow and all, trying to get off with Mia Farrow and a few other women" and things like that. And we went down to him, and we'd stayed up all night discussing was it true or not true, you know. And when George started thinking it might be true, I thought well, it must be true; because if George is doubting it, there must be something in it.'[3]

So, had John really been told that Maharishi had *raped*, or tried to *rape* Mia Farrow? If so, that goes some way to explain why John left the course in India in such a hurry! But, if there were any truth in such a rumour, wouldn't Mia have been screaming it from the rooftops, and wouldn't she have gotten her husband Frank Sinatra and his friends involved?

John - 'So we went to see Maharishi, the whole gang of us the next day, charged down to his hut, his bungalow, his very rich-looking bungalow in the mountains, and as usual, when the dirty work came, I was the spokesman - whenever the dirty work came, I actually had to be leader - wherever the scene was when it came to the nitty gritty I had to do the speaking. And I said "We're leaving." He asked "Why?" and all that shit, and I said, "Well, if you're so cosmic, you'll know why," because he was always intimating, and there were all these right-hand men intimating that he did miracles, you know. And I said "You know why," and he said "I don't know why, you must tell me," and I just kept saying "You ought to know," and he gave me a look like "I'll kill you, you bastard," and he gave me such a look and I knew then, when he looked at me, you know, because I had called his bluff, because I said if you know all, you know. Cosmic Consciousness, that's what we're all here for. I was a bit rough to him.'[5]

Jann Wenner - 'When did you decide you had to come to New York and denounce Maharishi?'
John - 'Denounce him?'
Jann Wenner - 'Well you came to New York and had that Press conference.'
John - 'The Apple thing. That was to announce Apple, that..'
Jann Wenner - 'But also at the same time..'
John - 'I don't remember that.'
Jann Wenner - 'You denounced Maharishi.'
John - 'Well what did I say? I don't know. You know, we all say a lot of things when we don't know what we're talking about. I'm probably doing it now, I don't know what I say, you know. See, everybody takes you up on the words you said, and I'm just a guy that people ask what about things, and I blab off and some of it makes sense and some of it's bullshit and some of it's lies and some of it's.. God knows what I'm saying. I don't know what I said about Maharishi, all I know is we said about Apple, which is worse, you know.'[3]

Okay, so the moral here seems to be that one should be cautious about accepting John's words at face value, as, according to him, they could just be *'bullshit'* or *'lies'*, but how does one know, know for sure?

❀ ❀ ❀

George - 'There were many stories about how Maharishi was not on the level or whatever, but that was just jealousy about Maharishi. We'd need analysts to get into it. I don't know what goes through these people's minds, but this whole piece of bullshit was invented. It's probably even in the history books that Maharishi tried to attack Mia Farrow - but it's bullshit, total bullshit. Just go and ask Mia Farrow.'[1]

Paul - 'John wrote 'Sexy Sadie' about it. Righteous indignation! I remember being quite shocked with that. It's really funny, John's reaction to this sexual thing. I mean, maybe say, "Hey, we thought he was better than that," but it seemed a little prudish to me, to do that. So I was quite glad I'd left the week before. I mean, even if they found him in bed, what is this? Anyway, it ended in disarray and that was the reason given.'[6]

Mick Jagger - 'But there's always stories about *guru's* sexuality 'cos, I think that people from the West always think of *gurus* - originally they did - they think of *gurus* as Catholic priests, but I don't think that was the idea of that. *Gurus* are not like Catholic priests.'[241]

Paul - 'In my mind I was saying: "What's the problem? He's not a god, he's not a priest. There are no rules in his religion that say he's not supposed to make a pass. He's only human, after all, and he's only given us a meditation system."'[1]

❀ ❀ ❀

On Thursday, 31st December 1970, Paul McCartney files a lawsuit against John, George and Ringo attempting dissolution of the Beatles' contractual partnership.
Paul - 'I was depressed. You would be. You were breaking from your lifelong friends. So I took to the bevvies. I took to a wee dram. It was great at first, then suddenly I wasn't having a good time …'[242]

❀ ❀ ❀

As many know, the independence of India in 1946 led to 'partition', and to the formation of West Pakistan to the west, and East Pakistan to the east in Bengal. In early 1971, East Pakistan's attempts to become independent from West Pakistan led to civil war.
The state of East Pakistan became a country in its own right, named Bangladesh, but before it has a chance to recover from the war it is hit by a cyclone, leading to the death of half a million people and the displacement of at least a quarter of a million. Ravi Shankar's family hails from Bengal, so for him the calamity feels particularly personal.

THE BEATLES, DRUGS, MYSTICISM & INDIA

'My friend came to me, with sadness in his eyes
He said he wanted help, before his country dies.'

- Excerpt of lyrics to *'Bangla Desh'* by George Harrison

So George sets about organising a huge benefit concert in New York featuring many big names including Bob Dylan. Two concerts are scheduled for 2-30pm and 8pm on Sunday, 1ˢᵗ August 1971. Ravi Shankar opens both all-star shows explaining the purpose of the concert and then playing a set of Indian music. George performs, as does Ringo, but though John Lennon is warm to the idea he does not attend. The shows are filmed, and the proceeds of the concert and movie, and the 3-record box set, all entitled *'Concert For Bangladesh'*, are intended for use as emergency relief, to be distributed by UNICEF.

❀ ❀ ❀

On Monday, 11th October 1971, a new song by John Lennon is released, entitled *'Imagine'*.

'Imagine no possessions, I wonder if you can
No need for greed or hunger, a brotherhood of man.'

- Excerpt of *'Imagine'* by John Lennon

When writing *'Imagine'*, perhaps John is remembering when he and George appeared on the *David Frost Programme*, and Frost asked them, *'But if you were to choose at this moment between having meditation and all that goes with it, and having all your possessions, you would choose to give up the possessions?'*, and George Harrison answered, *'Yes'* and John Lennon nodded his agreement.

Coincidentally, on Friday, 3ʳᵈ December 1971, George Harrison is re-united with Frost, and appears alongside Ravi Shankar on the *David Frost Show*.
Frost asks George - 'Do you ever play the *sitar* now?'
George - 'Yeah, I've got it at home, and it's more just for my own amusement.'
Frost - 'Can you remember the first exercises you played on your *sitar*?'
George - 'Yes.'
Frost - 'Could you try one now?'
George - 'Right.. first of all I'd have to go through and take these boots off and sit down. I don't know if I should touch this *sitar*, it's so beautiful.'
Frost, to Ravi Shankar - 'Would you mind him borrowing your *sitar* for a while?
Ravi Shankar - (inaudible)
(Audience applause)
George - 'Really? I'll have to take my boots off.'
(Ravi Shankar laughs)
George - 'You'd better keep yourselves amused.'
Frost - 'All right, I'll be the conscient; he's slowing taking off his right boot. His left boot is quickly going to follow.'
Ravi Shankar - 'According to our tradition he has to wash his hands first.'
George - 'Now I need to wash my feet. Maybe, maybe I should play it with talc on.'
Ravi Shankar - 'You can touch it, George.'
(laughter)
George starts to play - 'It's been three years!'³
George proceeds to demonstrate the first exercise he learned, and playing the simple scale he receives rapturous applause from the audience.

❀ ❀ ❀

It has also been several years since John and George slipped away from Maharishi's academy. So, how has Maharishi fared? Has he kept to his stated plan to retire and slip away to a cave in the Himalayas, now spending his days in silent reflection? Well, not quite, he spends much of his time holding courses in the U.S.A. and working on ever-newer ways to spread the practice of Transcendental Meditation.

In August 1972, he confides to his audience something of the difficulties he has met with over the years.

Maharishi - 'I'll tell you my experience.

I was thinking, "Why responsible people in society are not coming to the movement?" in the beginning days of the movement, and this remained the situation for about four, five years. I was going around the world, many times, twice a year, but responsible people, higher level of society were not responding. And the reason - I came to know after about seven or eight years of the movement, about three years ago - that the people were not coming to my lectures, they were not inspired by me, *because I was an Indian.* And what India can offer? We can't take care of our own children, and all that, all that. What Indian culture, or Indian religion, or what Indian nation can offer?

But when the movement kept going, year after year, year after year, and they were hearing from some paper, from some television, from some friends of theirs that "It's good, it's good, it's good, it's good". It's only about three years back that some responsible people started to come in, and come in, and come in, and come in, and come in. And on this explosion of world publicity, when The Beatles came here and there, and the serious minded people withdrew from this, they said "No". Because that was the time when the responsible society, responsible people in society had been responding to the movement, feeling the effects around and they thought; "Seems to be something genuine, something nice, something". But then The Beatle explosion was a setback for the movement; serious-minded people just come to "*that*" [much less interest]

It was talked about more in the papers, it brought publicity to the movement, but it discouraged the serious minded people.'[3]

Nowadays, Maharishi is glad that he is attracting *'more serious people'*, especially scientists, who are happy to assist him present Transcendental Meditation in scientific terms.

Maharishi - '... when I started the movement, I couldn't bear to come out in terms of *"yoga"* or "Vedanta", because the whole Vedanta faith is so misinterpreted, Veda, *yoga,* so misinterpreted. *Yoga* means somewhere standing on the head, or somewhere sleeping on the thorns, (audience laughter) or nails, or walking on water, or walking on fire, some such ridiculous things in the name of *yoga*...'[3]

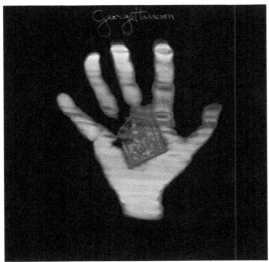

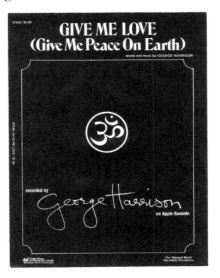

'Living in the Material World' **LP cover**

For his part, George Harrison is still extolling his audience to embrace a more spiritual vision of life, and this is reflected in the choice of title for his new LP, which is entitled *'Living in the Material World',* and a new single, called *'Give Me Love, (Give Me Peace on Earth)'.*

'Trying to touch and reach you with heart and soul
OM M M M M M M M M M M M M M M M M My Lord . . .'

- Excerpt from *'Give Me Love (Give Me Peace on Earth'* by George Harrison

Nowadays, George and Pattie live at Friar Park, a palatial mansion in Henley-on-Thames, Oxfordshire. The 120-room house, which stands in 62 acres of grounds, was built in 1889 as the residence of Sir Frank Crisp, a

lawyer with a passion for microscopy.
Prior to George purchasing Friar Park, it been in the care of Roman Catholic nuns.

Pattie is becoming increasingly concerned that her marriage to George has become challenged and compromised by their lifestyle.
In July 1974 George and Pattie's marriage has reached breaking point.
Pattie - 'Friar Park was a madhouse. Our lives were fuelled by alcohol and cocaine, and so it was with everyone who came into our sphere. We were all as drunk, stoned and single-minded as each other. Nobody seemed to have appointments, deadlines or anything pressing in their lives, no structure and no responsibilities.
Cocaine is a seductive drug because it makes you feel euphoric and good about yourself. It takes away your inhibitions and makes even the shyest, most insecure person feel confident.
And we had so much energy - everyone would talk nonsense for twice as long and drink twice as much because the cocaine made us feel sober. George used cocaine excessively and I think it changed him.
… I think it froze George's emotions and hardened his heart.'[243]

❀ ❀ ❀

Although George is no longer so keen on playing Indian music, he is happy to assist his friend Ravi Shankar. George produces *'Ravi Shankar, Family & Friends'*, an imaginative mix of tunes that Ravi has written, all very far removed from the classical music his audience is accustomed to hear him playing. One of the songs, *'I am Missing You'*, is selected as a single. The song is an ode to Krishna on which George Harrison plays acoustic guitars and autoharp.
Ravi Shankar - 'I don't know how I did it, but one day I wrote an English song without thinking ... George heard it and liked it so much he wanted to do a version of his own.'[244]
In fact George also assists by producing *'Ravi Shankar's Music Festival of India'*, a project in which Ravi and a host of Indian musicians play more traditional material.

When George tours in the U.S.A. in late 1974, to promote his *'Dark Horse'* album, he is joined by Ravi Shankar and his ensemble.
But on this *'Dark Horse'* tour trouble looms when George finds his voice failing him.

'He had a nasty case of laryngitis, and snorting mountains of cocaine didn't exactly make his voice any sweeter.'

- Rolling Stone [245]

In 1976 George flies over to India to attend the wedding of Ravi Shankar's niece, and is accompanied on the trip by his girlfriend, Olivia Arias, whom he met in 1974. Interestingly, Olivia is said to be a 'premie', a follower of the 'boy guru' Maharaj ji, founder of the Divine Light Mission.
On the flight over to India George gets into conversation with Gilbert Scott Markle, a record producer from the States, and presents him with a copy of *'Autobiography of a Yogi'*, one of many he carries in a briefcase.
Whilst in Bombay George asks Gilbert whether he has seen any holymen.

George - 'Did you see any today?'

Gilbert Scott Markle - 'No. I didn't see any.'

George - 'Me either.'

'Well, we're going up to Benares. It's either now or twenty years from now, and I'm not sure if I'm going to be around twenty years from now. We're targets for assassination, you know.'

Olivia Arias - 'Oh, George, stop that. Just stop that!'

George - 'Well, we're still going to Benares. You ought to come, Gil. Living gods guaranteed to line the road, on either side. Take your pick. Some of them live in caves and haven't eaten any solid food in years. You'll see them there, for sure.'

Gilbert Scott Markle - 'I don't know. I've got some things to attend to back home. Business things. I've got this whole other business scene happening. I think I'm screwing up enough already, without going to Benares with George Harrison for the *Kumbla Mela*!'

They travel together by taxi to their hotel in downtown Bombay.

Gilbert Scott Markle - 'George applied a match stick to a large, paper-wrapped mixture of London cigarette tobacco and crumpled black hashish. He smoked it alone for several minutes. Olivia would have none of it, when offered. Instead, it was passed to me. I knew joints like this. This was naughty sixties-London. "Can you, will you, smoke this thing? Do so and we will talk about the rest... about peace in our time... about a world which none of us understands, about..."'[246]

⊛ ⊛ ⊛

In May 1976, George Harrison and Ravi Shankar make a visit to see Sai Baba, the famous 'god-man'.

⊛ ⊛ ⊛

Another associate of George's is Emil Richards, a percussionist, who sometimes works with George (he played on Ravi Shankar's *I am Missing You*).

Like The Beatles, Emil has visited Rishikesh and spent time at Maharishi's academy.

Emil Richards - 'I'm still a meditator and George was all the way through. Maharishi approached transcendental meditation in a very scientific, practical way. It didn't really have anything to do with religion, so to speak. That's what made it very easy to talk about - and to live, actually.'[247]

⊛ ⊛ ⊛

Barely two and a half years after getting married to John Lennon, Yoko Ono comes to the conclusion that things are not right between them.

May Pang (Yoko's personal assistant) **-** 'One morning, Yoko came to my office in their apartment at the Dakota building, New York, and told me that she and John were not "getting along", which wasn't exactly surprising news to those of us who worked alongside them.

Yoko said John would start seeing someone new and she wanted it to be "someone who would treat John well".'

'Yoko continued: "You don't have a boyfriend." …. "I think you should go out with him."'

Surprisingly, all parties were eventually in agreement, and John takes a 'long weekend', his euphemism for a very long period of excess and partying.

May Pang - 'John and I were together "officially" for 18 months, but our relationship actually spanned ten years - from December 1970 to December 1980.'[248]

When John and Yoko eventually become reconciled, they have a child together, Sean, whom John dotes on and rears almost single-handedly, relishing his new role of househusband. During this period of reclusiveness, John writes, with the intention of compiling a short autobiography. Whilst working on his book, it becomes obvious that drugs, mysticism and India still remain compelling topics. Here is a sample of his outpourings:-

John - 'From pilgrimages to India with magic Alex Mardas, to what turned out to be a phony miracle worker called Babaji (?) [Sai Baba], who performed conjuring tricks such as pulling cheap watches with his picture on them "out of nowhere" to a packed house of mainly middle-aged American women (whilst outside the camp, thousands of crippled Indians were selling the same cheap stuff to make a living), we found ourselves living outside of San Francisco in San Mateo in the home of an alcoholic Kung Fu master and acupuncturist and his family. It was he who was responsible for helping us survive methadone withdrawal, which had almost killed Yoko.'

'I was talking… and as usual I found myself on the defensive about "mystics." I didn't get too frantic for a change. Anyway, I found myself saying something like the following - that many, if not all, great men and women were "mystics" in a sense: Einstein, who at the end of his life remarked that if he had to do it over, he would have spent more time on the spiritual; Pythagoras and Newton were mystics. But the main point I was getting at was the fact that in order to receive the "wholly spirit," i.e., creative inspiration (whether you are labelled an artist, scientist, mystic, psychic, etc.), the main "problem" was emptying the mind. You can't paint a picture on dirty paper; you need a clean sheet.'[236]

He makes short notes.
John - 'Cut to Maharishi's health farm on the tip of the Himalayas.'
'O.K., he's a lot balder now than when I knew him. How come God picks on these holimen? Ulcers, etc. "He's taking on someone else's karma." I bet that's what all the little sheep are bleating. He's got a nice smile, though. This is turning into *The Autobiography of a Yogurt*, but isn't everything? I ask myself. He made us live in separate huts from our wives . . . Can't say it was too much of a strain.'[236]

John is host to the occasional visitor.
George - 'I was in New York, at his house, at the… what's it called? The Dakotas.
'Yes, he was nice, sort of running round the house making dinner, and was actually playing a lot of Indian music, which surprised me cos he always used to like be a bit, you know when I was always playing it, and he had just hundreds of cassettes of all kinds of stuff.'
'He grew into it.'[249]

✿ ✿ ✿

On Wednesday, 16th January 1980, Paul McCartney is arrested at Tokyo's Narita International Airport for trying to take a half-pound of marijuana into Japan.
Paul - '… When I was in jail in Japan it [meditation] came in very handy; I meditated a lot there and it was very good. I wasn't allowed to write and I didn't want to just sit there and do nothing. My brain was racing, as you can imagine, so meditation was great. I found it very useful and still do. I find it soothing and I can imagine that the more you were to get into it, the more interesting it would get.'
The whole meditation experience was very good and I still use the mantra. I don't really practise it massively but it's always in the back of my mind if I ever want to. '
'But I must admit, I have spoken it, to Linda. At one point we decided that to reaffirm our faith in each other I would even tell her that, but that's the only time I've spoken it, once, to Linda. I know, I know, I've completely blown it, man! But I don't think you're really not allowed to. It's not like a chant, I think it's just generally a pretty good idea if you don't voice it, and I go along with that.'[6]

✿ ✿ ✿

John Lennon visits Japan from time to time, and on one such occasion, whilst in the company of Yoko, John picks up a magazine which happens to have a photo of someone who bears a resemblance to himself.
John - 'That guy is me in my past life.'
Yoko - 'Don't wish for that. Because he was assassinated.'[285]
The man in the photograph is Yasuda Zenjirō, a financier, who in 1921 was approached by a young man collecting funds for a workers' hostel, and when the extraordinarily wealthy man refused to make a donation, the young man killed him. Yasuda also happens to be Yoko Ono's maternal great-grandfather.

Apparently, John, Yoko and Sean meditate together daily, and it is said that whilst living in New York John makes a point of visiting his local meditation centre.
Robert Jayan Petzing, a long term meditator - 'In 1980 I was travelling through NYC [New York City] on my way back to Livingston Manor [a former hotel converted for use by Maharishi's organisations], and stopped by the Manhattan TM Center to do afternoon program. As I entered I felt a strong sense of electricity in the air. I asked someone what was going on, and she said that John Lennon had just left a few minutes earlier. She then explained that he had been coming in every month (without fail) to have his meditation checked....'[38]
Jerry Jarvis - 'I think I would have heard about that, but I didn't hear anything.'[38]
So perhaps the rumour that suggests that John spoke with Maharishi by telephone from the centre, is also

suspect?

❀ ❀ ❀

In 1980, John Lennon records a song entitled *'India, India'*, a retrospective composition about his visit to India in 1968, in which he describes his search for the answer to life's *'ancient mysteries'* whilst *'somewhere in my mind'* is the *'the girl I left behind'*.

'India, India, listen to my plea
I sit here at your feet so patiently'

- Excerpt from lyrics of *'India, India'* by John Lennon

John Lennon and Yoko are making a record together, and when it is finished, as part of its promotion, they agree to embark on a series of interviews, one of which is for *Playboy Magazine*. Over a period of three weeks, reporter David Sheff is given fairly unlimited access to John and Yoko, and in that time gets to cover a lot of topics.

So.. John and Yoko were apart awhile, and then they got back together again..?

John - 'It's like what they say about *karma*, you know? "You have to come back and go through that thing again, if you don't get it right this lifetime". Well, those moves that are cosmically talked about - accept it or not accept it - but, you know, the ones they all talk about, they're always referring to.. they apply down to the minutest detail of life too. It's like *Instant Karma*; it was my way of saying "It's right!" You know, it happens about a cup of coffee or anything. It's not just some big cosmic thing. It's that as well, but it's also about small things like your life here, and your relationship with the person you want to live with and be with. There are laws governing that relationship too and you can give up halfway up the hill and say, "I don't want to climb this mountain, cos it's tough", or "I'm going back to the bottom and start again", and well, we were lucky enough to get, go through that, and come back and pick up where we left off.. although it took a, took us some energy to blend in again, to get in the same sync again.'[3]

And, what about the future?

John - 'That seems to be the *karmic* trick, or *'Cosmic Joke No.9'*, that we can't just sit back and we'll have our.. because we know the universe is breathing in and out, so we're going to get Hitler then Christ, then Hitler then Christ, to use those two again. You know, cos they're just convenient, but it's not a matter of sitting back and waiting for Christ or, or accepting Hitler. If.. we have to do something, but whatever's gonna happen, gonna happen anyway as well. Both, at the same time.'

Yoko - 'Well, if whatever is gonna happen, is gonna happen, makes, you know, all of us...'

John - 'Yeah, right, *"Que sera, sera"*, but we're responsible.'

Yoko - 'We are. Exactly.'

John - '*"The future is ours to see"*. See, that's the only line I'd change in that beautiful song, If **we** can't see it, ain't nobody gonna see it for us!'[3]

Reporter David Sheff is given the freedom to ask a very wide range of questions.

Is John still taking drugs?

John - 'A little mushroom or peyote is not beyond my scope, you know, maybe twice a year or something. But acid is a chemical. People are taking it, though, even though you don't hear about it anymore. But people are still visiting the cosmos. It's just that nobody talks about it; you get sent to prison...

I've never met anybody who's had a flashback. I've never had a flashback in my life and I took millions of trips in the Sixties, and I've never met anybody who had any problem. I've had bad trips and other people have had bad trips, but I've had a bad trip in real life. I've had a bad trip on a joint. I can get paranoid just sitting in a restaurant. I don't have to take anything.

Acid is only real life in Cinemascope. Whatever experience you had is what you would have had anyway. I'm not promoting, all you committees out there, and I don't use it because it's chemical, but all the garbage about what it did to people is garbage.'[15]

What about Arthur Janov and Primal Therapy?

Yoko - 'I think Janov was a daddy for John. I think he has this father complex and he's always searching for a daddy.'

John - 'Had, dear. I had a father complex.'

David Sheff - 'Would you explain?'

Yoko - 'I had a daddy, a real daddy, sort of a big and strong father like a Billy Graham, but growing up, I saw his weak side. I saw the hypocrisy. So whenever I see something that is supposed to be so big and wonderful, a *guru* or primal scream, I'm very cynical.'

John - 'She fought with Janov all the time. He couldn't deal with it.'

Yoko - 'I'm not searching for the big daddy. I look for something else in men.. something that is tender and weak and I feel like I want to help.'

John - 'And I was the lucky cripple she chose!'

Yoko - 'I have this mother instinct, or whatever. But I was not hung up on finding a father, because I had one who disillusioned me. John never had a chance to get disillusioned about his father, since his father wasn't around, so he never thought of him as that big man.'

David Sheff - 'Do you agree with that assessment, John?'

John - 'A lot of us are looking for fathers. Mine was physically not there. Most people's are not there mentally and physically, like always at the office or busy with other things. So all these leaders, parking meters, are all substitute fathers, whether they be religious or political.. All this bit about electing a President. We pick our own daddy out of a dog pound of daddies. This is the daddy that looks like the daddy in the commercials. He's got the nice gray hair and the right teeth and the parting's on the right side. OK? This is the daddy we choose. The dog pound of daddies, which is the political arena, gives us a President, then we put him on a platform and start punishing him and screaming at him because Daddy can't do miracles. Daddy doesn't heal us.'

David Sheff - 'So Janov was a daddy for you. Who else?'

Yoko speaks for John.

Yoko - 'Before, there was Maharishi.'[3]

David Sheff - 'How do you feel about all the negative press that's been directed through the years at Yoko, your 'dragon lady,' as you put it?'

John - 'We are both sensitive people and we were hurt a lot by it. I mean, we couldn't understand it.'

David Sheff - 'But what about the charge that John Lennon is under Yoko's spell, under her control?'

John - 'Well, that's rubbish, you know. Nobody controls me.'

David Sheff - 'Still, many people believe it.'

John - 'Listen, if somebody's gonna impress me, whether it be a Maharishi or a Yoko Ono, there comes a point when the emperor has no clothes. There comes a point when I will see. So for all you folks out there who think that I'm having the wool pulled over my eyes, well, that's an insult to me.'

Yoko - 'Why should I bother to control anybody?'

John - 'She doesn't need me.'

Yoko - 'I have my own life, you know.'

John - 'She doesn't need a Beatle. Who needs a Beatle?'

Yoko - 'Do people think I'm that much of a con? John lasted two months with the Maharishi. Two months. I must be the biggest con in the world, because I've been with him 13 years.'[250]

And, John is emphatic that Yoko is his teacher.

John - 'It is a teacher pupil relationship, that's what people don't understand. She's the teacher and I'm the pupil. I'm the famous one, I'm the one that's supposed to know everything, but she's my teacher, she's taught me everything I fucking know. The lessons are damn hard and I can't take it sometimes, because those lessons are hard, and that's why I freaked out. When we were separate it was me who was making an asshole of meself, in the clubs, in the newspapers, it wasn't her. Her life was ordered and she missed me as a human being, and she loved me, but her life was ordered. I went back to her life, it wasn't the other way round.'[3]

So with hindsight, what does he make of Maharishi now?

John - 'Maharishi was a father figure, Elvis Presley might have been a father figure. I don't know. Robert Mitchum. Any male image is a father figure. There's nothing wrong with it until you give them the right to give you sort of a recipe for your life. What happens is somebody comes along with a good piece of truth. Instead of the truth's being looked at, the person who brought it is looked at. It's like when bad news comes, they shoot the

messenger. When the good news comes, they worship the messenger and they don't listen to the message. Have you ever met a Christian who behaves like Christian? Or in the other religions, have you met a person of the faith who behaves like the ideal? Well, nobody's perfect, right? Nobody's perfect, et cetera, et cetera, except for all these people who are *named* as being perfect.'
'Whether it be Christianity, Mohammedanism, Buddhism, Confucianism, Marxism, Maoism, everything. They're all about the person and not what the person said.'[15]

Yoko - 'You see, people like to personalise things. You know, people even personalize God. You know, when you say "God" most people think about this old man and his white beard or something, they don't think God as an action or anything.'
John - 'They don't know it's an old woman with a beard do they?' (chuckles)
'Of the Christians, I think that the Gnostics, meaning 'self-knowledge', were the true essence of Christianity, but they were stamped out, you know, or chased to the hills, and if you look at the Gnostic tradition, what little you can get of it, it's similar to the Zen Buddhists, which is not quite Buddhism, or any of the essences of each religion, that I think there's a group, the Sufis in the Muslims. And there's one, there's always one group that says, "Self, self, self!" you know, "here's a set of rules in which to enlighten the self with," and it *just so happens* to have come by this mailman, you know. And so the thing is there, you read, you read Christ's words and you read Buddha's words, you read any of the great words, Milarepa [a Tibetan *yogi*, 1052-1135] or some artist or poet. It's all there. But, you know, we don't need the imagery and the "Thou must worship like me or die."'
David Sheff - 'Right, that is a distressing side of it.'
John - 'Yeah, then when people got the image I was anti-Christ or anti-religion, I'm not at all, I'm a most religious fellow.'[3]

So, it seems that John remains consistent in his view of Transcendental Meditation, that it would have been better not to examine Maharishi as a person and just enjoy the benefits of meditation.
So, what about The Beatles, should we just enjoy the music and the films, and leave it at that?
John - 'The Beatles are not Jesus are not Janov are not Erhard. Maybe they had a nice way of swimming, but the swimming is the point. *[Exitedly]* The records are the point. Not the Beatles as individuals!'
Yoko - 'I don't think so. I think the Beatles -'
John - 'Oh Jesus! [Laughing, he screams and jumps up.] I thought I finally cleared it all up. Oh, shit!'[15]
Though John values the practices he has learned, both he and Yoko still find fault with the messengers.
John -'You see, they always show themselves. When we get around them, because we're famous, the daddies blow their cool because they can't contain their eagerness for power and glory. It showed itself in Maharishi; it showed itself in Janov, who suddenly came on like a silver-haired Jeff Chandler, impressed with our celebrity.'
Yoko - 'One day he brought cameras into the room. We walked out.'[15]
John - 'Now looking back, at first I was bitter about Maharishi being human, and a little bitter about Janov being human. Well, I'm not bitter about them being human, they're human and I'm only thinking what a dummy I am, you know. Although I meditate, and I cry, so I cannot deny it.'[3]

Yoko - 'Anyway, when I went to *est*, I saw Werner Erhardt - the same thing. He's a nice showman and he's got a nice gig there. I felt the same thing when we went to Sai Baba in India. In India, you have to be a guru instead of a pop star… Guru is the pop star of India and pop star is the guru here.'
John - 'But, as I was saying earlier, this doesn't mean there isn't validity in the message. The swimming may be fine, right? But forget about the teacher. If the Beatles had a message, it was that.'[15]

John is frustrated that so much attention is given to his past.
John - 'Time will tell where the real magic lies, I'm only 40 now when this tape comes out. Paul's 38. Elton John, Bob Dylan, we're all still young people relatively, and the game isn't over yet. Everyone's talking in terms of the last record or the last Beatle concert, the last thing. There's another - God, Goddess, willing - 40 years of productivity.'[3]
Nevertheless, John is all too aware of the evanescence of life and how, for no apparent reason, some people are taken earlier than others.
John - 'Gandhi and Martin Luther King are great examples of fa..'

Yoko - 'Yeah!'

John - '.. fantastic non-violents who died violently. I can't ever work that out. You know, 1'm.. we're pacifists but I'm not sure, it's always there, but what does it mean when you're such a pacifist that you, you get shot? I can never understand that.'[251]

Every day for three weeks, David Sheff asks his questions, and the resultant interview is published in the *The Playboy* magazine, the January 1981 issue, available on Saturday, 6th December 1980.

Monday, 8th December 1980 - BBC News

Former Beatle John Lennon has been shot dead by an unknown gunman who opened fire outside the musician's New York apartment.

Richie Havens, the singer-songwriter guitarist - 'We saw each other many times in his final months. I believe he had a strong premonition that something was going to happen to him. I know I did.'[252]

It is reported that Mark Chapman, John Lennon's assassin, had long planned the shooting. It is said that Chapman was very angry with John Lennon for making the claim about The Beatles being more famous than Jesus, regarding this as blasphemy. Allegedly, he was also angry at John for composing the idealistic lyrics to *'Imagine',* about peace, love and no possessions, whilst all the while living the life of a multi-millionaire; and angry at John for singing about how he didn't believe in Jesus, God or The Beatles.

The surviving former Beatles are shocked at John's death, and particularly at the way it occurred.

Paul - 'It's terrible news. We're all very shocked.'[3]

Ringo - 'I'll always miss him, you know.'[3]

George - 'When John died it was obviously an enormous shock, like, I couldn't believe it really, because, erm.. as we all know he was such a nice [laughs] person. Really! I mean he was stubborn, and there were certain things about him that maybe people would have wanted to change in him, but, you know, he was such a great person that it seemed ridiculous, you know. I mean in some ways it's understandable if someone goes to try and assassinate Adolf Hitler or something, but John Lennon had just given out all that love and great songs. Seemed ridiculous.'[253]

Chapter Thirty Three
Radiate Bliss Consciousness

In January 1985, George agrees to be interviewed on a TV chat show, called *'The Today Show'*.

Rona Elliot - 'Your commitment to spiritual values has been a constant part of your life, in the form that we experienced it in the sixties: devotees and gurus. Is that still the form that it takes in your life?'

George - 'I think the sixties, it was sort of necessary and important what happened, and I think like with anything, if you want to learn tennis, you go to somebody who can instruct you in tennis. If you want to learn how to be a "yogi", or to meditate, or whatever, then you need an instructor or somebody who knows that. And unfortunately the word "guru" became a bit of a joke because, again with the way the Press saw them as silly old fellows, you know like Maharishi with his long hair, and things like that, and also because there were a lot of "bhogis" [bhogi = a pleasure seeker]. You know as there are "yogis" there's also "bhogis", and you know, not mentioning names, there's been quite an influx of them over the years into America. And I still think it's like somebody once said, "you have to be like the wise ant, that crawls through the grains of sand and find the grains of sugar". And so each person has to find for himself a way for inner realization, I mean with the goal, I still believe that the only reason we are on this planet is like going to school again. Each soul is potentially divine and the goal is to manifest that divinity. Everything else is secondary.'[3]

'Back then long time ago when grass was green
Woke up in a daze'

- Excerpt of lyrics of *'When We Was Fab'* by George Harrison

1988 sees the release of George Harrison's *'When We Was Fab'*, a song which, through a pastiche of familiar sounds, summons and evokes nostalgic memories of The Beatles heyday. George and Ringo join Michael Aspel on his television show *'Aspel & Company'*, broadcast in England on Saturday, 5th March 1988.

Aspel, to Ringo - 'What did you make of the Indian episode?'

Ringo - 'Well the Indian episode was real interesting. I got two phone calls, one from George one from John "We're going to Wales" - see it's always been to Wales - to meet the Maharishi so I just got on the train because these guys wouldn't lie to me. So we met him in Wales and then we all decided to go to this *ashram* in India. I think that… I still thank Maharishi, you know, for what he said, but in the end I thought he was telling us stories, but that's my problem.'

Aspel - 'In the end, but how long did you actually stick that course?'

Ringo - 'Ten days.' (laughter)

George 'He ran out of beans. (laughter) He came all the way up the Himalayas with a big.. cans of beans.'

Ringo - 'Suitcase of beans and a suitcase of clothes.'

George - 'And didn't like flies and spiders.'

Ringo - 'No, can't stand them. But the interesting part was, you see, that I can only eat bland food because I was very sick as a child, and err, so I'd have me beans, and then I was getting fed up with that. and so they.., I said '"Got any eggs?" (laughter) I got eggs in the morning, you know. And so I caught these guys burying the shells in the ground, as if God wouldn't notice. (laughter) I decided to leave after that. (laughter) Oh no, cos he doesn't see those.'[3]

Michael Aspel asks about their reactions to John Lennon death.

Ringo - 'I was stunned on the day, and I'm still..'

George - 'Shocked and stunned.'

Ringo and George both explain the circumstances of how they each heard of John's assassination, then George offers his personal reflections.

George - 'But I feel, not so bad about it, inasmuch as, you know I had this, you know, unlike Ringo, when I went to Rishikesh in India I went into meditation and had some good experiences, and I got to..'

Ringo - 'I had some good experiences too..'

George - 'I know you did but you forgot to tell them about…' (laughter)

Ringo - 'Well yeah, they only asked about the eggs.' (laughter)

George - 'So, I believe what it says in the Scriptures and in the *Bhagavad Gita* it says, "There was never a time when you didn't exist, and there'll never be a time when you cease to exist". The only thing that changes is our bodily condition. Soul comes in the body and we go from birth to death. And it's death, how I look at it is like taking your suit off. You know, the soul is in these three bodies, and one body falls off. And err, I can feel him around here, and err, he's..'

Aspel, to Ringo - 'And do you feel that?

Ringo - 'Oh yeah!'

Aspel - 'You've.. you've seen him?'

Ringo - 'Oh Yeah.. I felt one time, very strong that I was in a hotel room in LA, and I was real down and miserable with everything that was going down, and he was in the corner saying "What are you doin'?", "Being miserable." He said "Come on, get it together!" So I believe like George on that respect - we just did the joking about the eggs - that we do continue, and I do believe in God.'

Aspel - 'What mental state was John in, at that time?'

George - 'Well, I'd never seen him for a couple of years before that.'

George explains that all the Beatles had a lot of experiences, including their use of LSD back in the 1960's, and he believes those experiences benefited them by giving insights into themselves.

George - 'I know John was, erm, you know, he knew who he was, that he was a soul that happened to be in this body for this period of time. And, you know, I don't think err.. It's just the method by which you die, you know, I think it's nicer if you can consciously leave your body at death as opposed to just some lunatic shooting you on the street or having a plane crash or something like that. I think it's unfortunate the way he went out, but it doesn't really matter, he's okay and life flows on within you and without you.'

Ringo, looking up - 'How you doin' Johnny?'[3]

❀ ❀ ❀

Actually, Ringo is in desperate need of help; for, since The Beatles' breakup, he has felt 'absolutely lost', which has resulted in him overindulging.

Ringo - 'I was drunk. Some of those years are absolutely gone.'

'I was mad. For 20 years. I had breaks in between of not being.'

'It got progressively worse, and the blackouts got worse, and I didn't know where I'd been, what I'd done. I knew I had the problem for years. But it plays tricks with your head. Very cunning and baffling is alcohol.'[254]

Ringo had re-married some years earlier, to his second wife, Barbara Bach, a former 'Bond' girl whom he met whilst co-starring with her in a movie called *'Caveman'*, in 1981.

Francesca Gregorini, Ringo's stepdaughter - 'It was their drugs heyday. Their troubles made me a better academic. I was always hidden away in a room reading because Mum and Dad were out of it.'[255]

Ringo - 'I got involved with a lot of different medications and you can listen to my records go downhill as the amount of medication went up.'

'I've got photographs of me playing all over the world but I've absolutely no memory of it. I played Washington with the Beach Boys [on Wednesday 4th July 1984] - or so they tell me. But there's only a photo to prove it.'

'I came to one Friday afternoon and was told by the staff that I'd trashed the house so badly they thought there had been burglars, and I'd trashed Barbara so badly they thought she was dead.'[255]

So, Ringo and Barbara decide to check into a rehab in Tucson, Arizona.

When Ringo emerges he commits to a cleaned up alcohol free lifestyle, and launches the newly formed All-Starr Band.

❀ ❀ ❀

George explains how it was that he and John became as close as they did.

George - 'After taking acid together, John and I had a very interesting relationship. That I was younger or I was smaller was no longer any kind of embarrassment with John. Paul still says, "I suppose we looked down on George because he was younger." That is an illusion people are under. It's nothing to do with how many years old you are, or how big your body is. It's down to what your greater consciousness is and if you can live in harmony with what's going on in creation. John and I spent a lot of time together from then on and I felt closer to him than all the others, right through until his death. As Yoko came into the picture, I lost a lot of personal contact with John; but on the odd occasion I did see him, just by the look in his eyes I felt we were connected.'[1]

On a chat show in 1990, George explains why he doesn't think it is necessary to be sad about John's passing.
George - 'The thing is, I hadn't seen him for so long, I mean, for all I know he could still be there now, you know, because I didn't see him for two years anyway, and occasionally maybe send a postcard. And it's knowing that he's on the other end of a telephone if you do want to call, that's the difference. Now, you know, you need the big cosmic telephone to speak to him, but, err, you know, I believe in.. I just believe in, you know, that life goes on, you know. And so to me, I can't get sad, I'm sad by.. you know, I can't go and have a err.. play guitars with John, but then I did that anyway, I did that for, you know, a long time, so, you know, we'll meet again somewhere down the line.'[249]

❀ ❀ ❀

In 1991 George is coaxed into doing a short tour of Japan with Eric Clapton's band, and afterwards he mulls over the possibility of touring Europe too.

Paul - 'A week before the British elections of 1992, the ones where the Maharishi's Natural Law Party took double-page ads in all the papers, George asked me to stand as the Natural Law Party Member of Parliament for Liverpool. Just one week before the last general election. George rang me giggling from LA. He said, "I've been up all night and you may think this is a bit silly, but Maharishi would like you, me and Ringo to stand as Members of Parliament for Liverpool." He said, "We'll win." I said "Yeeeessss!" He said, "It'll be great." I said, "Why, what'll we do?" He said, "Well, we'll introduce meditation for everyone." I said, "Wait a minute, this is a quite far-out idea this, you know." I think, as George's wife pointed out to him, he just wouldn't want the work. If you send George a bunch of papers, he says, "I'm not looking at that!", but if you're an MP, you've got to look at those papers, there's no getting round it. But it was quite funny. I said, "George, let's get one thing straight. No way am I gonna do it. I don't want to put a damper on, I don't want to rain on your parade or anything. You do it if you want. I'll support you. I'll back you up. But there's no way in heaven I am going to stand as a Member of Parliament a week before the election! You've gotta be kidding!" Well, they put 230 candidates out and I think every one of them lost their deposit. That may be a slight exaggeration but I don't recall any of them getting in. It showed they had a bit of dough, though. But they were talking mad things. George was saying, "You know places like Bradford and Blackburn or Southall where they have a big Indian community? They're going to bring in Indian guys, holy men, people like that to be candidates." He said, "Well, they'll definitely win in all those Indian communities." There was lots of talk, it was talk.'[6]

George - 'Maharishi got the TM instructors to put themselves up for election. It was a very long shot because they only put themselves up 10 days before the election. It was just to create a stir. They printed a manifesto which was really good. A lot of party politicians think of it as a joke. For me it was a stand just to say, "Look, I'm not impressed with any of you politicians, so I'm going to put my vote with the Natural Law Party." It's kind of a wind-up, really. The public ought to realise that they don't have to vote for the same old degenerates year in and year out.'[212]

On Monday, 6th April 1992, George Harrison announces he is going to play in a benefit benefit concert on behalf of Transcendental Meditation at the Royal Albert Hall, in London.
George - 'I still practice Transcendental Meditation and I think it's great. Maharishi only ever did good for us, and although I have not been with him physically, I never left him.'[256]

Seen arriving at the charity gig is the ever-glamorous Edna Linnell, a fellow participant on the 1968 course, who continues to show support for TM.
Edna Linnell - 'Harmony, peace, and caring for people, doing all the things that are beautiful the world needs.'[3]
Mike Love and fellow Beach Boy Al Jardine also arrive; they have both been teachers of Transcendental Meditation since 1972, since training with Maharishi in Majorca.
Mike Love - 'Support the Natural Law Party, that says that celebration should be an order of the electioneering!'
Al Jardine - 'We represent the "Beach Party"!'[3]

After performances from guitarists Joe Walsh and Gary Moore, George Harrison and his 'Hi-Jack Band' appear onstage and lose no time in getting started, delivering a strong set, peppered with Beatle songs and material from George's solo career, including his hit from the 1970's.

George - 'Feel free to sing along with this one, there's only three words in it.'[3]

'My Sweet Lord'

Well more than three words actually, and hidden amongst the lines of *'My Sweet Lord'* there is a small portion of the *puja* conducted for initiates of Transcendental Meditation.

गुरुर्ब्रह्मा गुरुर्विष्णुर् गुरुर्देवो महेश्वरः ।

गुरुःसाक्षात् परम्ब्रह्म तस्मै श्री गुरवे नमः ॥

'Gurur Brahmaa Gurur Vishnur Gurur Devo Maheshvarah
Guruh Saakshaat parambrahma tasmai shri gurave namah'

Translation:-

'Guru is Brahma, guru is Vishnu, Guru is the god Maheshwara (Shiva),
In the presence of the Guru, the transcendental brahman, to him the blessed Guru, I bow down.'

At the close of the song, George enthusiastically shouts; 'Thank you very much! Jai Guru Dev.'[3]

It's almost as though the concert is taking place sometime back in the late Sixties with George having just returned alone from the meditation course with Maharishi in India, but George has somehow lost his *sitar* somewhere along the way.

Ringo - 'I was there just to watch. The show went so well - George was just groovin'.
He should be doing what God wants him to do: perform. So then Joe [Walsh] sauntered off-stage and said [mimicking Walsh], "George wondered if you want to come on." It didn't take much coaxing, and I got up for the last two numbers.'[257]

❀ ❀ ❀

So George's first public concert in Britain since the Beatles breakup has been staged in support of meditation, therefore it stands to reason he must still be enamoured with the practice.

George - 'Look inside and do meditation. That's the answer. Meditation is the key to get from darkness into the light, from suffering into pleasure, from ignorance into wisdom. It doesn't matter if you're a beggar, you can still find God. It doesn't matter if you're the greatest guitar player in the world, if you're not enlightened, forget it [laughs] People go, "It's all right for you to say, you've got all that money."'[212]

And how does George view the way The Beatles left things with Maharishi, when John Lennon wrote the put-down song, *Sexy Sadie,* about him?

George - 'Yeah. I called it *Sexy Sadie.* The title John had was not nice at all. At least he realised that. Because there was nothing that ever happened except there was a fella who was supposedly a friend of ours who stirred up and created this fantasy. There was never anything that took place. But Paul and Ringo were never into it anyway. John and I were. The others came along to see what was going on. I think Ringo and Paul had actually left there before this. I was leaving because I was going to south India to do some filming with Ravi Shankar. We left in a bit of a hurry, that's really all that happened. I think John had been seduced by Yoko Ono and he was going into a downward spiral that he went through for the next five years or so. But the Maharishi didn't do anything. All he did was learn a lesson. The Beatles attracted so much publicity that it made it look like it was some kind of hippie cult. Now it's gone the other way, they look like business people. But the Maharishi has done a lot of work with universities, with science and medicine. Without the Beatles around it's more low profile. And I think it's better that it's like that. But for me, I was a bit disappointed in John.
But you know, that's what life is. We're all under a huge cloud of ignorance. Some of the people on this planet are still engulfed in ignorance.'[212]

❀ ❀ ❀

In the intervening years between the time of The Beatles visit to see Maharishi and now, many new buildings have been added to the academy, including a network of beehive shaped dwellings designed for use as meditation huts, but Maharishi no longer visits his academy in Rishikesh, and as a result the place has become neglected and run down. Nowadays, no courses are being held, but visitors still make their way up the hill to soak up the atmosphere, imagining those times when The Beatles came to stay, all those years ago. In fact the Beatles have now been apart for more than 20 years now, and the area has become some sort of shrine to them, and is referred to by visitors as 'The Beatles Ashram'.

From time to time, an old *swami* is seen coming and going to the deserted academy. His name is Dandi Swami Narayananand Saraswati, and sometimes he stays in one of the beehive stone huts. Dandi Swami, like Maharishi Mahesh Yogi, is a former pupil of Guru Dev. After Guru Dev's passing, in 1953, Dandi Swami followed the new Shankaracharya of Jyotirmath, Swami Shantanand Saraswati, serving him for several decades. When His Holiness Swami Shantanand sought to nominate him as his successor, Dandi Swami declined the post, preferring to pursue his solitary spiritual path quietly, out of the glare of publicity and public attention, often under a vow of silence.

❀ ❀ ❀

Geoffrey Giuliano, a reporter, manages to get a telephone interview with Maharishi.

Geoffrey Giuliano - 'Recently in London, for your Natural Law Party there was a benefit concert that was headlined by your old friend Mr George Harrison.'

Maharishi - 'Yes, I heard about it.' (giggles)

Geoffrey Giuliano - 'Could you tell me how George came to perform, to benefit your political organisation, the Natural Law Party?'

Maharishi - 'I think all these performers always look to opportunities, and this was the first onset of a new field of politics, so he thought he would do it.' (giggles)

Geoffrey Giuliano - 'Do you have special affection for George Harrison? He's meant a lot to a lot of people for many years now. How do you see Mr Harrison?'

Maharishi - 'I see him as a successful musician in his own talents. Whatever the effects, but he has become popular, and I attribute this to his talent also and to the British Press intelligence. British Press is very, very intelligent to promote their values, their national values.'

Geoffrey Giuliano - 'But Mr Harrison has been very intelligent because he's used Rock 'n' Roll music and popular music to promote the tenets and philosophy of Transcendental Meditation and spirituality. Oh surely you must applaud him for that, for properly using the medium of music to help to enlighten the world?'

Maharishi - 'I was happy when he started to meditate. I knew he would make a big impression in the world since he started to meditate. That's how the talents grow, with this program. And all the world of science then, and the world of artists, all the different values. But it has taken - the whole society has taken it - a good turn, in this, this knowledge. Very good. And now the whole politics is going to be sanctified with it.'[258]

Soon after George's surprise appearance at the Royal Albert Hall in support of Transcendental Meditation, he and his wife Olivia attend a concert given by Ravi Shankar at the Royal Festival Hall in London. It is many years since George brought out *'Wonderwall Music'*, and though he no longer utilizes Indian instruments, he enjoys listening to Indian music.

❀ ❀ ❀

Since the breakup of The Beatles there have been continued business hassles, but these are finally resolved so there is now a better basis for the surviving ex-Beatles to work together again. The three of them focus on a long-term project; to produce their own version of The Beatles story, to be released in video, audio and as a book, all to be called *'Anthology'*. Together, George, Ringo and Paul, hatch a scheme to also produce some new Beatles music, by using some tape recordings made by John Lennon shortly before his death. These songs, *'Free as a Bird'*, and *'Real Love'* are released as Beatles records and are well received by their fans.

Paul McCartney - 'I played these songs to the other guys, warning Ringo to have his hanky ready. I fell in love with "Free As A Bird". I thought I would have loved to work with John on that. I like the melody, it's got strong chords and it really appealed to me. Ringo was very up for it and George was very up for it. I actually originally heard it as a big, orchestral forties Gershwin thing, but it didn't turn out like that. Often your first vibe isn't always the one. You go through a few ideas and somebody goes "Bloody hell", and it gets knocked out fairly quickly. In the end we decided to do it very simply. It's crazy really, because when you think about a new Beatles record, it is impossible, because John is not around. So, I invented a little scenario; he's gone away on holiday and he's just rung us up and he says, "Just finish this track for us, will you? I'm sending the cassette - I trust you." That was the key thing. "I trust you, just do your stuff on it." I told this to the other guys and Ringo was particularly pleased, and he said "Ahh, that's great!" It was very nice and it was very irreverent towards John. The scenario allowed us not to be to ... ahh ... the great fallen hero. He would never have gone for that. John would have been the first one to debunk that. A fucking hero? A fallen hero? Fuck off, we're making a record! Once we agreed to take that attitude it gave us a lot of freedom, because it meant that we didn't have any sacred view of John as a martyr, it was John the Beatle, John the crazy guy we remember. So we could laugh and say, "Wouldn't you just know it? It's completely out of time! He's always bloody out of time, that Lennon!" He would have made those jokes if it had been my cassette.'[259]

On Tuesday, 11th March 1997, Paul McCartney is given a knighthood, thus making him Sir Paul McCartney.
Reporters, ask Sir Paul - 'Have you spoken to the other Beatles about this?'
Paul - 'Yep. They make fun of me. They keep ringing me up and calling me "your holiness", but they're having a good time. It seems strange being here without the other three. I keep looking over my shoulder for them.'[259]

In May 1997 a CD entitled *'Chants'* is released, sacred music performed by Ravi Shankar and a large assortment of other musicians; the CD has been produced by George Harrison in the studios at his country mansion, Friar Park.

George - 'I like producing Ravi's music, because for me it's educational as well as a joy to work with. It's actually soothing to your soul, and it helps you to focus or transcend.'[261]

On Sunday, 18th May 1997, Ravi and George both appear together on the VH1 channel and are interviewed by John Fugelsang.
George - 'I don't know what anybody else thinks and you know, as the years have gone by, I seem to have found myself more and more out on a limb, as far as, you know, that kind of thing goes. I mean, even close friends of mine, you know, they maybe don't want to talk about it because they don't understand it. But I believed in the thing that I read years ago, which I think was in the Bible, it said, "Knock and the door will be opened." And it's true, if you want to know anything in this life, you just have to knock on the door, whether that be physically on somebody else's door and ask them a question, or, which I was lucky to find, is the meditation, is, you know, it's all within.'[262]

In the middle of the night of Thursday, 30th December 1999, someone eludes the security system and breaks into George's home, arousing the family from their sleep. George uses the *Hare Krishna* chant to try to calm and distract the knife-wielding intruder, but it does nothing at all to improve the mood of his assailant. George's wife, Olivia, phones the police before attempting to deal with the attacker herself, she hits him with a fire poker; George's son, 21-year old Dhani Harrison, watches helplessly as his parents try to defend themselves from the assailant.

Olivia Harrison - 'There was blood on the walls and on the carpet. There was a moment when I realised we were going to be murdered - I realised that this man was succeeding.'

George - 'There was a time during this violent struggle that I truly believed I was dying.'

The police arrive and arrest the intruder, Michael Abrams.

Michael Abrams - 'You should have heard the spooky things he [George] was saying, the bastard.'

The court is told that Abrams believes he was possessed by George Harrison's spirit and that he was sent on a mission by God to kill him.

George is taken to hospital where he is treated for a punctured lung.[263]

❀ ❀ ❀

Despite enjoying enormous popularity in his solo career, Paul McCartney still has problems to deal with, and in particular the tragic loss of his wife, Linda McCartney, an animal rights activist and promoter of vegetarianism. On Monday, 11th June 2001, Sir Paul makes a televised appearance on The Charlie Rose Show on PBS (US Public Broadcasting System), where he appears in reflective mood.

Towards the end of the show Sir Paul is asked what he is looking forward to.

Paul - 'I look forward to, enjoying myself. I, sort of a great thing for me, err, it seems a bit sort of corny sometimes, when people say that. When, years ago when we studied meditation with the Maharishi in India, we had a real good time, and I always felt it was a very valuable experience, and it was a process that you can always go back to. If you're in turmoil, it's a centreing process that I like, like a lot. And he gave us his book, a very wise man; because he was one of the ones who wasn't a fake, there were a lot of them around at that time who were into Rolls Royce's and chicks. He wasn't one of them. He gave us his book and I looked to see what he would write, besides putting his name in it, and he wrote about.. he said; "Radiate bliss consciousness". Then at the end of it he just put, "Enjoy". And, I always thought, that was really cool, coming from him, and I actually met him, quite recently, just a year and half ago I think, he lives in the Netherlands now. And he is a **spry** old codger, seems to be in his eighties and he's still working, still spreading the message...'

Charlie Rose (the compere) - 'He's still a Maharishi and he's..'

Paul - 'He's still going. And I took Stella, my daughter, and James, my son, with me. And I said "Would it be okay if we all came to see you" so they said "Yeah, okay". So, we all went in for a meeting with him, and they said "We don't know how long you'll have, you know it could be over quite quickly, we don't know, he might get tired quickly, whatever". In the end it was four hours, we just sat down and it was four hours. We, had a good old time. But before we went in, Stella said to me "Say Dad, I've got my video camera, do you think I could shoot a bit of video?" I said, "Well, I don't know, I don't know what the scene is here". I said, "But, give it to me, I'll put it in my pocket, and at the end of our session I'll just ask, '*is it okay?*'". Well, of course, so the session came.. [then Stella nudged her father]. So, I said to Maharishi, "Could, would it be okay if she just does a little bit of video?". And he giggled and he said "Yeah, of course", you know, and so I gave Stell the camera, and she said, err, she lines it up; "Okay, Maharishi what have you got to say for the camera?" And he looks right in the camera and he says "Enjoy". Thirty years later, pretty consistent.

So, that's what I'm looking forward to, I think that's what's life's for, and if you can enjoy it, you're, as we say in English, you're "quids in" [in a profitable situation]. You are, if you, at the end of the day you can say "I enjoyed that day", then I think you're doing okay.'[264]

Then Paul is also interviewed by *Rolling Stone* magazine and he re-iterates his simple message.

Paul - 'Years ago when the Beatles were with the Maharishi, he gave us a book. He wrote in mine, "Radiate bliss consciousness." I thought, "That's pretty good." And then he just put, "Enjoy." I took that to heart. If at the end of each day — or most days — you could say, "That was a good one," it builds into a reasonably successful life.'[265]

❀ ❀ ❀

George Harrison's health has seemingly taken a downturn since the attack at his home.

George - 'Sometimes I feel like I'm actually on the wrong planet, and it's great when I'm in my garden, but the minute I go out the gate I think: "What the hell am I doing here?"'[266]

On Thursday, 29th November 2001, it is announced, that, after a long illness, George Harrison has died. His body is cremated within hours, and it is understood the ashes are to be flown to India, to be scattered at the confluence of Ganges and Yamuna rivers at Allahabad, and also at the Dashaswamedh Ghat on the Ganges in Varanasi. The cause of death is said to be lung cancer, first identified some four years earlier, and blamed on his many years of cigarette smoking.

❀ ❀ ❀

Dhani Harrison (George's son) - 'My earliest memory of my dad is probably of him somewhere in a garden covered in dirt, somewhere hot, a tropical garden, in jeans, khakis covered in dirt just continuously planting trees. I think that's what I thought he did for the first seven years of my life. I was completely unaware that he had anything to do with music. I came home one day from school after being chased by kids singing "Yellow Submarine", and I didn't understand why. It just seemed surreal: why are they singing that song to me? I came home and I freaked out on my dad: "Why didn't you tell me you were in The Beatles?" And he said, "Oh, sorry. Probably should have told you that."'[266]
'I can't even begin to describe how I miss him. He always supported me in everything I did. He was a very wise man and I realised at an early age I could learn a lot from him. He always gave me the right answer. But above all he was a very easy-going guy and all he wanted was to be my best friend. I'm an only child and so he shared everything with me. Of course he was very young to die and I was very young to lose a father. But there was nothing left unsaid between us.'[78]

❀ ❀ ❀

Ringo Starr - 'India was the first foreign country I ever went to. I never felt Denmark or Holland or France were foreign, just the language was different, but when you got to India it was very hard to know what the hell was going on. Over the years, I got to love the music myself and now I'm a Christian Hindu with Buddhist tendencies. Thanks to George, who opened my eyes as much as anyone else's.'[78]

❀ ❀ ❀

2002

In 2002, during a sound check before a concert in the U.S.A., Sir Paul McCartney plays a song about India, which opens with an incomprehensible incantation, probably intended to give one the impression of a Sanskrit chant. As with John Lennon's song *'India, India'*, the focus of the lyrics is on the heart:-

'India, over and over, where are you now
In my heart, forever and ever, I'll get back to you somehow'

- Excerpt of lyrics to *'India'* by Paul McCartney

❀ ❀ ❀

Maharishi speaks about the role of independent Transcendental Meditation teachers
On Wednesday, 14th May 2003, Maharishi is asked a question relating to his position on the current situation wherein many teachers of Transcendental Meditation (TM) are now operating independently of the organizations he set up. Some of the teachers are independent because they disagree with charging a fee for instruction, some because of the pricing structure, and some simply because they don't want to be allied or identified with any of his organizations.
Maharishi - 'What I have taught, because it has its eternal authenticity in the Vedic literature and you should know that, how many? 30 - 40 thousand teachers of TM I have trained and many of them have gone on their own and they may not call it Maharishi's "TM" but they are teaching it in some different name here and there. So there's a lot of these.. artificial things are going on, doesn't matter, as long as the man is getting something useful to make his life better, we are satisfied.'[3]

❀ ❀ ❀

June 2004
Paul McCartney mentions how he was recently invited by some youngsters in Los Angeles to share some

marijuana.

Paul - 'I don't actually smoke the stuff these days. It's something I've kind of grown out of.'
'To me, it's a huge compliment that a bunch of kids think I might be up to smoke a bit of dope with them.'[267]
'I don't do that any more. Why? The truth is I don't really want to set an example to my kids and grandkids. It's now a parent thing.'
'Back then I was just some guy around London having a ball, and the kids were little so I'd just try and keep it out of their faces.'[268]

Pattie - 'Marijuana wasn't destructive. Dope in the Sixties - a very different drug from the skunk kids smoke today - was about peace, love and increasing awareness.'[243]

❀ ❀ ❀

The *Times of India* publishes an article from its 'Guest Editor', endocrinologist Deepak Chopra (a former follower of Maharishi), in which he claims that in September 1991 he was asked by George Harrison to set up a meeting with Maharishi.

Times of India of 15th February 2006.

We got on to a chartered plane, which had just dropped off Paul McCartney to Monte Carlo.
George wrote a note to Paul, saying, "Guess whom we're going to meet", and signed it "Jai Gurudev". Then we flew to Vlodrop, in the Netherlands, where Maharishi was staying.
It was an emotional meeting. As Chopra tells it, Harrison first presented Maharishi a rose. This was followed by a long silence.
Then Maharishi asked, "How have you been?" George replied, "Some good things (have happened), some bad things."
Then he added, "You must know about John being assassinated." Maharishi replied, "I was very sorry to hear about it."
After some time, Harrison spoke. "I came to apologise," he said. "For what?" asked Maharishi. "You know for what," replied Harrison.
"Tell Deepak the real story," said Maharishi. Harrison said, "I don't know about it 100%, but here's what I know transpired." And he narrated the incident about the Beatles being asked to leave. Did Maharishi harbour any bitterness towards the Beatles?
Chopra smiled. "Part of the Beatles lore is that when they made their first appearance on American TV, on the Ed Sullivan show, there was no crime in the US for that one hour."
Maharishi told us, "When I heard this, I knew the Beatles were angels on earth. It doesn't matter what John said or did, I could never be upset with angels". On hearing that, George broke down and wept.
There was another long silence. Then Harrison told Maharishi, "I love you" and Maharishi responded, "I love you too."
The two left, and Harrison later phoned Chopra and told him, "A huge karmic baggage has been lifted from me, because I didn't want to lie."'

Further, despite Dr Chopra not attending the Rishikesh course in 1968, and not being involved with Transcendental Meditation until 1980, he claims, in a second article, that he knows the real reason for The Beatles leaving the course with Maharishi.

Times of India of 15th February 2006.

'The Beatles along with their entourage, which included Mia Farrow were doing drugs, taking LSD, at Maharishi's ashram, and he lost his temper with them. He asked them to leave, and they did in a huff.'
'In fact, the rumour was that Maharishi had misbehaved with Mia Farrow, but I met Mia years later at the airport while taking a flight to India, and she asked me to tell Maharishi that she still loved him.'

Mia Farrow - 'Deepak Chopra should talk about what he knows,'
'I was there. There were no drugs at the ashram, those guys were not kicked out. Ringo left because of the flies (she laughs), I left for my own reasons and the other guys left eventually because they just got bored. George stuck it pretty close to the end along with Prudence.'[269]

❀ ❀ ❀

Wednesday, 8th March 2006.
Reporter David Jones visits Maharishi's organisation in Vlodrop, Holland, and is granted a rare interview with the aged and frail Maharishi, who appears by televised link from his accommodation upstairs.
David Jones - 'I hesitate to mention the "Beatles" word, I know you don't particularly like going back all those years, but British.. English people, of course associate you with The Beatles and with that period and they haven't themselves.. they haven't enjoyed always a particularly good fate since their encounter with Transcendental Meditation.'
Maharishi does not answer the question directly, and instead advises the reporter, that rather than trying to get a news story he instead investigate Transcendental Meditation for himself,
Maharishi - 'You know that phrase, English phrase, "Taste of pudding is in eating"? Taste of Transcendental Consciousness is in experiencing.'
The reporter is not put off and he soon steers the interview back to the topic of his choice by asking Maharishi about the importance of celebrity in the modern world. Then he is more forthright.
David Jones - 'One more question then on that subject, about, and it is about The Beatles. Do you regret now having ever becoming involved with them? Because then your movement became associated with celebrity, with, you know, popular music and so on? Do you regret that period?'
Maharishi - 'Forget about it. If at all, Beatles became substantial due to my contact. I did not become great by the association of The Beatles. These boys may be musicians, Beatles, [but] it's wrong for the English Press to make the business perverted wherever, even after these fifty years. *"Beatles make the Maharishi great"*, it's a waste of thought, you know. It waned.
What? These little singers boys, singer boys, conquered the Field of Divine Integrity?
It's not good enough that they followed; they had a good - what they call it - a teacher or a guide? [manager] But when he was no more, they all scattered here and there and there. So he was the guide who made these four boys pull together, and made Beatles. And British Press made, "wherever they'll be I'll be" after so many years. All *"Beatles, Maharishi, Beatles"*. (laughs) It's a waste of thought, you know.'[3]

❀ ❀ ❀

The day of the full moon of July is known as Guru Purnima, and on this day the *guru* is celebrated.
On Guru Purnima, Friday, 27th July 2007, Maharishi recollects the teaching of his *guru*, Guru Dev, Swami Brahmananda Saraswati, Shankaracharya of Jyotirmath.
Maharishi - 'My spiritual master told me that life is bliss. And you sit like that, and you close the eyes and you let your mind go deep within yourself, and you get to Transcendental Consciousness. I did with him, and I found it so good, so good, so good. I saw in the world people suffering and all, so I came out to say, "No, no, no. Suffering is not good. Deep within you is Bliss Consciousness - life is bliss". How to explore it? Through the practice of Transcendental Meditation.'
'I did this in India for some time. Then, I thought the thing is so good, the thing is soooo good that I will go to those countries, where the people are fond of experiments, where the people are scientists.
'Now what happened is that so many, a few million, people—two, three, four million people—started to meditate and all. Everywhere there are people in the world who are practicing Transcendental Meditation, and what they found was what experiments found.[287]

Tuesday, 29th January 2008.

USA Today reports that Maharishi Mahesh Yogi *'has retreated into near silence'* and *'now spends his days in silence contemplating and preparing a commentary on the Vedas, a vast Sanskrit canon... from which he evolves solutions for today's troubled world.'*

On Tuesday, 5th February 2008, at 1am CET, the NASA's Deep Space Network, for the first time ever, is to beam out a song directly into deep space from its Madrid transmitter. The Interstellar Radio Message (IRM) is to be The Beatles' *'Across the Universe'*, and will travel across the universe at a speed of 186,000 miles per second towards the North Star, Polaris, located 431 light years away from Earth. That's a 2.5 quadrillion-mile trip (2,500,000,000,000,000,000,000,000 miles) to Polaris, where it will likely arrive in the year 2439. The Beatles' *'Across the Universe'* was recorded exactly 40 years ago.

Paul - 'Amazing! Well done, NASA! Send my love to the aliens. All the best...'
Yoko - 'I see that this is the beginning of the new age in which we will communicate with billions of planets across the universe.'[270]

The passing of Maharishi Mahesh Yogi
On Tuesday, 5th February 2008 the death of Maharishi Mahesh Yogi is announced. He is said to have been about 90 years of age.
Paul - 'I was asked for my thoughts on the passing of Maharishi Mahesh Yogi and I can only say that whilst I am deeply saddened by his passing, my memories of him will only be joyful ones.'
'He was a great man who worked tirelessly for the people of the world and the cause of unity. I will never forget the dedication that he wrote inside a book he once gave me, which read "radiate bliss consciousness", and that to me says it all. I will miss him but will always think of him with a smile.'[271]

Ringo - 'One of the wise men I met in my life was the Maharishi. I always was impressed by his joy and I truly believe he knows where he is going.'[271]

Donovan - 'Maharishi brought the pure transcendental meditation back to the world, reuniting us with our own true self. As a poet I can find no words to describe how grateful I am to Maharishi for his gift.'[272]

Mike Love - 'His passing is profoundly sad. But I, for one, am among the millions who are grateful for what he shared with us.'[272]

Times of India, Saturday, 9th February 2008.

'Call it cosmic coincidence. Close on the heels of NASA's announcement that the Beatles' song Across the Universe would be transmitted to the distant Polaris star system in the hope of making contact with intelligent, extraterrestrial life, came the news that the Indian mystic who inspired the Beatles to write the song had passed away. Ascended to a new plane of consciousness, perhaps, where he and those of the Fab Four no longer with us could produce more chart-busting music.
Maharishi Mahesh Yogi, also known for his introduction of transcendental meditation (TM) to the world, leaves behind a global business empire. But it was his impact on music and counterculture that first brought his movement attention from the world. Most famously, of course, he got the Beatles to replace LSD with a different kind of high.'

'Though his association with George Harrison, in particular, made him famous, the Maharishi's contribution in popularising Indian spiritualism across the world cannot be overstated. His theory of transcendental meditation has proved to be a treasure-trove of tips for management courses. TM, which he trademarked, offers a means of achieving enlightenment without self-denial. Dismissed by critics as a hippie mystic earlier, the Maharishi's interpretation of ancient yogic techniques has led to a multibillion dollar self-help industry. He moved into what he called consciousness-based education and set up several colleges and universities. Since TM became popular, there has been no shortage of scientists to study its techniques. Many of them have found that meditation does promote mental and physical well-being, and especially aids in reducing stress. He was both a businessman and a guru, a spiritual man who sought a world stage from where to advance the joys of inner happiness. As the refrain from Across the Universe went, Jai Guru Deva, here and perhaps one day in Polaris.'

Cynthia - 'Maharishi had a laugh like a tinkling bell. He had an aura. I was as cynical as anyone to begin with, but I suppose I'm a perpetual student. I felt he was someone I could learn from. He'd call us for two chats a day to talk about the spiritual life. I didn't follow the whole thing, just took what was necessary for me. I still meditate occasionally.'[273]

Yoko - 'John would have been the first one now, if he had been here, to recognize and acknowledge what Maharishi has done for the world and appreciate it.'[70]

Scott Schultz, a writer, asks Yoko - 'Do you have a personal mantra?'
Yoko - 'Yes. I believe you are speaking of the one you get from transcendental meditation? Yes, is the answer.'[274]

Paul - 'It was a great gift the Maharishi gave us. For me it came at a time when we were looking for something to kind of stabilize us in the, towards the end of the crazy sixties. And it is, it's a lifelong gift. You know, it's something that you can call on, at any time.'[275]

Pattie - 'I can't really take all the credit, because I think that whatever happens in life is meant to happen, you know, everything's pre-ordained, really, just needs a little nudge.'[40]

❀ ❀ ❀

On Saturday, 4th April 2009, at Radio City Music Hall in New York City, Sir Paul McCartney, Ringo Starr, Mike Love, Paul Horn and Donovan play 'Change Begins Within', a benefit concert to spread Transcendental Meditation to at-risk children. Also performing at the concert are Sheryl Crow, Eddie Vedder, Ben Harper, Moby, Bettye LaVette and Jim James.

Paul McCartney explains his commitment to spreading Transcendental Meditation to children at-risk.
Paul - 'In moments of madness, it has helped me find moments of serenity.'
'I would like to think that it would help provide them a quiet haven in a not-so-quiet world.'[276]

Ringo - 'It gives me great pleasure to be part of this evening. I feel the aims of this charity are wonderful.'[277]
Ringo joins Paul onstage and for the first time ever they perform a live version of The Beatles' *With a Little Help from My Friends*.
And towards the end of the concert Paul has another special surprise.

Paul - 'We'd like to do a song now which err, actually I wrote it erm.. when we were in Rishikesh at the *ashram* with Maharishi, and erm.. Maharishi would always say that he wanted everyone to be "cosmically conscious", and he'd also say "It's such a joy, such a joy".'[278]

'C'mon, be cosmically conscious,
cosmically conscious with me.'

- Excerpt of lyrics to *'Cosmically Conscious'* by Paul McCartney

Donovan - 'How great to be playing with Paul, Ringo, and Paul Horn again - as we did in India in 1968.'[276]

Millie Drummond - '… hadn't heard the song - it's a riot! But not really "my cup of tea"! Maharishi's way of saying "Such a Joy" was so beautiful.. almost sacred...& I have to say I'm not a fan of jazzing such things up!'[38]

Paul Horn - 'So it's always the youth, always the young, and I don't think anything could be more valuable than to have a young person start meditating. Which is to open up your potential, your inner potential, and make life happier and easier, and that's what these kids are finding out. So I'm very excited about that, it was a very successful concert, it raised a lot of money, and it brought together some musicians like I've never seen---Paul McCartney, Ringo and Donovan, and here we are, all again on the same stage, playing music individually and together with a lot of younger players, Sheryl Crow and Moby. And some that I was not familiar with myself, but anyways, it was a great show.'[141]

❀ ❀ ❀

Millions have learned Transcendental Mediation and many famous names are linked with the technique, such as Sting, Howard Stern, Jerry Seinfeld, Jennifer Aniston, Heather Graham, Tom Hanks, Russell Brand, Cameron Diaz, Mary Tyler Moore, Clint Eastwood, Stevie Wonder, Smokey Robinson, Billy Gibbons, Ben Harper, Andy Kaufman, Steve Lukather, Paul Rodgers, Steve Howe, Mike Oldfield, Tom Petty, Rick Rubin, Wes Carr, Martin Scorsese, Michael J. Fox, Sir Patrick Stewart, Arnold Schwarzenegger, Cameron Diaz, Jennifer Lopez, Kate Perry. Patrick Swayze, Elizabeth Taylor, Michael Jackson, Eddie Vedder, Steve Vai, Olivia Newton John, Oprah Winfrey, David Letterman, David Lynch, Rupert Murdoch, Hugh Jackman, Nicole Kidman, Laura Dern, Lindsay Lohan, Amy Schumer, Eva Mendes, Ellen Degeneres, Miranda Kerr, Daisy Lowe, Judy Greer, Maya Stojan, Hugh Jackman, Jeff Bridges, Dr. Oz, Ali Stephens, Raquel Zimmerman, Alyssa Miller, Miranda Kerr, Liv Tyler, George Lucas, Jim Carrey ….. and many, many more…

Jim Carrey, actor - 'Years ago when I was doing Andy Kaufman I learned how to meditate and it's been very valuable.'
'It's been around for a while, but I mean, on a widespread level it's being picked up by everybody now, it's being understood as something more than some kind of religious nutty thing. It's a system of teaching yourself how to get into a state of relaxation that effects your entire life, and the quality of your life, and I do it. I've done it for a while and I recommend it highly.'[279]

❀ ❀ ❀

Paul - 'I always thought I learned what I wanted to learn there. I took it just as a skill like riding a bike. I didn't then disbelieve. Now I say to my own kids, "Go and get a mantra, because then if you ever want to meditate and you're on some hilltop somewhere, you'll know how to do it." I'm not sure you have to go into it any deeper than that myself.'[6]

So, what about the children of the former Beatles, what value do they place on their parent's interest in Transcendental Meditation?
Having been brought up in the glare of publicity that comes with having celebrity parents, they seem to value their privacy. Notwithstanding, some of them have spoken up on the topic of meditation.

Dhani Harrison (musician) - 'The only things he [George Harrison] felt I *had* to do in my life are be happy and meditate.'[280]

James McCartney (musician) - 'Transcendental Meditation (TM) plays a big role in my life as it has done for my father and the other Beatles. I meditate regularly - twice a day - and I have learnt 4 advanced TM techniques.
I find that just 30 minutes of TM refreshes me as if I had slept a few hours!'
Arvind Devalia (a journalist) - 'James, but why TM? There are such a myriad of meditational techniques and teachers out there that newcomers to meditation can get so confused! Please explain why TM and why it's so special to you?'
James McCartney - 'Firstly TM is a tried and tested method going back many decades, with millions of practitioners around the world. It helps you in so many ways such as de-stressing, relaxing, calming down and getting clarity of mind which helps in problem solving.
My dad introduced me to TM after the Beatles went to Rishikesh and were taught by the man himself - Maharishi Mahesh Yogi who developed TM and spread it all around the world.'[281]
James's sister, Stella McCartney, the fashion designer, also values meditation.

Stella McCartney - 'It's about finding that balance between work, family, and self. But I don't always tick those boxes. I do meditate - but I'm not really at 20-minutes-a-day of TM [Transcendental Meditation], I'm not there yet.'
'My mum used to say - and this really resonates with me: "It's allowed."'
'So I think: I don't meditate for 20 mins twice a day? It's allowed. It's allowed to feel stressed. It's allowed to feel sad. You are allowed to let yourself off the hook.'[282]

Sean Lennon, John's son by Yoko, also meditates.

Reporter - 'Then it's safe to say your practice of transcendental meditation isn't about a higher power?'

Sean Lennon (musician) - 'Right. I don't think of TM as a religious practice, though I'm sure it can be for some. But for me, it's like a scientific method to calm my brain down and making my frontal lobe more active. It's an exercise, really. It helps me to have about 10 percent more conscious thinking, which is good, because we make a lot of decisions in our subconscious that aren't always good, like the decision to smoke cigarettes or to eat bad foods.'[283]

Yoko - 'Well, you see, John was not against Transcendental Meditation. He was a meditator, he was always meditating.'[284]

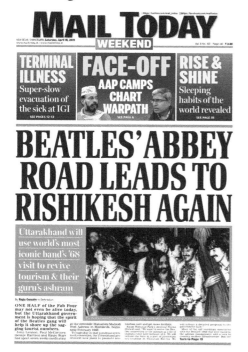

Mail Today **Saturday, 18th April 2015**

The Beatles were four young guys from Liverpool who caught the public's attention with their music, humour and great appetite for life. Most likely The Beatles' musical heritage will endure for centuries, and hopefully their idealistic quest for Peace, Love and Understanding through meditation will ultimately prevail, and governments of the world will *'Give Peace a Chance!'*.

~ Postscript ~

Julian Lennon on the 'sign' father John Lennon sent to him after death

When Julian Lennon was touring as a musician in Australia, he met a group of aboriginal leaders who asked him to use his voice and fame to bring attention to their plight.

It was a pretty normal request, until one of the tribal leaders presented Julian with a white swan's feather.

Julian, son of John Lennon, felt goosebumps wash over him.

"Dad had said to me that if there was a way of letting me know that he was going to be all right, or that we were all going to be all right, it would be in the form of a white feather," he told TODAY Parents.

That was two decades ago, and since then, Julian — a talented photographer, musician, filmmaker and now author — has been raising money for the White Feather Foundation to help support environmental and humanitarian causes.

"I just thought, well, it really is time to step up to the plate. Let me do what I can," Julian recalled Tuesday in an interview in the TODAY green room.

- *Today* Tuesday, 11th April 2017

Notes

1. *The Beatles Anthology*, Cassell & Co, 2000
2. http://beatles-merchandise.com/georgeharrison/george-harrison-finds-eastern-religion/
3. Author's transcript of audio recording
4. *Billboard*, December 1992
5. *Lennon Remembers*, Jann Wenner, Penguin Books, 1971
6. *Paul McCartney: Many Years From Now*, Barry Miles, Vintage, 1998
7. *Twist of Lennon*, Cynthia Lennon, Star, 1978
8. Author's transcript from recording of *Rolling Stone* 8th December 1970 interview
9. *Daily Mail*, 5th August 2007
10. *John*, Cynthia Lennon, Hodder & Stroughton, 2005
11. http://lennon.net/reflections/s_parkes5.shtml
12. *The Beatles Off The Record*, Keith Badman, Omnibus Press, 2000
13. An accomplished pupil of Ravi Shankar, Diwan Motihar (aka Dewan Motihar) appears on several records of the 1960's, notably on the groundbreaking *'Indo-Jazz Suite'* by The Joe Harriott Double Quintet with John Mayer, recorded 10th October 1966
14. *Abracadabra*, Ray Newman, 2006
15. *Last Interview: All We Are Saying*, David Sheff, St. Martin's Griffin, 2000 (*Playboy* interviews)
16. *I Read The News Today, Oh Boy*, Paul Howard, Picador, 2016
17. *Rolling Stone*, 18th Sept 1968
18. *Evening Standard*, 4th March 1966
19. *Daily Express*, 12th March 1969
20. *The Beatles*, Hunter Davies, Heinemann, 1968; rev. 2003,
21. *Wonderful Today*, Pattie Boyd & Penny Junor, Headline Review, 2007
22. *My Music, My Life*, Ravi Shankar, Simon and Schuster, 1968
23. *The Complete Beatles Recording Sessions: The Official Story of the Abbey Road Years 1962-1970*, Mark Lewisohn, 1995
24. Author's transcript of *'Revolver'* interview August 1966 https://www.youtube.com/watch?v=CP4eQJ6Rgus
25. *Lennon Revealed*, Larry Kane, Running Press, 2005
26. Interview by Donald Milner on 20th Sept 1966, for the BBC programme *Lively Arts*, 29th September 1966
27. *Times of India*, 20th September 1966
28. *The Beatles In Their Own Words* CD, Geoffrey Giuliano, Laserlight, 1995
29. *Holiday*, February 1968
30. *Raga Mala*, Ravi Shankar, Element, 1999
31. http://www.ndtv.com/india-news/when-pandit-ravi-shankar-taught-a-beatle-on-a-houseboat-507427
32. *Dear Prudence*, Prudence Farrow Bruns, 2015
33. http://www.telegraph.co.uk/culture/donotmigrate/3584221/John-Paul-George-and-.-.-.-Barry.html
34. *John Lennon In My Life*, Pete Shotton and Nicholas Schaffner, Coronet Books, 1983
35. http://www.uncut.co.uk/features/john-lennon-remembered-by-yoko-ono-we-were-in-love-desperately-71166/2
36. http://www.kathyetchingham.com/jimi-hendrix-brian-jones-and-tara-browne/
37. *Evening Standard*, 18th December 1966
38. Personal message
39. Author transcript, BBC's *Front Row*, John Wilson 20th November 2008
40. Author's transcript of Pattie Boyd talking to Martin Lewis at Beatlefest, February 2014 https://www.youtube.com/watch?v=St7hOTrpS8o
41. *INTRO*, issue 1, 28th September 1967
42. *All You Need Is Ears*, George Martin, Saint Martin's Press Inc., 1995
43. *The Beatles - An Oral History*, David Pritchard and Alan Lysaght, Allen & Unwin, 1998
44. *Observer*, 26th November 1967
45. http://www.beatlesebooks.com/within-you-without-you
46. Author's transcript of interview on *'The Beatles Anthology'* DVD, Apple, 2003
47. *New Musical Express - NME*, 27th May 1967
48. *The Beatles*, Anthony Scaduto, Signet, 1968
49. *AP Associated Press* 2nd June 2004 http://www.today.com/id/5121163/ns/today-today_entertainment/t/paul-mccartney-got-no-thrill-heroin/#.WECjMdWLSiR
50. *BBC News*, 10th May 1967 - http://news.bbc.co.uk/onthisday/hi/dates/stories/may/10/newsid_2522000/2522735.stm
51. *LIFE*, Vol. 62, No. 24, 16th June 1967
52. http://www.beatlesebooks.com/walrus
53. *The Beatles*, Hunter Davies, Jonathan Cape, 1968 rev 1985
54. *Guardian*, 25th August 1967
55. *Saturday Evening Post*, 18 May 1968
56. *The Lives of John Lennon*, Albert Goldman, Bantam Book, 1989
57. *Daily Telegraph*, 3 September 1967
58. Author's transcript of tape recording of Maharishi Mahesh Yogi c24th September 1968
59. *A Silent Melody: An Experience of Contemporary Spiritual Life*, Shirley du Boulay Daron, Longman and Todd Ltd, 2014
60. http://beatlesinindia.blogspot.co.uk/2009/01/cosmic-set-up-how-beatles-first-met.html
61. *Postcards From The Boys*, Ringo Starr, Cassell Illustrated, 2004
62. Author transcript of https://www.youtube.com/watch?v=Z8dryBMv4Zw
63. *The Quiet Mind*, John E Coleman, Pariyatti Press, 1971/2000
64. http://kenwoodlennon.blogspot.co.uk/2012/01/bangor-paolo-ammassari-interview.html
65. Author's transcript of interview between Jenny Boyd and Iain McNay, 8th March 2015
66. *Disc and Music Echo* 2nd September 1967
67. http://outerbluerecords.com/blog/beatle-john-lennons-home-studio/john-lennon-home-studio
68. http://www.teamrock.com/features/2014-05-28/archive-the-moody-blues-revolution-in-the-head
69. http://www.rockcellarmagazine.com/2013/04/02/justin-hayward-interview-moody-blues-spirits-western-sky/#sthash.J0DJJNLU.dpbs
70. *Rolling Stone*, 6th March 2008
71. http://www.donovan.ie/en/2013/10/donovan-trinity/
72. http://culteducation.com/group/1195-transcendental-meditation-movement/20517-transcendental-meditation-bliss-hippy-days-are-here-again.html
73. *Pageant*, April 1968
74. *John, Paul, George, Ringo & Me*, Tony Barrow - Pulse Records, Band CD002, 2001

75. *The John Lennon Letters*, Hunter Davies, Phoenix, 2013
76. *The Quiet Mind*, John E Coleman, Pariyatti Press, 1971, 2000
77. *New Musical Express - NME*, 9 September 1967
78. http://www.ringofstars.ru/across/?p=14243 http://www.hound-dog-media.com/2012/11/george-harrisons-letter-to-his-mother.html
79. *108 Discourses of Guru Dev*, translation by Paul Mason, Premanand, 2009
80. http://www.uncut.co.uk/features/john-lennon-remembered-by-yoko-ono-we-were-in-love-desperately-71166/2
81. http://beatlephotoblog.com/fool-on-the-hill-
82. *The Beatles Celebration* DVD, Laserlight, 1999
83. http://www.beatlesinterviews.org/db1967.0913.beatles.html
84. *The Hurdy Gurdy Man*, Donovan, Century, 2005
85. *Daily Express,* 20th September 1967
86. *John Lennon's Tooth*, Mr. Bonzai. BookBaby. Kindle Edition 2012
87. http://beatlephotoblog.com/fool-on-the-hill-3
88. *The Love You Make*, Peter Brown and Steven Gaines, Pan, 1983
89. Author transcript from video of October 1967 interview on Sveriges Television, Stockholm
90. *The Village Voice,* 9th November 1967
91. http://www.marmalade-skies.co.uk/wall.htm
92. *Wonderwall Music,* Remastered CD, Apple, 2014
93. *The Beatles Monthly Book*, No. 56, March 1968
94. *Apple Years 1968-75,* booklet, Apple, 2014
95. *Melody Maker,* 2nd December 1967
96. http://lifeofthebeatles.blogspot.co.uk/2006/06/interview-george-harrison-educational.html
97. *Disc and Echo,* 9th December 1967
98. *Melody Maker,* 16th December 1967
99. Transcript from video of Al Jardine 6th July 2013 https://www.youtube.com/watch?v=BQK-GCRW4Xk
100. *Heroes and Villains: The True Story of The Beach Boys*, Steven Gaines,Grafton, 1988
101. *The Story of Wonderwall,* Collectors Booklet written by Joe Massot July 2000, DVD booklet, Fabulous, 2014
102. *Wonderwall the Book*, Pilar, 2000
103. http://www.beatlesinterviews.org/db1967.1227.beatles.html
104. *The Beatles A Celebration*, Geoffrey Giuliano, Sidgwick & Jackson, 1986
105. *Times of India,* 10th January 1968
106. *UNI - United News of India*, 16th January 1968
107. Author's transcript, Kate Saunders *BBC Radio 4* FM, 30th June 1998
108. *International Times, IT,* 26, 16th February 1968
109. Author's transcript from a recording of Donovan, released on *'Rising',* Donovan, Permanent Records, 1990
110. *Llànties de Foc (Lamps of Fire)* documentary directed by Nofre Moya & Silvia Ventayol, 2011
111. *The Secret of the Mantras*, Richard Blakely, 2012
112. *What Falls Away*, Mia Farrow, Transworld, 1997
113. Author's transcript of https://www.youtube.com/watch?v=WOKuWy2zsCA
114. *Phil Spector: Out of His Head*, Richard Williams, Omnibus, 2003
115. https://theymaybeparted.com/tag/gayleen-pease/
116. *Rolling Stone,* issues 5 & 6, February 1968
117. *Beyond Gurus*, Nancy Cooke de Herrara, Blue Dolphin, 1992
118. Author's transcript of Maharishi speaking at Poland Spring, U.S.A., on 12th July 1970
119. *Rolling Stone,* 21st January 1971
120. *New York Magazine,* 25th May 1981
121. *The Beatles Book*, No.58, May 1968
122. *Daily Mirror,* 19th February 1968
123. Author transcript - *The Beatles A Mad Day's Out* 1968 DVD
124. *With the Beatles*, Lewis Lapham, Melville House, 2005
125. *AP - Associated Press,* 19th February 1968
126. *Maclean's* June, 1968
127. Author's transcript of https://www.youtube.com/watch?v=PiAhzpGO1Qk
128. *The Beatles Book*, No.59, June 1968
129. *The Way to Maharishi's Himalayas*, Elsa Dragemark, Stockholm, 1972
130. *The Beatles in Rishikesh*, Paul Saltzman, Viking Studio, 2000
131. *Salut Les Copains,* June 1968
132. *Rave,* May 1968
133. *Times of India,* 27th February 1968
134. Author's transcript of https://www.youtube.com/watch?v=R1TwPvJysTQ
135. *Billboard,* 4th October 2012 by Phil Gallo
136. http://www.popsike.com/HURDY-GURDYSTRare-Danish-Psych-Prog-LPCBS-64781/140099707219.html
137. Author transcript of https://www.youtube.com/watch?v=Q3tWkyYXcLc
138. https://dancingledge.wordpress.com/tag/jenny-boyd/
139. *Times of India,* 27th Oct 2014
140. *Paul Horn A Special Edition*, Island Records, 1974, booklet
141. *Paul Horn in Conversation History & Influences* - transcript of http://snapshotsfoundation.com/index.php/paul-horn-interview
142. Message from Holger Mielke
143. *Statesman,* April 1968
144. *Inside Paul Horn*, Paul Horn with Lee Underwood, HarperSanFrancisco, 1990
145. http://www.beatlesinterviews.org/dba09white.html
146. *Gudbrandsdølen Dagningen,* 30. Juli 2016 (translation)
147. http://www.mayonews.ie/component/content/article/52-living/going-out/9400-in-full-mike-love-interview?Itemid=0
148. *I Me Mine*, George Harrison, WH Allen, 1980
149. *New Musical Express - NME,* 21st September 1968
150. *New York Magazine,* 25th May 1981
151. https://www.beatlesbible.com/1968/02/29/live-yoko-ono-and-ornette-coleman-royal-albert-hall-london/
152. Interview promoting *'The Beatles'* album, 20th November 1968 Radio Luxembourg, http://www.beatlesinterviews.org/db1968.1120.beatles.html
153. http://thebeatlesinindia.com/stories/donovan/
154. http://donovan-catch-the-wind.blogspot.co.uk/2010/03/gypsy-dave-interview.html

155. *Disc and Music Echo,* 16th March 1968
156. *Melody Maker,* 16th March 1968
157. *Melody Maker,* 9th March 1968
158. Author transcript of https://www.youtube.com/watch?v=R1TwPvJysTQ
159. http://donovan-unofficial.com/music/albums/the_hurdy_gurdy_man.html
160. *Times of India News Service,* Rishikesh, Sunday, 3rd March 1968
161. *New Musical Express - NME,* 9th March 1968
162. *Fleetwood: My Life and Adventures in Fleetwood Mac,* Mick Fleetwood with Stephen Davis, William Morrow, 1990
163. https://gatelessgate.wordpress.com/2006/07/13/jo-lysowsky-an-artists-journey/
164. http://www.ralph-abraham.org/1960s/joe/joe.txt
165. http://www.vulture.com/2016/11/donvan-on-helping-the-beatles-write-a-classic.html?mid=emailshare_vulture
166. http://DONOVAN TRINITY - Donovan - Official Website.html (retrieved 21st January 2016)
167. http://vaniquotes.org/wiki/Maharishi_Mahesh_Yogi_(Conversations)
168. *At the Apple's Core: The Beatles From the Inside,* Denis O'Dell with Bob Neaverson, Peter Owen, 2002
169. *Thank U Very Much: Mike McCartney's Family Album,* Panther, 1982
170. *Sunshine Superman: The Journey of Donovan* DVD, SPV, 2008
171. *OZ,* issue 12 - May 1968
172. https://groups.yahoo.com/neo/groups/FairfieldLife/conversations/topics/17479
173. Carole Hamby's notes
174. *Uncut,* 9th May 2005
175. *It's Not Only Rock 'n' Roll,* Jenny Boyd Ph.D with Holly George-Warren, John Blake, 1992/2013
176. *Melody Maker,* 30th March 1968
177. *New Musical Express - NME,* 30th March 1968
178. Letter from Geoffrey Baker c1995
179. *A Hard Day's Write,* Steve Turner, Carlton, 1994
180. http://www.thenomadicphotographer.com/2009/04/15/the-true-story-of-bungalow-bill/
181. *Days In The Life: Voices from the English Underground,* 1961-71, Jonathon Greene, Minerva, 1988
182. http://www.beatlesinterviews.org/db68.html
183. http://www.rollingstone.com/music/news/the-real-dear-prudence-on-meeting-beatles-in-india-20150904
184. http://bytesdaily.blogspot.co.uk/2014/07/the-white-album-songs-continued.html
185. *MOJO,* October 1996
186. http://peterdoggettbeatles.blogspot.co.uk/2010/07/meeting-magic-alex.html
187. http://kingencyclopedia.stanford.edu/encyclopedia/encyclopedia/enc_kings_trip_to_india/
188. http://www.goldminemag.com/article/sudden-ending-on-the-road-with-the-beach-boys-in-1968
189. 'John's Poem' - given to Joe Massot, author's transcript from *'Wonderwall'* movie
190. *New Musical Express - NME,* 6th April 1968
191. http://minet.org/www.trancenet.net/personal/dolan/midnight.shtml
192. *Magical Mystery Tours,* Tony Bramwell, Thomas Dunne Books, 2005
193. http://graphics8.nytimes.com/packages/pdf/arts/Mardas.pdf
194. Excerpts from Wikipedia entry for 'Mysticism'
195. Message from Diane Rousseau, a close student of Charlie Lutes
196. https://beatlesunlimited.wordpress.com/2008/02/10/cynthia-lennon-the-beatles-the-maharishi-and-me/
197. *New Musical Express - NME,* 20th April 1968
198. *Disc and Music Echo,* 20th April 1968
199. *Good Vibrations: My Life as a Beach Boy,* Mike Love, Faber & Faber, 2016
200. *Inside,* Paul Horn, LP Liner notes, Epic, 1968
201. http://www.beatlesinterviews.org/db1968.0514pc.beatles.html
202. Author's transcript of video footage in *'Anthology Director's Cut'* DVD set
203. *New Musical Express - NME,* 1st June 1968
204. *Canberra Times,* 17th May 1968
205. *Disc and Music Echo,* 25th May 1968
206. Interviewed by Andrew Darlington 2005 http://www.soundchecks.co.uk/articles/donovanle.html
207. Author's transcript of excerpt of video documentary https://www.youtube.com/watch?v=vA0xQUv2QSk
208. *George Harrison Reconsidered,* Timothy White, Larchwood & Weir, 2013
209. *Daily Mail,* 7th March 2015
210. Transcription by Tom Anderson of lecture given on 16th March 1970
211. http://www.kctv.co.uk/plus/018_Yoko_Ono.html
212. *RCD Magazine,* No.4, 1992
213. *The Beatles 1963-1970 The Beatles Diary Volume 1: The Beatles Years,* Barry Miles, Omnibus, 2001
214. *The Ottawa Journal,* 22nd June 1968
215. *Canberra Times,* 28th June 1968
216. *Record Mirror,* 27th July 1968
217. *Rolling Stone,* 22, 23rd November 1968
218. *John, Paul, George, Ringo & Me,* Tony Barrow, Sevenoaks, 2005
219. http://wogew.blogspot.co.uk/2015/01/interview-with-maureen-cox-1988.html?m=1
220. *The Right Words At The Right Time,* Marlo Thomas and Friends, Atria Books, New York, 2002
221. https://www.youtube.com/watch?v=gZl2aArxB8o
222. *Canberra Times,* 25th September 1968
223. http://harrisonstories.tumblr.com/post/108390499933/harrisonstories-a-letter-george-wrote-to-art
224. *Luck and Circumstance: A Coming of Age in Hollywood,* New York, and Points Beyond, Michael Lindsay-Hogg, Alfred A. Knopf, 2011
225. Excerpts from *'The Beatles Get Back'* book, Apple Publishing, 1969
226. Author's transcript of audio material recorded during *'Let it Be'* movie
227. *MOJO,* Winter 2000
228. Personal message from Raghvendra's brother, Thakur Vishwa Vijay Singh, via daughter Gesu Aftab
229. http://www.nytimes.com/2008/02/07/arts/music/07yogi.html?_r=1&ref=arts&oref=slogin
230. Author's transcript of recording of John Lennon's story about his time in India
231. *John Lennon & Yoko Ono,* David Wigg Interview: Apple Offices, London 8th May 1969
232. *International Times - IT,* issue 63 29th August 1969
233. http://vanisource.org/wiki/Room_Conversation_With_John_Lennon,_Yoko_Ono,_and_George_Harrison_--_September_11,_1969,_London,_At_Tittenhurst
234. *Daily Mail,* 11th June 2007

235. http://www.today.com/id/5121163/ns/today-today_entertainment/t/paul-mccartney-got-no-thrill-heroin/#.WECjMdWLSiR
236. *Skywriting By Word of Mouth*, John Lennon, Pan, 1986
237. https://www.yahoo.com/music/letter-john-lennon-paul-mccartney-215615384.html
238. http://www.noise11.com/news/george-harrison-classic-interview-with-paul-cashmere-20110926
239. Author's transcript of *Fact or Fantasy*, BBC1 broadcast, 26th April 1970
240. http://www.beatlesinterviews.org/db1970.04gh.beatles.html
241. Author's transcript of *'Gurus'* by Jerry Hall, BBC documentary 2003
242. *Guardian,* 24th May 2016
243. http://www.dailymail.co.uk/femail/article-473206/Pattie-Boyd-My-hellish-love-triangle-George-Eric--Part-Two.html#ixzz4UofUnSIB
244. *Collaborations,* box set, Ravi Shankar-George Harrison, accompanying book, Dark Horse Records, 2010
245. www.rollingstone.com/music/pictures/10-classic-drugged-out-performances-from-santana-to-green-day-20130606/7-george-harrison-1974-tour-cocaine-0622544
246. http://www.studiowner.com/essays/essay.asp?books=0&pagnum=28
247. *George Harrison: Behind the Locked Door*, Graeme Thomson , Omnibus, 2013
248. *Montreal Gazette,* 14th April 1983
249. Author's transcript from 1990 recording of Swedish Dabrowski SVT 1990 interview https://www.youtube.com/watch?v=rUrlX6_qSqw
250. *Playboy* interview - http://www.beatlesinterviews.org/db1980.jlpb.beatles.html
251. Author's transcript of recordings at http://www.npr.org/templates/story/story.php?storyId=130429818
252. *They Can't Hide Us Anymore*, Richie Havens with Steve Davidowitz, Avon Books, 1999
253. Author's transcript from video https://www.youtube.com/watch?v=o5YTMiqxZcw
254. http://www.huffingtonpost.com/2015/04/12/ringo-drunk_n_7049282.html?utm_hp_ref=fifty&ir=Fifty
255. http://www.dailymail.co.uk/news/article-3566678/16-bottles-wine-day-Piles-coke-75-does-Ringo-look-younger-son.html#ixzz4U8yc5TKa
256. *Telegraph,* 28th June 2011
257. http://www.interviewmagazine.com/music/new-again-ringo-starr/print/
258. Author's transcript of excerpt of *The Beatles in their own Words - A Rockumentary,* Geoffrey Giuliano, CD, Delta Music,1995
259. *The Beatles Diary Volume 2: After The Break-Up 1970-2001*, Keith Badman, Omnibus, 2001
260. *Playboy,* December 1984
261. *Mystical One: George Harrison*, Elliot J. Huntley, Guernica Editions 2006
262. http://lifeofthebeatles.blogspot.co.uk/2006/06/george-harrison-on-vh1-yin-yang-with.html
263. https://www.theguardian.com/uk/2000/nov/15/stevenmorris
264. Author's transcript of https://www.youtube.com/watch?v=lHFKEIYEcZw
265. *Rolling Stone,* 6th December 2001
266. https://www.rutherford.org/publications_resources/john_whiteheads_commentary/george_harrison_living_in_the_material_world
267. *BBC* 2nd June 2004 http://news.bbc.co.uk/1/hi/entertainment/3769511.stm
268. http://home.bt.com/news/uk-news/why-mccartney-keeps-off-the-grass-11363983944848
269. *The Times Magazine,* June 2006
270. https://www.nasa.gov/topics/universe/features/across_universe.html
271. http://metro.co.uk/2008/02/08/ex-beatles-pay-tribute-to-maharishi-627556/
272. http://uk.reuters.com/article/uk-dutch-maharishi-idUKL0611095720080206
273. *Sunday Times,* 10th February 2008
274. http://imaginepeace.com/archives/10279
275. http://blog.silentadministration.org/2009/03/41-years-after-they-meditated-together.html
276. http://paulhornmusic.com/2010/12/mccartney-and-lynch-benefit-concert/
277. http://news.bbc.co.uk/1/hi/entertainment/7924392.stm
278. Author's transcript from video of *'Cosmically Conscious'* by Paul McCartney
279. https://www.youtube.com/watch?v=UTncD79koeA
280. *Rolling Stone,* 15 September 2011
281. http://www.arvinddevalia.com/blog/2013/04/06/james-mccartney-interview/
282. http://www.telegraph.co.uk/fashion/people/stella-mccartney-on-worrying-what-the-nation-thinks-and-transcen/
283. http://www.dallasobserver.com/music/ghost-of-a-saber-tooth-tigers-sean-lennon-once-you-frack-you-cant-go-back-7049443
284. Author's transcript of NPR's *On Point* radio show with Tom Ashbrook, Yoko Ono and caller Craig Berg on 25th June 2012
285. http://imaginepeace.com/archives/10408
286. *Rave* magazine June 1968
287. http://press-conference.globalgoodnews.com/archive/july/07.07.27.html
288. http://cooperowen.com/john-lennon-shroud-of-tourin-recently-discovered-hidden-drawings-revealed/
289. *It was Fifty Years Ago Today!* - DVD, Spectrum, 2017

THE BEATLES, DRUGS, MYSTICISM & INDIA
Titles by Paul Mason:

*Maharishi Mahesh Yogi: The Biography of the Man Who Gave
Transcendental Meditation to the World*

*Roots of TM: The Transcendental Meditation of Guru Dev
& Maharishi Mahesh Yogi*
^
Den Transcendentala Meditationens Ursprung - Turning Pages
Swedish edition 2017

*108 Discourses of Guru Dev:
The Life and Teachings of Swami Brahmananda Saraswati,
Shankaracharya of Jyotirmath (1941-53) - Volume I*
~
*The Biography of Guru Dev:
The Life and Teachings of Swami Brahmananda Saraswati,
Shankaracharya of Jyotirmath (1941-53) - Volume II*
~
*Guru Dev as Presented by Maharishi Mahesh Yogi:
The Life and Teachings of Swami Brahmananda Saraswati,
Shankaracharya of Jyotirmath (1941-53) - Volume III*

*The Knack of Meditation:
The No-Nonsense Guide to Successful Meditation*

*Dandi Swami: The Story of the Guru's Will, Maharishi Mahesh Yogi, the Shankaracharyas of Jyotir Math &
Meetings with Dandi Swami Narayananand Saraswati*

Via Rishikesh: A Hitch-Hiker's Tale

Mala: A String of Unexpected Meetings

Kathy's Story

*The Maharishi: The Biography of the Man Who Gave
Transcendental Meditation to the World*
Element Books - First English edition 1994
Evolution Books - Revised English edition 2005
Maharishi Mahesh Yogi - Aquamarin - German edition 1995
O Maharishi - Nova Era - Portuguese edition 1997

*Established in Yoga, Perform Action:
Gita Bhavateet; The 'Song Transcendental' of Acharya Satyadas*

Paul Mason became a fan of The Beatles at an early age, and recalls that as an 11-year-old he listened to a live broadcast of them playing, picked up on his transistor radio set on Boxing Day, 26th December 1963. Living in London, Paul got to see many of the major acts live in concert, meet a lot of colourful characters on the fringes of the music business, and enjoy good times together, occasionally brushing shoulders with those close to the core.

In 1970, Paul hitchhiked to India where he visited Maharishi's ashram at Rishikesh and learned the technique of Transcendental Meditation. This spurred him to dig deeper into the history of the teaching of meditation, which led to his being commissioned to write Maharishi's lifestory. This authoritative work has been revised, expanded, and re-published as *Maharishi Mahesh Yogi: The Biography of the Man Who Gave Transcendental Meditation to the World.*. He has also translated the teachings and lifestory of Maharishi's master, Guru Dev - Shankaracharya Swami Brahmananda Saraswati - from Hindi and Sanskrit into English.

In 2000, at a little ceremony on the banks of the River Ganges at Swargashram, Rishikesh, Paul was given the honorary *sannyasi* name of 'Premanand'. More recently, a chance meeting with singer/songwriter Donovan Leitch proved the necessary spur to bring to fruition a project that had been bubbling under for years - the compilation of the detailed account of The Beatles' involvement with Maharishi, and their clear endorsement for the practice of Transcendental Meditation.

Printed in the USA
CPSIA information can be obtained
at www.ICGtesting.com
LVHW060707171223
766619LV00050B/2061